COMANDANTE CHE

COMAND

COMANDANTE CHE

Guerrilla Soldier, Commander,
and Strategist, 1956–1967

PAUL J. DOSAL

The Pennsylvania State University Press
University Park, Pennsylvania

Library of Congress Cataloging-in-Publication Data

Dosal, Paul J. (Paul Jaime), 1960–
   Comandante Che : guerrilla soldier, commander, and
   strategist, 1956–1967 / Paul J. Dosal.
     p.   cm.
   Includes bibliographical references and index.
   ISBN 0-271-02261-2 (cloth : alk. paper)
   1. Guevara, Ernesto, 1928–1967—Military leadership.
   2. Cuba—History—1933–1959.
   3. Insurgency—History—20th century.
   4. Guerrilla warfare—History—20th century.
   5. Guerrillas—Cuba—Biography.
   I. Title.

F2849.22 .G85 D67 2003   2003004755
355.4'25'092—dc21

It is the policy of The Pennsylvania State University Press
to use acid-free paper. Publications on uncoated stock
satisfy the minimum requirements of American National
Standard for Information Sciences—Permanence of Paper
for Printed Library Material, ANSI Z39.48–1992.

We must carry the war into every corner the enemy happens to carry it: to his home, to his centers of entertainment; a total war. It is necessary to prevent him from having a moment of peace, a quiet moment outside his barracks or even inside; we must attack him wherever he may be, make him feel like a cornered beast wherever he may move.

—CHE GUEVARA, "MESSAGE TO THE TRICONTINENTAL," 1967

I dedicate this book to my father,

LOUIS DOSAL (1928–2002)

CONTENTS

LIST OF MAPS

PREFACE

In October 1992, the twenty-fifth anniversary of Che Guevara's death, I started to research the life of Ernesto Che Guevara. Although there were dozens of books and articles about Che, I realized that I knew little about the life and career of this important figure. The definitive biography of the legendary guerrilla had not yet been written. I initially set out to write the life history of Che Guevara, hoping that I would have the honor of writing the first scholarly biography of Che. That honor fell on others more capable than myself. Four comprehensive biographies of Che Guevara appeared in 1997, the thirtieth anniversary of his death. They covered Che better than I could have done, and the many citations to their work in this book show how much I owe to their impressive work.

About two years after commemorative activities ceased, I reopened my Che files and began to think about what I might do with all the data I had accumulated about Che. I had already read every speech, article, book, letter, and diary written by him. I had read just about everything ever written about him as well. I wanted to make a contribution to the growing literature about Che Guevara, but I was not sure what I could add. Finally, after liberating my repressed interest in military history, I decided to change the project from a comprehensive biography to a study of Che's career as a soldier, commander, and strategist.

I was originally trained as a political-economic historian at Tulane University under Dr. Ralph Lee Woodward Jr., focusing on Central American history. In writing about Che's military career, I have broadened the boundaries of my geographical and topical interests. I taught myself basic military history by reading extensively on the U.S. Civil War and World War II. I have come to admire the technical expertise and narrative skills of writers and historians such as Shelby Foote and Stephen Ambrose, both of whom demonstrated that military history is a viable, exciting, and important field of inquiry.

Yet this book is more than a military history. Fighting and winning a guerrilla campaign is not simply a question of devising the proper strategy, applying the right tactics, or selecting the appropriate weapon. The object of the guerrilla is not so much to win a military engagement as to avoid losing it. Guerrilla warfare, as Che fought and taught it, is a political and social struggle as well as a military conflict. If political factors do not favor the guerrillas, they will lose, as Che discovered in Bolivia. Ambushes, battles, and skirmishes figure prominently in the following account, but the analysis does not start and end with them. To assess Guevara's career as a guerrilla soldier, commander, and strategist, one must analyze it in its proper political context, examining Che's ideological development; his personal relations with Fidel Castro; and even Soviet, Chinese, and American policies toward the Cuban Revolution and Latin America.

The life of a guerrilla is filled with long moments of inactivity, broken occasionally by the forced night march or the surprise attack. During the many pauses in his guerrilla campaigns, Che read and wrote extensively. His complete works, constituting more than nine volumes, form the primary source of information for this study. He kept campaign diaries wherever he fought, and most of these have been published and translated. Parts of his diaries have been censored, and more documents are locked away in Cuban archives, but the available literature, including a rich vein of memoirs written by people who fought for and against Che, forms a solid foundation for the study of Che Guevara's military career.

Che Guevara remains a well-known figure, whether adored or reviled, to millions around the world. The thirtieth anniversary of his death, highlighted by the discovery of his unmarked Bolivian grave and the transfer of his remains to Cuba, demonstrated the remarkable durability of his image and his message. I have tried not to get caught up in the Che mania that swept the world then. Students, colleagues, and friends who knew of my research on Che gave me Che posters, shirts, socks, and underwear, thinking that I would appreciate such gifts. I usually gave those items away, preferring to keep just a few images of Che in my office to remind myself that he was a real man who influenced the lives of millions, for better or worse. He killed for a cause; he ordered people to kill for that cause; he advocated war to the death against imperialism; and he died for his principles. His life and death is in many ways a modern tragedy, not a cause for celebration. We must study who he was, why he fought, why he died, and why so many followed him into battle. I have tried to analyze his career as objectively as possible, sorting myth from reality in an effort to assess Guevara's actual impact on twentieth-century military history.

My research on Che has taken me to Washington, D.C.; Austin, Texas; Havana; Buenos Aires; and Córdoba. A Research and Creative Scholarship Grant from the University of South Florida and a Faculty Research Grant from the University of Massachusetts allowed me to complete my research.

I have received generous assistance and encouragement along the way. Ann Shuh was with me from the start to the finish of the project, sharing my frustrations. Her careful reading of the manuscript showed that she also shared my ambitions. John Belohlavek, my friend and colleague from the University of South Florida, reviewed the manuscript and offered his military expertise. I thank him for his assistance and the many happy hours we spent together talking about the Civil War. I also want to thank Mike Conniff, a wonderful friend and supportive colleague, for all the encouragement he has offered. Neill Macaulay and Charles Ameringer offered perceptive and constructive critiques of the manuscript as well. I hope that I have addressed their questions and concerns in this final product.

A number of friends and colleagues in Cuba have helped me. Marel García shared her expertise and put me in contact with some of Che's closest associates. I also want to thank Miriam Rodríguez of the University of Havana for facilitating my research and travel. Gabriel Cartaya kindly escorted me in and around the Sierra Maestra to see La Plata, Santo Domingo, Alegría del Pío, and other sites associated with the Cuban insurrection. The late Enrique Sosa, a dear friend, shared with me his love of Cuba before his passing in March 2002.

I offer a special thanks to my old soccer buddy Rick Pope, who graciously offered to prepare my maps. My good friends Joe Costa and Christy Paul read and commented on earlier versions of the manuscript, helping me to bring out aspects of Che's life that I might otherwise have overlooked. Joe, like Theresa, Ross, Tami, John, Belinda Allen, Dave, Kenny, Jocelyn, Jimmy, Mike, Dodd, Scott, Valerie, Mike Ortiz, and Tara, have helped me just by making sure that I had a good time. The same goes for all my friends at the revived Cuban Club of Tampa, particularly Jorge and Ileana Díaz, Mario González, Alex Solera, Alex de Quesada, Frank Castillo, Raúl Lavín, Reinaldo Garrido, Fernando Mesa, Dr. Angelo Pérez, José Vivero, and many others.

I have a large, loving, and supportive family to thank: Mom, Dad, Michael, Cindy, Jessica, Duane, Rhonda, Lindsey, Brooke, Madison, Darlene, Michael, and Andrew. We have all suffered in recent years, but we are stronger for having lived through it.

I am not sure that I am any better for having worked so long on this project, but I hope that the literature on Che is richer for it. This book is offered as a modest contribution to a controversial historical subject and is designed for both scholars and the general public. I do not intend to settle the arguments about Che's record, but I will enjoy participating in the debates to come.

ONE NOBODY SURRENDERS HERE!

Until he arrived at the port of Tuxpan, Mexico, on November 24, 1956, Ernesto Guevara, a twenty-eight-year-old doctor from Argentina, did not know how Fidel Castro, a thirty-year-old revolutionary from Cuba, intended to transport his rebel army across the Caribbean Sea. A week earlier, a Havana newspaper had published Castro's threat to invade Cuba if dictator Fulgencio Batista did not resign immediately. In contrast to putting forth that impudent declaration, Castro divulged few details of his invasion plans to his soldiers. Few rebels knew how, when, or where the invasion would take place. They all learned one sobering truth at Tuxpan. Castro planned to load one hundred soldiers and their supplies on a fifty-eight-foot yacht called the *Granma*. Built in 1943 and sunk a decade later, the refurbished vessel could safely carry only twenty-five people. When Universo Sánchez, a confidante of Castro, saw it anchored in the Tuxpan River, he asked timidly: "When do we get to the real ship? Where is the mother ship?"[1]

On this pleasure craft, Fidel loaded 2 antitank guns, 90 rifles, 3 Thompson submachine guns, and 40 pistols, plus 48 cans of condensed milk, 2,000 oranges, 6 hams, a box of eggs, 100 chocolate bars, and 10 pounds of bread. Boxes filled up the cabin then spilled onto the deck, leaving rebels wonder-

1. Franqui, *Diary*, 121–22; Szulc, *Fidel*, 371 (quoted).

1

ing where they might sit. When all the equipment and supplies had been loaded, eighty-two rebels filled up every remaining space. Castro left behind another fifty men, many of whom probably felt lucky that there had not been enough room for them on the *Granma*.[2]

At 1:30 A.M., one of the vessel's two diesel engines revved up and the yacht began the adventure that would alter Cuban history and make Ernesto Guevara the legendary "Che." Within an hour, the overloaded *Granma* left the calm waters of the river and entered the turbulent waters of the Gulf of Mexico. Che did not know where they would land and he could not identify his first military objective, but he joined the Cuban patriots in singing the Cuban national anthem.[3]

Within five minutes, "the whole boat took on a ridiculously tragic appearance," Che later wrote. Men with whitened faces hurled their last supper into buckets; others lay in anguish until they could hold their churning stomachs no longer. Luckily Che did not get seasick and could tend to the men, but he had no motion sickness pills to prescribe. Then the yacht began to take on water. A handful of seaworthy men began to bail water while the mechanic tried frantically to get the pumps working. Che laughed when one sane sailor turned off an open faucet and stopped the flooding. The stench of failure already hung over the sickened warriors.[4]

As the sun rose on the twenty-seventh, the rebels found themselves in calm seas north of the Yucatán Peninsula. Fidel set a course directly eastward, hoping to make up for lost time. He had calculated that the journey from Mexico to Cuba would take five days. Because of rough seas, excessive weight, and one nonfunctioning motor, the *Granma* had been plugging along at 7.2 knots instead of the 10 knots that Castro had anticipated. The progress of the boat through placid waters lifted spirits and soothed stomachs, but it also resulted in an increasing demand for food, forcing Fidel to ration his scarce supplies. While most of the men recovered, Che fell victim to a severe asthma attack; the doctor had no medication to prescribe for himself either. Che had fought with asthma since he had been two years old, and it got the best of him during the journey. At 5:00 P.M. on November 28, the *Granma* changed course to the southeast, heading through Yucatán Channel into the Caribbean.[5] (See

2. Bornot Pubillones et al., *De Tuxpan a La Plata*, 78; Quirk, *Fidel Castro*, 119; H. Thomas, *Cuban Revolution*, 108–9.

3. Guevara, *Episodes*, 85–86; Bornot Pubillones et al., *De Tuxpan a La Plata*, 74.

4. Guevara, *Episodes*, 85–86; Franqui, *Diary*, 122.

5. Bornot Pubillones et al., *De Tuxpan a La Plata*, 78; Deutschmann, *Che*, 69.

Map 1.) With the abrupt change in course, it became obvious that Fidel did not intend to invade anywhere near Havana or western Cuba.

Castro intended to land the main body of the Movimiento 26 de Julio (26th of July Movement, or M-26-7) in eastern Cuba on November 30, at the same time that M-26-7 militants in Santiago and elsewhere would launch diversionary strikes on selected army garrisons and police stations. Fidel planned to land his rebel army at Playa las Coloradas, about twelve miles south of Niquero on the western coast of Oriente province. Frank País, the general coordinator of the M-26-7, planned to draw Batista's army away from Castro's invasion force by attacking the police headquarters, the maritime police office, and the Moncada garrison in Santiago. País, who had worked out the details of the general strategy with Fidel in Mexico, hoped to prevent Batista from sending reinforcements to engage Castro. By pinning down Cuban soldiers in Santiago, Holguín, and Guantánamo, the urban militants expected to facilitate Castro's landing near Niquero, where M-26-7 militants led by Celia Sánchez would reinforce him with arms, ammunition, supplies, and trucks. Castro would then lead his augmented force in attacks on the isolated army base at Niquero and possibly Manzanillo, capturing more arms and ammunition to supply a larger rebel army. From Manzanillo he could proceed to Santiago or into the Sierra Maestra. If País took Moncada he could join the M-26-7 forces there; if not, he could lead his men to a more secure location in the Sierra Maestra, from where he would direct a guerrilla campaign against Batista.[6]

Given that the strategy required precise coordination between units in two countries, any delays en route could endanger the entire mission. By dawn on November 30, the *Granma* was still puttering along west of Gran Cayman Island, two days behind schedule. Even worse, the Cuban military had already learned of Castro's departure from Mexico. At 5:45 A.M. on November 30, the Cuban air force initiated an islandwide search for a white sixty-five-foot yacht flying the Mexican flag. Cuban intelligence agents, working in collaboration with American and Mexican agents, had been monitoring Castro's activities in Mexico for at least a year. American, Cuban, or Mexican agents

---

6. Bornot Pubillones et al., *De Tuxpan a La Plata,* 78; Bonachea and San Martín, *Cuban Insurrection,* 78–79; Szulc, *Fidel,* 375; testimony of Celia Sánchez in Franqui, *Diary,* 128–29. There is still substantial debate about Castro's military strategy. Official historians of the Cuban insurrection insist that Fidel always intended to march the *Granma* rebels into the Sierra Maestra. Bonachea and San Martín argue that Fidel conceived of a guerrilla campaign as a contingency plan. For more on this, see Chapter 3.

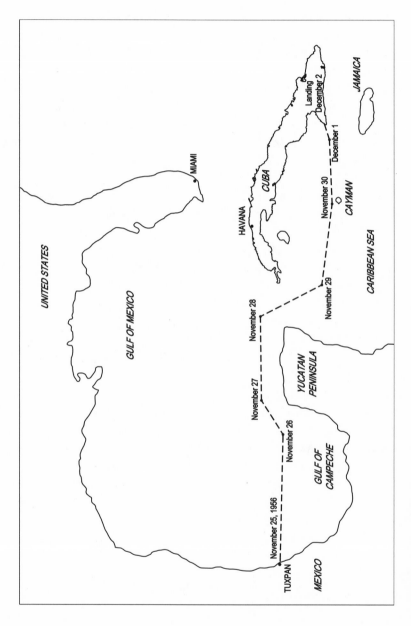

Map 1. Route of the *Granma*

probably detected the *Granma*'s departure soon after it sailed from Tuxpan, if not earlier. Given that Cuban insurrections had always been based in eastern Cuba, Batista expected Castro to invade Oriente province. Beginning on November 5—three weeks before the *Granma*'s departure—the Cuban air force began flying patrols along the north and south coasts of Oriente province. Batista also reinforced army garrisons in Santiago and Holguín the day after the *Granma* left Tuxpan. The troop movements that Fidel hoped to deter by launching diversionary strikes had actually been promoted by his public declaration that he intended to invade Cuba. Batista's patrols and troop movements prior to the Santiago uprisings clearly indicated that he intended to meet and defeat Castro's rebel army, wherever it landed.[7]

Unaware of Castro's delay, Frank País attacked as scheduled. At 7:00 A.M. on November 30, M-26-7 soldiers attacked the police headquarters and the maritime police building in Santiago, while snipers tried to keep the soldiers in the Moncada barracks pinned down. Twenty rebels took the maritime police building, but País and his combatants met with stiff resistance at the police headquarters. At 11:00 A.M., País realized that the attacks would fail and ordered his men to change back into civilian clothes and filter into the general population. In Guantánamo, a group of rebels gained control of an army outpost, but they abandoned it and took to the hills when they learned of an approaching army patrol. In Holguín, the M-26-7 hit a few targets, but Havana remained absolutely quiet. Unable to communicate with País from the *Granma*, Castro could not discuss the situation with País and modify their strategy accordingly. He could only listen to radio reports about the Santiago uprising and contemplate his own dwindling alternatives, with an engagement with the Cuban army, navy, or air force increasingly likely. The men on the *Granma* never expected to land wholly undetected, but at the rate they were going, they most likely would be martyrs by the end of 1956.[8]

By the evening of November 30, the rebels knew that the plans for a coordinated invasion and national uprising had failed. However, Castro could not change course and "invade" Jamaica, Mexico, or some other country. He could only disembark his rebel army in Cuba. The aborted Santiago uprising had definitely alerted the Cuban army to the pending arrival of Castro. On November 30 Batista suspended constitutional guarantees, declared the entire

7. Bornot Pubillones et al., *De Tuxpan a La Plata*, 78; Guevara, *Che*, annex 1, 141; Szulc, *Fidel*, 372–73.

8. Bonachea and San Martín, *Cuban Insurrection*, 79–83; Franqui, *Diary*, 122; Szulc, *Fidel*, 374–75.

province of Oriente to be in a state of "Operations," and placed the rest of the country on alarm. Air and naval patrols continued. If Castro managed to elude the patrols and disembark in Oriente, he would now have to contend with an army under orders to search for and capture his rebel forces.[9]

On the afternoon of December 1, Fidel finally divulged his military plans to his soldiers. Despite the defeat of the Santiago uprising, Castro announced that he would disembark the rebel army at a point near Niquero, from where, one can deduce, he still intended to attack the Niquero garrison.[10] He could no longer count on receiving reinforcements from Celia Sánchez, because his landing had been delayed. In fact, Celia withdrew her units when the *Granma* did not land on November 30. Nothing in Fidel's original plan had materialized, yet he refused to abandon his military strategy and disembark at a point with easier and safer access to the Sierra Maestra. A landing near Niquero made sense only if Castro intended to attack Niquero.

Ramón Bonachea and Marta San Martín, in their study of the Cuban insurrection, contend that Castro applied his contingency plan after he learned of the failure of the Santiago uprising.[11] If he had opted for his contingency plans while en route to Cuba, he should have set a course for the southern coast of Oriente, from where the rebels would have had a relatively short and safe march to the Sierra Maestra. Castro definitely shelved his plans for an attack on Niquero, but he implemented his contingency plan *after* the *Granma* landing. He could have saved precious time and lives by landing his men at a site with shorter and safer access into the Sierra Maestra. Castro had evidently selected the farm of Mongo Pérez as his first operational headquarters and a rallying point. Located at Purial de Vicana, just five miles north of the coast, it provided an excellent staging area for a march into the Sierra Maestra. (See Map 2.) Celia Sánchez, leader of the M-26-7 forces in Manzanillo, favored a landing at or near Pilón, El Macho, or La Magdalena, all of them "ideal landing places" on the southern coast of Oriente province. "At Pilón, they would have been one step away from the Sierra; it is right on the flank of the mountain. There would have been no problems," Celia later explained.[12]

As it happened, a shortage of fuel dictated Castro's decision to attempt a landing at Coloradas beach. The expedition suffered a critical setback around

9. Guevara, *Che,* annex 1, 141.
10. Bornot Pubillones et al., *De Tuxpan a La Plata,* 81.
11. Bonachea and San Martín, *Cuban Insurrection,* 364.
12. Testimony of Celia Sánchez, in Franqui, *Diary,* 128–29.

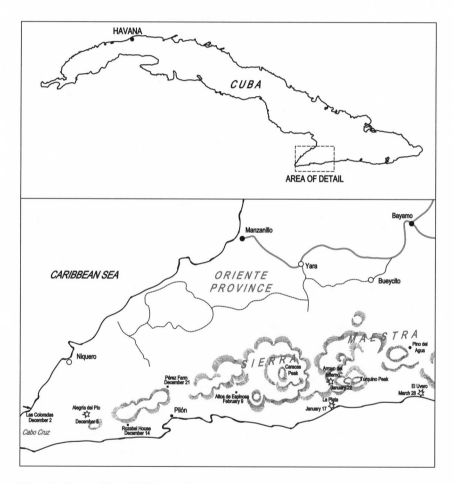

Map 2. Route of the Rebel Army, December 1956–May 1957

one o'clock in the morning on December 2, when Roberto Roque, the navigator, fell overboard. Fidel could not make landfall without his navigator. The *Granma* circled around in search of Roque, with only a lantern available to illuminate the dark waters. After an hour, the rebels pulled Roque on board.[13] In recovering Roque, Castro had expended precious supplies of fuel and pushed the scheduled landing perilously close to daybreak.

With Roque back at the helm, the *Granma* finally broke from its easterly course and headed northeast toward Coloradas beach. As the *Granma* sailed into Niquero channel, Captain Onelio Pino and Roberto Roque realized that their navigational charts were wrong. They did not know where they were. With dawn approaching and the tanks nearly out of fuel, Fidel could not waste any more time. He ordered full speed ahead, directly toward whatever coast lay in front of them. At 4:20 A.M., the *Granma* slid into the mud one hundred yards offshore, in a mangrove swamp more than a mile south of Coloradas beach. Fidel's long-anticipated invasion of Cuba looked more like a shipwreck than an amphibious assault.[14]

Around six o'clock that morning, Captain José Smith Comas, a veteran of the Korean War, began to disembark his vanguard platoon. The men lowered the lifeboat and loaded it with their heavy weapons. It sank. Unable to bring the yacht any closer, the men jumped into the water, carrying only their personal weapons overhead. Some men sank hip deep in mud. Captain Juan Almeida's center platoon went into the water next, followed by Castro and his general staff (which included Che), and Captain Raúl Castro and his rearguard. As the men watched their boots sink into the mud, their hearts sank with them, as they gradually realized that they had landed in the wrong place at the wrong time. They had disembarked in a thick mangrove swamp, and an impenetrable net of branches, gnarly stumps, and tepid water faced them as far as they could see.[15]

By 7:00 A.M. on December 2, Second Lieutenant Aquiles Chinea, commanding Squadron 12 of the Rural Guard in Manzanillo, received a confidential report that two hundred to three hundred well-armed men had landed at Coloradas beach, about sixteen miles south of Niquero. Lieutenant Chinea immediately ordered the commander of the Coast Guard 106 to scout the

13. Bornot Pubillones et al., *De Tuxpan a La Plata*, 82–83.

14. Szulc, *Fidel*, 375. Referring to the *Granma* landing, Juan Manuel Márquez said, "It wasn't a landing, it was a shipwreck." See Franqui, *Diary*, 124.

15. Quirk, *Fidel*, 122; Bornot Pubillones et al., *De Tuxpan a La Plata*, 83; Franqui, *Diary*, 124.

area. With only eight men under his command, Lieutenant Chinea knew that he could not engage the invaders until he received reinforcements from Bayamo. While he waited for help to arrive, he flew over the landing sight to determine the exact location, size, strength, and direction of the invading force.[16]

As the rebels hacked their way through the mangroves, two planes randomly strafed the swamp. The pilots could not penetrate the swamp any easier than could the rebels cursing their way through it. Unable to spot the rebels moving slowly through the thicket below, the pilots strafed the area anyway, having little impact on the tortuous rebel movement through the swamp. It took the rebels more than two hours to cut through a mile of mangroves. Che, afflicted by the high humidity and rising heat, suffered through a vicious asthma attack while he plowed through the suffocating swamp. As soon as he joined the men on solid ground near the thatched-roof hut of Angel Pérez Rosabal, the sound of artillery and machine-gun fire from the swamp from which they had just escaped indicated that the army was in pursuit. Castro ordered the troops to move out.[17]

At this point, with enemy planes in pursuit and without Celia Sánchez's reinforcements, a move toward Niquero would expose the troops to unnecessary risks. Castro finally abandoned his conventional strategy and ordered the rebels to march toward the Sierra Maestra. Unfortunately, a march to the Sierra Maestra now carried risks almost as high as an attack on Niquero because the rebels would have to travel more than sixty miles through Alegría del Pío and La Esperanza, along the only route to the sierra. Castro could only have suspected that the army would attempt to block his movement, as indeed it had. The army had already mobilized one thousand troops to block Castro's path toward the mountains. Fortunately for him, some misinformation filtered into the Cuban army on December 2, when army patrols picked up rumors that Castro intended to attack Niquero that night, temporarily diverting the army's attention away from the path that Castro actually took from the beach. Castro kept his men marching until nightfall, then they camped just a few miles from where the *Granma* actually landed.[18]

At dawn on December 3, the men resumed the march south and eastward, looking for the quickest route into the Sierra Maestra. Few of them knew the

16. Confidential army communiqué, December 5, 1956, in Franqui, *Diary,* 126; Bonachea and San Martín, *Cuban Insurrection,* 86.

17. Bornot Pubillones et al., *De Tuxpan a La Plata,* 88; Guevara, *Episodes,* 86.

18. Bornot Pubillones et al., *De Tuxpan a La Plata,* 89; Guevara, *Che,* annexes 2 and 3, 141–45.

terrain. Only nine of the men came from Oriente province; the rest of the rebels came from western and central Cuba, with Havana supplying thirty-eight of the eighty-two men in the rebel force. Che, one of four foreigners in the group, was just a year older than the average rebel, but he had more education than most of them.[19] He had never even been to Cuba before this, but he was willing to sacrifice his life and career for the cause. Around noon, he and his new comrades ate their first hot meal in days—yucca, bread dipped in honey, and some chicken broth—at the home of Zoilo Vega, a local peasant. Vega's brother Tato then guided Fidel's troops to a path that ran through a large sugar plantation. The rebels settled for the evening at a clearing, while scouts and foragers searched for stragglers and food.

During the night, eight stragglers rejoined the rebel army, bringing it back to its full strength of eighty-two combatants. The foragers also brought in some crackers, sausages, and condensed milk. Castro ordered the march to resume at 8:00 A.M. on December 4. "We were an army of shadows, of ghosts," Che wrote later. Marching in single file through a well-covered path, the rebels still had to take cover from enemy planes more than thirty times during the day. They finally rested at midnight at a village called Agua Fina. They got only four hours of sleep before Castro ordered them back into line. They marched under cover of darkness to Alegría del Pío but could go no farther.[20]

Dogged by enemy planes since their arrival, the rebels had marched through rugged terrain for three consecutive days, consuming most of their food rations along the way. The sugarcane fields provided them with some cover and food. Some of the men chewed on sugarcane stalks as they marched, leaving behind a trail of cane peelings. They did not know that their guide, Tato Vega, had betrayed them to the army. The Rural Guard had no problem picking up the rebel trail on December 4. That night, the army set ambushes near Alegría del Pío and La Esperanza, through which the rebels would have to pass.[21]

Fidel decided to let his men rest during the day of December 5 and resume the march later that night. Around noon, Che noticed aircraft circling overhead at low altitudes. The rebels, however, rested and consumed their few

19. Of the eighty-two men, only ten, including Che, had a university education. Forty-four rebels had only a primary education. See Bornot Pubillones et al., *De Tuxpan a La Plata*, 82.

20. Ibid., 89–91; Guevara, *Episodes*, 87 (quoted); Alvarez Tabio, *Diario de la guerra*, 28–30.

21. Szulc, *Fidel*, 380; confidential army communiqué, December 5, 1956, in Franqui, *Diary*, 126.

rations, unaware of the approaching storm. Castro had encamped on a low unprotected hill bordered by cane fields to the front and left and a thicket to the right. The guards were posted so close to the camp that they were practically in it, making it impossible for them to warn the rebel army of an approaching army patrol. Most of the soldiers found a shady place to sleep and lay down with their weapons. Che tended to the men, most of whom suffered from blisters or fungal infections caused by the march through the mangrove swamp. Around 4:30 P.M. on December 5, Che sat down next to Jesús Montané to eat his ration of half a sausage and two crackers. Ernesto and Jesús were leaning against a tree, exchanging happy memories of their respective children, when a single shot suddenly fathered a terrifying silence.[22]

Within seconds, a hurricane of bullets ripped through the camp. Rebel soldiers scattered, looking for cover or their commanding officer; others, including Ernesto, hugged the ground as bullets whizzed above them. They could not see their enemies and their enemies could not see them. But Squadrons 12 and 13 of the Rural Guard, commanded by Second Lieutenant Aquiles Chinea and Captain José C. Tandrón, respectively, unleashed a withering fire on the unsuspecting rebels. The Rural Guards had picked up the rebel trail at Agua Fina and followed them to the rebel camp at Alegría del Pío. They had decided to attack with machine-gun and rifle fire before nightfall, and they caught the rebels completely by surprise.[23]

Fidel and a few members of his general staff fled from the attackers and took cover in the adjacent cane field. From there, Fidel attempted to withdraw and reorganize his men. But the surprise attack dispersed the rebels as soon as it began. Rebels hit the dirt, ran for cover, and fired back at an enemy they could not see. Although they had taken the rebels by surprise, the 140 men of the Rural Guard inflicted only three casualties in their initial assault, finding it difficult to hit their targets because of thick vegetation and a slight elevation that separated them from the rebels.[24] The remaining seventy-nine combatants could have been reorganized for a counterattack, but Castro had not selected a rallying point before setting camp. In the heat of battle, he and his commanders could not organize a retreat or redeployment. A degree of panic ensued among the soldiers and their commanders, some of whom (including Che) were facing hostile fire for the first time. In Che's account

22. Guevara, *Episodes,* 89; Jesús Montané Oropesa, preface to Deutschmann, *Che,* 16.
23. Confidential army communiqué, December 5, 1956, in Franqui, *Diary,* 126; Szulc, *Fidel,* 381.
24. Guevara and Castro, *La conquista de la esperanza,* 80–84.

of the battle, he implied that the rebel command structure broke down: "I recall that [Juan] Almeida, then a captain, came beside me to get orders, but there was nobody there to issue them."[25] Only Fidel Castro could have given orders to Captain Almeida, and from Fidel's position in the cane field, he could not communicate effectively with his squad leaders. To get to his position, the rebels had to cross a path that exposed them to enemy fire.[26] Captain Almeida returned to his group and tried to organize a defense on his own initiative.

Che, not one to shy away from risk, tried to follow Castro into the cane field. As he and Emilio Albentosa attempted to cross the path, a burst of gunfire dropped both men to the ground. One bullet struck a box of ammunition in Guevara's shirt pocket and the ricochet grazed his neck. It was a minor injury, but in the heat of battle, with blood spilling over his uniform, Che was convinced that he and Albentosa, whose mouth and nose were spewing blood, had suffered mortal wounds. Guevara thought about killing himself, knowing that Batista's soldiers would torture and execute any rebel they captured. He thought about the heroic character in "To Build a Fire," a short story by Jack London, one of his favorite authors. When the hero of London's story realizes that he is about to freeze to death in the Alaskan wilderness, he calmly leans against a tree and accepts death with dignity. Che did not want to die screaming in agony. To prevent such an undignified end, he might have to kill himself before the enemy captured him.[27]

The firing suddenly stopped and the enemy called on the rebels to surrender. One rebel, crawling near Che, shouted, "We'd better surrender!"

"NOBODY SURRENDERS HERE!" yelled Camilo Cienfuegos, a wild, wiry young soldier. Camilo answered the ultimatum with a blast of his submachine gun, cursing at the enemy troops as he thrust himself back into the battle.[28]

---

25. Guevara, *Episodes*, 90.

26. Daniel James argues that the original Spanish version of Che's account of Alegría del Pío contains an implicit criticism of Fidel's leadership. In the Monthly Review Press translation, a passage is given as "Fidel tried in vain to regroup his men in the nearby cane field, which could be reached simply by crossing a small clearing." In the original Spanish, the last clause of this sentence reads: "al que había que llegar cruzando la guardarraya solamente." According to James, the clause should be translated as "which could be reached only by crossing the path." The incorrect translation, he argues, gives the impression that Castro's men had not *followed* him, whereas Guevara meant to suggest that Castro had not *led* them. See James, *Che Guevara*, 89.

27. Bornot Pubillones et al., *De Tuxpan a La Plata*, 94; Che did not mention the story by name, but his description of it suggests that it was "To Build a Fire." See Guevara, *Episodes*, 91.

28. Guevara, *Episodes*, 91. In the official account of the battle, Camilo and Juan Almeida

Captain Almeida, who also refused to entertain the notion of surrender, rushed over to Che. "Leave me, they've killed me," Che pleaded. Almeida refused to abandon Che and, with help from Ramiro Valdés, carried him off the field, heading toward a thicket that would provide them with some highly demanded cover.[29] Soon after Che fled the battlefield, low-flying planes strafed the rebel positions again, sowing even greater confusion among the retreating rebels. The Cuban army then set fire to the cane in an effort to smoke the rebels out. With smoke and flames rising from the cane fields behind them, Almeida led Che and three other men into some wooded ground, having survived a dreadful, thirty-minute baptism of fire.

The Cuban army routed Castro's rebel army at Alegría del Pío. Without much effort and at the cost of only one dead, two Rural Guard companies had broken up Castro's rebels into twenty-six separate groups, some of which consisted of only one soldier. Within a day or two the army hunted down and executed twenty-one rebels. The army captured and imprisoned another twenty-three, and another nineteen rebels disappeared. Only sixteen of the eighty-two men who landed from the *Granma* survived the battle of Alegría del Pío and the army's subsequent pursuit.[30]

Yet two years later, the survivors of that disaster marched triumphantly into Havana as liberators, among them Che Guevara, Camilo Cienfuegos, Raúl Castro, Juan Almeida, and Ramiro Valdés. Their survival was attributable to their good fortune and the army's bad judgment. Before the battle of Alegría del Pío, the army had pulled back its ambush at La Esperanza, where army units could have ambushed rebels attempting to move into the Sierra Maestra.[31] Batista called off the pursuit on December 13, having concluded that Castro had been killed and his army crushed. Batista withdrew his combat units from the Sierra Maestra and canceled aerial surveillance, leaving a path to the sierra open to any rebel fortunate enough to have eluded army patrols for eight days.

Nevertheless, if Fidel Castro had continued to pursue the same strategy and tactics that had led his men directly into an army ambush just three days after their arrival, Batista's army would have crushed him. By publicly announcing that he would invade Cuba by the end of the year, Castro provided Batista

---

are both credited with the courageous response to the enemy's ultimatum. See Alvarez Tabio, *Diario de la guerra,* 33.

29. Guevara Lynch, *Mi hijo el Che,* 100–101.
30. Szulc, *Fidel,* 383.
31. Confidential army communiqué, December 5, 1956, in Franqui, *Diary,* 127.

with an opportunity to place troops in position to defeat the invaders. Although Castro's declaration could have been a ruse—and General Francisco Tabernilla, the Cuban army chief of staff, publicly dismissed it as such—Batista nevertheless ordered warships and aircraft to patrol the coast from Pinar del Río to Oriente, and placed army and Rural Guard garrisons on alert. Castro's declaration lifted the cover off his invasion force and vitiated the strategy behind the diversionary strikes. Batista expected Castro's landing and had sent reinforcements to Oriente province before the Santiago uprising on November 30.[32]

Castro, like Che and other rebel commanders, would learn from the costly mistakes that had led to Alegría del Pío. A brilliant and charismatic political leader, Fidel lacked training and faith in unconventional warfare, which explains why he opted for guerrilla warfare only after he landed in the wrong place and at the wrong time. The seasoned rebel troops who came down from the mountains two years later would not have withered under enemy fire as had the rebels at Alegría del Pío. Two years of combat in the mountains turned idealistic rebels into veteran guerrillas. But from the swamp to Alegría del Pío, the rebels left a trail of cane stalks and followed a treasonous peasant, who helped to lead the army to Castro's encampment. Castro selected a poor location to rest, failed to post sentries, and did not make arrangements for an orderly retreat. When the firing commenced, the rebels scattered in every direction and Castro could not regroup them. He lost more than 75 percent of his men as a result.

If Castro had come to Cuba with the intention of fighting a guerrilla war, he surely did not act like it. The war he launched from a swamp was overt, anticipated, and conventional. Che learned from the *Granma* how not to launch a guerrilla campaign. The first guerrilla band should be organized by a handful of conspirators, "without mass support or knowledge," Che explained in *Guerrilla Warfare*. "Absolute secrecy, a total absence of information in the enemy's hands, should be the primary base of the movement."[33]

The *Granma* rebels who followed Fidel across the Caribbean lacked the training, strength, and secrecy required for launching any hostilities, whether a guerrilla campaign or conventional operations. Yet they trusted Fidel's military judgment, convinced that they would somehow drive Batista out of

---

32. Vinton Chapin (counselor of embassy) to State, November 23, 1955, U.S. National Archives, record group 59, Department of State Records 737.00/11-2355; Szulc, *Fidel*, 373.

33. Guevara, *Guerrilla Warfare*, 128.

office. Only a handful of trusted advisers knew that behind Fidel's strategy was the assumption that a combination of conventional and unconventional strikes against the Batista regime would spark a mass uprising. Castro did not believe that his rebel force, by itself, could topple Batista in one decisive blow. If other anti-Batista forces, including, and perhaps especially, disaffected military units, did not join the insurrection, Castro planned to implement his contingency plan, calling for his troops to reassemble in the Sierra Maestra, from where they would launch a guerrilla campaign.

At the outset of the Cuban insurrection, Castro's strategic planning placed more emphasis on conventional warfare than on a guerrilla campaign. He and his close advisers, including Che, believed that the Batista regime lacked the strength and legitimacy to withstand coordinated uprisings. The rebels believed that they could initiate the disintegration of the Batista regime with a few decisive strikes. Che later explained how he first envisioned the triumph that would follow the invasion of Cuba: "We all thought about arriving at some place in Cuba and after a few cries, several heroic battles, a few radio broadcasts and several deaths, we would expel dictator Batista and achieve power."[34] The *Granma* rebels did not conceive of themselves as a *foco,* as Guevara later defined a guerrilla band, and they did not initially intend to launch a guerrilla campaign against Batista. They conceived of themselves as the spearhead of a broadly based insurrectionary movement that would topple the dictatorship with attacks on military garrisons, general strikes, *and* guerrilla warfare. The Cuban insurrection *became* a guerrilla campaign but it *began* with a conventional attack supplemented by some unorthodox assaults on well-fortified positions. The rebels never envisioned an armed struggle based principally in the mountains. According to Faustino Pérez, one of Fidel's two chiefs of staff, the *Granma* rebels intended to spark a general insurrection with attacks, strikes, and sabotage on urban and rural fronts.[35]

The success of this ambitious plan hinged on the ability of urban militants to pin down the Cuban army in Havana and Santiago long enough to convince Batista and his generals that they faced a nationwide insurrection rather than just an invasion force of eighty-two men in Oriente province. Batista would not likely vacate the Havana or Santiago garrisons to engage Castro in Oriente if Castro did not secure the two largest cities. Castro had negotiated an alliance with the Directorio Revolucionario (DR, Revolutionary

34. Guevara, "Development of a Marxist Revolution," 248.
35. Szulc, *Fidel,* 379.

Directorate), an insurrectionary group based at the University of Havana, but he did not command those units. In fact, mutual suspicions weakened the alliance between the two organizations, which partly explains why the DR remained inactive on November 30. Castro could only depend on a handful of militants, led by Frank País. However, País could not strike Moncada unless and until he captured enough arms and ammunition to mount a full-scale assault on Moncada with civilian volunteers. In the initial assault on the police station, País commanded twenty-eight rebels. If the people of Santiago did not join the uprising, the badly outgunned and outnumbered rebels could not mount a viable attack on the one thousand troops stationed at Moncada.[36] Although the Santiago rebels only had to divert the Cuban army away from Castro's invasion forces, their strategy, like Castro's, still assumed that thousands of Cubans would immediately join them in rebellion against Batista.

Castro borrowed his military strategy from a traditional and conventional source: José Martí, who led Cuba's third war for independence in 1895. Martí had organized a rebel army in Florida and planned to invade eastern Cuba on three yachts sailing from Fernandina Beach, near Jacksonville. Martí intended to coordinate his invasion with a general uprising on the island, thereby preventing the Spanish army and navy from concentrating its superior forces against the widely scattered rebel units.[37] Spanish and American authorities uncovered Martí's plot and seized the three vessels on January 14, 1895. Undeterred, Martí authorized secret revolutionary cells in Cuba to launch the insurrection on February 25, 1895. The Spanish authorities crushed that conspiracy too. Martí eventually slipped into Cuba six weeks later on a small boat, and he came, not with an invading army, but with General Máximo Gómez and four other men in a quiet, covert operation, undetected by the Spanish naval patrols.[38]

Castro adopted an honored military strategy from Cuba's greatest patriot for the compelling political reason of linking himself to Martí. However, instead of adopting the covert plan that had worked, Castro borrowed the insurrectionary plan that had failed. Martí's experiences had demonstrated that scattered groups of rebels could infiltrate the island safely and relatively easily, while larger, overt operations offered easy prey to the authorities. Castro wanted to accomplish what Martí had failed to do, despite overwhelming

36. Bonachea and San Martín, *Cuban Insurrection*, 79; H. Thomas, *Cuban Revolution*, 49; Franqui, *Diary*, 118–21.

37. Foner, *Spanish-Cuban-American War*, 1:1–4.

38. Musicant, *Empire by Default*, 43–49; Foner, *Antonio Maceo*, 162–65.

logistical barriers. His strategy required absolute secrecy, precise timing, and effective coordination of units in two countries. Castro had to maintain secure lines of communication with his allies in Santiago and Havana, particularly during the twelve-hundred-mile odyssey of the *Granma* from Tuxpan to Oriente province. Once the *Granma* left port, however, Castro could not transmit radio messages to the island. If something went wrong and the diversionary strikes did not succeed, he could not alter or postpone his plans. He could not even communicate with his own men by radio or walkie-talkie. As a result, Castro lost command and control of his rebel army when navigational errors or enemy fire forced them into swamps and cane fields. In his first three days back on Cuban soil, Castro knew little about the strength or location of his enemies or his allies.

The absence of communications equipment did not deter Castro or his men. Even though he could not transmit or receive messages to or from Celia Sánchez about the delivery of critical supplies and reinforcements, Castro pinned his initial hopes on an amphibious landing followed by an attack on the nearest army garrison. He faced formidable statistical and logistical odds. Che Guevara recognized the weaknesses in Castro's military strategy. Soon after meeting Fidel in July 1955, Guevara expressed grave concerns about the prospects for success. "What do you think of this crazy idea of the Cubans, invading an island completely defended by coastal artillery?" Guevara once asked Hilda Gadea, his first wife. Guevara enlisted enthusiastically in the rebel army anyway—with Gadea's support.[39]

Guevara, like so many other rebels who enlisted in the rebel army, eventually developed a conviction that with bold, courageous, and determined leadership, the rebels could inspire a nationwide rebellion and overthrow Batista. Castro had tried and failed in his assault against the Moncada army barracks in 1953, but he still had enough power and charisma to raise another rebel army for another attack on terms that still favored the Cuban army. Instead of attacking the weak points in the enemy's armor first, Castro launched his second rebellion in the same way that he initiated the first, with an attack on strong army and police units in Santiago. Although Castro's 1956 strategy called for the main body to hit a relatively easy target in Niquero, the campaign would once again begin with an attack in Santiago, on ground and terms chosen by his enemy.

To Castro's credit, he developed a contingency plan to regroup his rebel

39. Gadea, *Ernesto*, 102.

forces and launch a guerrilla campaign from the Sierra Maestra if he failed to take the Niquero garrisons. Yet Castro clearly preferred a victory through quick and rather conventional strikes to the more daunting prospect of victory through a protracted guerrilla campaign. Castro questioned the viability and potential of guerrilla warfare. If his initial strikes had generated the popular uprising he had anticipated, he might have rolled into Santiago at the head of a conventional army a few short weeks after the *Granma* landing. As it turned out, he rolled into Havana two years after the *Granma* landing at the head of a guerrilla army whose most accomplished commander was Ernesto Che Guevara.

Although Che Guevara had mastered the theory of guerrilla warfare in Mexico, he (and Castro) perfected the practice of it in the Sierra Maestra. Abstract concepts became hard realities at Alegría del Pío, where the disaster left no doubt that the initial strategy contradicted fundamental principles of guerrilla warfare. From these negative experiences Guevara developed the basic tenets that he subsequently elaborated in *Guerrilla Warfare:* "The fundamental principle is that no battle, combat, or skirmish is to be fought unless it will be won." In the initial phase of a guerrilla campaign, "the essential task of the guerrilla fighter is to keep himself from being destroyed."[40] Guevara learned these painful truths three days after the *Granma* landed. To launch his guerrilla campaign in Bolivia in 1966, he dispatched small rebel units around the continent and assembled them in eastern Bolivia, a textbook example of covert infiltration. A credible guerrilla campaign did not begin with the *Granma*'s departure, an overt shipment of men and matériel across twelve hundred miles of hostile waters. There was no certainty of victory in Castro's strategy; complete annihilation was the more likely outcome.

Although Batista had only a few units trained in counterinsurgency warfare, he had more than enough resources to crush any conventional attacks. The Cuban army consisted of forty thousand troops divided into eight regiments stationed at each of the provincial capitals. In Oriente, the Antonio Maceo Regiment maintained operational headquarters in Santiago and Holguín, with Rural Guard units scattered throughout the towns and villages of Oriente. In western Oriente, where Castro intended to land, Niquero, Media Luna, Campechuela, Manzanillo, and Pilón were defended by at least a company of rural guardsmen (one hundred men). From these bases, the Cuban army was ideally positioned to send out multiple search-and-destroy

---

40. Guevara, *Guerrilla Warfare*, 54, 56.

missions against Castro's rebel army.[41] In addition, the army could call in air and naval support to locate and destroy the invading army. Cuba's air forces included a bomber squadron of twenty B-26s, a fighter squadron of seventeen F-47s and eight T-33 jet trainers, and a transport squadron of thirty-three mixed aircraft, including eleven C-47s. The navy could deploy up to a dozen small submarine chasers, several World War II–era PT boats, and several small gunboats for coastal defense.[42]

In addition to the advantage in material resources, the Cuban army had more accurate and reliable intelligence. From the moment the Cuban rebels began training in Mexico, they attracted Mexican, Cuban, and American intelligence agents. The Mexican police first raided Castro's training camp in June 1956 and, in collaboration with Cuban and American agents, continued to track the movements of the rebels for the following five months. On November 21, three days before the Cubans assembled at Tuxpan, Mexican police arrested three Cuban conspirators and then gave Castro seventy-two hours to leave the country. Mexican police dutifully reported to the Cuban government that Castro and his men were about to leave Mexico. Armed with that information, the Cuban army placed all army and Rural Guard outposts on alert and ordered constant surveillance of the coast from Pinar del Río in the west to Oriente province in the east.[43] The only thing that Batista did not know was the precise location of Castro's intended disembarkation.

The military strategy that ultimately led the rebels to victory was covert, unpredictable, and unconventional. The survivors of Alegría del Pío applied basic rules of guerrilla strategy and tactics because Castro's more conventional approach failed. Fortunately for Fidel, his best guerrilla commander and strategist—Che Guevara—survived the battle and guided the transition of the rebels from a conventional insurrectionary force into the most accomplished guerrilla army in twentieth-century Latin America. The recovery of Castro's army and its subsequent success was attributable in no small part to the training, strategy, and leadership provided by Ernesto Guevara.

Despite the deluge of biographies, memoirs, and documentaries that appeared on the thirtieth anniversary of Guevara's death in 1997, none of the

---

41. Regan, "Armed Forces of Cuba: 1933–1959," 70; Fermoselle, *Evolution of the Cuban Military*, 209–10; H. Thomas, *Cuban Revolution*, 157.

42. Regan, "Armed Forces of Cuba," 122; Fermoselle, *Evolution of the Cuban Military*, 209–10.

43. Szulc, *Fidel*, 370; Quirk, *Fidel*, 117; Bornot Pubillones et al., *De Tuxpan a La Plata*, 78; Guevara, *Che*, annex 1, 141.

recent analysts has reexamined Guevara's career as a guerrilla soldier, military commander, and revolutionary theorist. New evidence has come to light, including some of Guevara's previously unpublished campaign diaries and declassified Central Intelligence Agency (CIA) documents. These new sources can be used to reevaluate Guevara's fame and impact as a guerrilla warrior and theorist. In the 1960s, several scholars debunked Guevara's contributions to the theory and practice of guerrilla warfare, but around the world, Guevara was and is still ranked in the pantheon of the great guerrilla theorists, along with Colonel T. E. Lawrence, Mao Tse-tung, Augusto César Sandino, and General Vo Nguyen Giap.

The aim of this study is to evaluate Guevara's record as a guerrilla soldier, commander, and theorist, from his first skirmish in Cuba to his defeat in Bolivia eleven years later. How did Guevara perform in battle, as a soldier and as a commander? Were his theories of guerrilla warfare sound and applicable? The examination of these and other questions will separate the mythical Guevara from the real guerrilla, the doctor who received his baptism of fire at Alegría del Pío, drafted a revolutionary doctrine of guerrilla warfare, and died fighting for his ideals in Bolivia. The objective is to examine Guevara's complete military record—as a soldier, commander, and theorist—and draw conclusions based on the best available evidence.

With a nod to both Guevara's critics and admirers, the record indicates that Che was underrated as a conventional military strategist, overrated as a guerrilla commander, and often misrepresented as a guerrilla theorist. Che achieved his greatest military victory by applying a conventional military strategy in his campaign to take the city of Santa Clara (November–December 1958). Widely regarded as an offensive and aggressive commander, he orchestrated a brilliant defensive campaign during the army's summer offensive of 1958. As a guerrilla commander, he scored impressive victories in ambush after ambush in Cuba and later in Bolivia, but he rarely commanded more than one hundred troops in battle. The strategies and tactics he presented in *Guerrilla Warfare* did not substantially deviate from the doctrines advocated by other strategists, and he violated most of his own precepts during his disastrous Bolivian campaign (1966–67). Credited with developing foco theory, Che never attempted to devise a new *theory* of guerrilla warfare. He wanted to practice guerrilla warfare, and during a relatively brief military career (1956–67), he practiced it more than he theorized about it. Che was a man of action rather than theory. He fought on the front lines, commanded his own columns, trained guerrillas, and organized guerrilla fronts in almost every Latin American country.

The fact that Che served under and took orders from Fidel Castro does not diminish the value of his contributions to revolutionary strategies and practices. For most of the campaign in the Sierra Maestra, Che served as the rebel army's top military strategist. Fidel, after six months and several skirmishes as the field commander, eventually ceded tactical military command to Che and his other military subordinates, Raúl Castro, Juan Almeida, Camilo Cienfuegos, and Ramiro Valdés. Fidel directed general insurrectionary strategy, but even there, he sought and accepted advice and criticism from Che, whom he regarded as his best strategist and commander, despite Che's overly aggressive tendencies in battle.

Moreover, it was Che—not Castro—who literally wrote the book on guerrilla warfare. The manual of that title, which served as the basic text for Cuba's Revolutionary Armed Forces, exposed a truth that had been concealed during the insurrection: Che Guevara was the principal architect of Castro's military strategy. He undoubtedly learned and benefited from Castro; Fidel certainly profited from the military advice and leadership provided by Che. Ironically, Ernesto Guevara never studied military affairs formally. In Chapters 2 and 3, I will examine how Che developed from a medical doctor into a revolutionary and a *guerrillero,* identifying the events and people that shaped his principles and strategies. A well-read intellectual with a sharp analytical mind, Guevara discovered an inclination and aptitude for armed conflict, learning quickly from Castro's initial military fiasco and developing into Fidel Castro's trusted and most accomplished guerrilla commander. In Chapters 4 through 6, I analyze Guevara's record as a soldier and comandante in Cuba, from his earliest days as the army's medical doctor to the triumphant commander of the rebel forces that took Santa Clara and forced the resignation of Fulgencio Batista.

Guevara's education in guerrilla warfare did not begin or end in Cuba. In 1954 he witnessed the quick and easy collapse of Jacobo Arbenz's revolutionary regime in Guatemala. From that experience he learned to expect a counterrevolution sponsored by the United States. When he marched into Havana in January 1959, he knew what had to be done to consolidate a radical revolution. If and when the United States intervened militarily, Guevara intended to wage a defensive guerrilla campaign against the occupying forces. Thus, Che wrote *Guerrilla Warfare* primarily as an instruction manual for the Cuban army and militia, but he also intended to teach other Latin American revolutionaries how to wage unconventional warfare. *Guerrilla Warfare,* however, does not represent Guevarism in full bloom. Che devoted his later years to the development and implementation of a tricontinental strategy of insurrection supported by an international fighting front. The strategies and tactics conveyed in *Guerrilla Warfare* are neither innovative nor dangerous. Guevara's tricontinental strategy, explained so passionately in his "Message to the Tricontinental," represented something new and radical in revolutionary circles, which explains why so many self-proclaimed revolutionaries denounced it then. Guevarism, the subject of Chapters 7 and 8, was a tricontinental revolutionary strategy that began with a guerrilla foco and ended with a total war against imperialism in Africa, Asia, and Latin America.

In the three final chapters, I examine the project that consumed and ultimately defeated Che Guevara: the execution of his tricontinental strategy. Unsatisfied and even slightly uncomfortable as a bureaucrat, Guevara left Cuba to apply his revolutionary doctrines in the field. By that time, American military strategists, diplomats, and intelligence agents had studied his writings as carefully as had any Latin American revolutionaries. They adapted their counterinsurgency strategies to meet and defeat the challenge of Guevarism. Guevara unwittingly compelled his enemy to develop more effective counterinsurgency strategies and tactics, innovations that ultimately defeated him. Guevara also failed partly because friends and allies let him down. He advocated international solidarity when there was none; he *practiced* revolution when too many revolutionaries preferred simply to talk about it.

Few people, however, could have predicted that an asthmatic, twenty-eight-year-old doctor from Argentina, with only a few months of a basic military education, would have developed into one of the world's most famous guerrilla commanders and strategists. His image alone, more than thirty years after his death, remains powerful enough to capture the rebellious spirit of Guevara and the generation of revolutionaries he inspired.

TWO THE MAKING OF A REVOLUTIONARY

In August 1958, Carlos Rafael Rodríguez, one of the few leaders of the Partido Socialista Popular (PSP, Popular Socialist Party, the Cuban Communist Party) to join the M-26-7 forces in the Sierra Maestra, gave Che a copy of Mao Tse-tung's *Problems of Strategy in Guerrilla War Against Japan*. Che had just finished directing 350 guerrillas in a brilliant defensive campaign, holding his bases against fourteen infantry battalions that had been hurled against them. Although Che found some similarities between the Chinese and Cuban struggles, he dismissed any implication that the Cuban rebels had imported their guerrilla strategies from China. He later explained: "The popular forces [of Cuba], without knowing these manuals on strategy and tactics on guerrilla war beforehand, written in China, carried on our guerrilla war in a similar manner. We did not know the experiences of the Chinese troops in twenty years of struggle in their territory, but we knew our territory, our enemy, and we used something that every man has on his shoulders. We used our heads to fight the enemy."[1]

Ernesto Guevara certainly did not graduate from a guerrilla training school in Beijing. He had received rudimentary training in guerrilla strategy and tactics

---

1. Guevara, "Development of a Marxist Revolution," 249; Debray, *Revolution in the Revolution?* 20.

under the tutelage of a Spanish military instructor in Mexico. Although Guevara came predisposed to fight a guerrilla campaign, he, like Fidel, developed and refined his guerrilla strategy and tactics under fire in the mountains. The sixteen rebels who escaped from the army ambush had no choice but to alter their strategic concepts. Necessity forced the Cuban rebels to "invent" their version of guerrilla warfare.

This is not to suggest, however, that Guevara did not learn from great guerrilla commanders. Che first read about Mao and Communist China in 1954, while in Guatemala. In Mexico, Guevara studied guerrilla warfare under Alberto Bayo, a Cuban-born Spanish military officer who had directed guerrilla operations during the Spanish Civil War. Bayo had also studied the campaigns of Augusto César Sandino, who learned the value of guerrilla warfare during his fight against the American marines who occupied his native Nicaragua (1927–33).[2] Thus, one can detect significant foreign influences in the strategy or tactics of guerrilla warfare that Che applied and taught.

However, guerrilla commanders in Spain, China, and Nicaragua fought campaigns designed for the unique circumstances of their countries. Military strategy must be shaped by and adapted to the fighter's terrain, technology, and weapons; the size and strength of the enemy; and the national and international political climate. The conditions under which the Chinese Communists pursued their guerrilla campaigns could not be replicated in Cuba, nor could Che Guevara replicate his Cuban model in the Bolivian highlands. Che's greatest guerrilla success came in Cuba, where he fought on the front lines and commanded troops in battle, developing guerrilla strategies and tactics as he fought the enemy in the field. Neither Che nor Fidel sailed for Cuba with the intention of applying a Chinese, Soviet, or any other revolutionary model to Cuba. According to Ramón Bonachea and Marta San Martín, two students of the Cuban Revolution, the "Cuban insurrectionists borrowed no model from abroad to carry out their fight against the dictatorship."[3]

Ernesto Guevara certainly did not bring any revolutionary model with him to Cuba. He arrived with only a basic military training that included some lessons in guerrilla strategy and tactics. He had absolutely no formal military training when he met Alberto Bayo in Mexico. Prior to that time, Guevara had studied everything but military affairs—primarily literature, political philosophy, and medicine. Guevara only became a student of war after he became

2. Gadea, *Ernesto*, 19–20, 35–36; Quirk, *Fidel*, 13; Bayo, *Mi aporte*, 15–21.
3. Bonachea and San Martín, *Cuban Insurrection*, 3.

a revolutionary. He became a revolutionary in Guatemala, in 1954.

An asthmatic child born into an upper class Argentine family in 1928, Guevara lacked the physical strength, inclination, and education for a military career. From the age of two until his death in Bolivia, Guevara suffered through serious asthma attacks that frequently incapacitated him.[4] Even on his military campaigns in Cuba, the Congo, and Bolivia, Guevara needed medicines and rest to relieve his suffering. His asthma had a direct and often negative impact on his military campaigns. He occasionally suffered so seriously that he had to halt his guerrilla column while he recuperated or send men to acquire medication to alleviate his symptoms.

Aside from a boyhood fascination with playing war games, the young Ernesto showed little inclination for a military career. As a teenager, in fact, he seemed more inclined toward a literary than a military profession. Although he made only passing grades in school, he excelled in the informal educational environment maintained at home by his parents, who encouraged open discussions of politics, poetry, philosophy, and literature. By the age of fourteen, Ernesto had read Sigmund Freud, Robert Frost, Alexandre Dumas, and Jules Verne. He delighted in adventure stories, particularly in the novels of Jack London, but he also found inspiration in French poets such as Charles Baudelaire, whose works he read in French. He also read Spanish and Latin American poets, among them Federico García Lorca and Pablo Neruda. In literature Ernesto found an escape from modern civilization, which was, he concluded, spiritually decadent and depraved, in desperate need of regeneration.[5]

By the age of seventeen, Ernesto had developed an extraordinarily inquisitive temperament and a disarming intellect. That year, he began to compile a philosophical dictionary, an effort that reflected a highly disciplined mind. This handwritten notebook eventually totaled 165 pages, with the entries arranged alphabetically and indexed by topic and author. The entries ranged from short biographical sketches of famous philosophers to definitions of love, reason, narcissism, and morality. Some of his entries reveal an extensive familiarity with and perhaps a certain expertise in the basic principles of Marxist-Leninist philosophy. To explain dialectical materialism, for example, Ernesto quoted from a relatively obscure work by Engels, *Anti-Dühring*. He characterized *The Communist Manifesto* as "the most brilliant Pamphlet" written by Marx.[6]

4. Castañeda, *Compañero*, 17–18.
5. Guevara Lynch, *Mi hijo el Che*, 238, 265; Gadea, *Ernesto*, 19–20, 35–36.
6. Anderson, *Che Guevara*, 38; Cupull and González, *Ernestito vivo y presente*, 107–9.

Guevara's interest in political philosophy, however, never compelled him to take an active role in Argentine politics. To some extent he inherited the antifascist ideology of his parents, who regarded Colonel Juan Domingo Perón and his wife, María Eva Duarte, called Evita, as homegrown versions of Franco and Mussolini.[7] The Italian and Spanish working-class immigrants of Argentina adored the Peróns, but the Argentinean oligarchy, which included relatives of Ernesto's mother and father, despised them. Following the Argentine military coup of June 1943, Ernesto's history teacher argued that the officers, including the charismatic Colonel Perón, would bring culture to the poor. "If the people were cultured," Ernesto responded, "they would not accept the military."[8]

In the presidential campaign of 1945–46, Ernesto's mother, Celia, easily the most militant anti-Peronist in the house, favored the Democratic Union, a coalition of the Radical, Socialist, Communist, and Progressive Democrat parties that campaigned under the slogan "For Liberty, Against Nazism." Ernesto, however, watched this and other political campaigns from the sidelines, determined not to get involved. Ernesto Guevara simply did not participate in the political or social struggles that engulfed Argentina during the Peronist regime.[9]

Yet Guevara's independent readings in political philosophy expanded after he entered the University of Buenos Aires in 1947. In his private world of study and reflection, he systematically read all twenty-five volumes of his father's *Contemporary History of the Modern World*. His explorations of socialist and communist thought expanded to include writings on Joseph Stalin, a French biography of Lenin, and some of Lenin's speeches. He reread *The Communist Manifesto* and reexamined *Das Kapital*. By this time he had developed a special interest in the life and thought of Marx. From R. P. Ducatillon's *Communism and Christianity*, he developed biographical portraits of Marx and Lenin, describing the latter as a man who "lived, breathed and slept" socialist revolution.[10]

As a medical student at the University of Buenos Aires (1947–52), he explored an even wider range of political ideas and parties. One of his best

7. Rock, *Argentina*, 238–61; Page, *Perón*, 73–78.
8. Cupull and González, *Ernestito vivo y presente*, 95.
9. Page, *Perón*, 139; Gambini, *El Che Guevara*, 51–53; Cupull and González, *Ernestito vivo y presente*, 102–3; Guevara Lynch, *Mi hijo el Che*, 283–84; Anderson, *Che Guevara*, 34; Castañeda, *Compañero*, 30–33.
10. Anderson, *Che Guevara*, 48.

friends at the university was a young woman named Berta Gilda Infante, known as Tita. A cultured, attractive, and intelligent woman, Tita became Ernesto's closest intellectual comrade. Through her, Ernesto escaped from the always crowded Guevara household and learned more about the ideology and practices of the Communist Youth, to which she belonged. Ernesto met other party militants and, evidently out of intellectual curiosity, attended at least one Communist Youth meeting. According to Ricardo Campos, who invited him to the meeting, Ernesto stormed out while it was still in progress. Carlos Infante, Tita's brother and also a member of the Communist Youth, recalls that Ernesto criticized the sectarianism of the Communist party.[11]

Despite Ernesto's intensive studies in Marxist-Leninist philosophy and his contacts with Communist party members, he had not yet fully articulated his ideological positions or affiliated himself with a political party. He was a pensive young bohemian, quite content to spend his time away from medical school and the laboratory in quiet reflection or, as he discovered in 1951, on the open road. One of his diary entries during a two-month trip reveals a troubled young man trying to come to terms with life. He wrote: "I realize that something has ripened in me that was growing over time within the hustle and bustle of city life: and it is the hatred of civilization, the crude image of people moving like crazy to the beat of this tremendous noise which seems to me like the hated antithesis of peace."[12]

In October 1951, Ernesto and his best friend, Alberto Granado, set out on a nine-month motorcycle journey around South America. They intended to ride across the Andes to Chile, then north through Bolivia, Peru, Ecuador, and Colombia. This trip, full of the adventure and new experiences that Ernesto craved, brought him closer to the ideological maturity that he sought.[13]

During their nine-month journey, the two young men occasionally acted like young men, chasing women and carousing in bars. Unlike most casual tourists, however, they toured a Chilean copper mine, worked in a Peruvian leper colony, and rafted down the Amazon River. For Ernesto, the trip brought to life concepts and people that had only been abstractions to him. Guevara first saw and felt the alienation of the masses when he toured Chuquicamata, a great open-pit copper mine in northern Chile. A significant moment in

11. Espinosa Goitizolo, *Atlas histórico*, 42–43; Cupull and González, *Ernestito vivo y presente*, 117, 169; Guevara Lynch, *Aquí va un soldado*, 9–10; Anderson, *Che Guevara*, 49–50.

12. Diary excerpts cited in Guevara Lynch, *Mi hijo el Che*, 334 (my translation).

13. Granado, *Con el Ché*, 15–16; Guevara, *Motorcyle Diaries*, 13.

Guevara's ideological development occurred in the mining town of Baquedano, just outside Chuquicamata, on March 11, 1952. Ernesto and Alberto spent the evening with a poor miner and his wife, both of them Communists. The man's "shrunken features struck a mysterious, tragic note," as Ernesto observed him by the light of a candle. The man explained how he had been imprisoned for three months because of his membership in the Communist party. Now he could not find a job in the copper mines, which explained why he and his wife had little food to share with their guests. Ernesto could have lectured them about the Marxist concept of alienation, but instead, he learned more from them, the "living symbol of the proletariat the world over." He confided to his diary: "They didn't have a single miserable blanket to sleep under, so we gave them one of ours and Alberto and I wrapped the other round us as best we could. It was one of the coldest nights I've ever spent, one which made me feel a little closer to this strange, for me anyway, human species."[14]

This passage in Ernesto's travel diaries has been studied carefully by Che's biographers. Jean Cormier argues that the night spent at Baquedano marked the political awakening of Ernesto Guevara. From that moment on, Cormier argues, Ernesto started to become Che.[15] Even Jorge Castañeda, the most critical of Che's recent biographers, agrees that the visit to the copper mines represented part of a gradual political awakening for Che, noting that "Che was disturbed by the chasm between the mine foremen—'the masters, the blond and efficient, insolent administrators . . . the Yankee masters'—and the miners."[16]

The politicization of Ernesto Guevara accelerated during his first South American venture. The poverty and injustice that he observed struck a sensitive chord and intensified his desire to study, but he stopped short of making a political commitment to search for and apply solutions to those problems. He still had to analyze the Latin American condition more carefully and he looked more frequently to Marxist-Leninist thought for answers. In Castañeda's critical assessment of Guevara's ideological development, "his approach remained naïve and incomplete: indignation and common sense made up for serious deficiencies in analysis."[17]

14. Granado, *Con el Ché*, 85–86; Guevara, *Motorcycle Diaries*, 59–60.
15. Jean Cormier, *Che Guevara* (Paris: Editions du Rocher, 1995), 37, 50, cited in Castañeda, *Compañero*, 48.
16. Castañeda, *Compañero*, 47.
17. Ibid., 46.

The journey, which ended with a monthlong layover in Miami, generated a strong anti-American strain in Ernesto's increasingly Pan-American nationalism. He had gradually come to identify United States imperialism as the source of the injustices and poverty he had observed in South America. A brush with the law in Miami fueled his growing anti-Americanism. Some biographers have dismissed the alleged arrest in Miami, but a declassified CIA document confirms that Guevara had a police record in Miami. Although the CIA did not identify the crime for which he was charged, other reliable sources, Alberto and Tomás Granado, indicate that Ernesto and a Puerto Rican friend had caused a disturbance in a Miami bar by expressing some strong criticisms of the United States and the Truman administration.[18]

If Ernesto's South American journey did not constitute a full political awakening, the trip certainly changed his career plans. He returned to Buenos Aires only to complete his medical degree; he had decided to find his destiny somewhere outside Argentina and the medical profession. Sometime after his return to Buenos Aires, Ernesto reviewed and rewrote his travel diary, as he usually did with the diaries he kept throughout his life. He also added a mysterious epilogue called "Notes on the Margin." These notes are the first indication of Guevara's commitment to the revolutionary struggle in Latin America. Without mentioning any time, place, or people, Guevara cryptically described his political activation as the result of a strange meeting with an unidentified man who challenged Guevara's convictions.

"The future belongs to the people and gradually or suddenly they will take power, here and all over the world," the anonymous man proclaimed. "The problem is that the people must be educated first, and they can't do that until they take power," he continued. "They can only learn by their own mistakes, and these will be very serious and will cost many innocent lives." Then he turned his attention to Ernesto: "I also know—and this won't change the course of history or your personal impression of me—that you will die with your fist clenched and your jaw tense, the perfect manifestation of hatred and struggle, because you aren't a symbol, you are an authentic member of the society to be destroyed."

Ernesto, puzzled by the "playful grin with which the man foretold history," shook the man's hand and said good-bye. As he described the

18. Guevara Lynch, *Mi hijo el Che,* 420; Gambini, *El Che Guevara,* 73–74; Cupull and González, *Ernestito vivo y presente,* 160; Martin, "Making of a Revolutionary"; Central Intelligence Agency (hereafter CIA), teletyped information report, April 3, 1958, in Ratner and Smith, *Che Guevara and the FBI,* 31.

encounter, the starry night closed in around him, and his future was revealed in an instant. When humanity is divided into two antagonistic halves, I will be with the people, Ernesto decided.

> And I know it because I see it imprinted on the night that I, the eclectic dissector of doctrines and psychoanalyst of dogmas, howling like a man possessed, will assail the barricades and trenches, will stain my weapon with blood and, consumed with rage, will slaughter any enemy I lay hands on. And then, as if an immense weariness were consuming my recent exhilaration, I see myself being sacrificed to the authentic revolution, the great leveler of individual will, pronouncing the exemplary mea culpa. I feel my nostrils dilate, savoring the acrid smell of gunpowder and blood, of the enemy's death; I brace my body, ready for combat, and prepare myself to be a sacred precinct within which the bestial howl of the victorious proletariat can resound with new vigor and new hope.[19]

Che's biographers and his associates have hotly debated this enigmatic passage. Alberto Granado, who traveled with Che throughout South America, could not recall ever meeting a man who fit the description. Aleida March, Che's second wife, cannot identify the person either, but has suggested that he might have been a composite of several individuals whom Ernesto created as a literary device to explain his self-revelation. Castañeda dismisses the entire passage, arguing that Guevara was simply "ranting and raving." It was impossible, he argues, for Guevara to complete his political conversion by that time, because he had not yet met Fidel Castro or experienced the events that would eventually transform him.[20]

Even Guevara recognized that he needed to continue his ideological development and political studies. What he recognized and described so eloquently in "Notes on the Margin," however, is not his political awakening, but a fatal commitment to die fighting for a cause. He saw himself fighting on behalf of the "people," fighting for the "authentic revolution," even though he could barely define his version of this. He knew only that he was destined to fight and die for that cause. Biographer Jon Lee Anderson concluded that the passage was "uncannily precognitive of Ernesto Guevara's own future

---

19. Guevara, *Motorcycle Diaries,* 152.
20. Anderson, *Che Guevara,* 755; Castañeda, *Compañero,* 55.

death." Guevara's "Notes on the Margin" represented a commitment to a course of action, not an ideology, and "must be seen as a decisive personal testimonial, for the sentiments it contained would soon emerge from the penumbra of his submerged thoughts to find expression in his future actions."[21]

Moreover, Guevara's vision, ending with martyrdom or at least a glorified suicide, is consistent with his previous commentaries on death. Back in 1947, during a tour of northern Argentina, he began to recognize his own suicidal tendencies. He had never been far from death anyway. Every asthma attack he suffered as a child produced a sensation of drowning or suffocating. At an early age he had learned not to fear death. Death might even be liberating, but he did not want to suffer an ignoble end. He developed a stubborn determination to die on his own terms, fighting for a cause. A poem he wrote on January 17, 1947, at least five years before he wrote "Notes on the Margin" expressed the same commitment to die on the battlefield. "The bullets, what can the bullets do to me if / my destiny is to die by drowning. But I am / going to overcome destiny. Destiny can be / achieved by willpower. / Die, yes, but riddled with / bullets, destroyed by the bayonets, if not, no. Drowned, no . . . / a memory more lasting than my name / is to fight, to die fighting."[22]

Ernesto returned to Buenos Aires determined to embark on a new profession as a soldier, a curious decision for a young man who had no formal military education or training. He had received a medical deferment because of his asthma and thereby avoided compulsory military service in Argentina.[23] Aside from some independent readings in history, the only previous expressions of an interest in a military career came when he was a child, when Ernesto and his buddies reenacted battles of the Spanish Civil War in a large field behind his house. He also followed the movements of the Spanish armies on a large map. Ernesto may not have understood the politics of the conflict so well, but through his father he identified the fascists as the enemy.[24]

Still, many boys play war. Few people abandon a medical career after obtaining a medical degree. Ernesto did just that, however, after completing fifteen medical examinations in April 1953 and rejecting a promising job offer in Buenos Aires. He had once dreamed of becoming a famous medical researcher,

---

21. Anderson, *Che Guevara,* 125.

22. Ibid., 44.

23. Cupull and González, *Ernestito vivo y presente,* 164; James, *Che Guevara,* 50.

24. Gambini, *El Che Guevara,* 36–39; Cupull and González, *Ernestito vivo y presente,* 69, 80.

but now the thought of dedicating his life to medicine absolutely depressed him. "I am determined to finish [medical school] but not to incarcerate myself in the ridiculous medical profession," Guevara explained to a friend.[25] Guevara was determined to fulfill a glorious destiny on the field of battle, not in the research laboratory.

Ernesto received his diploma in June 1953 and left Argentina for good several weeks later. After a going-away party, friends and family went to see Ernesto depart from the Retiro train station. Among the anxious crowd was his mother, Celia, who somehow sensed that she would never see her closest son again. As passengers boarded the train for Bolivia, Ernesto hugged and kissed everybody, pulling away from the crowd at the last moment. Still reluctant to turn his back on his loved ones and begin a new journey, he walked alongside the train then turned, raised a clenched fist, and proclaimed: "Here goes a soldier of the Americas." Just in case they did not hear him, he jumped on board and repeated the slogan before disappearing into the car.[26]

Ernesto considered himself a foot soldier in an army not yet formed; he had no idea where this army would be assembled, where it might strike, or who would command it. He and he alone knew that he would fight and die—like a soldier—for the authentic revolution.

One possible location was Bolivia, where, in 1952, an army of workers and peasants had defeated the military and installed a reformist government led by Víctor Paz Estenssoro of the Movimiento Nacionalista Revolucionario (MNR, Nationalist Revolutionary Movement). Paz proceeded to nationalize the tin mines—representing the country's leading economic sector—and when Ernesto arrived Paz was preparing to implement an agrarian reform. Consequently, Ernesto found the cafés, bars, and restaurants in La Paz buzzing with political activity. He made the most of this opportunity to study a revolutionary movement in progress and clarify his own political principles.[27]

In addition to reading the newspapers and discussing politics in the coffee shops, Ernesto inspected the tin mines with Ricardo Rojo, a young anti-Peronist journalist from Buenos Aires. The Argentines visited the Catavi tin mines, home of the largest and most militant congregation of workers in the country. In contrast to the copper mines of northern Chile, which were in private hands, the tin industry in Bolivia was owned and operated by the

25. Martin, "Making of a Revolutionary."

26. Guevara Lynch, *Aquí va un soldado*, 7; see also Ernesto Guevara Lynch's description of this event in *Mi hijo el Che*, prod. Birri.

27. Rojo, *My Friend Che*, 17–18.

national government. The workers Ernesto spoke with expressed enthusiastic support for the nationalization of the mines, but Ernesto remained critical. Since the workers held only two of the seven seats on the board of the state company, they did not control it. "The nationalization of the mines represented a mere change in bosses," he argued.[28]

Nevertheless, the militancy of the miners impressed Ernesto because of their revolutionary potential. For the first time in his life he saw a brigade of workers "armed to the teeth." They had effectively eliminated the army during the April 1952 rebellion, and the workers' brigades had marched in La Paz to demonstrate their willingness to defend their revolution. Guevara recognized that the working classes, given the means to defend and promote their interests, could push the revolution in a radical direction. With the support of the militias, President Paz, who represented the political center of the MNR, implemented the agrarian reform on August 2, 1953, despite opposition from the right wing of the MNR.[29]

The only hope Ernesto saw in the MNR resided in the left-wing faction of Juan Lechín, but Ernesto doubted that Lechín would mobilize the workers or the peasants for a decisive blow against the right-wing MNR faction, led by Siles Suazo. The outcome of an internal struggle between the three MNR factions, Ernesto predicted, would determine the direction of the revolution. Although Lechín had the support of the armed miners, his opponents controlled the military, which they had already purged and reorganized. As a result, Guevara concluded that the balance of power favored the moderate and right-wing elements of the MNR; Lechín, whom Guevara described as a "womanizer and party animal," inspired no confidence in Ernesto. He would not fight and die for Lechín or the MNR. Guevara left in disappointment in August 1952.[30]

Ernesto had planned to go to Venezuela, where Alberto Granado awaited him and where he had planned to work with Alberto in a leprosarium. However, having decided to become a soldier of the authentic revolution and now more interested in revolutionary politics than leprosy, he lost his enthusiasm for the project. Moreover, the repressive regime of Marcos Pérez Jiménez

28. Dunkerley, *Rebellion in the Veins,* 6–10, 58–60; Rojo, *My Friend Che,* 31–32; Gambini, *El Che Guevara,* 77; Ernesto to father, July 24, 1953, in Guevara Lynch, *Aquí va un soldado,* 15.

29. Dunkerley, *Rebellion in the Veins,* 40–48, 65–74.

30. Ibid., 40–48; Ernesto to Tita Infante, September 3, 1953; Ernesto to mother, August 22, 1953, both in Guevara Lynch, *Aquí va un soldado,* 19, 21–22; Gadea, *Ernesto,* 15.

had suppressed the reformist political opposition, and Ernesto saw no signs of a militant opposition developing in Venezuela. Ernesto left for Guatemala, where a revolutionary government had already implemented reforms that challenged American enterprises and delighted Latin America's militant Left.[31]

On his way to Guatemala, Ernesto had an opportunity to inspect the operations of the most powerful American corporation in Central America, the United Fruit Company (UFCO). The revolutionary government of Jacobo Arbenz charged that UFCO, known as "the octopus" in Guatemala, strangled the country's economic development by monopolizing railroads, shipping, and the banana industry. The North American copper companies that Ernesto condemned in Chile did not manage an empire as extensive as that of United Fruit. United owned banana and sugar plantations, railroads, and port facilities in Ecuador, Colombia, Panama, Costa Rica, Honduras, Guatemala, Jamaica, and Cuba. From these bases of supply, the company monopolized the banana trade, working closely with corrupt and authoritarian regimes that allowed the company to exploit its workers.[32] United had recently transferred its Costa Rican operations from the Caribbean to the Pacific Coast, and Guevara inspected those relatively modern port facilities and plantations en route to Guatemala. He hitched a ride on a UFCO ship from Golfito to Puntarenas, Costa Rica, but that UFCO courtesy did not cool his red-hot anger toward the company.[33] In a letter to his aunt Beatriz, Ernesto claimed that his observations of United Fruit's operations had confirmed his negative feelings about these "capitalist octopuses." More important, he began to channel his hostility into some form of political action. "I have sworn before a portrait of the dearly departed Stalin," he half-mockingly explained to Beatriz, "that I would not rest until I see this capitalist octopus annihilated." He then vowed, "In Guatemala, I will improve myself and attain that which I need to become an authentic revolutionary."[34]

When Ernesto arrived in San José, President José "Pepe" Figueres, leader of Costa Rica's "revolution" of 1948, had abolished the army and national-

31. Che to father, October 4, 1953; Che to mother, October 21, 1953, both in Guevara Lynch, *Aquí va un soldado,* 25–27.

32. On the history of United Fruit in Central America, see Dosal, *Doing Business with the Dictators;* Chomsky, *West Indian Workers;* Ernesto to Aunt Beatriz, December 10, 1953, in Guevara Lynch, *Aquí va un soldado,* 29.

33. Ernesto to mother, October 21, 1953, in Guevara Lynch, *Aquí va un soldado,* 26–27; Rojo, *My Friend Che,* 39–40.

34. Ernesto to Aunt Beatriz, December 10, 1953, in Guevara Lynch, *Aquí va un soldado,* 29.

ized the banks. He maintained U.S. support, however, by banning the Communist party and maintaining cordial relations with United Fruit. Although Figueres also angered Washington by offering safe haven and support to the Caribbean Legion, a militant organization dedicated to the overthrow of dictators Anastasio Somoza García of Nicaragua and Rafael Trujillo of the Dominican Republic, Ernesto did not endorse Figueres or join the legion.[35]

Ernesto's concept of authentic revolution embraced armed struggle against Latin American dictators, North American businesses, and the United States government. Figueres and other members of Latin America's democratic, anticommunist Left infuriated Guevara with their calls for moderation and accommodation with the United States. He allegedly got into a heated argument with Rómulo Betancourt, former and future president of Venezuela, because Betancourt favored an alliance with the United States.[36] Ernesto saw "Yankee" capitalism and the United States government as the source of the poverty and oppression in the Americas. Nevertheless, he still had only a rudimentary understanding of Marxist-Leninist political doctrines and only the vaguest notions of how to conduct a revolutionary struggle. He intended to study and perfect his own revolutionary theories and practices in Guatemala.

At the time, Jacobo Arbenz had brought the Guatemalan revolution to a critical juncture by implementing substantial land and labor reforms. The revolution had begun as a moderate movement initiated by students and workers opposed to dictator Jorge Ubico in 1944. During the first government of the revolution, President Juan José Arévalo (1945–50) attempted to steer the revolution on a moderate course, maintaining a tenuous alliance between a moderate faction led by Colonel Francisco Arana, and a more radical wing led by Colonel Jacobo Arbenz. In July 1949 gunmen linked to Arbenz assassinated Arana, provoking a rebellion by the Aranistas. Arbenz crushed the rebellion with the assistance of armed workers, clearing his path to the presidency and setting the revolution in a more radical direction.[37]

Ernesto Guevara gravitated naturally to President Arbenz (1951–54), who pushed the revolution to the left. He encouraged and supported the working classes, which gained formidable political strength through two labor fed-

35. Gleijeses, *Shattered Hope,* 107–14; Ameringer, *Democratic Left in Exile,* 59–110; for the definitive study of the Caribbean rebels, see Ameringer, *Caribbean Legion.*

36. Gadea, *Ernesto,* 4; Anderson, *Che Guevara,* 120; Guevara Lynch, *Aquí va un soldado,* 29–30.

37. Gleijeses, *Shattered Hope,* 22–36, 50–71.

erations with more than four hundred thousand members. He allowed the Communists to operate openly as the Partido Guatemalteco de Trabajo (PGT, Guatemalan Labor Party). Although only a handful of Communists held elected or appointed offices, they occupied important positions in the labor unions, the bureaucracy, and in Arbenz's inner circle. Arbenz did not enlist in the PGT, but he shared its Marxist-Leninist philosophy and welcomed the advice of leading Communists, particularly José Manuel Fortuny. Arbenz and Fortuny, determined to transform Guatemala's semifeudal economy into a modern capitalist system, wrote and passed Decree 900, a monumental agrarian reform and the "most precious fruit of the revolution."[38]

Compared to Mexico's agrarian reform, Decree 900 was relatively moderate, providing for the confiscation and distribution of uncultivated lands, with compensation. The government would assume ownership of most tracts of land and lease them to individuals or cooperatives. By the time Ernesto arrived in Guatemala City in December 1953, Arbenz had already confiscated 80 percent of United's banana plantations on the Pacific Coast. With militant labor unions, peasants, and the military apparently behind him, Arbenz had issued an unprecedented challenge to UFCO and the American government that supported it. If he carried out his agrarian reform, Arbenz would transform the Guatemalan countryside and score a decisive victory over the Americans.[39]

Guevara quickly realized that Arbenz had drawn a decisive battle line between the revolutionaries and imperialists, and he knew which side he would join. From his perspective, Arbenz led the revolution for which he had been looking. "There is a climate of authentic democracy" in Guatemala, he wrote his mother. Whereas the international media portrayed the government as a cave of "robbers, communists, and traitors," Ernesto saw a revolutionary movement committed to social change and justice. "I'm going to stay here awhile," he informed his aunt in January 1954.[40]

Guatemala offered safe haven and a congenial political environment to a wide variety of progressive, liberal, and radical intellectuals and activists. Within a few days of Ernesto's arrival, Ricardo Rojo introduced him to Hilda Gadea, a Peruvian economist working at a Guatemalan development bank.[41] Ernesto

---

38. Ibid., 140–47; Handy, "Most Precious Fruit of the Revolution."
39. For a comprehensive analysis of Guatemala's agrarian reform program, see Handy, *Revolution in the Countryside.*
40. Ernesto to mother, December 28, 1953; Ernesto to Aunt Beatriz, January 5, 1954, both in Guevara Lynch, *Aquí va un soldado,* 30–34.
41. Ernesto to mother, December 28, 1953, in Guevara Lynch, *Aquí va un soldado,* 30–31; Anderson, *Che Guevara,* 120–21; Rojo, *My Friend Che,* 46–48; Gadea, *Ernesto,* 2.

quickly became a popular member of a vibrant intellectual circle that included the twenty-three-year-old Edelberto Torres Rivas Jr., a graduate of Guatemala's University of San Carlos and the secretary general of the Communist Youth. He had just returned from a trip to Communist China when he met Ernesto at the Casa de la Cultura, a popular gathering place for artists, poets, and intellectuals. Guevara, dressed modestly and always short of cash, nevertheless surprised the other intellectuals by expressing his political ideas with such conviction, according to Edelberto.[42]

In this radical political environment Guevara met four Cuban rebels with actual combat experience. Following the disastrous attack on Moncada, a number of Cuban exiles had taken asylum in Guatemala, where they spread tales of their courageous exploits among their comrades. Ernesto suspected that the Cubans tended to embellish their stories with a bit of bravado and machismo, but he grew particularly fond of a lanky twenty-one-year-old named Antonio (Ñico) López, who towered over Ernesto at six feet six inches. From Ñico, Ernesto first learned about the struggles and objectives of Fidel Castro's revolutionary movement.[43]

Amid avant-garde artists, unconventional intellectuals, and Cuban insurrectionists, Ernesto's studies of revolutionary doctrines flourished. Hilda Gadea became his intellectual soul mate and main romantic interest. The most educated and politically active woman whom Ernesto had ever met, she joined Ernesto's private world of study and reading. Together, they read or discussed classic novels, poetry, and philosophy. They analyzed advanced Marxist-Leninist works, including *Imperialism: The Final Stage of Capitalism; Das Kapital; The Origins of the Family, Private Property, and the State; Landmarks of Scientific Socialism;* and *Anti-Dühring,* which Ernesto had read as a teenager. Hilda Gadea observed and participated in the political transformation of Ernesto Guevara. "In theory he was already a partisan, but it was not until Guatemala that he adopted the role," she explained.[44]

Hilda recognized that Ernesto's understanding of Marxist-Leninist philosophy surpassed her own. When Professor Harold White, a Marxist professor from the University of Utah, asked her to translate his book on Marxism, she asked for Ernesto's assistance. Once Ernesto convinced himself that White

---

42. Anderson, *Che Guevara,* 128–29; Aldo Isidrón del Valle, "Aquel joven argentino de ideas profundas" (interview with Edelberto Torres Rivas), in Rojas, *Testimonios sobre el Che,* 72.

43. Bonachea and San Martín, *Cuban Insurrection,* 20–21; Deutschmann, *Che,* 13; Gadea, *Ernesto,* x, 7–8, 23.

44. Gadea, *Ernesto,* 35.

did not work for the CIA, he undertook the translation project and began, in effect, to study Marxism under the tutelage of Professor White. Over the following six months, Ernesto developed "a synthesis, an outline of the profound and comprehensive structure that makes Marxism a science." According to White, Ernesto had developed an "exhaustive knowledge of Marxism" by the time he left Guatemala, having learned Marxism as a means of interpreting and changing the objective forces of imperialism.[45]

Guevara had even studied the unorthodox contributions to Marxist theory and practice that were being made in Communist China. He probably learned something about the Chinese Revolution through his friend Edelberto Torres Rivas. Hilda Gadea also encouraged his studies of the Chinese Revolution by lending him Mao Tse-tung's *New China*. According to Gadea, he studied the Chinese Revolution carefully and came to admire Mao and the struggle of the Chinese people. In the Chinese road to socialism, based on a massive peasant uprising in the countryside, Ernesto recognized a revolutionary option that might be more appropriate for Latin America's Indians and peasants than was the Soviet road. His intellectual curiosity piqued by the Chinese, he half-jokingly invited Gadea to join him on a trip to China.[46]

At the time, Latin American Communist parties adhered to the official Soviet line that the objective conditions for revolution did not exist in Latin America, much less in the countryside. The slim hopes for revolution that Moscow recognized in Latin America resided in the urban proletariat, which had not yet attained the size or the political consciousness required to make a revolution feasible. Yet in Guatemala, Guevara witnessed a growing militancy and revolutionary consciousness among the peasants who benefited from Arbenz's agrarian reform. Guevara's observations of the Guatemalan revolution, combined with his newfound understanding of the Chinese Revolution, sparked his interest in the revolutionary potential of the Latin American countryside, an interest that would develop into a fatal conviction.

The ideological conversion that Guevara completed in Guatemala established him as a Marxist-Leninist-Maoist maverick. Marxism was not simply a political agenda derived solely from *The Communist Manifesto*. Guevara learned Marxism as a methodology, dialectical materialism, a means of interpreting and changing reality, as Lenin and Mao had done. Hilda Gadea, the most astute observer of Guevara's "conversion," certainly recognized the philo-

45. Ibid., 221.
46. Ibid., 19–20, 35–36.

sophical foundations of Guevara's ideology. According to Gadea, Ernesto developed a "materialist philosophy of life and a socialist conception that takes account of the individual as part of society."[47]

Ernesto first disclosed his newfound political convictions to his family two months after his arrival in Guatemala. On February 12, 1954, he informed his aunt Beatriz: "I have taken a definite position in support of the Guatemalan government, and, within it, the PGT, which is Communist."[48] As a sign of his revolutionary commitment, he began to work as a doctor with the labor unions, but like Arbenz, he refused to join the Communist party. An official at the development bank where Hilda Gadea worked offered Ernesto a job on the condition that he joined the PGT. When Hilda relayed the offer to Guevara, he responded angrily: "You tell him that when I want to join the party I will do so on my own initiative, not out of any ulterior motive."[49]

Ernesto, already a revolutionary renegade, criticized Arbenz for being too tolerant of his opposition. In February 1954 Arbenz nationalized 68 percent of United Fruit's Caribbean plantations, less than a year after he had expropriated its Pacific Coast properties. In response, UFCO mobilized its supporters in the United States and Guatemala in an attempt to reverse or terminate the revolutionary movement. Arbenz nevertheless allowed his opponents to express their treasonous positions on the streets and in the press. Ernesto wanted Arbenz to suppress the opposition and prepare for an armed struggle against the United States, which, he suspected, had organized the counterrevolutionaries. Arbenz took a step in that direction in February 1954, when he crushed a minor rebellion.[50]

However, the increasingly militant Guevara wanted Arbenz to eliminate all internal opposition. In Ernesto's view, Arbenz granted "excessive liberties" to his political opposition, allowing reactionaries to organize, publish, and conspire against the revolution. With the Guatemalan reactionaries plotting openly against Arbenz, Guevara urged his comrades to discard their democratic pretenses and fight: "True patriots know that victory will be achieved by blood and fire and that the traitors cannot be pardoned; the total exter-

47. Ibid., 36.
48. Che to Aunt Beatriz, February 12, 1954, in Guevara Lynch, *Aquí va un soldado,* 38–39.
49. Gadea, *Ernesto,* 39.
50. Gleijeses, *Shattered Hope,* 164; Gadea, *Ernesto,* 10–12; Ernesto to Aunt Beatriz, January 5, 1954; Ernesto to Ana María (sister), January 15, 1954; Ernesto to father, February 2, 1954, all three in Guevara Lynch, *Aquí va un soldado,* 33–38.

mination of the reactionary groups is the only way to assure the reign of justice in America. . . . It is time to answer the garrote with the garrote, and if one has to die, let it be like Sandino."[51]

Ernesto saw the world divided into two antagonistic and irreconcilable camps. The capitalist world, led by the United States, controlled the developing countries of Asia, Africa, and Latin America. The Soviet Union and China, two great revolutionary powers, challenged the United States but did not threaten Latin America militarily or economically. The United States, however, exploited the resources and cheap labor of developing countries, and whenever any Latin American country tried to assert its economic independence and promote a more equitable distribution of wealth, the United States used the pretext of "international communism" to justify armed intervention. Guevara therefore urged Latin Americans to recognize this hard reality and prepare to fight the United States in a war for economic liberation and social equality.[52]

Ernesto believed that Colonel Arbenz would fight if and when the Yankees intervened. Tensions between Guatemala and the United States escalated after the Guatemalan military confiscated a shipment of Communist bloc weapons on May 16. To the Eisenhower administration, the arrival of the arms demonstrated the aggressive intentions of the Soviet Union and its client, Jacobo Arbenz. In response, Eisenhower imposed a naval quarantine on Guatemala to prevent further shipments of arms and ammunition. To defend the revolution, Ernesto offered himself for night guard duty with the Communist Youth brigades.[53]

On June 17, 1954, the long-anticipated intervention began when Colonel Carlos Castillo Armas led an invasion force of 150 Guatemalan exiles from a secret base inside Honduras toward Zacapa, a small town in eastern Guatemala. Ernesto studied the counterrevolutionary movement carefully and prepared to defend the Guatemalan revolution against "mercenaries." He recognized that only a direct intervention by the United States military would pose a significant threat to the Guatemalan army. Arbenz would surely fight and die at his post before surrendering to these imperialist agents, Guevara informed

51. Ernesto Guevara, "El dilema de Guatemala," April 1954, in Guevara Lynch, *Aquí va un soldado*, 68–70.

52. Ernesto Guevara, "La clase obrera de los EE.UU . . . ¿Amiga o enemiga?" in Guevara Lynch, *Aquí va un soldado*, 70–74.

53. Gleijeses, *Shattered Hope*, 295–98; Gadea, *Ernesto*, 46–47; Schneider, *Communism in Guatemala*, 258–61.

his mother. Guevara would defend the revolution as well, supporting the resistance either as a doctor or fighting on the front lines with the youth brigades.[54]

Over the following week, rebel planes bombed storage dumps and other targets in Guatemala City, causing little material damage but inflicting a serious psychological blow on the civilian population. On June 25, the Guatemalan army at Zacapa refused to fight Castillo Armas. Ernesto checked out of his pension, grabbed his sleeping bag, and prepared to fight, confident that Arbenz would distribute arms to the people and let them defend the revolution. He talked with Marco Antonio Villamar and Alfonso Bauer Paíz about arming the workers and peasants. Several hundred volunteers showed up for duty at a military base on June 26, but the officer corps refused to obey Arbenz's late order to arm the militias. Fearing a direct military confrontation with the United States, the officers instead demanded Arbenz's resignation. Arbenz resigned and fled the country the following day.[55]

Ernesto was stunned. Arbenz should have repudiated his traitorous general staff, armed the labor unions, and taken to the hills, where he could have led a struggle against imperialism indefinitely, Ernesto concluded. "He did not think that a people in arms is an invincible power, in spite of the example of Korea and Indochina. He could have given arms to the people and he did not want to, and this is the result." Despite his harsh condemnation of Arbenz, Ernesto ultimately blamed the army for the defeat: "The betrayal continues to be the patrimony of the army, and once again it proves the saying that democracy truly begins with the liquidation of the army."[56]

From the crucible of this Cold War confrontation emerged an angry young revolutionary. Although Guevara took asylum in the Argentine embassy, he refused an opportunity to return home, preferring to avenge the Guatemalan revolution. He had been willing and eager to defend that revolution, but Arbenz's refusal to fight sent the young Guevara into a controlled rage, desperate for an opportunity to do battle with American imperialists or their mercenaries. He would now have to fight with another army of liberation in another country, commanded by a leader who recognized the necessity of

54. Gleijeses, *Shattered Hope,* 320–21; Ernesto to mother, June 20, 1954, in Guevara Lynch, *Aquí va un soldado,* 56.

55. Ernesto to mother, July 4, 1954, in Guevara Lynch, *Aquí va un soldado,* 57–59; Gadea, *Ernesto,* 57–61; Gleijeses, *Shattered Hope,* 342–47.

56. Ernesto to mother, July 4, 1954, in Guevara Lynch, *Aquí va un soldado,* 57–58; Gadea, *Ernesto,* 57.

taking up arms. "In any event," he informed his aunt Beatriz, "I will be ready to go to the next [revolution] that takes up arms."[57]

The Guatemalan counterrevolution sponsored by the United States turned Ernesto Guevara into a revolutionary. Within a decade, he became the most popular and dangerous revolutionary in the hemisphere, the ironic, bitter creation of the United States' Cold War policies. From the failures of the Guatemalan revolutionaries Guevara learned three lessons that he subsequently incorporated into his revolutionary strategy. First, in order to carry out and defend their program, revolutionaries had to destroy or purge the old army and create a new revolutionary army. They could not create a new society using an institution created to preserve the old one. Although Arbenz had placed loyalists in key army positions, they obviously did not share his revolutionary convictions. In the end, they betrayed Arbenz and the revolution.

Second, revolutionary leaders should give the people the means to defend their revolution. Arbenz had given Guatemalan workers and peasants rights and land, but he refused to give them weapons. If Arbenz had organized and armed worker and peasant militias, he could have repulsed Castillo Armas even without the support of the regular army.

Third, Guevara recognized that a counterrevolution sponsored by the United States constituted an inevitable part of Latin America's revolutionary struggle. Any revolutionary who confiscated American property and challenged American hegemony—and Guevara believed that any true revolutionary should do so—should prepare for some type of American intervention, whether a covert operation sponsored by the CIA or a direct invasion by the United States military. Given that Guevara now aimed to destroy American imperialism, he saw armed struggle as necessary and inevitable. He saw no reason to delay the inevitable; he saw every reason to prepare for the confrontation. If and when the Americans intervened militarily, they would come with overwhelming power, so Guevara began to see the potential for resisting American aggression through guerrilla warfare, as Sandino had done.

Arbenz failed to implement any of these strategies and succumbed to an invasion of 150 poorly armed exiles. Che would not make the same mistake in Cuba. From Arbenz's failures he drew the lessons on which he would sharpen his revolutionary ideology, strategy, and tactics. Guevara certainly

57. Rojo, *My Friend Che*, 63; Gambini, *El Che Guevara*, 95–96; Gadea, *Ernesto*, 66–67; Ernesto to Aunt Beatriz, July 22, 1954, in Guevara Lynch, *Aquí va un soldado*, 60 (quoted, my translation).

recognized his Guatemalan experience as a turning point in his life: "I was born in Argentina, I fought in Cuba, and I began to be a revolutionary in Guatemala," Che later wrote.[58]

Guevara left for Mexico in mid-September, determined to transform his Marxist convictions into revolutionary action, fighting for some revolutionary movement somewhere in Latin America. "After the experience I went through," Guevara later explained, "my long walks throughout all of Latin America and the Guatemalan closing, not much was needed to convince me to join any revolution against a tyrant."[59]

Guevara learned how to defend revolutionary power by observing how the Guatemalan revolutionaries had not. He still needed to learn how to *take* power. Although he sensed the might of armed workers and peasants, he did not know how they could defeat a disciplined army. He only knew that politicians and diplomats would not defeat American imperialism by using ballots instead of bullets. Revolution could only triumph through revolution. Ernesto concluded that moderate politicians such as Rómulo Betancourt and José Figueres advocated political strategies that represented "a betrayal of the true revolution and independence of our countries." In hoping that Arbenz would have led the resistance from some mountain refuge, Guevara gave the first indication that he recognized guerrilla warfare as a viable defensive strategy. However, he had not yet begun to recognize the possibility that a small guerrilla band could constitute the main offensive weapon against an old regime. He would learn the offensive potential of guerrilla warfare under the tutelage of Alberto Bayo in Mexico. He left Guatemala angry and bitter, determined to avenge Guatemala's loss by attacking the Yankees or their puppets. He left Guatemala thinking, "The struggle begins now."[60]

58. Che to Compañero Guillermo Lorentzen, May 4, 1963, in Ernesto Guevara, *Reminiscences of the Cuban Revolutionary War,* 265.
59. "Interview with Jorge Masetti," in Guevara, *Che: Selected Works,* 364.
60. Gadea, *Ernesto,* 56.

THREE THE MAKING OF A GUERRILLA

Ernesto Guevara arrived in Mexico City on September 21, 1954, convinced that the revolution would eventually triumph in Latin America and hoping that he would fight in it.[1] But he did not know how to fight; he advocated the armed struggle before he knew how to struggle. He learned how to fight for his revolutionary convictions in Mexico, where Alberto Bayo began to make him into a *guerrillero*.

At the time, Guevara knew of no organization that followed the militant line he now advocated. His determination to fight imperialism did not diminish as the Guatemalan revolution faded into memory. By late 1954 he realized that he had developed political convictions so strong that he expressed them in religious terms. He believed in the triumph of the revolution and that destiny reserved a role in it for him. "Exactly when I left reason for something like faith I cannot tell you," he acknowledged in a letter to his mother.[2]

Guevara's odyssey continued for another ten months before he decided to place his faith in Fidel Castro. During that time he considered several options, including a return to Argentina to promote his revolutionary ambitions there. Determined to fight, he could have enlisted in any revolutionary army. Castro

1. Ernesto to Tita Infante, September 29, 1954; Ernesto to mother, October 10, 1954, both in Guevara Lynch, *Aquí va un soldado*, 75–78.
2. Ernesto to mother (late December) 1954, in Guevara Lynch, *Aquí va un soldado*, 86.

just happened to catch Guevara at the right time. "I am waiting for some recommendation to march to the fields where a new day is dawning," Ernesto
explained to his father on May 27, 1955. Should his first marching orders come
from Cuba, he had already decided to obey them: "I will not lose an opportunity to make an extra trip: Havana, in particular, appeals to me; it would
fill my heart with landscapes well blended with passages from Lenin."[3]

By this time Guevara had developed a close relationship with some of the
Cuban exiles he had met in Guatemala. He grew particularly close to the
long-legged Ñico López, who already had the military experience Guevara
only craved.[4] Through López and the other exiles, Guevara learned enough
about the Cuban revolutionary movement to consider joining it even before
Fidel Castro arrived in Mexico. Guevara admired the Cuban exiles primarily
because they had fought for their ideals. The Cubans saw in Ernesto an ideological comrade and a mentor, whose understanding of Marxist-Leninist
thought exceeded their own. They eventually became his students in an informal school. Guevara described himself as a "little roving prophet" who was
announcing that "judgment day" was at hand.[5]

The Communist parties of Latin America, including the PSP of Cuba, then
adhered to the "popular front" strategy adopted by the Seventh Congress of
the Communist International in 1935. Soviet ideologues and their doctrinaire
followers held that Latin America lacked the objective conditions for revolution, namely an industrial proletariat. Therefore, orthodox Communists offi-
cially opposed armed struggle, even against brutal dictatorships. While they
waited for the objective conditions to develop, Communists worked within
the political system, forming alliances with other political parties and hoping
to gain a measure of power through the established democratic processes.[6]

The collapse of the Guatemalan revolution demonstrated the fallacy of this
strategy to Ernesto. He believed that an "authentic revolutionary" could not
work within the existing system; he or she had to fight against it. In June
1955, Ernesto met Raúl Castro, a twenty-four-year-old Cuban Marxist committed to armed struggle. Raúl had joined the youth wing of the Cuban
Communist party and toured the Soviet Union and eastern Europe, giving
him some travel experience that Guevara also longed for. Despite his ties to

---

3. Ernesto to father, May 27, 1955, in Guevara Lynch, *Aquí va un soldado*, 96.
4. Gadea, *Ernesto*, 80–81; Anderson, *Che Guevara*, 162–64.
5. Ernesto to mother, June 17, 1955, in Guevara Lynch, *Aquí va un soldado*, 99–101.
6. Poppino, *International Communism in Latin America*, chaps. 2 and 3; Alexander,
Communism in Latin America, chap. 1; Ratliff, *Castroism and Communism in Latin America*;
Liss, *Marxist Thought in Latin America*, 34–38.

the orthodox Communists, Raúl supported the direct action of his brother, leading one squad of rebels at Moncada garrison, despite the PSP's opposition to the attack. Raúl agreed with Ernesto that the people could only take power through armed struggle. He expressed a great faith in the ability of Fidel to lead the people to power in Cuba and promised to introduce Ernesto to him as soon as he arrived.[7]

Fidel Castro considered it a right and a duty to rise against an unjust government. After his release from prison in May 1955, he refused to renounce his right of insurrection and publicly denounced Batista and top Cuban generals. Rather than join the Communists, a revolutionary organization that would not fight, Fidel had formed an organization that would, the M-26-7. Established secretly on June 12, 1955, the M-26-7 created an underground network in Cuba to recruit and sustain an army of liberation, which Fidel intended to train in Mexico, far removed, he hoped, from Batista's secret police. On July 7, 1955, Fidel left for Mexico, because all doors of peaceful struggle had been closed to him. As a disciple of José Martí, Fidel believed that "the hour has come to take rights and not to beg for them, to fight instead of pleading for them."[8]

Soon after Fidel arrived, Raúl introduced him to Guevara, who felt drawn to Fidel "from the beginning by a liking for romantic adventure."[9] Castro, the full-time insurrectionist, recognized in Guevara the Marxist intellectual that he was not. Guevara, the aspiring revolutionary soldier, recognized in Castro the charismatic military leader he was not. Thus each man immediately recognized in the other qualities that he either lacked or needed. Fidel and Che would form a political and military partnership that ultimately transformed Cuba, but only a solid determination to fight drew the men together initially. Ernesto saw that Castro had "an unshakable faith that once he left he would arrive in Cuba, that once he arrived he would fight, that once he began fighting he would win." Ernesto, already tired of pseudorevolutionaries, also thought that it was "imperative to act, to fight, to concretize. It was imperative to stop crying and fight," and Ernesto resolved to do just that the night he met Fidel.[10]

---

7. Szulc, *Fidel*, 219–20; Anderson, *Che Guevara*, 173; Gadea, *Ernesto*, 98; Bonachea and San Martín, *Cuban Insurrection*, 19–20; H. Thomas, *Cuban Revolution*, 56.

8. Paterson, *Contesting Castro*, 15–17; Szulc, *Fidel*, 323–24; Castro, *Revolutionary Struggle*, 257 (quoted).

9. Deutschmann, *Che: A Memoir*, 68; Guevara, *Episodes*, 84 (quoted).

10. Masetti interview, April 1958, in Guevara, *Che: Selected Works*, 364.

When their first meeting broke up at dawn the following day, Ernesto had enlisted as the doctor of Fidel's rebel army. He joined not because he fell under Castro's spell but because Fidel offered him his first opportunity to fight for his revolutionary convictions. After the Guatemalan experience, Guevara admitted that he probably would have joined almost "any revolution against a tyrant."[11] Ernesto doubted that Fidel would lead the authentic revolution, but he joined the struggle against Batista because "it would be well worth dying on a foreign beach for such a pure idea."[12] The soldier of the Americas had finally found his army and its commander.

Guevara joined the M-26-7 not because of Castro's ideology but *in spite of his moderation*. Castro had proposed a moderate agrarian reform and a rather conventional industrial development policy, but he said nothing about the construction of a socialist society or the destruction of imperialism. Castro intended to overthrow Batista and restore the Constitution of 1940, hardly the objectives of an authentic revolutionary. When Ernesto met Castro in 1955 he had already embraced Marxism-Leninism; Fidel had not. Although Fidel later claimed that he had gained a basic understanding of Marxism in 1948, Guevara certainly did not view Fidel as an ideological comrade in 1955. Two years after he met Fidel, he admitted that he had characterized Castro's movement "as one of the many inspired by the bourgeoisie's desire to free themselves from the economic chains of imperialism." As for Castro, he confessed: "I always thought of Fidel as an authentic leader of the leftist bourgeoisie, although his image is enhanced by personal qualities of extraordinary brilliance that set him above his class."[13]

Ernesto enlisted in the rebel army "without any hope of going any further than the liberation of the country, and fully prepared to leave when the conditions of the later struggle veered all the action of the Movement toward the right."[14] Guevara had no idea that he would have such a profound impact on the political ideology and military strategy of the movement that the rightward drift he anticipated would never occur. He planned, in fact, to return to Argentina after Castro's rebels defeated Batista. "The only thing I want after the victory of the revolution," Ernesto explained to Fidel, "is to go fight

11. Ibid.

12. Guevara, *Episodes*, 84.

13. Fidel Castro, "History Will Absolve Me," in Castro, *Revolutionary Struggle*, 185; Szulc, *Fidel*, 207–8; Ernesto to Daniel (René Ramos Latour), December 14, 1957, in Franqui, *Diary*, 269 (quoted).

14. Ernesto to Daniel, December 14, 1957, in Franqui, *Diary*, 269.

in Argentina—that you don't keep me from doing so, that no reasons of state will stand in the way." Fidel promised him that he could return to his native country after the liberation of Cuba.[15]

Fidel and Ernesto shared a determination to fight as well as a total lack of formal military training. Given their objective of overthrowing a dictatorship defended by a forty-thousand-man army trained and supplied by the United States, they had to school themselves and their rebel force in military strategies and tactics that had a reasonable chance of success. Castro and Guevara had already begun to recognize the potential of guerrilla warfare before they met. Castro viewed guerrilla warfare as a viable contingency plan that could be implemented after a conventional assault failed. Guevara saw guerrilla warfare as a viable defensive strategy that could have enabled Jacobo Arbenz to resist the American-sponsored intervention. Alberto Bayo, who had fought, taught, and studied guerrilla campaigns, knew that guerrilla warfare could constitute much more than a contingency plan or a defensive strategy. Bayo believed that Latin American rebels could overthrow Caribbean dictatorships by using guerrilla warfare as the principal military strategy against armies trained and supported by the United States. From Bayo, Guevara learned the strategies and tactics that would lead the Cubans to victory over Batista. Guevara referred to Bayo as his master, the only one he ever recognized.[16]

Bayo, then a sixty-four-year-old veteran with a distinguished military career behind him, bridged the traditional forms of guerrilla warfare with the modern innovations of Sandino and Mao Tse-tung. He had served for eleven years with the Spanish army in Morocco, where Islamic guerrillas known as Riffs used guerrilla tactics against the occupying Spanish and French forces. Although the Riffs failed to gain their independence, Bayo came to respect their guerrilla tactics. When the Spanish Civil War erupted, Bayo sided with the Republicans against General Francisco Franco, who had also served in Morocco. In August 1936, Bayo commanded an amphibious invasion of the Balearic Islands in the western Mediterranean, held by Franco's forces and supported by the Italian air force. With three thousand men and a small naval flotilla under his command, Bayo fought to recover Majorca, the largest of the islands. Italian airplanes pounded Bayo's forces and forced him to withdraw after one month of intense fighting.[17]

15. Deutschmann, *Che,* 116.
16. Bayo, *Mi aporte,* 10.
17. Mallin, *Strategy for Conquest,* 315–16.

Upon his return to Spain, Bayo became a strong advocate of guerrilla warfare, a form of combat as old as war itself. Some military historians, however, credit the Spanish with developing the name and methods of guerrilla warfare during their fight against the occupying French forces from 1808 to 1814. Although Napoléon easily captured the largest cities and towns on the Iberian Peninsula, he had trouble eliminating Spanish resistance in the countryside, where patriots carried on a *guerrilla* (little war) against the French. Unconventional little wars, supported by regular British armies, sprang up everywhere and tied down French forces all over the peninsula. As the guerrilla armies gained strength and sapped their enemy of men and morale, they adopted conventional strategies and fought alongside British regulars in Spain and into France. In the end, the British general Wellington claimed victory over the French, but he knew well that the heroic guerrilla campaigns of the Spanish resistance made his victory possible.[18]

What the Spanish called a little war came to mean in practice the operations of irregular, nonprofessional civilian-soldiers who adopted unconventional tactics to expel an invading force or occupying power. According to one military historian, "Guerrilla warfare is conducted by civilians who usually have little formal military experience and little patience with the science of tactics by which modern mass armies operate. The abiding impetus which spurs the guerrilla is the intense desire to expel the invader, the occupier, or the colonizer."[19]

Guerrilla warfare has in fact been used most often and with greatest effect as a means of resisting to an invading or occupying force. Cuban rebels used guerrilla tactics effectively during their wars for independence in the late nineteenth century. In the 1890s, the insurgent army commanded by General Máximo Gómez never numbered more than fifty-four thousand soldiers. Facing regular Spanish forces of 240,000, Gómez knew that the Cubans could not afford to fight any decisive battles. Instead of fighting a traditional war of positions, with each army defending territory, the rebels fought a war of movement, constantly pressing the Spanish forces but never attacking unless they held a numerical advantage. Few rebel leaders applied guerrilla strategies and tactics as effectively as General Antonio Maceo, the "Bronze Titan" of Cuban independence. Maceo and the peasant soldiers who followed him,

18. Wilkins, "Guerrilla Warfare," 4–5.
19. Colonel Virgil Ney, "Guerrilla Warfare and Modern Strategy," in Osanka, *Modern Guerrilla Warfare*, 26–27.

known as *mambises*, struck fear into the Spanish troops by hitting supply lines, communication facilities, and sugar plantations, rarely offering the enemy an opportunity to strike back at a fixed position. "The rebel strategy [of Máximo Gómez] envisaged no fixed battle lines, no large campaigns, and no great concentrations which the Spanish army could overwhelm," explains historian Philip S. Foner.[20]

Ernesto Guevara clearly did not introduce the concept of guerrilla warfare to Cuba. In fact, Bayo, Castro, and he studied and learned from Cuban military history. A long tradition of unconventional warfare existed in Cuba, a heritage particularly important in the mountains of Oriente province, where *guajiros*, or peasants, recalled the campaigns of Maceo and the *mambises* with pride. But even the guerrilla model developed in Cuba by the founders of the republic could not be applied without modification to Cuba in the 1950s. Great advances in military science and technology rendered Gómez and Maceo obsolete. Bayo knew of these advances, and more important, he learned how guerrilla innovators such as Augusto César Sandino had modified modern guerrilla warfare.

Bayo gathered firsthand information about Sandino's campaigns from some of the Nicaraguan veterans who sought his advice in Guadalajara, Mexico, where he taught at the aviation school. Some Sandinista veterans had joined the Caribbean Legion and asked Bayo to provide military instruction to their rebel volunteers. Bayo, still burning with a hatred of fascism and dictatorship, readily agreed. After studying the Sandinista campaigns against the American marines and the Nicaraguan National Guard, Bayo came to believe that Sandino provided a military blueprint for fighting the Caribbean dictatorships.[21]

Sandino launched his campaign with a conventional assault on Ocotal in July 1927. The hard core of his rebel army consisted of about sixty officers and soldiers, but as many as eight hundred local peasants joined the attack on the thirty-nine American marines and forty-eight Nicaraguan National Guardsmen who occupied several buildings in the town square. The Sandinistas caught the defenders by surprise and pinned them down behind the walls. The marines called in an air strike to repulse the Sandinistas. Five De Havilland planes, each carrying four bombs and twelve hundred rounds of ammunition, caught the startled Sandinistas in an open field outside of

20. Foner, *Spanish-Cuban-American War*, 1:30.
21. Ibid.; Macaulay, *Sandino Affair*, 260–62.

town. Diving from fifteen hundred feet, the planes opened with deadly machine-gun fire and dropped a bomb at the end of the dive. As the planes climbed away, a rear gunner mowed down Sandinista volunteers as they fled for cover. Within an hour of the air assault, Sandino ordered a retreat, having lost as many as four hundred men in the first dive-bombing attack in history.[22]

The battle of Ocotal taught Sandino that recent developments in military technology and tactics, namely the use of airplanes, machine guns, and dive-bombing, made it impossible for roving bands of cavalry to mass in open fields or deserts. Latin American guerrilla leaders, including Generals Antonio Maceo in Cuba and Pancho Villa in Mexico, had typically massed their cavalry forces for unconventional attacks on enemy positions, even on unfavorable terrain. But the new military technologies compelled commanders to modify their tactics and usher in a new era of guerrilla warfare. "The new guerrilla who emerged that year [1927] spurned the horse and the lance and avoided massed formations in the open, where he could be cut down by automatic fire or aerial bombardment," writes Neill Macaulay. "The habitat of the new guerrilla was the forests and the mountains, where he moved about in small groups, often under cover of dense foliage, practically secure from observation and attack from the air."[23]

Sandino divided his army into self-supporting columns of only one hundred men, each unit operating independently. The Sandinistas remained mobile and flexible, striking only when the odds favored them and avoiding combat under unfavorable circumstances. Sandino realized that his success depended not on defending terrain but on retaining the support of the people, who provided him with intelligence, supplies, and recruits. From his secure mountain bases, Sandino gradually attempted to expand his area of operations and take the war to the cities.[24] He had to engage the enemy in a protracted campaign, avoiding decisive engagements wherever possible and attacking the enemy at its weakest points. He still aimed to liberate Nicaraguans of the American occupation, but he realized that it would be easier to convince the occupiers to leave than to drive them out. Macaulay explains the strategy as "a process of attrition directed against the morale of the target government and its supporters—military and civilian, native and foreign."[25]

22. Macaulay, *Sandino Affair,* 11–12, 62–82.
23. Ibid., 11.
24. Hodges, *Intellectual Foundations,* 134–35; Macaulay, *Sandino Affair,* 263–65.
25. Macaulay, *Sandino Affair,* 10–11.

Perhaps because Sandino did not write much about the theory and practice of guerrilla warfare, he has not generally been acknowledged as one of
the intellectual creators of modern guerrilla warfare. Yet his campaigns reflected
the strategic approach of Colonel T. E. Lawrence, who is generally credited
with making "the first theoretical contribution to understanding guerrilla
warfare as a political movement furthered through unconventional tactics
rather than as military tactic supplementary to conventional warfare."[26]

In World War I, the British assigned Colonel Lawrence as an adviser to
the Arab rebels fighting for their independence from the Turkish Empire.
Lawrence, a student of classical military doctrines, adopted a guerrilla strategy after his conventional approaches against the Turkish army failed. Instead
of trying to defeat that army in open battle, he changed his objectives to
attacking supply lines and communications. Between 1916 and 1918, Lawrence
directed attacks on railway bridges, tunnels, railroads, and lines of communication. He occasionally threatened isolated posts and garrisons, not with
the intention of gaining territory, but to force the Turks to reinforce the garrisons. After the reinforcements arrived at the garrisons, Lawrence let the soldiers exhaust their rations while he attacked their supply lines. According to
one military expert, Lawrence's plan was "to convince the Turks they could-
n't stay, rather than drive them out."[27]

Sandino may not have studied Lawrence's military classic, *Seven Pillars
of Wisdom*, but in his campaigns against the American marines, he certainly
applied Lawrence's revolutionary principles. Alberto Bayo, who was fighting Moroccan guerrillas at the same time that Lawrence was waging his
guerrilla campaign in Arabia, certainly recognized the wisdom of Sandino's
strategy. Even in exile, Bayo continued to press the Republicans to launch
a guerrilla campaign against Franco. His compatriots objected, claiming
that a poorly equipped guerrilla band had no chance of defeating an army
equipped with heavy artillery, tanks, and airplanes. In response, Bayo pointed
out that Sandino's army of peasants fought against a much stronger
American army for seven years and eventually persuaded the Americans to
withdraw. Bayo insisted that all Latin American revolutionaries study
Sandino, a model guerrilla warrior and a revolutionary martyr. In a pamphlet he wrote for the Caribbean Legion in the 1940s, Bayo wrote: "Always
remember Sandino."[28]

---

26. Loveman and Davies, "Guerrilla Warfare, Revolutionary Theory," 5.
27. Wilkins, "Guerrilla Warfare," 7.
28. Bayo, *Mi aporte*, 19; Macaulay, *Sandino Affair*, 261–62.

To understand the contributions of twentieth-century guerrilla strategists, including Sandino and Che, one must distinguish between the irregular tactics of a conventional army and the guerrilla tactics of a guerrilla army. Conventionally organized forces, even massed formations of infantry and artillery, have often used irregular tactics. The Confederate cavalry divisions led by Nathan Bedford Forrest, for example, harassed enemy supply lines, cut lines of communications, and terrorized the Union armies, striking secretly, quickly, and with overwhelming firepower.[29] These unconventional tactics, applied at a time when in the main most generals fought with conventional methods, complemented the conventional war waged by General Robert E. Lee. Forrest did not operate independently. The presence of a formidable Confederate army in the Union front made it possible for Forrest and his cavalry to attack the Union flanks and rear.

Conventional military strategists, even those as brilliant as Lee, viewed irregular or partisan units as bandits who dishonored the cause for which the regular armies fought. Although Lee praised the military skills of Nathan Bedford Forrest, he rejected unconventional or partisan warfare as a viable means of resistance to the Army of the Potomac. After he surrendered to General Ulysses S. Grant at Appomattox, Lee rejected a suggestion that he disperse the Army of Northern Virginia into bands of partisans, fearing that such "bushwhacking" would only bring more destruction to the South.[30]

Military commanders from ancient times to the present have used guerrilla tactics, but few conceived of guerrilla warfare as a viable, honorable, and effective strategy. Prior to such twentieth-century innovators as Sandino, military strategists considered guerrilla warfare as an occasionally effective complement to the operations of a regular army. The influential Prussian military strategist Carl von Clausewitz recognized that guerrilla warfare, as part of a campaign coordinated by a regular army, could inflict heavy damages on and sap the morale of an occupying force. In the American Revolution, Colonel Francis Marion, the famous "Swamp Fox," used guerrilla tactics effectively against General Lord Charles Cornwallis in the Carolinas. Marion's guerrilla operations depleted the economic resources of the enemy, pinned down large numbers of conventional troops, and demoralized their soldiers. But in the end, General George Washington's conventional army, supported by a large French fleet, defeated Cornwallis at Yorktown. Marion's irregu-

---

29. Henry, *Nathan Bedford Forrest,* 464.
30. E. Thomas, *Robert E. Lee,* 362–63.

lar operations constituted an important yet peripheral aspect of the regular military campaign.[31]

Even Lenin failed to recognize the possibilities of using guerrilla warfare as a means of revolutionary combat. In fact, he did not even conceptualize guerrilla warfare in the terms later defined by Lawrence, Mao, and Guevara. Lenin reluctantly advocated selective assassinations and bank robberies, the only irregular forms of combat that he approved. Even then, he argued that revolutionaries could only carry out these forms of "partisan warfare" if they coordinated them with other forms of combat. If not "ennobled by the enlightening and organizing influence of socialism," these partisan actions would "lower the class-conscious proletariat to the level of drunkards and bums."[32]

Colonel T. E. Lawrence, the first to develop the principles of guerrilla warfare into an offensive military strategy for national liberation, helped to elevate the stature of unconventional warfare. Few armies fight without some drunkards and bums in the ranks, but they fight for patriotic purposes. The Arab forces that Lawrence advised enjoyed widespread popular support in their fight against a foreign enemy who happened to enjoy military superiority in the field. Knowing that the Arabs lacked the weapons and economic resources of their foes, Lawrence advised them to wage guerrilla war against the Turks. He used the Arabs' political advantage, widespread popular support, as a military asset, demonstrating that the invaders could not possibly deploy enough troops to control every square inch of territory.

However, Guevara's mentor, Alberto Bayo, had no need to look beyond the shores of the Americas to learn guerrilla warfare. Although his understanding of guerrilla warfare bears an undeniable resemblance to that expressed in the theories of Lawrence and Mao, Bayo recognized only Sandino as his mentor, making the Nicaraguan patriot the intellectual grandfather of Che Guevara. Sandino had already demonstrated in practice the virtues of tactics that Lawrence and others developed into theory. Sandino divided his guerrilla army into small, self-supporting units and carried out a war of attrition against a superior enemy. Moreover, these guerrilla units did not complement the operations of a regular army. They *were* the army. A people in arms, Bayo had learned from Sandino, could present a formidable military challenge to a more powerful conventional army. It did not take Mao to teach Bayo that

---

31. Loveman and Davies, "Guerrilla Warfare, Revolutionary Theory," 2–3; Wilkins, "Guerrilla Warfare," 3–5; Asprey, *War in the Shadows*, 63–71.

32. V. I. Thomas, "Partisan Warfare," in Osanka, *Modern Guerrilla Warfare*, 76.

guerrilla columns could fight on their own as long as they fought for legiti-mate objectives and earned the support of the peasants.[33]

When Castro caught up with Bayo in 1956, the latter had been advocating guerrilla warfare against Caribbean dictatorships for nearly a decade. The fail-ure of Nicaraguans and Dominicans to launch campaigns against Somoza and Trujillo, respectively, had not shaken Bayo's confidence in guerrilla warfare. The charismatic and energetic Castro ignited Bayo's dormant Republican fer-vor to the extent that he gave up his job to devote himself full time to the training of Castro's rebel army.[34]

The training of the Cuban rebel army began in earnest in January 1956. Bayo, assuming that Fidel intended to launch an unconventional military cam-paign, began his training program with a lecture on the hardships and risks of the guerrilla fighter. He warned the Cuban rebels that they would face overwhelming odds in combat, one individual against one thousand. Ninety percent of the guerrillas would be killed or captured; the surviving 10 per-cent of the guerrilla army would triumph, Bayo predicted confidently. Che and the Cuban recruits proudly accepted the risks and agreed to submit them-selves to the rigid discipline required of a guerrilla army. To prepare the men for the life of the guerrilla, Bayo ordered them on long night marches over rough terrain without food or water. The recruits also rowed boats in Chapultepec Lake, played basketball, and learned hand-to-hand combat. After a month devoted to physical conditioning, Bayo began to teach the men how to fire a weapon properly.[35]

In the evening, Bayo lectured on the theory of guerrilla warfare. He found it difficult to convince the young men that they should not engage the enemy face to face. He advised them to attack only when they had a clear advantage, and even then they should hit and run, always disappearing into the moun-tains or forests when confronted by the enemy. Some of the Cuban recruits refused to fight in such a "cowardly" manner. Bayo argued that Batista's army assassinated, tortured, robbed, and abused the Cuban people. The strength and brutality of the Batista dictatorship, Bayo continued, compelled the rebels to use guerrilla warfare, an honorable form of resistance. One hundred armed soldiers, no matter how courageous, could not defeat an army of forty thou-sand if they used conventional methods. They had to hit weak links in the

33. Alberto Bayo, "One Hundred Fifty Questions to a Guerrilla," in Mallin, *Strategy for Conquest*, 319.

34. Szulc, *Fidel*, 325–27; Bayo, *Mi aporte*, 15–28; *Tempestad en el Caribe*, 86.

35. Bayo, *Mi aporte*, 28; Bornot Pubillones et al., *De Tuxpan a La Plata*, 23.

army, flee to the security of the mountains, and reorganize for another attack, always careful to avoid combat at places and times chosen by the enemy.

Even though Fidel had initially asked Bayo to train his men in guerrilla warfare, he also expressed skepticism about the use of guerrilla tactics. After hearing Bayo's lecture on guerrilla combat, he asked Bayo to train his men in conventional attacks. Bayo agreed to do that, but he advised Fidel not to practice regular warfare, because they would all be killed within a month of landing on Cuban soil.

But Fidel still objected. "I find it repugnant to win a fight by cowardice, low blows, not showing your face."

Bayo replied: "If we use guerrilla warfare in Cuba, I am certain that we will win, absolutely certain, I don't know if it will take one year or ten years, but we will win. If we fight a regular war, that is to say, showing your face, I am certain that we will lose, absolutely certain, I don't know if it will be one week or three weeks, but we will lose."[36]

Fidel thought carefully about Bayo's arguments, but he remained skeptical about using guerrilla warfare as his principal method of attack. Bayo continued to lecture on the philosophy and tactics of such warfare to the other men, but Fidel rarely attended the evening classes or participated in the military training. He had studied some military history, including the Cuban wars for independence, the Spanish Civil War, and World War II. He evidently did not study Mao, Lawrence, Sandino, or any other guerrilla strategists. His knowledge of guerrilla warfare came primarily from the history of Maceo and the *mambises* who had used guerrilla tactics effectively against the Spanish army. He considered himself a descendant of those independence heroes and borrowed from them a mix of conventional and unconventional military tactics, as was evident in his first attack against Batista.[37]

On July 26, 1953, Castro attempted to take the Moncada army garrison in Santiago, Cuba, with 123 combatants. Convinced that favorable conditions already existed for a nationwide rebellion, Castro conceived the Moncada attack as the catalyst for insurrection. He hoped to capture the arsenal, distribute arms to the people, and turn Moncada into the base for the insurrectionary forces. The loss of the barracks might even divide Batista's army and compel some officers to lead a coup against the dictator. In either case, Castro's revolutionary strategy was built on the assumption that the people,

36. Bayo, *Mi aporte*, 37–38.
37. Szulc, *Fidel*, 241–42.

alone or with elements of the army, would join his rebellion against Batista.

The strategic plan rested on risky suppositions and dangerous tactics. Castro loaded the rebels and their armaments into sixteen automobiles and directed them toward three targets in downtown Santiago. He led the main assault on the Moncada garrison, which was defended by four hundred soldiers, with ninety-five men. Attacking at 5:15 A.M., he banked on the element of surprise to give his men the advantage as they stormed the garrison through gate number 3 in the southeastern corner. The men in the lead car, dressed in regular army uniforms, would disarm the guards, unlock an iron chain across the roadway, and let the other cars in the caravan drive into the courtyard. From there, the rebels would storm into the building to the immediate left of the gate, capture or kill the sleeping soldiers, take over the fort's radio transmitter, and confiscate arms and ammunition. To provide covering fire for the main force, a twenty-man group led by Abel Santamaría would take control of an adjacent military hospital, and Raúl Castro would take the Palace of Justice. From the upper floor of those buildings, the rebels would have a clear line of fire to the courtyard of Moncada.

As it actually happened on July 26, the rebels in the lead car carried out their mission, disarming the guards and pushing through the gate. But the rebels lost the element of surprise immediately. A two-man army patrol showed up at gate 3 with two submachine guns. In addition, an army sergeant appeared on the street leading to the gate. Only three rebels had pushed through the gate and entered the barracks before the soldiers responded to the alarm and attacked the rebels with deadly machine-gun fire. Fidel, unable to enter the compound, called a retreat just thirty minutes after the attack began. He tried in vain to lead the remnants of his rebel army into the mountains and launch a guerrilla campaign, but he and eighteen men surrendered shortly thereafter. The army hunted down, tortured, and killed another sixty-one rebels. Only eight men had been killed in the initial assault on Moncada.[38]

If a guerrilla fighter attacks only when and where there is a certainty of victory, Fidel Castro twice demonstrated that he was no guerrilla, first at Moncada, and again in the *Granma* invasion. He favored risky attacks on well-fortified positions, convinced that bold leadership and the element of surprise could overcome the advantages in armaments and numbers held by the enemy. Castro did not attack when and where the terrain and firepower favored him. Instead, he attacked a regimental headquarters, then attempted

---

38. Bonachea and San Martín, *Cuban Insurrection,* 10–23; Szulc, *Fidel,* 262–81.

an overt invasion after announcing that he would do so. Castro may have demonstrated personal courage, but he also displayed a recklessness that had led his rebels into two disastrous engagements with Batista's army. He needed a military strategist whose abilities could complement his formidable political skills.

Under the tutelage of Alberto Bayo, Ernesto Guevara became that strategist. He attended every lecture and training session and became Bayo's closest confidant. Bayo's first lecture on guerrilla warfare convinced Guevara that the rebels could defeat Batista by applying guerrilla warfare. "I had thought it quite doubtful when I first enrolled with the rebel commander," Guevara admitted later, but should Castro apply the strategic and tactical concepts that Bayo taught, he sensed victory.[39]

Bayo continued to lecture on guerrilla warfare, trying to convince the highly motivated troops that they did not have to engage Batista's army face to face. Imagine one hundred soldiers armed with bazookas, machine guns, and repeating rifles, pursuing three guerrillas. If the latter turned to fight, the soldiers would certainly crush them. If they adopted a strategy of running when necessary and attacking when possible, inflicting three or four casualties in every brief skirmish, they would eventually win. To convince the Cubans, Bayo used a boxing analogy, that of Batista's best boxer meeting the rebels' best boxer in a fight to the death. In a "clean" fight with the best rebel boxer, Batista's man, possessing advantages in strength, agility, and training, would kill the rebel. But if the rebel underdog could resort to low blows, sucker punches, and head butts in an "anything goes" match, he would surely win, justifying the means to the end—victory.[40]

Bayo spent many hours trying to convince the rebel soldiers that they could not fight Batista on his own terms. They had to determine the terms of combat, and they had to select conditions that favored them. Fidel, however, clung to a blend of the conventional and unconventional; he would initiate a guerrilla campaign from the Sierra Maestra if the *Granma* landing and the Santiago uprising failed to generate the popular rebellion he anticipated. Fortunately for the rebels, Ernesto Guevara embraced Bayo's principles and survived the disaster at Alegría del Pío, so that he could guide the implementation of Fidel's contingency plan and train the rebel recruits in guerrilla warfare.

Bayo divided a guerrilla campaign into three phases. In the first stage, the

39. Guevara, *Episodes*, 84.
40. Bayo, *Mi aporte*, 40–41.

guerrillas waged war from a base in the mountains, launching sporadic hit-and-run attacks against vulnerable enemy units and supply lines. Once the rebels had established a strong defensive position in the highlands, they could take the war into its second phase, on the plains. With their ranks swelled by recruits, the guerrillas could take on larger enemy forces, but they would still use hit-and-run tactics to avoid encirclement. Only when the guerrillas had control of the transportation routes and secondary cities in the plains could they launch the third and final phase of the campaign, an assault on the great cities, by which they would finally defeat the enemy.[41]

Bayo's three stages of guerrilla warfare bear some resemblance to Mao's concept of protracted war, which he developed in the 1930s to resist Japanese aggression. Mao recognized that his Chinese forces could not match the Japanese in military or economic terms. China, however, possessed certain advantages that Mao could use to gain leverage over the superior Japanese armies. With huge expanses of land and a seemingly infinite supply of soldiers, China could sustain a long war against Japan, which because of its limited human and material resources had to strive for a quick and decisive victory. Mao therefore decided to give the Japanese armies space in exchange for time, allowing them to push deep into the interior, causing them to lengthen their lines and forcing them to station troops to defend cities and transportation routes. Mao believed that if he employed the correct military strategy and tactics to prolong the conflict, he could expect the balance of power between the contending armies to tilt in China's favor.[42]

The protracted war against Japanese imperialism, Mao predicted, would develop through three distinct but overlapping phases. In the first stage, the Japanese would take the offensive while the Chinese adopted a strategic defensive posture, avoiding decisive engagements and concentrating on developing bases beyond Japanese control. In the second stage, the Japanese would focus on consolidating their positions while the Chinese patiently prepared to launch a counteroffensive, producing a strategic stalemate. The two large regular armies would remain in place, while Chinese guerrillas harassed the Japanese lines of communication and supply. In the third and final stage of the protracted war, Mao argued, China would launch a strategic counteroffensive and compel the enemy's strategic retreat. The Chinese would recover lost cities and territories in conventional combat with an enemy sapped of its

41. Ibid., 47.
42. Mao Tse-tung, "On Protracted War," in Mallin, *Strategy for Conquest*, 57–70.

morale and matériel during the course of a bloody, protracted war.[43]

Bayo shared Mao's confidence in the ability to defeat a superior foe through a protracted campaign, wherein a small and relatively weak force gradually expanded in size and in the scope of its operations. However, Mao developed his theory of protracted war to resist a foreign invasion; Bayo envisioned a three-phase civil war against a dictatorial regime. Maoist theory begins as a defensive campaign against an alien aggressor with a superior military capability; Bayo's strategy begins as an offensive campaign by a force with an acknowledged inferiority in military capability. Moreover, Mao's strategy of protracted war called for both conventional and unconventional warfare in each of the three stages, with a large regular army coexisting with smaller guerrilla bands. Bayo advocated a guerrilla campaign by a guerrilla army. Bayo shared the Maoist conviction that final victory could only be achieved by taking the cities in conventional assault, but he envisioned the gradual transformation of the guerrilla army into a regular army. Bayo's Cuban trainees would not have the luxury of support from a large regular army.

Although Bayo did not acknowledge any intellectual debt to the Chinese Communists, his star student, Ernesto Guevara, undoubtedly studied the Chinese and Soviet civil wars. According to Jon Lee Anderson, Guevara supplemented Bayo's lectures with his own intense studies of Mao, Lenin, and Stalin, reading Soviet texts he borrowed from the Instituto Cultural Ruso-Mexicano. Guevara updated his philosophical notebooks and edited them into a single volume totaling more than three hundred typewritten pages. This encyclopedia demonstrated Guevara's profound understanding of the revolutionary theories and practices of Marx, Lenin, Stalin, and Mao.[44]

In any case, Bayo clearly adhered to the Maoist doctrine that successful guerrilla warfare required the cooperation of peasants in the countryside. Bayo explained to his students that a guerrilla army would melt like ice cream in the hot sun if it did not have the support of the peasants. The guerrillas depended on the peasants for intelligence, supplies, and recruits. If the peasants did not support the campaign, the guerrilla army would wither away and die.[45]

Consequently, the guerrillas had to convince the peasants to join their campaign against an unjust regime. Although Bayo wrote little about the political aspects of a guerrilla campaign, he left no doubt that those who engaged in

---

43. Ibid., 71–74.
44. Anderson, *Che Guevara*, 189.
45. Bayo, *Mi aporte*, 47.

guerrilla war had to fight for a just cause, whether liberation from a foreign invasion, a cruel dictatorship, or an oligarchic regime. "If these conditions do not exist, the guerrilla war will always be defeated. Whoever revolts unrighteously reaps nothing but a crushing defeat," Bayo asserted.[46]

Bayo's training regimen, however, emphasized the military and physical aspects of guerrilla warfare. The physical training of the Cuban rebel army intensified in May 1956, when Bayo set up a camp at the Santa Rosa ranch, twenty-five miles east of Mexico City. With a sixty-six-hundred-square-foot ranch house, it accommodated more than fifty men and still offered enough privacy to train a guerrilla army in the nearby fields and mountains. Behind nine-foot stone walls with four observation towers, Bayo directed a rigorous training program designed to prepare the force for conventional combat and guerrilla warfare. Ernesto "Che" Guevara, now called simply Che by his Cuban comrades, served as Bayo's assistant. Fidel had appointed Che the chief of personnel, a sign of the respect Che had gained from Fidel and Bayo.[47]

The rebels rose at 5:00 A.M. and practiced military tactics until dark. Bayo taught them how to attack in a series of steps rather than with a frontal assault; he showed them how to flank an enemy position, defend themselves against airplanes and tanks, conduct night marches, use camouflage, and set ambushes. To simulate combat conditions, Bayo set up two mountain camps and had the opposing forces engage in small-scale war games, complete with forced night marches and guard duty. Although the training included conventional tactics, undoubtedly at Fidel's insistence, Bayo still trained the men in guerrilla strategy and tactics.[48]

The best student also turned out to be the best soldier. Che dedicated himself to the training regimen more intensely than any of the Cuban volunteers. After one long day of training, many of the rebels collapsed on the ground. Fidel wanted to calibrate the rifle sights, but only Ernesto had the energy to keep working with him. When they finished, Fidel gathered the rebels and expressed his disappointment in the inability of the Cubans to endure the long, difficult tasks required of the rebel soldier. He noted with admiration the model behavior of Guevara, a foreigner who was pushing himself beyond endurance for a country he had never visited. After this rebuke from Fidel, none of the Cubans thought about getting tired again.[49]

46. Bayo, "One Hundred Fifty Questions," 319.
47. Szulc, *Fidel*, 357; Bayo, *Mi aporte*, 76.
48. Bayo, *Mi aporte*, 37, 57–58.

As chief of personnel, Che prepared daily reports for Fidel. He often consulted with Bayo on the performance of the trainees, becoming Bayo's de facto assistant instructor. Guevara actually led some of the training sessions and earned a reputation as a demanding disciplinarian. In one instance, Calixto Morales refused to obey a direct order from Che to continue on one of Bayo's forced night marches. According to Juan Almeida, Calixto sat down to protest the "tyranny" of the Spanish and Argentine instructors. Guevara ordered the men back to camp, where he convened a court martial to try Morales on charges of insubordination, a crime punishable by death. Although Che and Bayo argued against the death penalty, the jurors convicted Morales and sentenced him to death. Fidel, however, still wielded supreme authority and later pardoned him.[50]

At the Santa Rosa training camp, Che developed an intimate association with Bayo. During their evening talks, the apprentice peppered the master with more questions about the military subjects that Bayo had lectured about or demonstrated during the day. Bayo engaged Guevara in intellectual debate, often while they played chess by candlelight. Bayo came to enjoy these matches so much that he often helped Che prepare his reports so that they could devote more time to chess in the evening. Bayo claimed that he beat Guevara more often than not, a considerable accomplishment, given Guevara's experience. In 1945, at the age of seventeen, Ernesto was one of fifteen challengers who played Argentine national champion Miguel Narsdorf. Ernesto lost that match, but he played Narsdorf to a draw in Cuba seventeen years later.[51]

In any case, Che impressed Bayo with his dedication, intelligence, and discipline. He absorbed Bayo's military knowledge, seeing in guerrilla warfare the means to the end he sought: revolution. Bayo advocated not a means to quick victory, but a slow process, a carefully planned sequence of offensive and defensive moves that would lead to ultimate conquest. Guevara, with the patience and deliberation of a chess master, learned how to devise a long-term military strategy. He fully embraced Bayo's philosophy of guerrilla warfare and won Bayo's highest praise. When Bayo evaluated each man in shooting, discipline, conditioning, and capacity to command, he gave Che the highest score, a perfect ten. Fidel asked Bayo why he ranked Che number one. Bayo answered: "Because he is, without a doubt, the best of everybody."

49. Szulc, *Fidel*, 350.
50. Anderson, *Che Guevara*, 195.
51. Bayo, *Mi aporte*, 76; Guevara Lynch, *Mi hijo el Che*, 283–84.

Fidel, who had observed but rarely participated in any of the training exercises, held the same high opinion of Che.[52]

When Mexican police raided the Santa Rosa camp in June 1956, Bayo had already gone into hiding, leaving Che in command. On the direct orders of Castro, Che and twelve men surrendered to the Mexican authorities, who charged them with violating immigration laws. The Cuban government, however, accused them of plotting Batista's assassination with Cuban and Mexican communists. When interrogated by the Mexican police, Che spoke freely about his communist convictions and the need for an armed revolution throughout Latin America. Guevara's reckless confessions infuriated Castro because they gave his enemies evidence of a communist presence within his movement.[53]

Guevara's radical ideology, uncompromising character, and Argentine citizenship obstructed his move into Castro's inner circle. Che evidently did not influence the strategic planning that led the rebels to disaster at Alegría del Pío. After their release from prison, all the rebels went underground, dispersed by Castro and kept in motion to avoid the Mexican authorities. They had been released on condition that they would leave Mexico within a few days. During an underground period of three months, Che saw little of Bayo or Castro. He could not have participated in any strategic planning with Castro, but should Fidel order him to move out, he would obey.[54]

Ernesto Guevara was now Che, a revolutionary and a *guerrillero*. Like any good soldier who has been submitted to intensive training, he placed the interests of his comrades above his own. He had refused to accept any deal that his parents could have arranged through their political contacts to secure his release from prison. He insisted on being given the same treatment as his Cuban comrades. In a letter to his mother, Guevara proudly explained how "the concept of 'I' had been replaced by the concept of 'us.' It was a communist morale and naturally it may seem a doctrinaire exaggeration, but really it was (and is) beautiful to be able to feel that removal of 'I.'" He signed the letter "El Che," the first expression of his new identity.[55]

He trusted Fidel's leadership and his comrades, fully prepared to triumph with them or die fighting. Che's training and studies had prepared him for a leadership role, and as the doctor assigned to the general staff, he held a posi-

52. Bayo, *Mi aporte*, 76.
53. Anderson, *Che Guevara*, 199.
54. Ibid., 202.
55. Ernesto Guevara to Celia Serna de Guevara, July 15, 1956, in Guevara Lynch, *Aquí va un soldado*, 141.

tion near to Fidel, but he did not exert much influence on strategic planning prior to the departure of the *Granma*. Bayo had devised detailed instructions on how to execute an amphibious landing and initiate a guerrilla campaign, but Castro either ignored or discarded those precious lessons. Bayo believed that a guerrilla army could land and unload its matériel safely, but he stressed the importance of moving quickly to the highest ridge that offered cover from the enemy.[56]

In spite of Bayo's advice, Fidel devised a slightly modified version of the strategy that had led his rebels to disaster at Moncada. For his next move, Castro planned to coordinate an amphibious landing of his rebel army in Oriente province with another attack on Moncada and other sites in Santiago. Thanks to Castro's impudent declarations prior to departure, even Batista knew that Castro intended to invade the island before the end of 1956. From the landing site he intended to move, not toward the Sierra Maestra, but toward the army garrison at Niquero. If the attack on Niquero failed, his men were to reassemble at a farm in the foothills of the Sierra Maestra, according to instructions that he apparently issued. From there the men would move into the mountains and launch a guerrilla campaign. Just as he had done at Moncada in 1953, Castro planned to spark a nationwide rebellion with a bold strike that relied on the element of surprise and precise coordination. He would retreat to the mountains and launch a guerrilla campaign if the initial attacks did not generate the popular uprising he anticipated.

Castro's strategy violated the principles of guerrilla warfare that Bayo had taught in Mexico. "The perfect guerrilla," Bayo wrote, "is one who never invites the enemy to do battle. Nor does he accept a challenge to fight the enemy who hopes to meet us where he would hold the advantage. Every good guerrilla should attack by surprise, in skirmishes and ambushes, and when the enemy least suspects any action."[57] Castro had not only issued a public invitation to his enemies to do battle, he even offered to fight them at places where they would hold the advantage—the garrisons in Santiago and Niquero. If Castro had asked for Bayo's advice about the first military action his eighty-two-man army should take after landing in Cuba, Bayo would have recommended an attack on the roads and railroads in Oriente province, to deny the enemy the use of vehicles and force them to travel on foot.[58]

Bayo recognized the possibility of guerrilla companies attacking military

56. Bayo, "One Hundred Fifty Questions," in Mallin, *Strategy for Conquest,* 320–25.
57. Ibid., 328.
58. Ibid., 327.

garrisons, but only in the later stages of a war that had begun as a guerrilla campaign. He even offered detailed instructions on how guerrilla units should execute these and other conventional missions, including an amphibious landing. However, Castro drafted the military strategy that guided the eighty-two men who sailed on the *Granma* on November 25, 1956. Among those eighty-two passengers, fortunately for Castro, was an attentive young Argentine who had studied Bayo's strategies and tactics carefully. From the charred cane fields of Alegría del Pío came a company of soldiers who had no choice but to apply Bayo's theories with the guidance of Che Guevara.

FOUR COMANDANTE CHE

After the initial battle at Alegría del Pío, Che, Ramiro Valdés, Juan Almeida, and two other soldiers took cover in a cave just a short distance from the battlefield. The occasional sounds of nearby gunfire indicated that the Cuban army intended to capture and kill the scattered remnants of Fidel's rebel forces. For all Captain Almeida knew, he commanded the only remaining combatants. They each had a weapon and some ammunition, but thirst or starvation might kill them before the enemy did. Under these desperate circumstances, the five men took a solemn vow to fight to the death. If Batista's soldiers found them, they would convert that cave into their tomb.[1]

They decided to resume their march toward the Sierra Maestra, as Castro had ordered them to do shortly after their landing. They made it safely to the Caribbean coast by dawn on December 7, then guided themselves eastward by keeping the sea to their right. On the ninth, they marched on the beach under a nearly full moon, Che and Almeida in the lead. They came to an abrupt halt when they detected three shadowy figures in a wooden shanty a short distance ahead. Too close to retrace their steps, Almeida decided to attack. He approached cautiously, Che and the others following closely behind, their weapons ready. The rebels jumped the supposed enemy troops and found

1. Che to Hilda Guevara, January 28, 1957, in Guevara, *Episodes,* 404; Guevara Lynch, *Mi hijo el Che,* 101–2.

themselves pointing their guns at Camilo Cienfuegos and two other rebels. Camilo, one of the few heroes of the battle of Alegría del Pío, accepted the "surrender" of his comrades, and welcomed them into his hideout.[2]

Left to their own misfortune, the rebels might have stumbled into an army patrol, in which case they would have been summarily executed. They knew that they had to get into the mountains as soon as possible, but to do that, they needed guidance, food, and shelter. In the unlikely event that the entire rebel army reassembled in the Sierra Maestra, they still faced the prospect of another military disaster if Fidel Castro adopted a more appropriate—that is, less risky—strategy. Castro's daring surprise attack on Moncada, followed three years later by the ill-starred "invasion" of Oriente province, had decimated and demoralized the ranks of the rebel army. Twice, Batista's army had shown greater resilience and the people less discontent than Castro had anticipated. If Castro continued to rely on the elements of surprise and popular support to take fortified military positions, his outgunned rebels might not survive another engagement. Their only hope for survival lay in the adoption and deliberate execution of a guerrilla strategy, and Fidel had not yet shown much appreciation for guerrilla warfare.

Luckily, Ernesto Guevara survived the battle of Alegría del Pío. In the six months after the *Granma* landing, Guevara emerged as the rebel army's military instructor, top guerrilla commander, and closest military adviser to Castro. Although Fidel learned quickly and incorporated some elements of guerrilla warfare into his strategy, he still displayed a preference for positional warfare, as evident in the first major rebel victory, the battle of El Uvero. Guevara's preference for ambushes, hit-and-run attacks, and a defensive campaign in general, moderated Castro's conventional and offensive military style. The two men learned from and complemented each other nicely, forming a military partnership that gave the M-26-7 army its first competent command structure.

In the transition from a conventional to a guerrilla strategy, Che Guevara played a pivotal role. Castro, who had excused himself from Alberto Bayo's training sessions, knew little of the strategy and tactics of guerrilla warfare. Bayo, too old to accompany the rebels to Cuba, could not give Castro the advice he needed. Castro would have to rely on Che, Bayo's top pupil. Castro retained overall command of the rebel army throughout the insurrection, but his strategic objectives and tactical maneuvers gradually fell into line with the guerrilla campaign favored by Guevara, who also had to refine and adapt his

2. Guevara, *Episodes*, 93–95; Alvarez Tabio, *Diario de la Guerra*, 40–54.

concepts of guerrilla warfare under fire. By the summer of 1957 Guevara had emerged as the top guerrilla strategist in the rebel army, a fact reflected in his promotion to command the first rebel column to operate independently of Fidel.

From Bayo, Che had learned that a guerrilla army could not survive without the support of the peasants. Fortunately for the rebel army, M-26-7 activists had already prepared a network of peasant sympathizers in Oriente province prior to the landing of the *Granma*. During a crucial two-week period after Alegría del Pío, a few peasants found, protected, and reassembled the battered remnants of Castro's rebel army. On December 13, a week after Alegría del Pío, Juan Almeida decided to beg for food and water at a small hut in Puercas Gordas, on the other side of the Toro River. Che, not knowing whether he could trust these peasants, suspected a trap. To Che's surprise, the peasant man not only offered them food and shelter, he also informed them that Castro had survived the battle.[3]

Che, visiting Cuba for the first time, did not know the people or the terrain. He had little awareness or appreciation of the preparatory work that had been done prior to the *Granma* landing. A national network of M-26-7 activists already existed, trained and prepared to gather supplies, funds, and recruits to support a guerrilla band in the mountains. The lifeline from the cities to the mountains also already existed, thanks to Frank País in Santiago and Celia Sánchez in Manzanillo. One of Celia's recruits was Guillermo García, one of eleven poor children, who had been in the M-26-7 movement for nearly two years prior to the arrival of the *Granma*. On November 30 he had been waiting with several trucks near the landing area, but the rebels arrived several days later. He attempted to organize peasant supporters soon after the *Granma* landing, but the quick movements of Batista's army prevented him from meeting the rebel force at the beach. Guillermo, like Batista's army, had no problem picking up the trail of the rebels, but he did not find them in time to prevent the disaster at Alegría del Pío. Knowing every *bohío* (hut), trail, and *guajiro* (peasant) in the area, he personally rescued six rebels, including Fidel.[4] Without the assistance of peasant sympathizers such as Guillermo, none of the rebels would have made it safely to the Sierra Maestra.

With Guillermo's assistance, Fidel established a base at the farm of Mongo Pérez, about five miles east of the Pilón–Niquero highway. Pérez, another M-26-7 activist who had been waiting for the rebels, owned this farm, which

3. Alvarez Tabio, *Diario de la Guerra*, 70.
4. Ibid., 82–83; Szulc, *Fidel*, 383–87; Franqui, *Diary*, 127.

Fidel intended to use as an operational headquarters in the event that his attack on Niquero did not succeed. The Pérez farm would evidently serve as a rallying point for the rebels, a place to reassemble if Castro had to implement his contingency plan and move his men into the Sierra Maestra. Some rebels may have known of these plans in advance, but they would not have been able to reach the farm safely without the support of Guillermo García and other peasant sympathizers.[5]

No amount of peasant assistance, however, would have saved the rebels if Batista had decided to pursue them more aggressively. On December 11, only six days after Batista's forces routed the rebels at Alegría del Pío, Batista ordered a cease-fire. Two days later, the army withdrew all combat units, leaving only the standard Rural Guard units to patrol the area. The armed forces even canceled aerial surveillance. Thinking that the rebels had been either defeated or completely dispersed, Batista claimed victory, while rumors spread that Castro was already dead.[6] Relentless pursuit of the scattered rebel army, ending only with the capture of Castro, would have terminated the insurrection before the rebels had a chance to regroup in the Sierra Maestra. Throughout the counterinsurgency campaign that followed, Batista's forces consistently demonstrated an inability or unwillingness to engage and pursue the enemy until they achieved a complete and definite victory.

After Batista's army fled the battlefield and claimed victory, the surviving rebels came out of their hiding places and reassembled at the Pérez farm. At 4:00 A.M. on December 21, Che's group finally reached the camp, suddenly home to fifteen rebels. To Che's delight, he found that Raúl, Ciro Redondo, and Efigenio Ameijeras had also survived the battle. Many other valiant comrades had fallen in the two-week manhunt that followed Alegría del Pío, but if Che had had to pick fifteen men to continue the fight, he would have selected most of these individuals.[7]

Fidel, who should have been delighted at the appearance of his most competent military commander and soldier, noticed that only three of the new arrivals carried guns. Che and Almeida tried to explain that one of their peasant guides had asked them to leave their weapons behind so that they would be less conspicuous. Their explanation did not calm Fidel, who reproached Che in bitter terms that Guevara would never forget: "You have not paid for

5. Alvarez Tabio, *Diario de la Guerra*, 70–71, 86–93; Szulc, *Fidel*, 385–86; Guevara, *Episodes*, 99; Guevara and Castro, *La conquista de la esperanza*, 126.

6. Pérez, *Army Politics*, 140; Szulc, *Fidel*, 382.

7. Alvarez Tabio, *Diario de la Guerra*, 95–97.

the error you committed, because the price for abandoning your weapons under such circumstances is your life. Your only hope of survival, in the event of a head-on encounter with the army, was your weapons. To abandon them was criminal and stupid."[8]

The bitter rebuke from the man responsible for Alegría del Pío stung Che. Che had to harbor serious doubts about Castro's command capabilities, given that Fidel had marched his army directly into an ambush. Although there is no indication in published accounts that Che criticized Fidel for his military errors, one cannot dismiss the possibility that Che and Fidel got into a heated argument. Few people, including Fidel, intimidated Che, who never shied away from an argument. In any case, relations between the two men were obviously strained. The day Che reunited with Fidel, a shipment of weapons arrived as scheduled, making it clear that Fidel's harsh rebuke of Che had been gratuitous and unnecessary. Fidel nevertheless took away Che's pistol—a highly valued weapon among the rebels—and gave him what Che called "a bad rifle." Che's field diary, which has been censored by Cuban authorities, gives no indication that he defended his actions, but according to Jon Lee Anderson, "Fidel's upbraiding must have been galling [to Che]. Fidel may have hung onto *his* weapon in flight, but his judgments had led them into catastrophe in the first place, beginning with the *Granma*'s grounding offshore."[9]

Fidel would not have admitted it, but he needed Che Guevara, the best, if not the only, guerrilla strategist in his decimated rebel army. With his force reduced to twenty men, Castro had no choice but to implement some of the strategies and tactics that Guevara had so carefully studied under Alberto Bayo. Castro had neither the expertise nor the inclination to reorganize and redeploy his rebel forces as a guerrilla army. Che Guevara, however, had learned how to conduct a guerrilla campaign and recognized that a guerrilla army, no matter how small and poorly armed, could defeat a superior military force. Over the following six months, Che Guevara trained that people's army and its commander, his power increasing with each new victory on the battlefield.

Ernesto Guevara's rise in the ranks from doctor to second in command took nearly a year, and the volatile Castro and the stoic Guevara clashed repeatedly over strategy and tactics. Castro often rejected Che's military recommendations, but his adoption of the ambush and hit-and-run reflected

8. Guevara, *Episodes,* 100–101.
9. Anderson, *Che Guevara,* 217.

Che's influence on rebel strategy. The day after Castro criticized Che, he ordered him to prepare the men for battle, and two days after that, he presented Che with a telescopic rifle; these were two clear signs that Castro still valued him and the guerrilla campaign that Che favored. The day after Christmas, Fidel appointed Che to the general staff of a twenty-two-man army, a presumptuous gesture that nonetheless marked Guevara's official entry into Castro's inner circle, from which he would push Fidel toward unconventional warfare.[10]

Castro's gestures did not, however, muffle Guevara, who did not see any sense of purpose or urgency in Fidel's command. On December 22, he decried the "almost total inactivity" of the rebel band. On December 23, Che noted that they were "still in the same place." On Christmas Eve, Fidel held them in "a wait that seems useless to me." On Christmas Day, they began a slow march after feasting on roast pork. But the men marched carelessly, leaving broken fences behind them for the army or peasants to follow. The only action that they took, Che noted ironically, was "an exercise of assaulting a house, and as we did the owner, Hermes, appeared." When they finally resumed the march after a two-hour coffee break, they made so much noise that they alerted every peasant along the way. Despite such lack of caution, Guevara was ready to go into battle with the twenty men available. "Che wanted to see more organization, discipline, and action. He wanted the war to begin," concludes Anderson.[11]

However, Castro commanded the rebel army and still made the strategic decisions. He also rejected his brother's advice to attack six soldiers guarding a nearby estate, arguing that he had to acquire more arms, ammunition, and recruits before taking the offensive or moving to a defensive position in the Sierra Maestra.[12] Che, demonstrating the defensive instincts that would serve him well in the campaign to come, wanted to move quickly into the mountains and establish a strong defensive position. From there he could apply Bayo's strategy, setting ambushes to disrupt the enemy's lines of communication and supplies. The longer the rebels lingered in the plains, the more likely they would march into another ambush. Fidel wanted to wait for more recruits and supplies before they climbed into the mountains. Che argued against delaying the march into the Sierra Maestra, asserting that the

10. Ibid., 216–17.

11. Guevara and Castro, *Conquista de la esperanza,* 140–51; Anderson, *Che Guevara,* 218 (quoted).

12. Guevara and Castro, *Conquista de la esperanza,* 155–56.

recruits and supplies could be sent directly to them in the mountains, but Fidel held his ground. "It doesn't seem wise to me but Castro insists on it," Che wrote.[13]

By the end of December, peasant support had begun to materialize. Crescencio Pérez, a popular man with a legendary reputation for violence and sexual promiscuity attracted *guajiros* to the rebel banner, and with Pérez on his general staff, Castro won the confidence of local peasants. Six peasants joined the rebel army in late December. With these "reinforcements," Fidel decided to move on December 30, to the delight of Che Guevara. An army battalion, they learned from the peasants, was preparing to pursue them into the sierra.[14]

Luckily for the rebels, Batista's military demonstrated an inexplicable reluctance to fight. While a battalion prepared to resume the manhunt that had been called off by Batista for political reasons, Castro had two weeks to regroup, a luxury of time that Castro still did not exploit fully. If Che deserved criticism for abandoning his weapon, Castro certainly deserved censure for taking so long to take up a defensive position in the mountains. Only on January 5, a month after Alegría del Pío, could the rebels see the hazy blue outline of the peak of Mount Caracas, in the heart of the Sierra Maestra. If and when they reached that position, they would finally be on terrain that favored them. The steep slopes would slow the movement of the enemy soldiers and force them to fight as infantry, while the forest would provide cover from aerial reconnaissance. "The perspectives are good," Che wrote, "because from here to La Plata is all steep and forested, ideal for defense."[15]

Rather than going directly east across the mountains to the peak of Mount Caracas, Fidel decided to descend to the coast first and then climb into the mountains along the natural ridges and canyons cut by the rivers. On an eleven-day march to the coast, the rebels gained confidence and strength, recognizing that conditions favored the kind of hit-and-run attack that Alberto Bayo preferred. Feeling secure, the rebel leaders began to debate their military options, hoping to select an appropriate and vulnerable target for their first offensive action. According to Bayo, a newly established guerrilla band should strike first at the roads and railroads leading into its base of operations, in an effort to force the enemy to fight on foot.[16]

13. Anderson, *Che Guevara,* 222.
14. Ibid.
15. Alvarez Tabio, *Diario de la Guerra,* 134–36; Szulc, *Fidel,* 393; Anderson, *Che Guevara,* 217–18.
16. Bayo, "One Hundred Fifty Questions," in Mallin, *Strategy for Conquest,* 327.

However, the rebel army had not yet established a base of operations. Once this was put in place, the rebels could launch attacks on enemy outposts and supply lines, but political circumstances dictated Castro's military strategy. Popular opinion held that the army had crushed the rebels and killed Fidel Castro. The morale of the rebels had sagged in the month after Alegría del Pío, and they needed a victory. Fidel wanted to boost the morale of his troops and make headlines in Havana, thereby refuting government claims that the rebels had been defeated. Che and Fidel argued about how to score the first rebel victory. On January 10, the rebels observed eighteen marines walking along a road from a coastal garrison. Che urged Fidel to ambush the soldiers, but Fidel held him back. Eighteen soldiers, even if caught by surprise, could have put up a stiff resistance. Castro had already decided to launch his first attack against the Rural Guard outpost at La Plata. From there he would move into the mountains with all the food, weapons, and ammunition that they could carry from the garrison, hoping that the army would pursue him. Che had doubts about Fidel's strategy: "[Fidel's plan] doesn't seem bad to me but it's a lot of weight [to carry]. My plan was to form a [central] camp with abundant food and [from there] send out assault troops." Castro, knowing that he would finally have the advantages of surprise and numerical superiority, rejected Che's proposal.[17]

Guevara had little understanding or appreciation of the political conditions that shaped Castro's military concepts. He thought primarily in military terms. His plan to establish a base camp first made complete military sense because it would have increased the mobility of the troops before and after the attack on La Plata. Mobility in the initial stages of guerrilla warfare is essential; the guerrilla should never offer the enemy a fixed target. Although Fidel's plan to carry off the prizes of war he captured at La Plata would limit mobility in retreat, it aimed at a political target that had so far eluded him: an army outpost. Castro had failed miserably at Moncada, but by downsizing the scale of his target from a regimental headquarters (one thousand men) to a Rural Guard outpost (fifteen men), he could score his first unqualified military success and make an important political statement, locally and nationally. The villagers of La Plata and Palma Mocha had recently been the victims of army atrocities that included several executions and the destruction of several homes. The army's repressive actions offered Castro a clear opportunity

---

17. Alvarez Tabio, *Diario de la Guerra,* 138–61; Guevara and Castro, *Conquista de la esperanza,* 185–87; Che Guevara's diary, cited in Anderson, *Che Guevara,* 223–24.

to rally the peasants to the M-26-7 cause and show the Cuban nation that Batista had not killed him or his movement.

After a careful surveillance of the area, Castro concluded that his rebel army could take La Plata, where the river of the same name empties into the Caribbean. (See Map 3.) From local peasants the rebels learned that only fifteen men guarded the barracks, and the soldiers would have to fight with their backs to the sea. If the rebels attacked under the cover of darkness, they would have a decided advantage over the unsuspecting soldiers. Conditions favored Castro's rebel army. He had finally accepted a fundamental rule of guerrilla warfare: no battle should be fought unless it can be won. The addition of a few more peasant recruits increased the number of rebels to thirty-two, but only eighteen men had any combat training and not all of them carried a weapon. A scarcity of weapons limited the number of effective combatants to twenty-two. Given the shortage of weapons and ammunition, Che knew that the rebels had to take La Plata at all costs. If they failed, they would have expended all their ammunition without gaining anything, leaving them virtually defenseless. Fidel ordered Che to prepare the men for battle.[18]

Shortly after nightfall on January 16, the rebels crossed the shallow La Plata River and took up positions on a path leading to the garrison. Chicho Osorio, a notoriously brutal foreman on a nearby plantation, subsequently rode into the rebels on his mule. The first few words out of his slobbering mouth indicated that he was drunk in the saddle, oblivious to danger. Fidel, pretending to be an army colonel, duped Osorio into guiding the rebels to the barracks.[19]

The barracks consisted of three buildings: a wooden bunkhouse located on the northern end of the camp; a house; and a small thatched-roof hut on the southern end of the camp, nearest to the coast. Fidel divided his twenty-two men into four squads. The first, commanded by Lieutenant Julio Díaz, took up a position on the extreme right of the rebel line, opposite the thatched-roof hut. Che, as a member of the general staff, took his position near Fidel in the center. Raúl Castro commanded the squad to Fidel's left, fronting on the bunkhouse. Juan Almeida commanded the fourth squad on the extreme left of the line. Almeida lined his men up on the dirt road that ran parallel to the bunkhouse. The rebel line enclosed the barracks on two sides, resembling

18. Guevara, *Episodes,* 102–5; Anderson, *Che Guevara,* 224.
19. Guevara, *Episodes,* 103–5. The rebels killed Osorio as soon as the battle of La Plata began.

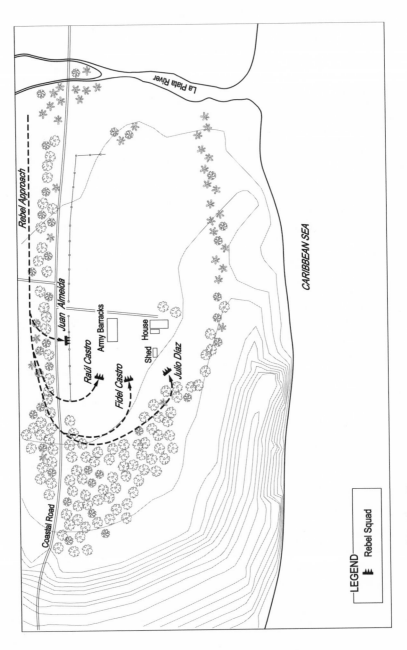

Map 3. Battle of La Plata, January 17, 1957

an inverted L, with the La Plata River and the Caribbean Sea blocking the retreat of the enemy on the other two sides.[20]

It took thirty minutes for the rebels to form their lines; they maintained a strict silence as they settled into position about fifty yards away from their targets. The enemy soldiers had no warning of the rebel advance. On January 17, 1957, the soldier of the Americas finally took aim at the enemy, an opportunity denied him in Guatemala. Fidel broke the unnerving silence with a submachine-gun blast at 2:30 A.M. The rebels then opened up with all they had: thirteen rifles, five semiautomatic rifles, two submachine guns, two machine pistols, and a sixteen-gauge shotgun. Then the guns fell silent.

Fidel, hoping to save ammunition, called on the soldiers to surrender. They answered with their own burst of gunfire and the rebels responded with another torrent of bullets. On Fidel's order, Che lobbed his old Brazilian-made grenade. It did not explode. Raúl Castro threw a stick of dynamite into the bunkhouse; it fizzled out. In frustration, Fidel ordered the houses set on fire. Che grabbed a torch, ran across a clearing with Luis Crespo, and set fire to the thatched-roof hut. The soldiers in the nearby bunkhouse quickly realized the futility of their resistance and surrendered. By 3:00 A.M., it was all over. The rebels had killed two and wounded five, while suffering not even a scratch. As Che tended to the wounded soldiers, the rebels took stock of their prizes: eight Springfield rifles, a Thompson submachine gun, a thousand rounds of ammunition, cartridge belts, fuel, knives, clothing, and food. Che took an army corporal's hat as his prize. They set fire to the remaining buildings and withdrew in the direction of Palma Mocha at 4:30 A.M., the fires behind them now representing victory rather than disaster.[21]

The first offensive action of the guerrilla campaign, a brief skirmish between a handful of poorly armed rebels and an isolated Rural Guard outpost, gave Castro his first military victory. The rebels defeated an enemy unit and acquired valuable matériel without losing a man. The skirmish demonstrated that Fidel had finally applied some of the fundamental precepts of guerrilla warfare. Castro had scouted his target carefully and acquired valuable intelligence about the strength and location of the enemy before he attacked. When he attacked, he enjoyed the element of surprise and the cover of darkness. Further, the deployment of his men left the enemy without a viable means of escape, while his men could flee into the mountains if necessary. Castro's debut as a guerrilla commander was a small but significant success. In Guevara's debut as a soldier,

---

20. Alvarez Tabio, *Diario de la Guerra*, 182.
21. Ibid., 182–88; Guevara, *Episodes*, 105–9.

he demonstrated the courage he later expected of his subordinates.

The assault on La Plata formed part of a two-phase strategy. By hitting and running into the sierra, Castro made his presence known and invited the army to pursue him. Army Major Joaquín Casillas took the bait. He set up a command center at La Plata with a company of one hundred men divided into three platoons. One of the platoons, commanded by Lieutenant Angel Sánchez Mosquera, followed the rebels up the Palma Mocha River.[22]

By the time Lieutenant Sánchez Mosquera left La Plata, however, the guerrillas had had two days to prepare an appropriate reception for him. They reached the Palma Mocha River just before dawn on January 17. Turning north, their march slowed by the extra weight they had picked up at La Plata, they entered a different world, leaving behind them the hungry days in the dry coastal plains. Walking along the soft riverbanks and through luscious forests, they marched into territory with geographical, political, and economic conditions that favored the guerrilla campaign that Castro had finally initiated. As they ascended, they passed first one, then dozens of peasant families heading in the opposite direction. These peasants, ostensibly evicted from their homes because of guerrilla operations, represented potential sympathizers and suppliers.[23]

Shortly before noon on January 18, the mountain trail led into a clearing with two uninhabited *bohíos*. Surrounded as it was on all sides by thickly forested heights, Fidel recognized it as an ideal location for an ambush. He expected the army to follow him into the mountains; indeed, he wanted to be pursued, and thus he had marched in daylight. Fidel decided to prepare an ambush at the clearing, near a little creek known as the Arroyo del Infierno (Hell's Creek).[24] (See Map 4.)

On January 20, Fidel deployed seven squads in a semicircular line along and just below the crest of the wooded heights and ordered them to dig in. Fidel expected the army patrol to march into the clearing, where they would be surrounded; one squad would close the trap behind them. After the squads took their positions, Che, wearing his corporal's cap, joined Fidel and Raúl in an inspection of the lines, yet another confirmation of Che's status as a top military adviser to Fidel. A shot suddenly rang out and they ran for cover, thinking the army had initiated an attack. It turned out that Camilo

22. Fermoselle, *Evolution of the Cuban Military*, 221.
23. Alvarez Tabio, *Diario de la Guerra*, 195–201.
24. Ibid., 202–4.

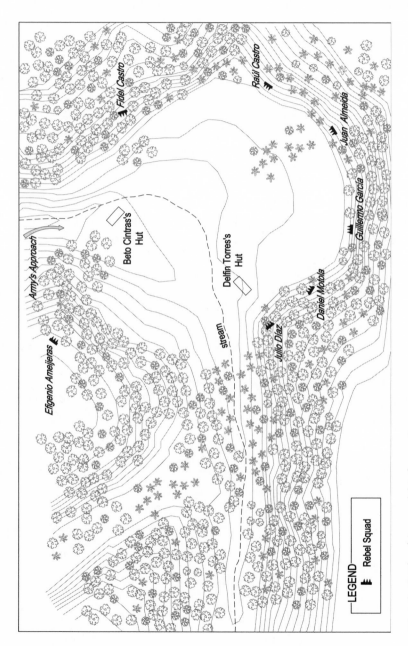

Map 4. Battle of Arroyo del Infierno, January 22, 1957

Cienfuegos had fired at Che, mistaking him for an enemy soldier because he wore an army cap. Luckily for Che, Camilo's gun jammed before he could get a second shot off. The shot, however, scared some of the guerrillas and sent them scurrying into the bush.[25]

Che and the rest of the general staff took a position on the extreme left. Then they waited for two days. An occasional shot interrupted their boredom. Several shots at 5:00 A.M. on January 22 signaled the approach of Lieutenant Sánchez Mosquera's platoon. Batista's army had received no training in counterinsurgency tactics, though Lieutenant Sánchez Mosquera would soon develop into their most effective field commander. At noon, a soldier cautiously approached the first *bohío*. Six other soldiers followed. After inspecting the huts, three of them began to walk away. Another, apparently left behind as a guard, sat down in the shade, showing no apprehension. Fidel killed the poor soldier with a single shot of his telescopic rifle. All units opened up, catching the vanguard of the enemy patrol in a cross fire. Che saw another soldier take cover in the *bohío* closer to his position, just twenty yards away. Che fired his rifle and missed. He fired again, and the man fell, leaving his rifle stuck in the ground, into which the bayonet had plunged. Covered by Crespo, Che rushed into the house and admired his work. With the trained eye of a medical doctor, he noticed that a single shot had pierced the heart, killing the soldier instantly. Che took his rifle, bullets, and a few other items, then ran off, his weapon finally stained with blood.[26]

After thirty minutes, the army withdrew. The guerrillas had killed only five enemy soldiers and picked up a rifle, but they had accomplished their objective—the repulsion of the enemy's vanguard unit. Fidel ordered the rebels to retreat higher into the mountains. As he marched away from his second consecutive victory, Che understood the meaning of this battle: the guerrilla ambush had eliminated the vanguard of the enemy on the march, and an army without a vanguard is paralyzed. Aside from a few minor tactical mistakes and accidents in these initial skirmishes, Castro's application of a classic guerrilla strategy had resulted in two small victories. Castro and Guevara would apply the strategy again and again. According to Ramón Bonachea and Marta San Martín, "The pattern of attacking an isolated army post, withdrawing immediately, and then preparing an ambush for pursuing troops

25. Guevara, *Episodes*, 110; Anderson, *Che Guevara*, 227.
26. Guevara, *Episodes*, 111–13.

became the guerrillas' strategy throughout the campaign."[27]

Five days after the Arroyo del Infierno ambush, Che reflected on the recent victories. The adrenaline still flowed through his veins as he wrote to Hilda Gadea on January 28, 1957: "From the woods of Cuba, alive and thirsting for blood, I write these fiery lines in the spirit of Martí." Che clearly understood how the guerrilla tactics would demoralize and ultimately defeat the enemy, which would not register a victory more significant than their first one at Alegría del Pío. "Just when they [the army troops] think we're in their grasp, they see us disappear like soap through their fingers. Naturally, the fight is not completely won and many battles lie ahead, but things now lean in our favor, as they will increasingly."[28]

After the skirmishes at La Plata and Arroyo del Infierno, Batista could no longer deny that rebels existed in the Sierra Maestra. To eliminate what the regular army considered a minor nuisance, the general staff deployed to the region fourteen hundred troops under the command of Colonel Pedro Barrera Pérez. The colonel intended to establish a military cordon around the sierra, contain the conflict in the mountains, and prevent recruits from joining the guerrillas. In addition, the army designed some minor social programs for the peasants, sending medical units into the area to provide basic medical services.[29]

The army plan required officers and soldiers with the strength and determination to carry out the strategy, which was to pursue the rebels with all available infantry units, supported by the air force. If the officers coordinated operations on the ground and in the air, they could certainly tighten a noose around the guerrillas. The military unleashed its new offensive on January 30 with an impressive aerial assault on the guerrilla camp on the slopes of Caracas Peak. The air force attacked with five American planes used extensively in World War II: the B-26 Invader, the fastest bomber used in World War II; and the P-47 Thunderbolt, used in bomber escort and ground attack. The Americans had faster and deadlier planes on their airfields, but the Cuban pilots could destroy the rebels with the heavy payloads they carried. The B-26 alone could carry up to four thousand pounds of bombs.[30] The attack

27. Alvarez Tabio, *Diario de la Guerra,* 205–17; Guevara, *Episodes,* 114; Bonachea and San Martín, *Cuban Insurrection,* 90 (quoted).

28. Che to Hilda Guevara, January 28, 1957, in Guevara, *Episodes,* 404.

29. Pérez, *Army Politics,* 140.

30. Angelucci and Matricardi, *World War II Airplanes,* 2:95; Gunston, *Encyclopedia of World Air Power.*

caught the guerrillas completely by surprise. Fortunately for them, they happened to be more than two hundred yards above the location of their forward detachment and field kitchen, which the bombers knocked out with a direct hit. Fidel and Raúl led two groups scurrying for cover in the woods, while Che volunteered to pick up stragglers and supplies from the forward camp and catch up with the main body later. Miraculously, the guerrillas did not lose one man in this assault.[31]

Che caught up with Fidel three days later at Altos de Espinosa, several miles to the southwest of Caracas Peak. The air force returned with a bombing and strafing run on February 7 and again on February 8. Although the strikes inflicted little damage, they kept the rebels on the run and demonstrated Batista's recognition that he had to use his material advantages to defeat the guerrilla forces. Guided to the camps by a peasant informant, the pilots had a rare opportunity to score a direct hit. The guerrillas escaped destruction only by sheer luck. Airpower alone probably could not have defeated them, but aircraft can be used effectively in a counterinsurgency campaign, particularly if aerial reconnaissance and attacks form part of a strategic operation. "Airpower properly coordinated with surface power plus highly coordinated military and civil agency operations can insure the defeat of the insurgent guerrillas in military combat," according to one counterinsurgency expert.[32]

Air strikes can also have a devastating psychological impact on guerrilla forces, and the morale of Castro's guerrilla band certainly plummeted as a result of the aerial assaults. The men began to talk of a traitor within their ranks. None could believe that such accurate bombing missions could have been executed if the pilots did not know the exact location of the rebel camp. Even worse, the guerrillas feared the approach of infantry units.

On the morning of February 9, Fidel learned that 140 soldiers had taken positions above the camp. At 1:30 P.M., the army unit, commanded by Major Casillas, attacked. Clearly outnumbered and fighting on terrain that favored the enemy, the guerrillas had no choice but to withdraw. They scattered again in three units commanded by Fidel, Raúl, and Che, who was forced to run so quickly that he had to leave his knapsack behind, full of medicines and rations. This time the guerrillas had a prearranged rallying point: El Lomón, just a few miles west of Caracas Peak. Arriving there three days later, they

31. Guevara, *Episodes,* 115–17; Szulc, *Fidel,* 396; Alvarez Tabio, *Diario de la guerra,* 242–44; Anderson, *Che Guevara,* 230.
32. Pustay, *Counterinsurgency Warfare,* 116.

learned that the two surprise attacks, one by air and one on the ground, had been made possible by the traitorous conduct of Eutimio Guerra, a peasant turned informant who had guided the army to the rebel camps.[33]

Che had suspected treachery within the ranks of the new recruits and had urged Castro to execute three spies in January. Castro showed mercy on those men, but he made "desertion, insubordination, and defeatism" crimes punishable by death. When Juan Almeida captured Eutimio Guerra holding a safe-conduct pass from the enemy commander, Che demanded his immediate execution. Guerra fell down on his knees and asked that he be shot. Castro showed no mercy and Guerra asked for none. He only asked that the revolution take care of his children. "Just then a heavy storm broke and the sky darkened," Che wrote later. Nobody stepped forward to carry out the execution. Fidel apparently walked away, hoping that somebody else would carry out the grisly job. To end what Che described as an "uncomfortable" situation, he stepped forward and put a .32-caliber pistol to the right side of his head and shot him.[34]

From that point on, guerrillas and peasants feared "el Che." The cold-blooded execution of a poor peasant eliminated any doubt about Guevara's willingness to kill and die for the cause. If soldiers or peasants wanted mercy, they now knew to appeal to Fidel and not to Che, whose reputation as a ruthless revolutionary gradually spread throughout the region. "This incident," concluded biographer Jon Lee Anderson, "was seminal in the growth of Che's mystique among the guerrillas and peasants of the Sierra Maestra. From then on he acquired a reputation for a cold-blooded willingness to take direct action against transgressors of the revolutionary norms."[35]

These character traits made Che an efficient subordinate commander, but they did not necessarily qualify him for independent command. Fear alone is not enough to inspire individuals to follow a commander into battle. Che lacked the charm and diplomatic skills of Fidel, who recognized the political dimensions of the struggle and directed nonmilitary affairs with little input from Guevara. Eighty-two men had landed near Coloradas beach in December 1956, and two months later, Castro could only put about thirty effective combatants into the field. He did not yet pose a serious military threat to Batista. If Batista's forces continued to pursue them with a coordinated air and ground

33. Guevara, *Episodes*, 120–27.
34. Ibid., 130–31; Che Guevara's diary, cited in Anderson, *Che Guevara*, 236–37.
35. Anderson, *Che Guevara*, 238.

campaign, they might entirely eliminate what threat the rebels did pose. Castro therefore needed to bring more men and supplies into his rebel army.

Despite the efforts of Crescencio Pérez, few peasants had enlisted, and the case of Eutimio Guerra showed that they had to be handled with extreme care. The M-26-7 had already recruited volunteers in Santiago, but the organization had not yet decided to make Castro's rebel army the focus of its insurrectionary activities. Consequently, when Castro met with the M-26-7 National Directorate in mid-February to discuss strategy, he hoped to convince his associates that a guerrilla campaign based in the mountains could lead to the overthrow of Batista. Castro had prevailed only in two minor skirmishes, leaving most leaders skeptical about the prospects of a guerrilla campaign. Other leaders advocated a variety of tactics, including general labor strikes and urban sabotage campaigns, following the general insurrectionary line that Fidel maintained until Alegría del Pío. Frank País, the M-26-7 coordinator of Oriente province, had come to the meeting determined to convince Castro to leave Cuba and reorganize the movement from another Latin American country. Faustino Pérez, a *Granma* veteran, returned with a proposal to open a second guerrilla front in the Escambray Mountains in central Cuba. Fidel, however, opposed both proposals and persuaded his comrades to make his rebel army the highest priority of the M-26-7 movement. País promised to send Fidel more combatants and supplies. With these reinforcements, Castro could keep his army in the mountains and possibly expand his area of operations, but he still depended entirely on the urban organizers to keep his army clothed, supplied, funded, and armed. "Without Frank País's support," Bonachea and San Martín argue, "Castro would have found himself in a position similar to 'Che' Guevara's in the jungles of Bolivia in 1967: easy victims of the regular army, unable to establish their own bases of operation or to patrol their own areas, full of ideals but lacking the arms and the logistics to fight for them."[36]

Che did not appreciate the work being done by a wing of the M-26-7 known as the Llano (Plains), the urban wing of the movement. He eventually came to believe that a guerrilla army should sustain itself in the field, with little or no support from urban networks. In the initial stages of the Cuban campaign, however, Castro's guerrilla army survived because of the clandestine support it received from innumerable agents who worked within arm's

36. Szulc, *Fidel,* 401–6; Guevara, *Episodes,* 128–29; Bonachea and San Martín, *Cuban Insurrection,* 93.

reach of Batista's dreaded intelligence agents and police, risking torture and execution if captured. They faced greater dangers than did the guerrillas in the mountains, where the soldiers at least had the security of residing on territory that they controlled. In spite of their valuable help, Che severely criticized the M-26-7 urban leaders after his first meeting with them in February 1957. He judged them quickly, not by the work they did on his behalf, but on their ideology. "I discovered the evident anticommunist inclinations of most of them, above all [Armando] Hart," Che wrote in his diary. "Of the women, Haydée [Santamaría] seems the best oriented politically, Vílma [Espín] the most interesting, Celia Sánchez is very active but politically strangled. Armando Hart [is] permeable to the new ideas."[37]

At least Guevara came to admire the political skills that Castro brought to the struggle. On February 17, Fidel manipulated *New York Times* journalist Herbert Matthews so brilliantly that Matthews reported that Castro's rebels controlled the Sierra Maestra and were winning the war against Batista. Castro could not have written a more positive and sympathetic article, one that would help to win public support in the United States and neutralize American policy-makers. The thirty rebels controlled nothing but the ground they stood on. In this initial, nomadic phase of the guerrilla campaign, with the guerrillas moving from mountain to mountain and struggling simply to stay alive, Castro could measure success by the number of battles his men *did not* fight. They rarely fought Batista's army and they never fought the Americans. Castro kept the Americans out partly through political maneuvers such as the Matthews interview. "At the time, the presence of foreign reporters, preferably North American, was more important to us than a military victory," Che wrote later.[38]

Shortly after the meeting of the M-26-7 directorate, Che came down with such a serious asthma attack that he could not keep up with the marching pace of the other men. Castro nevertheless assigned Che the important mission of meeting the recruits promised by Frank País and guiding them into the sierra. Fifty men, only thirty of them armed, arrived on March 16, eleven days behind schedule. It took País less time to get more combatants into the mountains than it had Fidel; he doubled the size of Castro's rebel army without suffering a single casualty. If País recruited fifty soldiers in Cuba and sent them safely into the mountains, one can only wonder why the *Granma*

---

37. Quoted in Anderson, *Che Guevara,* 235.
38. Guevara, "Social Ideas of the Rebel Army," in Guevara, *Che: Selected Works,* 198.

veterans had not been sent to the mountains in the same way. It is difficult to resist the conclusion that Castro could have trained his eighty-two men in Cuba and filtered them into the Sierra Maestra without making a publicly announced invasion on an overcrowded ship. It may have made for great political theater, but it lacked a compelling military rationale.

The fifty volunteers sent by País constituted a second guerrilla army. Guevara had been assigned the job of guiding them to Fidel's camp, the final leg of their journey. Captain Jorge Sotús, a veteran of the November 30, 1956, Santiago uprising, had commanded the five squads of ten men from Santiago to the sierra. When Che met him, he informed Sotús that Fidel had ordered him to take command of the troops and lead them the rest of the way, but Sotús refused to relinquish command to anybody other than Castro. Che did not want to press the issue, feeling a bit insecure about being a foreigner in a Cuban army and not wanting to waste time on an irrelevant political argument. So the men marched, nominally under Sotús's command, to the rebel camp.

The presence of so many inexperienced men in the column gave Che even more incentive to avoid all contact with the army. Guiding these men safely to the rebel camp presented Che with a real logistical nightmare. He had to feed fifty hungry men—more than Castro then commanded—and avoid the enemy patrols. Although Che completed the mission safely, Castro actually criticized Che for not exercising the authority he had conferred on him and letting raw troops march under an inexperienced commander.

Fidel convened a nine-man revolutionary council on March 24 to reorganize the rebel army and discuss military strategy. Castro reassembled the troops into three platoons, under the command of Captains Raúl Castro, Juan Almeida, and Jorge Sotús. Raúl advised Fidel to appoint Che as his political commissar, but Fidel, disappointed with Che's recent performance and reluctant to appoint a Marxist to the position, kept Che as lieutenant and general staff physician.[39]

As for strategy, Che favored an immediate strike against the closest army garrison to give the recruits a taste of combat similar to the one the first guerrillas had experienced at La Plata. Fidel and the others, however, wanted to give the men time to train properly and get accustomed to the rigorous life of the guerrilla before they went into battle. So the council agreed that they would march eastward, toward Turquino Peak, while Guevara trained the

39. Guevara, *Episodes,* 138–42; Anderson, *Che Guevara,* 248.

new recruits in the fundamentals of guerrilla warfare. The men marched, carrying heavy backpacks and rifles, for the following two months. Moving constantly and avoiding contact with the army, the rebels gained valuable experience and learned the terrain during an extended period of apprenticeship under Che.[40]

By late May, following the arrival of a large shipment of arms and ammunition, Castro's guerrilla army was ready for battle. The arsenal included three Madsen submachine guns, nine M-1 carbines, ten Johnson automatic rifles, and six thousand rounds of ammunition, acquired and dispatched by Frank País. Castro distributed the weapons in accordance with past performance on the battlefield. He gave Che one of the Madsens and assigned four men to his squad, including a fifteen-year-old named Joel Iglesias. When Che first held the Madsen, a submachine gun firing 450 rounds per minute, he felt as if he had finally become a full-time combatant.[41]

With the arrival of the new weapons, Fidel had another opportunity to disprove the government's claims that the guerrillas had been eliminated. During the training march through the mountains, he had eluded the army patrols. The army, evidently unable to pinpoint the location of the rebels, could not mount an attack by air or land. The lack of contact with the guerrilla forces led Colonel Barrera Pérez, commander of the offensive launched in January, to announce that he had completed his mission and reduced the size of the rebel army to twenty men. Oriente province, the government claimed, had been returned to normal.[42]

On May 25, the guerrillas heard that a boat called the *Corinthia* had landed a group of rebels on the northern coast of Oriente province. Former president Carlos Prío Socarrás, leader of the Auténtico party, had organized this expedition, adding his considerable resources to the armed struggle. At a secret meeting in Texas a year earlier, Prío and Castro had agreed to coordinate actions against Batista, and the former president had now made a substantial military contribution to the struggle. The news of the landing reminded the *Granma* veterans of their own terrible landing, and some might have wanted to initiate offensive operations to divert the army away from the *Corinthia* rebels, but few could have ignored the political implications of a rival organization opening a second military front. Cubans had not heard of

40. Guevara, *Episodes*, 148–50.
41. Bonachea and San Martín, *Cuban Insurrection*, 139; Guevara, *Episodes*, 162–63.
42. Pérez, *Army Politics*, 141.

any M-26-7 military action in two months, so Castro wanted to demonstrate that he still presented the main military challenge to Batista. Che advocated an immediate ambush of an army patrol. Fidel, again showing a preference for attacking fixed installations, favored an assault on the garrison at El Uvero, on the Caribbean coast. If they just captured a truck, he argued, the government would dismiss it as an isolated act of banditry, but if they took El Uvero, they would deal a psychological blow to the dictatorship. Fidel won the argument, of course. On May 27, Fidel ordered his commanding officers to prepare for battle.[43]

Fidel divided his eighty men into nine squads and marched them down to the coast. Che volunteered to lead his squad in attack on the far left. The toughest assignment fell on Juan Almeida, who would lead his platoon in an assault on the center of the enemy compound. (See Map 5.) With the exception of the barracks, most of the buildings—belonging to a private lumber company—had no fortifications whatsoever; the strongest enemy positions were the guard posts, each with three or four soldiers strategically placed on the perimeter of the compound. Fidel intended to surround the compound on three sides with his nine squads; at the rear of the enemy would be the Caribbean Sea.

Fidel opened the battle with a single shot from his telescopic rifle at dawn on May 28. Rebel squads followed with volleys on the enemy targets in their front. The army, caught completely by surprise, recovered quickly and returned the rebel fire with a volley from the barracks. In the first exchanges of gunfire, the guerrillas took out a radio transmitter and the telephone lines, thereby preventing the enemy from calling in reinforcements.[44] Fidel ordered all squads forward, hoping to close a noose around the enemy barracks. Che swung his squad around farther to the left, Camilo's squad moving in directly to his right. As they advanced through a flat open space, barely sixty yards from an enemy trench, bullets whistled around them. Che dropped to the ground and crawled over to one of his fallen comrades. It was Mario Leal, shot in the head and losing consciousness. Che could do little for him. Che ordered his men to advance, then Lieutenant Juan Vitalio Acuña fell, wounded, and Che halted his squad.

An hour passed, then another. Off to the right, Che could hear thunderous exchanges between Almeida's squads and the enemy troops. To relieve his comrades in the center, Che decided to take the post in his front and

43. Guevara, *Episodes,* 164–65; Bonachea and San Martín, *Cuban Insurrection,* 134–38.
44. Javier Rodríguez, "La batalla del Uvero," *Bohemia,* May 24, 1963.

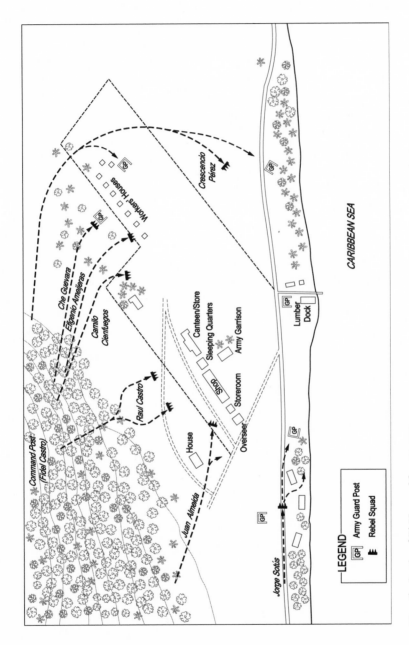

Map 5. Battle of El Uvero, May 28, 1957

attack the barracks from its exposed right flank. Fortunately for his men, a white flag went up above the barracks before his men launched a desperate attack. After two hours and forty-five minutes, the garrison at El Uvero surrendered.[45]

The battle of El Uvero gave Castro the conventional military victory he had been denied after the landing of the *Granma*. Six months after the botched invasion and uprising, he finally gained victory facing the enemy in combat. Che had opposed the attack on El Uvero, but he accepted the mission assigned to his squad and performed it well. The only aspect of the battle that reflected a *guerrillero*'s approach to combat was the hasty departure of the attacking forces after they took the garrison. The fact that Castro did not seek to gain and defend territory did not make him a guerrilla commander. It simply indicated that he did not value the property. Fidel struck El Uvero to make a definitive political statement that he alone had the strength, power, and audacity to defeat an army garrison. The price for making this statement was six guerrillas dead and nine wounded; the enemy sustained fourteen dead and nineteen wounded.[46] The rebels could not afford to suffer a 19 percent casualty rate, whereas the army could call up an infinite number of troops.

If the defenders of El Uvero had been able to call in air support, the rebels would have been dangerously exposed to overwhelming firepower. Despite the loss of communications, regimental headquarters in Santiago eventually learned of the attack and dispatched six F-47 fighters, three B-26 bombers, a C-47 transport, and one Beaver plane. By the time they flew over the battlefield, however, the rebels had already withdrawn and the air force could not pick up their trail.[47]

The victory at El Uvero boosted the morale of the rebel forces and marked the coming of age of the rebel army. "It showed," Guevara later wrote, "that the Rebel Army could function in a territory from which intelligence never leaked out to the enemy and from which we could dart to the plains and attack enemy positions."[48]

Castro had left El Uvero as quickly as possible, detaching Che and four assistants from the main body to care for seven wounded rebels. Che loaded the men onto a truck and drove northward into the sierra, where he would

45. Bonachea and San Martín, *Cuban Insurrection*, 95–96; Almeida, "El ataque a Uvero," 29–31; Franqui, *Diary*, 180–81; Guevara, *Episodes*, 166–75.
46. Bonachea and San Martín, *Cuban Insurrection*, 95.
47. Confidential report, Colonel Carlos M. Tabernilla to Jefe de la FAE, Ciudad Militar, May 28, 1957, in Guevara, *Che*, annex 4, 146–47.
48. Guevara, *Episodes*, 173; Guevara, "Notes for the Study of the Ideology of the Cuban Revolution," October 8, 1960, in Guevara, *Che: Selected Works*, 52 (quoted).

a secure location and tend to the wounded. Two of the men, Juan
Almeida and Félix Peña, were too weak to walk, so they had to be carried in
a hammock, after the trucks coughed to a stop on the steep mountain roads.
Moving from one *bohío* to the next at a painfully slow speed, Che, with his
column, eventually reached the safety of El Peladero, where he rested for the
following month.[49]

For the second time in two months, Che found himself the de facto commander of a small but independent rebel column. Captain Juan Almeida out-
ranked him, but with wounds in his head, shoulder, and left leg, Almeida was
in no condition to command. Responsibility for the men fell on Che, who
established direct contact with Frank País to obtain medical supplies, asthma
medicine, more recruits, and weapons. By the time Che reunited with the
main body of rebels in mid-July, he had about thirty men under his command. Thanks to the addition of new recruits from the cities, the rebel army
boasted more than two hundred combatants, and now it truly controlled the
heights of the Sierra Maestra. Batista virtually conceded the Sierra Maestra
to the guerrillas by dismantling the Rural Guard posts that presented easy
targets to Castro.[50]

Stung by the rebel victory at El Uvero, Batista launched a third offensive
against Castro's forces. From a command post at the Estrada Palma sugar
mill near Bayamo, Colonel Barrera Pérez intended to carry out a coordinated
air, naval, and ground campaign designed to force the guerrillas out of their
mountain strongholds and into battle on terrain that favored the army. Then
army companies would search out and destroy the guerrilla columns in a
"campaign of extermination." The army declared the Sierra Maestra a "free
fire zone," authorizing army, naval, and air forces to fire and bomb indis-
criminately. Government forces relocated about two thousand peasant families from the area of operations, reviving terrible memories of Spanish atrocities
during Cuba's war for independence. The government's relocation policy
only alienated the peasantry and generated more sympathy and recruits for
the rebel army.[51]

The army offensive made sense from a military point of view. Forced relocation programs have been part of many successful counterinsurgency campaigns. The British stamped out the Malayan guerrillas in what is considered

---

49. Guevara, *Episodes*, 174–77; Almeida, "El ataque a Uvero," 29–31.
50. Frank País to Alejandro (Fidel Castro), June 26, 1957, in Franqui, *Diary*, 186–87;
Guevara, *Episodes*, 182–89; Pérez, *Army Politics*, 142.
51. Pérez, *Army Politics*, 141–42; H. Thomas, *Cuban Revolution*, 166.

a model counterinsurgency campaign that included a massive relocation of peasants from the area of military operations. The British realized that they had to sever the logistical ties between the guerrillas and the farmers who lived on the fringes of the jungle. Between 1950 and 1953, the British resettled more than a half million Chinese into six hundred new communities they controlled. The resettled farmers then received title to land and economic development assistance.[52] While forced relocation can generate widespread national and international opposition, if it is done as part of a larger political, economic, and social development project, it can contribute to the eradication of guerrilla bands.

Batista's government, however, lacked the political legitimacy and the resources required to implement the social and economic aspects of a well-coordinated counterinsurgency project. The army removed only two thousand peasant families before Batista suspended the project because of political considerations. The army did not deploy enough troops to establish a security cordon around the Sierra Maestra to cut the ties between the guerrilla camps and the cities. However, even after the battle of El Uvero, Batista refused to recognize Castro's guerrilla army as a credible military threat. In four engagements at Alegría del Pío, La Plata, Arroyo del Infierno, and El Uvero, the guerrillas had killed twenty-one soldiers, wounded another twenty, and captured a substantial quantity of arms, ammunition, and supplies. The rebels had sustained heavier losses, losing more than sixty men at Alegría del Pío and in the manhunt that followed. A specially trained counterinsurgency force would have decimated Castro's rebel band during this start-up phase, but neither Batista nor his army had training in irregular warfare. The air raid and ambush at Altos de Espinosa had demonstrated the deadly potential of a coordinated air and ground campaign, but Batista's army lacked the will or the ability to maintain pursuit of the rebels. Given time and space by Batista, Castro rebuilt and reorganized his rebel army in the mountains.

Batista did not fully exploit his advantages in men and matériel. He did not attempt to rally his troops behind him by visiting the area of operations and talking to the troops. Castro represented only a political nuisance to Batista, not a military threat. If Batista had visited the area of operations, he would have given Castro more credibility than Batista cared to acknowledge. In retrospect however, the failure of Batista's army to maintain pursuit of the

---

52. James E. Dougherty, "The Guerrilla War in Malaya," in Osanka, *Modern Guerrilla Warfare*, 303–4.

guerrillas constituted a critical error. During this formative period of the guerrilla band, Batista's army should have pursued the guerrillas relentlessly. But Batista dismissed or ignored Castro's challenge and thereby lost his best opportunity to destroy the guerrillas before they established a base of operations.[53] The battle of El Uvero, the first armed conflict between the guerrillas and the army that deserves to be called a battle, shocked the Cuban army into the realization that a guerrilla army controlled the Sierra Maestra. In a six-month gestation period, the guerrillas had prevailed in three engagements with the army, organized a force of two hundred men, secured lines of supply and communication extending all the way to Santiago, gained the sympathy of the local population, and garnered considerable political support in Cuba and abroad.

The rebel victory at El Uvero did not guarantee the success of the insurgents, but it marked the end of the formative phase of Castro's guerrilla army. At this point in the campaign, Che's influence came to bear primarily on military training; he had trained the men who triumphed in the battle of El Uvero. As a member of the general staff, Che contributed to the tactical execution of a strategy that Fidel adopted. If Castro had accepted Che's advice, the guerrillas would not have attacked a fortified position such as El Uvero. Castro still favored conventional assaults, attaching great political significance to such victories as El Uvero, but at least he did not attempt to hold the garrison after he had defeated it.

During the first six months of the Cuban campaign, Che Guevara learned that the essential task of the guerrilla fighter in the formative stage is simply "to keep himself from being destroyed."[54] The rebel army had made only three attacks during this formative phase, and it triumphed in each case. Meanwhile, the soldiers adapted to the rigorous life of the mountains and learned from Che how to fight a guerrilla war. As the rebels gained confidence, experience, and knowledge of the terrain, they would expand the scope of their operations. The rebels could not win simply by establishing a base in the mountains and daring Batista's army to come after them. In the following phase of the campaign, the guerrillas would indeed go after the enemy, but on terms that still favored them. Castro's conventional attack on El Uvero did not mean that he had abandoned a guerrilla strategy. His quick retreat into the mountains showed that he did not intend to fight on conventional

53. Pérez, *Army Politics,* 143.
54. Guevara, *Guerrilla Warfare,* 56.

terms. Over the following year, Castro and Che would apply guerrilla strategy more consistently and effectively, winning battle after battle.

With nearly two hundred men under his command, logistics and military strategy compelled Fidel to rely more heavily on Che. A large concentration of guerrillas created a tempting target for the enemy and made supply difficult, whereas a second column could establish independent supply lines and improve the defensive posture of the rebel army. For command of the second column Fidel turned to Che, who had impressed his commander and comrades as a soldier, doctor, instructor, and leader. On July 17, Fidel promoted Che to captain and gave him command of seventy-five men dubbed the "Fourth Column," this name a ruse designed to convince the enemy that Castro commanded four rebel columns. Raúl Castro and Juan Almeida had been captain longer than Che, but neither of them had yet demonstrated as much potential as had Che for independent command. Raúl would have made a logical choice for command of the first independent column, but his star had fallen rapidly because his entire platoon had committed some form of insubordination in an incident that remains a closely guarded secret.[55]

Che, in contrast, had led units of wounded, lost, and inexperienced men in the Sierra Maestra. He had advised Fidel on military strategy before every engagement, guided Castro away from a conventional strategy, and trained his soldiers. Guevara's uncompromising nature and communist convictions made him something of a political liability, but Castro did not have a more competent commander. After a few victories over Batista's army, Castro had come to recognize the value and potential of guerrilla warfare. Any number of men could have commanded a *regular* army, but only Che could lead the first independent *guerrilla* column.

On July 21, Che filed into a *bohío* to sign his name to a letter offering condolences to Frank País, whose brother had been killed by the dictator's forces. The rebels signed their name in one column and listed their rank on the right. As Che began to sign, Fidel ordered: "Put down Comandante." With that, Castro promoted Che to major, the highest rank in the rebel army. Although Che rarely displayed emotions, he was then the proudest man in the rebel army. Celia Sánchez gave him a small star for his uniform, and Ernesto Guevara de la Serna became Comandante Che Guevara, second only to Commander in Chief Fidel Castro.[56]

55. Anderson, *Che Guevara*, 267; Taibo, *Guevara*, 130.
56. "Letter to Frank País," July 21, 1957; "Letter from the Rebel Army to Frank País," both in Castro, *Revolutionary Struggle*, 348–50; Deutschmann, *Che*, 70–71; Guevara, *Episodes*, 196.

FIVE ALL GUNS TO THE SIERRA

The promotion of Che to comandante coincided with the initiation of the second phase of the guerrilla campaign. Having established a mountain base for two guerrilla columns totaling nearly two hundred men, the rebel leaders felt strong enough to take the war into the plains. They now intended to hit army garrisons on the fringes of the Sierra Maestra and then run back to their bases, hoping that the army would pursue them onto their terrain. Fidel retained overall strategic command of the entire army and directed the operations of the first column, operating west of Turquino Peak. Castro assigned Che to the region east of Mt. Turquino and gave him tactical independence to complete his mission of drawing Lieutenant Sánchez Mosquera, the most aggressive enemy commander, into a trap.[1] Che could bait him into an ambush using three platoons, each commanded by a battle-hardened captain: Ramiro Valdés, Ciro Redondo, and Lalo Sardiñas. Che decided to attack the Rural Guard garrison at Bueycito, a mining village about thirteen miles southwest of Bayamo, and then take a defensive position in the mountains and wait.[2]

On the afternoon of July 31, 1957, Che's men hiked down from the mountains, boarded three trucks, and drove for three hours through cane fields and flat lands, a new and less secure environment for Che's brand of guerrilla

1. Guevara, *Episodes,* 196.
2. Ibid., 199.

warfare. Leaving a rear guard under the command of Lieutenant Juan Vitalio Acuña, Che moved against Bueycito with the three platoons, planning to surround the twelve-man post and take it by surprise. Che deployed Ramiro Valdés and Lalo Sardiñas on the flanks and rear, while he approached the barracks from the front with Ciro Redondo. He sent a squad to blow up two bridges connecting Bueycito with the central highway, with the aim of detaining any reinforcements that the army might send from Bayamo.[3]

The attack fell apart soon after it began. Ramiro Valdés lost part of his platoon in the darkness. Che, advancing down the main street armed with a Thompson submachine gun, lost the element of surprise when a dog started barking. A soldier came out to inspect the disturbance and came face-to-face with Che, who ordered the man to halt. The soldier moved and Che pulled the trigger, but he heard only a *click*. His aide Israel Pardo pulled his trigger, and his gun also misfired. Che immediately turned and sprinted away, reaching the safety of a building before the crackling of Garands, submachine guns, and automatic rifles indicated that all rebel units had engaged. Ramiro's platoon took the barracks from the rear, wounding six (two of them fatally), capturing another six, and taking rifles and ammunition, all in twenty minutes.[4]

"My debut as a major was a success from the point of view of victory and a failure as far as the organizational part was concerned," Che subsequently informed Castro. Guevara judged himself too harshly. He had organized the attack properly, attacking with overwhelming force under the cover of darkness, surrounding the target, and destroying two bridges to slow down any enemy reinforcements. He had accomplished his objective of making a demonstration in the plains to lure the enemy into the mountains. As Che's column drove back to its mountain base, a few reconnaissance planes passed overhead, but they failed to prevent the guerrillas from returning to their base.[5]

The losses Batista suffered at Bueycito paled in comparison to the hit he took in March 1957, when commandos of the Revolutionary Directorate (DR) attacked him in the presidential palace. While Castro's battered rebel army struggled to survive, University of Havana students carried out a daring though ill-advised raid, hoping to crush the dictatorship with one stunning blow. Although the students had failed in their objective of killing Batista "in his lair," their courageous effort inflicted a serious political blow on the regime.

3. Ibid., 203.
4. Ibid., 198–204; Bonachea and San Martín, *Cuban Insurrection*, 96–98.
5. Che to Fidel, August 31, 1957, in Franqui, *Diary*, 224–25; Guevara, *Episodes*, 204.

The commandos had, after all, stormed the guard posts, overwhelmed machine gun nests, and penetrated as far as Batista's office on the second floor. The students clearly exposed the vulnerability of the Cuban strongman and created a national crisis. Batista unleashed a wave of vengeance and repression that decimated the leadership of the DR and revealed the brutal character of his regime. The students suffered a military defeat but gained a political victory. According to Bonachea and San Martín, "The attack on the presidential palace shook the confidence of pro-Batista people. That a group of men had dared attack the caudillo was something beyond their comprehension."[6]

Che nevertheless dismissed the DR as a "terrorist group" and, though he admired the courage of the attackers, felt that their valor would have been placed better in the Sierra Maestra. Che advocated more than the elimination of one man.[7] He intended to carry out a revolution, and a strike "at the top" would not advance the interests of those at the bottom. Castro's attack on Moncada had also been an ill-advised strike at the top, but Fidel, thanks in large part to Che, now advocated a strategy of prolonged guerrilla warfare.

Within this strategic outlook, Che's victory at Bueycito, despite its relatively inconsequential military results, represented a more serious military challenge to Batista than had the attack on the presidential palace. No armed group of commandos, no matter how courageous, could revolutionize Cuban society through one crushing blow. They could, however, roll up victories over isolated army posts, gaining strength while they dared the army to attack them in their mountain strongholds. On the plains and especially in Havana, Batista's army and police held a decisive advantage over the rebels. Fidel and Che preferred now to fight in the sierra, and they insisted that the M-26-7 give the guerrilla campaign the highest priority. Some rebel leaders still saw greater value in urban struggle than did Fidel and Che, and some had even rendered assistance to the DR after the palace attack. In the eyes of these urban activists, the guerrilla campaign complemented their efforts and depended almost entirely on their support.

After more than six months in the mountains, however, even Castro had come to recognize that a guerrilla campaign offered the greatest chance of success. Urban actions carried excessive risks, a fact demonstrated forcefully on July 30, 1957, when the Santiago police assassinated Frank País. País, the titular head of the M-26-7, had reorganized the National Directorate of the

---

6. Bonachea and San Martín, *Cuban Insurrection*, 132.
7. Anderson, *Che Guevara*, 246; Bonachea and San Martín, *Cuban Insurrection*, 130.

M-26-7, made preparations for a future general strike, and attempted to launch a second guerrilla front independent of Castro. Fidel, the national coordinator for military affairs and nominally subordinate to País, had convinced País five months earlier not to open a second front near Santiago, but the two leaders conceived rebel strategy in significantly different ways. País favored a general insurrectionary strategy that Fidel had advocated prior to the departure of the *Granma*. Although his advocacy of a second guerrilla front reflects his growing faith in guerrilla warfare, it does not suggest a growing confidence in Fidel, for País wanted to command that column independently of Fidel. His untimely death eliminated all talk of a second guerrilla front and strengthened Fidel's hold on the organization and its strategy. The urban wing of the M-26-7 and its general insurrectionary strategy, often referred to as the Llano (Plains), lost power to the Sierra (Mountains), and the guerrilla strategy Castro favored. On August 11, Fidel left no doubt about his insurrectionary strategy when he ordered Celia Sánchez to send "all guns, all bullets, and all supplies to the Sierra."[8]

Che despised the anticommunist politics of the Llano and had no confidence in their insurrectionary line. He urged Fidel to appoint a trusted *guerrillero* to succeed Frank País in Santiago, either Raúl, Juan Almeida, Ramiro Valdés, or himself, people who would promote the *authentic* revolution. Guevara had absolutely no experience in running a clandestine urban operation, yet he assumed that he could replace Frank País. His offer to take that post reflected his ignorance of urban operations, an underestimation of the Llano, and a growing ego. Luckily for the M-26-7, Castro rejected Guevara's nominees and proposed his confidant Faustino Pérez for the position. Still, the M-26-7 directorate overruled him and appointed René Ramos, a clear indication that Castro did not yet have complete control over the organization and its strategies.[9] His guerrilla army, dependent on the Llano for money, supplies, and recruits, could not long survive without people like Ramos.

Che viewed the guerrilla army as the vanguard of the revolutionary struggle. If the guerrillas could draw Batista's army into combat on the rebels' terrain, the rebels could defeat the army, and with this purpose in mind, Che had tried to lure the soldiers into his "lair" by attacking Bueycito. It took the army nearly four weeks to respond to Guevara's challenge. Major Merob Sosa,

8. Frank País to Fidel, July 7, 1957; Fidel to Celia Sánchez, August 11, 1957, both in Franqui, *Diary,* 202–5, 220–21; Bonachea and San Martín, *Cuban Insurrection,* 138–46.
9. Che to Fidel, August 31, 1957, in Franqui, *Diary,* 224–25; Anderson, *Che Guevara,* 235, 276.

commanding a company of about 140 men, finally began to ascend a path leading to Guevara's base at El Hombrito on August 29. (See Map 6.) Che deployed his men for an ambush. He sat with a squad overlooking a point where the trail made a ninety-degree turn around a boulder. Another squad, under the command of Juan Vitalio Acuña, sat in ambush opposite Che, both of them situated to block the enemy advance. Che posted the platoons of Ramiro Valdés, Ciro Redondo, and Lalo Sardiñas on the flanks of the path, with orders to attack the rear of the column. Che intended to let ten or twelve soldiers pass before firing at the last man, the sign for the three platoons to open fire on the trailing elements. The soldiers came walking through at a leisurely pace, as if they were hiking. Che counted, one, two, and three soldiers pass the target. He realized that the enemy column was too strung out to let twelve men pass through the bend. He counted the sixth, then saw one of the soldiers jerk his head up, surprised. Che pulled the trigger and the sixth man fell.

Both flanks opened fire and Che pulled a second burst from his gun, then he lost sight of the five men who had passed the boulder. He ordered a squad to advance toward that position. The guerrillas found only a wounded medic; the other five men had escaped the trap. Soon, deeper and deadlier explosions indicated that the army had recovered from its initial shock and brought up its heavier weapons—bazookas and mortars. Che ordered a withdrawal and set another ambush about one thousand yards from the original site. The enemy did not pursue him.[10]

Che had halted the enemy advance at El Hombrito, but he judged the performance of his men harshly. Posted in ambush less than twenty yards from the approaching column, the guerrillas wounded only one soldier and captured one weapon. The army's performance, however, had been even worse. The company did not receive aerial support in its advance against an important rebel position, and then it retreated after a brief skirmish. Che still considered the engagement a victory, for his men had stopped an advance of 140 soldiers with a tactic that became standard practice for an ambush. By aiming at the point man of the approaching company, the guerrillas had immobilized the entire army column. "Little by little this tactic was being crystallized," Che realized, "and it finally became so systematic that the enemy literally stopped entering the Sierra Maestra, and there were scandals involving soldiers who refused to march in the forward spot."[11]

10. Guevara, *Episodes,* 205–9; Fermoselle, *Evolution of the Cuban Military,* 223–24.
11. Guevara, *Episodes,* 211.

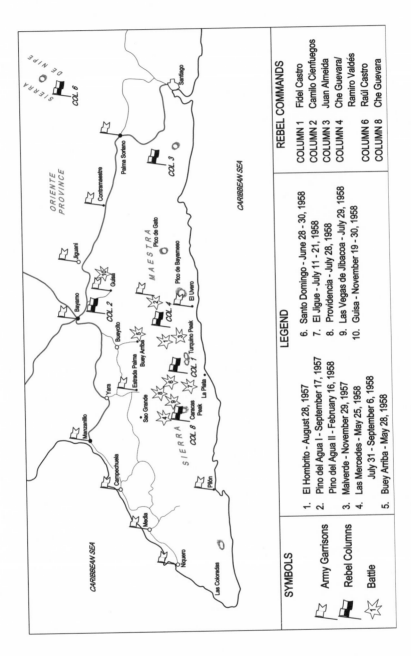

Map 6. Battles of the Sierra Maestra, 1957–58

SYMBOLS

Army Garrisons

Rebel Columns

Battle

LEGEND

1. El Hombrito - August 28, 1957
2. Pino del Agua I - September 17, 1957
   Pino del Agua II - February 16, 1958
3. Malverde - November 29, 1957
4. Las Mercedes - May 25, 1958
5. Buey Arriba - May 28, 1958
   July 31 - September 6, 1958
6. Santo Domingo - June 28 - 30, 1958
7. El Jigue - July 11 - 21, 1958
8. Providencia - July 28, 1958
9. Las Vegas de Jibacoa - July 29, 1958
10. Guisa - November 19 - 30, 1958

REBEL COMMANDS

COLUMN 1	Fidel Castro
COLUMN 2	Camilo Cienfuegos
COLUMN 3	Juan Almeida
COLUMN 4	Che Guevara/ Ramiro Valdés
COLUMN 6	Raúl Castro
COLUMN 8	Che Guevara

Several months of guerrilla combat had reinforced lessons that Che had learned from Alberto Bayo. In order to defeat a superior force, the guerrillas had to draw army companies onto rebel terrain, neutralizing the advantages Batista held in numbers and in arms and other matériel. Rebel columns could not expect to defeat an army battalion in one pitched battle on the plains, but they could punish isolated companies if they forced the fight on mountainous ground that they had prepared, where tanks, airplanes, and heavy artillery posed little threat to them.

Che intended to defeat the entire army eventually; he did not want to ally with factions of it to overthrow Batista, for a coup d'état would not produce the revolutionary changes he wanted. On September 5, 1957, naval officers at the Cienfuegos naval base, working in collaboration with elements of the M-26-7 and other opposition groups, revolted against Batista. Known as *puros,* because of their alleged military purity, and led by Lieutenant Dionisio Pérez San Román, they intended to restore constitutional government. Although the conspirators liberated Cienfuegos within a few hours, they did not receive support from any other garrison. Isolated and with their backs to the sea, the rebels had to surrender the following day. Che admired their courage but criticized their strategy, wondering why they had not launched a guerrilla front in the nearby Escambray Mountains instead.[12]

By this time, Fidel and Che were fighting on their own terms on ground that they selected. The DR, the urban wing of the M-26-7, and dissident military officers fought on Batista's terms on terrain that he controlled. The guerrillas would take the war to Batista in due time, when they had gained the military strength to fight on conventional terms outside the mountains. In the meantime, Castro and Che continued to bait army units into the mountains. The two leaders met in late August to devise a strategy to lure the army into battle, using Castro's column as the bait. On September 10, the two columns converged on Pino del Agua, a hamlet built around a sawmill along the crest of the Sierra Maestra. Fidel informed some villagers of his intention to march toward Santiago, expecting one of them to pass on the information to the army. The following day, Fidel's column continued its march, moving south along the road leading to Santiago. Che's column, meanwhile, circled back that night and prepared an ambush at Pino del Agua, hoping that the army would take the bait and send at least a company in pursuit.

Seven days later, on the morning of September 17, Che learned that five

---

12. Bonachea and San Martín, *Cuban Insurrection,* 147–52; Guevara, *Episodes,* 266.

army transports were climbing up the road, just as he had expected. Che deployed his platoons along both flanks of the road, creating a killing field in which his men could fire on the trucks from both sides. He planned to immobilize the first truck at a bend in the road, forcing those that were trailing to halt or reverse their movement. If they carried out the plan, Che expected to capture three or four vehicles. Twenty minutes before the trucks came within the ambush, the skies opened up and drenched the waiting men. Nevertheless, they remained focused on the task at hand, the destruction of an army column. When the lead truck approached the curve, the rebels opened fire. The soldiers abandoned three of their five trucks and fled, after a brief but spirited resistance. Che confiscated all the equipment from the three captured trucks and then burned the damaged vehicles. The rebels had killed three soldiers, taken one prisoner, and walked off with a valuable supply of arms and ammunition that included a tripod machine gun. They lost only one man.[13]

Despite this result, Che concluded that his men had performed badly. Although they had lured a convoy into an ambush, they had failed to destroy it. Che felt that his squads should have destroyed at least the first three trucks and their occupants. But soon after the battle had begun, an incorrect order to retreat had circulated among his troops, sowing confusion among the squads and delaying their efforts to capture the vehicles. "All this proved the imperative necessity of improving combat preparations and discipline among our troop," Che concluded.[14]

The courage and combat morale of his guerrillas, however, exceeded that of his enemy. Colonel Barrera Pérez, the chief of operations in Oriente in the summer of 1957, had been replaced because of his inability to deal with the guerrilla challenge. General Francisco Tabernilla, the army chief of staff, replaced him with Colonel Manuel Ugalde Carrillo. Lieutenant Angel Sánchez Mosquera received a promotion to major and retained command of Battalion 1. Despite the changes in command, the army demonstrated no greater effectiveness in the field. B-26 bombers flew over Pino del Agua shortly after the battle and again the following day, but they inflicted no damage and did not disturb Guevara's men. Lieutenant Colonel Curbelo del Sol, Ugalde's assistant, refused to send an infantry company after Guevara's column because he

---

13. Guevara, *Episodes*, 220; Jorge Le Sante to Director de Operaciones G-3, "Resultado de investigación practicada acción Pino del Agua, Zona de Operaciones, Provincia de Oriente," September 20, 1957, in Guevara, *Che*, annex 6, 149–50.

14. Guevara, *Episodes*, 223.

feared that it would just march into another ambush.[15] By this time, the rebels' training in guerrilla tactics had given them a distinct advantage over the soldiers, who had no training in irregular warfare. The guerrillas had the initiative, and Fidel and Che determined the time and place of battle.

Moreover, the rebel troops were more experienced, disciplined, and motivated than Batista's. Che demanded total subordination to military discipline and would not tolerate failure to live up to the high standards he set for guerrilla fighters. Shortly after the battle of Pino del Agua, Captain Lalo Sardiñas angrily reprimanded one of his men for an unspecified breach of conduct. Sardiñas put a gun to the man's head, not intending to fire, but he accidentally shot and killed the soldier. Many guerrillas, already bristling at Che's attempts to impose tighter discipline, demanded the immediate execution of Sardiñas. Guevara and Castro found themselves in a delicate situation. Captain Sardiñas had been a brave and highly disciplined platoon leader, in stark contrast to many of his accusers. At the same time, they wanted to maintain discipline and a system of justice, and Sardiñas had clearly erred by pointing a gun at the victim's head. Fidel and Che spoke against the execution of Sardiñas and persuaded a majority of rebels to demote rather than execute Sardiñas. A group of men left in protest the following day.[16]

If anything good came out of this incident, it was in the person of Camilo Cienfuegos, whom Fidel assigned to Che's column as the replacement for Sardiñas as commander of Che's vanguard. Camilo had been one of the last to join the rebel movement in Mexico and one of the first to counterattack at Alegría del Pío. Unlike Che, he was a genuine product of the working class, having toiled as a tailor in Havana before joining the expeditionary force. Known more for his courage and audacity than for his intelligence, Camilo had distinguished himself in virtually every engagement with the enemy. Che thought that Camilo occasionally became too aggressive in combat, but he admired his fighting spirit. He assigned Camilo the special task of eradicating the bandits who operated in the mountains, claiming to serve under Castro's revolutionary banner.[17]

---

15. Bonachea and San Martín, *Cuban Insurrection,* 97; Lt. Col. Curbelo del Sol to Dir. Operaciones G-3, September 19, 1957, in Guevara, *Che,* annex 5, 147–48.

16. Guevara, *Episodes,* 224–29.

17. Jaime Sarusky, "Camilo: El guerrillero y el político," *Bohemia,* October 27, 1962; Bonachea and San Martín, *Cuban Insurrection,* 104; Ernesto Guevara, "Discurso en homenaje al Comandante Camilo Cienfuegos," October 28, 1964, in Guevara, *Ernesto Che Guevara,* 8:211–17; Guevara, *Episodes,* 229.

Camilo hunted down Chino Chang, a local bandit, and brought him before a revolutionary tribunal. He had tortured, killed, and stolen from peasants, falsely claiming membership in Fidel's rebel army. In the absence of Batista's judicial system in the region, the rebels now had to maintain law and order there. If they allowed Chang and his gang to operate with impunity, their reputation among the peasants would suffer. In mid-October a rebel tribunal convicted and executed Chang and another man. The rebels put three members of Chang's gang before the firing squad, but Fidel decided to give them a second chance—if they survived the terror of a simulated execution. The executioners fired above the heads of the condemned, who took a few seconds to realize that their lives had been spared. Thus there was justice as well as mercy—if misguided—in the rebel camp.[18]

The tribunal formed part of Che's larger effort to institutionalize the rebel presence and establish a permanent base. Having taken the war to the army at Bueycito and Pino del Agua, Che now wanted to strengthen his El Hombrito camp. Che built a self-sufficient industrial town at El Hombrito raising pigs and poultry and producing shoes, saddles, and clothes. He even initiated the construction of a hydroelectric dam and an armaments factory making mines, grenade launchers, and mortars. By late November, Che declared the independence of El Hombrito by planting an immense red-and-black July 26 flag on the highest hill.[19]

If Sánchez Mosquera, now a major, did not see the fluttering challenge to his authority, he could read all about it in *El Cubano Libre*, a revolutionary newsletter produced on a mimeograph machine at El Hombrito. In a front-page editorial in the inaugural edition, Che declared that the Sierra Maestra had become an "unassailable fortress." The rebels had entrenched in the mountains, building antiaircraft shelters, basic industries, and fortified outposts guarding all paths to El Hombrito. Che now called upon the people to rise in rebellion by burning the cane fields—a proposal once championed by Antonio Maceo—and paralyzing the country in a general revolutionary strike. He wanted all-out war.[20]

The army accepted the gauntlet soon after Che threw it down. Some army officers had finally begun to reconsider their counterinsurgency tactics, since they could only claim one victory over the rebels—Alegría del Pío. At least

18. Guevara, *Episodes*, 230–33.
19. Ibid., 236–37.
20. Cited in Bonachea and San Martín, *Cuban Insurrection*, 203.

one prominent officer wanted to draw the guerrillas out of their fortified positions so they could be destroyed on the plains. Although chief of staff General Tabernilla rejected pleas for any radical change in strategy, he reinforced Oriente in early November 1957, bringing the army's strength in the region to five thousand men. If he intended to seal off the Sierra Maestra, he still only had twenty men to secure each mile of perimeter. If he intended to search out and destroy the two guerrilla columns, he had enough men to drive the rebels from their bases, assuming that the soldiers had the courage to fight and sustain casualties. With the guerrillas entrenched on high ground, with secure lines of supply and communication, Batista's army had no choice but to go in and get them, because Batista had promised the "total extermination" of the guerrillas.[21]

Major Sánchez Mosquera advanced toward El Hombrito in late November with a company of one hundred men and forty peasants on point, where they would be the first to draw enemy fire and detonate any land mines. Che's column observed the advance from fortified positions, but the men refused to fire on innocent people, so the army column passed through six ambushes. Then, the army sent in two P-47s to bomb the guerrilla positions. The army had not attempted coordinated ground and air attacks since February, and the assault caught the guerrillas by surprise. Che hid behind the only available cover—a banana tree—while the bombs destroyed two houses and some provisions, forcing Che to admit that he had been hurt. "We ate shit with hair in it," he reported.[22]

Unwilling to cede the initiative to the army, Che urged Fidel to establish a third column on the other side of Pino del Agua. With a third column located in that area, the guerrillas would spread out and pin down more enemy forces. Che recommended Raúl Castro, Juan Almeida, or Ramiro Valdés for the command of the new column.[23]

In the meantime, Che pursued his pursuer, hoping to surround and then annihilate Sánchez Mosquera, an objective that seemed to be within his grasp on the morning of November 29, 1957. His eighty men surrounded the enemy at Mar Verde, a village south of Turquino Peak near the Caribbean coast. Che opened the battle of Mar Verde hoping to frighten the enemy into a retreat,

21. Regan, "Armed Forces of Cuba," 136; Bonachea and San Martín, *Cuban Insurrection,* 97–98; Major Pedro J. de Castro Rojas, "Resúmen de operaciones," in Guevara, *Che,* annex 9, 155–65; Pérez, *Army Politics,* 141–42.

22. Che to Fidel, November 24, 1957, in Franqui, *Diary,* 255–56.

23. Ibid., 257.

but the stubborn Major Sánchez Mosquera held his ground. Che decided not to press the attack, knowing that he did not hold a clear advantage. Several hours after the assault commenced, army reinforcements began coming up from the coast. Che sent two squads to block their advance, but after a furious exchange of fire at midafternoon, Che ordered a retreat. For the first time in the guerrilla campaign, the rebels had failed to halt the advance of an army column. They lost two men, including Captain Ciro Redondo, and suffered five wounded during an indecisive showdown.[24]

In anticipation of Major Sánchez Mosquera's advance on El Hombrito, Che fortified his defenses and mined the paths leading to his base. When the army advanced on December 6, the mines failed to detonate, forcing Che to withdraw his ambushes and opening a path to his "unassailable fortress." The crude installations at El Hombrito mattered much less than the lives of his men. Che wisely ordered the abandonment of El Hombrito and redeployed his forces for another ambush higher in the mountains, at a place called Altos de Conrado.[25] In retrospect, Che clearly established a base before he had the strength in numbers and armaments to defend it. Then, repeating a mistake Fidel had made prior to the departure of the *Granma,* he challenged the army to a fight and even divulged his location by conspicuously displaying the M-26-7 flag.

On December 8, the army fell into the ambush that Che had set at Altos de Conrado. Once again, the guerrillas fired prematurely and inaccurately from carefully selected positions. This time the soldiers anticipated an ambush, and Major Sánchez Mosquera brought machine guns, bazookas, and mortars into the fight. In a furious exchange, a bullet struck Che in the foot and put him out of action. The guerrillas withdrew once again and took up another defensive position at La Mesa, just a mile or two west of El Hombrito. From there, Che dispatched a letter to Fidel asking for reinforcements to help him remedy a rapidly deteriorating situation.[26]

As it happened, Major Sánchez Mosquera called off his pursuit of Che after the battle of Altos de Conrado, taking satisfaction in the destruction of El Hombrito. After destroying the rebel installations, he marched off with all the supplies his men could carry, leaving only a trail of burned huts. In less than a week, one army column had marched into and out of two ambushes and destroyed the incipient guerrilla base. The drive to Altos de Conrado

24. Matthews, *Revolution in Cuba,* 244; Guevara, *Episodes,* 245–57; Che to Fidel, December 1, 1957, in Franqui, *Diary,* 258–59.

25. Guevara, *Episodes,* 248–50.

26. Ibid., 248–55; Cabrera Alvarez, *Memories of Che,* 114–16; Che to Fidel, December 9, 1957; Che to Fidel, December 15, 1957, both in Franqui, *Diary,* 264–65, 270.

marked the point of farthest penetration in the sierra. It also demoralized Guevara's column. Che sensed a "certain air of defeat and fear among our troop," as he waited for help to arrive at his new base, La Mesa.[27]

Through the actions he had taken, Major Sánchez Mosquera provided a brief hint of how to wage counterinsurgency war. He had pursued the guerrillas into the mountains and continued the pursuit even after falling into an ambush. Had he continued the pursuit after Altos de Conrado, coordinating his moves with those of other infantry battalions and supported by the air force, he could have inflicted even greater damage on Guevara's reeling rebel column. The army patrols typically halted or retreated after contacting the guerrillas throughout the campaign. Lacking training in counterinsurgency, the Cuban army searched for, but did not destroy, the guerrilla columns. As Bolivian army patrols were to learn a decade later, guerrillas are not invincible, just hard to catch.

Batista's army had no idea that a serious political conflict within the M-26-7 had weakened Guevara's column. Che claimed that the Santiago underground had been unable or unwilling to provide assistance to his column. A political war had been raging between Che and René Ramos, the successor to Frank País. Che had not supported the nomination of Ramos and subsequently refused to work with him. Instead, Che made unauthorized deals with other suppliers, a practice that undercut the authority of Ramos, who insisted that Che use only the authorized channels.[28]

Che regarded Ramos, Armando Hart, and the other urban leaders as nationalistic members of the leftist bourgeoisie, who fought for nothing more than the overthrow of the dictatorship. Che suspected that the Llano organizers deliberately undercut his guerrilla column because they opposed his Marxist-Leninist orientation. The conflict over the supply lines masked a deeper ideological conflict. Che, still advocating an authentic revolution, insisted on the recruitment of peasants and workers into the army. In late November, Hart had assured Che that the directorate shared his concern about incorporating workers and peasants into the army, but Che still suspected that Hart and the other moderates on the National Directorate would even strike a deal with the United States to remove Batista.[29]

27. Guevara, *Episodes,* 253–54.

28. Armando Hart to Che, November 23, 1957; Che to René Ramos Latour, December 14, 1957, both in Franqui, *Diary,* 253, 269.

29. René Ramos Latour to Fidel, September 15, 1957; René Ramos Latour to Che, both in Franqui, *Diary,* 229–30, 237–39; Anderson, *Che Guevara,* 291–94; Taibo, *Guevara,* 207–9.

The publication of the Miami Pact on November 1 suggested to Che that Fidel had aligned with the moderates. Former president Carlos Prío Socarrás had convened a unity conference in Miami, Florida, and invited representatives from other opposition groups, including the Ortodoxo party, Revolutionary Directorate, and the M-26-7. Felipe Pazos, an official fund-raiser for the M-26-7 in the United States, signed the agreement on behalf of the organization. The pact called for Batista's resignation, the formation of a Cuban Liberation Junta to coordinate the armed struggle against Batista, the restoration of the 1940 constitution, and an end to American military aid to Batista. According to the pact, the army then under Castro's command would be incorporated into the regular Cuban army after Batista's resignation, meaning, in effect, that it would be dissolved. The pact said nothing about social and economic reforms and did not reject U.S. intervention.[30]

Che could not believe that Castro could have approved the provisions of the Miami Pact, so many of them antithetical to Fidel's political program and authority. He asked Castro to clarify his position on the agreement, fearing that Castro supported René Ramos and Armando Hart, two of Che's political opponents. Che actually suspected that Ramos and Hart were deliberately sabotaging his column by denying him badly needed supplies. In a letter to Fidel dated December 9, 1957, Che asked Castro for authority to deal "sternly" with the persons responsible for impeding his operations. He threatened that if he did not receive such authority from Fidel, and, by inference, a reasonable explanation for the Miami Pact, he would resign.[31]

Four days later, in response Fidel sent a letter to Che in which he assured him that Pazos had signed the agreement without his authorization. He had not betrayed his revolutionary principles. The contents of this letter, which have never been released, caused Guevara to reaffirm his faith in Castro and the ideological direction of the movement. Given that Castro issued a public denunciation of the Miami Pact, the letter to Guevara must have included a frank expression of his ideology and political ambitions. Castro made it clear that he would never approve the incorporation of the rebel army into the regular armed forces. He also rejected the exiles' plans to form a post-Batista government.[32]

30. Quirk, *Castro*, 152–53; H. Thomas, *Cuban Revolution*, 186–87.
31. Che to Fidel, December 9, 1957; Che to René Ramos Latour, December 14, 1957, in Franqui, *Diary*, 264–65, 268–69.
32. Che to Fidel, December 15, 1957, in Franqui, *Diary*, 270–71; Fidel Castro, "Letter to the Cuban Liberation Junta," in Castro, *Revolutionary Struggle*, 363.

In any case, Castro's letter filled Che "with peace and happiness. Not for any personal reason, but rather for what this step means for the Revolution."[33] Che would not resign, and now, finally convinced that Fidel shared his revolutionary ambitions, he would campaign more openly for the radicalization of the M-26-7. In a letter to René Ramos, Guevara admitted that he belonged "to those who believe that the solution of the world's problems lies behind the so-called Iron Curtain, and I see this Movement as one of the many inspired by the bourgeoisie's desire to free themselves from the economic chains of imperialism."[34]

Guevara's ideological confession did not surprise Ramos, who responded: "I've known your ideological background ever since I met you, and I never found it necessary to make reference to it. Now is not the time to be discussing 'where the salvation of the world lies.'" He left no doubt that he opposed Guevara's politics, arguing that "those with your ideological background think the solution to our evils is to free ourselves from the noxious 'Yankee' domination by means of a no less noxious 'Soviet' domination."[35] Ramos supported Che in spite of Che's politics and promised to continue working with him. However, he did this in the interest of maintaining unity within the M-26-7. If Che had been the commander in chief of the guerrilla army, one wonders if Ramos and the other moderates would have supported him. Castro, not Che, possessed the political power and prestige that held the M-26-7 together and made it an attractive alternative to moderates and conservatives who opposed Batista.

Despite his denunciation of the Miami Pact, Fidel was prepared to unite with all other anti-Batista organizations, provided that they supported the armed struggle under his leadership. Castro's rebel army could not yet hope to defeat Batista on its own. Fidel still needed support from the Llano, the University of Havana students, and the *puros* in the army. Che worked grudgingly, if at all, with people who did not share his radical political opinions. In politics Che attacked as boldly as he did in battle; only comrades and enemies inhabited Che's political world. Fidel saw the guerrilla campaign as part of a larger struggle waged in the Sierra Maestra as well as in Havana and Washington, and the campaign required militants, fund-raisers, diplomats, union organizers, gunrunners, and urban activists. Fidel fought on all fronts

33. Che to Fidel, December 15, 1957, in Franqui, *Diary,* 271.
34. Che to René Ramos Latour, December 14, 1957, in Franqui, *Diary,* 269.
35. René Ramos Latour to Che, December 19, 1957, in Franqui, *Diary,* 273–74.

simultaneously; Che preferred to fight the enemy in his immediate front, with only ideological comrades in the trenches with him. He had no experience or interest in fund-raising, recruiting, or diplomacy, even though Fidel's success in those areas created and sustained his guerrilla army.

Che once believed that Fidel represented the typical political perspective of the nationalistic and leftist Latin American bourgeoisie. Fidel's secret letter to Che convinced him that he shared his revolutionary ambitions, which included a confrontation with the American imperialists. Guevara had learned from his Guatemalan experience that a true revolution could not compromise with the United States. He suspected that the Eisenhower administration was already "pulling the wires behind the scenes." In a letter to Fidel he argued that that they would "have to face Uncle Sam before the time is ripe. But one thing is clear, the 26th of July, the Sierra Maestra, and you are three separate entities and only one true God."[36]

Uncle Sam's agents might not have been pulling any strings at the time, but they had established a presence in or near Che's camp. The first CIA report about Che, dated December 17, 1957, referred to Che as the "most powerful henchman" of Fidel Castro. The informant described Guevara as taller than most Cubans, with brown eyes, auburn beard, and extremely bad teeth. Che reportedly had a flair for the good life; a black orderly kept him supplied with Cuban cigars and fine brandy. His mannerisms suggested "old-world Spanish imperial hauteur and the old-world Spanish charm." The CIA's unnamed informant noted that Che, the only comandante other than Castro, controlled the largest and most important rebel column. Only Che and Fidel, the agent reported, had the authority to "mete out executions and punishments for severe infractions of discipline." It was widely rumored that in the event of a rebel victory, Fidel would hold the political power and Che would become head of the army, becoming Cuba's new "strong man."[37]

Although Che held the second highest rank in the rebel army, he had no desire to challenge Fidel's political authority, and he did not have bad teeth. The quality of CIA reports began to improve in early 1958, after the CIA had assigned Robert Wiecha to the Santiago consulate. Operating under the cover of a position as vice consul, Wiecha established contacts with Castro and may have funneled some money to him. A lengthy report on Che Guevara, "hench-

---

36. Che to Fidel, December 15, 1957, in Franqui, *Diary,* 271.

37. "Personality Data Concerning 'Che,' Chief Lieutenant of Fidel Castro," December 17, 1957, report no. 00-B-3,094,401, CIA, Che Guevara Files, National Security Archive (hereafter NSA), Washington, D.C.

man of Fidel Castro," crossed the desks of the CIA on February 13, 1958. The unidentified informant described Che as twenty-five to thirty years old, five feet nine inches tall, and weighing about 160 pounds. With a square face, straight nose, olive complexion, and dark brown eyes, he bore a remarkable resemblance to the Mexican comedian "Cantinflas." He had two outstanding physical characteristics, chronic asthma and outstanding "filth." Even when Che took his men to a stream to wash up, he just sat on the bank and watched. "He is really outstandingly and spectacularly dirty," the agent reported.[38]

The agent found Guevara's politics a bit murkier than his appearance. In late January, a Cuban radio station in Manzanillo had charged that Raúl Castro and Che were communists, their accusation based on documents found on Armando Hart when he was arrested. A letter from Hart to Che referred to Che's comment about the Iron Curtain countries holding the solution to the world's problems.[39] The CIA informant, however, concluded that Guevara's political philosophy did not reflect the patterned thinking of "real Communists." Che described himself as a "warrior" who would prefer to "die like a man at the head of his troops" rather than surrender. The CIA informant concluded that Che's hostility toward the United States was "dictated more by somewhat childish emotionalism and jealousy than by a cold, reasoned, intellectual decision."[40]

Ernesto Guevara had been a cold, reasoned, and intellectual communist, hostile toward the United States, for at least four years prior to the CIA's first analysis of his ideological orientation. There could not have been any doubt about Guevara's communist ideology. In his interrogation by the Mexican police, Guevara openly discussed his communist convictions and received a reprimand from Fidel for doing so. Batista's Servicio de Inteligencia Militar (SIM, Military Intelligence Service) had access to the Mexican files and collaborated with the Federal Bureau of Investigation (FBI) and CIA. The CIA helped Batista create the Buró de Represión a las Actividades Comunistas (BRAC, Bureau for the Repression of Communist Activities) in 1954.[41] Only

---

38. Paterson, *Contesting Castro,* 64, 105–7; Szulc, *Fidel,* 427–28; Geyer, *Guerrilla Prince,* 189–90; "Biographic and Personality Information Concerning 'Che' (Ernesto Guevara), Henchman of Fidel Castro," February 13, 1958, CIA, in Ratner and Smith, *Che Guevara and the FBI,* 20–26.

39. Guevara, *Episodes,* 295.

40. "Biographic and Personality Information Concerning 'Che,'" February 13, 1958, CIA, in Ratner and Smith, *Che Guevara and the FBI,* 20–26

41. Paterson, *Contesting Castro,* 63–65; H. Thomas, *Cuban Revolution,* 69.

agents prejudiced against Latin Americans or completely ignorant of their political culture could have dismissed Guevara's hostility as the product of "childish emotionalism." The only accurate information the CIA possessed about Guevara was that he had asthma and that he was filthy. But Cantinflas, dirty or clean, could not possibly lead a revolutionary movement that would ultimately threaten the security of the Western Hemisphere.

Batista's government repeatedly charged that the Fidelistas, most notably Che Guevara, were communists, but the CIA was not inclined to believe the Batistianos either. However, the CIA did not establish an independent and reliable intelligence network in the mountains, as it would do in Bolivia. Only a few agents operated in the field, and the information they gathered did not reveal Castro as a threat to American interests in Cuba. The American military, unaware of a security threat in eastern Cuba, did not provide the Cuban military with any advice, hardware, or technology to conduct an effective counterinsurgency campaign. The Cuban army fought alone in a war that it was not trained to win. The Americans remained on the sidelines, a neutral position they did not hold in Bolivia.

After driving Che out of El Hombrito in early December, the army made no further attempts to penetrate the rebel lines, leaving the guerrillas with ample time to regain their strength. Castro decided to break a two-month lull in mid-February 1958 with a second attack on Pino del Agua. In the months since the first battle of Pino del Agua, the army had strengthened its presence there, placing an artillery company at that location and stationing another company at Oro, just four miles away. With Major Sánchez Mosquera stationed at San Pablo de Yao, eight miles away, and a naval garrison at El Uvero, sixteen miles to the south, Pino del Agua marked the army's farthest advance into the sierra. The elimination of this advance post would facilitate rebel communications and supply and make national headlines.[42]

Even with both guerrilla columns involved in the attack, Castro doubted whether the guerrillas could take the village. The strategy called instead for the rebels to surround the company, attack, and wait in ambush along the four roads leading to Pino del Agua. Che and Castro posted platoons to intercept reinforcements sent from any of the nearby garrisons. The rebels had neither the time nor the strength to lay siege to Pino del Agua, but they could punish the army in ambushes, the tactic most preferred by the rebels and feared by their enemy.

42. Guevara, *Episodes*, 296–99.

At dawn on February 16, 1958, Camilo Cienfuegos initiated the battle with an assault on the posts guarding the southern entrance to the town. A general bombardment followed, including crude mortars.[43] The guerrillas, however, did not press the attack. They waited for the army to bring in reinforcements. Later that day, as expected, a reconnaissance patrol came up from Oro and marched directly into a rebel ambush. The battered patrol returned quickly to Oro and called for more reinforcements. Hours after the fighting began, the most vicious combat of the day took place on the hills outside town, pitting Raúl Castro's platoon against the company of Captain Sierra Talavera. Raúl withdrew first, but Talavera did not pursue him. Reinforcements never came up from San Pablo de Yao or El Uvero, and the guerrilla units posted along those roads remained largely inactive throughout the day. B-26 bombers strafed the hills around Pino del Agua throughout the daylong battle, but they had little impact on the guerrilla forces.[44]

Che, convinced that another attack could overcome the post in Pino del Agua, begged Fidel for authorization to launch another assault that night. Fidel reluctantly agreed. Che intended to get as close as possible to the sawmill, set fire to the wooden houses, and force the soldiers out. As Che approached the barracks, he received an urgent message from Fidel, who had had second thoughts about the attack. Unsupported by other rebel units, Che risked heavy casualties if he attacked only with his column. Fidel advised him against launching such a suicidal attack and gave him a strict order to stay out of the fight. Che, who had ignored at least one previous order to refrain from combat, hesitated, then called off the attack. The rebels had already demonstrated their power, killing 18 to 22 and capturing 33 rifles, 5 machine guns, and ammunition, while suffering 5 dead and 3 wounded. The following day, Fidel ordered a retreat. The army eventually pulled out of Pino del Agua without another fight, conceding the western part of the Sierra Maestra to the guerrillas.[45]

The second battle of Pino del Agua, the largest and longest fought by the guerrillas since their landing, revealed the combat capabilities of an experienced guerrilla army. They did not wither under artillery fire nor cringe under aerial attack. They fought in well-organized, coordinated units and displayed patience and valor in equal measure. They still lacked the strength to take the

43. Ibid., 294–300; Bonachea and San Martín, *Cuban Insurrection,* 98–100.
44. Guevara, *Episodes,* 299–306.
45. Ibid., 301–3; Fidel to Che, February 16, 1958, in Franqui, *Diary,* 285.

war to Santiago, much less Havana, but they could hold their own in any fight with any company that Batista threw at them.

Castro created three new columns after Pino del Agua to expand his area of operations. He promoted his brother Raúl to comandante and gave him command of Column 6, which would operate in the Sierra Cristal, east of Santiago. Fidel also made Juan Almeida comandante and gave him command of Column 3, which he placed west of Santiago. Promoting Camilo Cienfuegos to comandante, Castro placed him in charge of Column 2, which would be assigned to a region later. Che remained in command of Column 4 at La Mesa.[46]

Che applied his administrative skills as he developed La Mesa into a manufacturing center and fortress. He rebuilt the industrial establishments that had been destroyed at El Hombrito, making the guerrilla army less dependent on its supply lines to Bayamo and Santiago. At La Mesa his workers made shoes, uniforms, foodstuffs, and land mines. His mimeograph machine still produced *El Cubano Libre,* and on February 24, 1958, Radio Rebelde hit the airwaves. Thanks to Che, rebels also had a reliable supply of crude but tasty cigars. Che had built a self-sufficient industrial camp that his men dubbed "Che City."[47]

Such organizational efforts reflect the strategic planning and foresight of Che. He knew that the guerrillas would eventually have to descend from their mountain bases, march across the island, and attack the army in the cities. To that end, he had to transform the guerrilla army into a larger, more conventional force, which required the recruitment and training of more troops. In March, Che began to establish a military training school at Minas del Frío. Che would retain his duties as comandante of Column 4, while Evelio Lafferte, a twenty-six-year-old lieutenant who had defected from the army, administered the school. Che, however, did not want just soldiers, he wanted *revolutionary* soldiers, combatants inspired by and trained to fight for the authentic revolution. For that mission, Che assigned Pablo Ribalta, who had studied communism in Prague, to teach courses on Cuban history and Marxism. In the summer of 1957, Che had secretly asked the PSP (Partido Socialista Popular) to send a political cadre to the sierra, the first overture made by the M-26-7 to the Cuban Communist party. Guevara first tested Ribalta's knowl-

46. Guevara, *Episodes,* 304; Franqui, *Diary,* 286; Che to Camilo, April 3, 1958, in Guevara, *Obras, 1957–1967,* 2:664.

47. Agustín Alles Soberón, "Los primeros periodistas cubanos en la Sierra Maestra," *Bohemia,* February 22, 1959; Nydia Sarabia, "Che Guevara: Fundador de Radio Rebelde," *Bohemia,* October 27, 1967.

edge of Marxism and put him through guerrilla training before assigning him to the school in the spring of 1958. Only a handful of leaders knew that Ribalta belonged to the PSP. Among Ribalta's students was a sixteen-year-old named Harry Villegas Tamayo. Villegas would become one of Guevara's most loyal comrades, serving with him from Cuba to the Congo to Bolivia.[48]

Although Che Guevara identified ideologically with the Cuban Communists and initiated contacts with them, he questioned their utility as combatants. He wanted only communists who advocated armed struggle. Che once ridiculed a PSP member: "You are capable of creating cadres who can silently endure the most terrible tortures in jail, but you cannot create cadres who can take a machine gun nest."[49]

When the National Directorate met in the mountains on March 7, 1958, the leaders sensed victory. They argued for four days on the best strategy for delivering the final blow to Batista. Although Castro and Che continued to insist on the primacy of the guerrilla campaign, they also recognized that a properly timed and coordinated general strike could deliver a crippling blow to the regime. René Ramos doubted that the urban cells could defend themselves against the army and police units that Batista would send out to crush protestors on the streets. Ramos feared that if the guerrillas in the mountains did not support the strikers in the city by sending them military aid and launching diversionary attacks on the day of the strike, the strike would fail, with many of his militants lying dead in the streets. Che subsequently claimed that the Llano wing ordered the general strike with the grudging consent of the Sierra. However, since Che and Castro had long-standing plans to complete the insurrection with a crippling general strike, they only argued with the Llano about the timing of this strike.[50]

In any case, the National Directorate unanimously agreed to declare "total war" against the tyranny of Batista. In a manifesto dated March 12, 1958, Castro publicly announced that the final blow against Batista would be delivered by a revolutionary general strike. Various organizations affiliated with the M-26-7 would prepare workers, professionals, and students for a nation-

48. Anderson, *Che Guevara*, 296–99, 305–7; testimony of Harry Villegas Tamayo, in Cupull and González, *Entre nosotros*, 30–31.
49. Bonachea and San Martín, *Cuban Insurrection*, 221; Karol, *Guerrillas in Power*, 153; Guevara, *Episodes*, 273 (quoted).
50. Bonachea and San Martín, *Cuban Insurrection*, 203–4; Llerena, *Unsuspected Revolution*, 188; Guevara, "The Role of a Marxist-Leninist Party," in Guevara, *Che: Selected Works*, 107; Karol, *Guerrillas in Power*, 173–74; "El 9 de abril de 1958," *Bohemia*, April 19, 1959.

wide strike, the date of which Castro did not divulge. The guerrilla army would support the urban actions by attacking the army and stopping all highway and railway traffic in Oriente province. To give the revolutionary leaders time to prepare for the final assault, Castro announced that his "campaign of extermination" would not begin until April 5, but from March 12 on, Cubans should consider themselves in total war against tyranny.[51]

On March 12, the same day that Castro declared a war of extermination, Batista suspended constitutional guarantees. Three days later, the Eisenhower administration halted all arms shipments to Cuba on the grounds that it did not want American weapons used in a civil war. The embargo hardly reduced the military capacity of Batista, since he had sufficient supplies in stock, but the suspension of military aid inflicted serious political damage to his regime and diminished army morale. The Cuban soldiers had less incentive to fight for an unconstitutional president who no longer enjoyed the support of the United States. The political damage inflicted by the embargo hurt Batista more than any military defeat his army had yet suffered in the Sierra Maestra. "No step by Castro could have so disheartened Batista. His old friends were seen to be deserting him," argues historian Hugh Thomas.[52]

Eisenhower's decision to stay out of the conflict had to brighten the outlook of the guerrillas. Few rebel leaders could have relished the prospect of a guerrilla campaign against the Americans. It is true that the United States military had not performed well in its counterinsurgency campaign against Sandino in the 1920s; however, military strategy, tactics, and technology had changed dramatically in the three decades since the Nicaraguan campaign. The United States had gained valuable experience combating communist guerrilla movements in Greece and the Philippines after World War II.[53] The Americans did not have the counterinsurgency capabilities that they would develop after Castro's victory, but they had firepower and technology that could have turned the tide against the rebels. Electronic and aerial surveillance might have divulged the precise location of the rebel camps to the Americans, who could have brought in bombers with heavier payloads and deadlier accuracy. If Eisenhower had authorized the military to intervene,

51. Fidel Castro, "Total War Against Tyranny," March 12, 1958, in Castro, *Revolutionary Struggle*, 373–78.

52. Paterson, *Contesting Castro*, 130–33; R. Gordon Arneson to undersecretary, 737.00/4-158; Ambassador Earl Smith to State, record group 59, Department of State Records, 737.00/4-158; H. Thomas, *Cuban Revolution*, 203 (quoted).

53. Osanka, *Modern Guerrilla Warfare*, 177–242.

either directly with troops or indirectly with advisers, the nature of the conflict would have changed immediately and the prospects for a guerrilla victory would have diminished considerably.

The American decision to remain neutral highlights the critical importance of pursuing a political and diplomatic strategy that is complementary to a guerrilla campaign. The American military certainly did not fear a military confrontation with Castro's rebel army. American politicians, however, did not perceive a threat to U.S. interests, because Castro had convinced them that he did not represent one. He had won the support of the American press by manipulating Herbert Matthews. In his public political pronouncements he had renounced communism and affirmed his commitment to the restoration of the 1940 constitution. Despite the receipt of some reliable information about the communist inclinations of Raúl Castro and Che Guevara, the Eisenhower administration did not detect a communist threat in Castro's guerrilla campaign. If Castro shared Che's revolutionary ambitions, he revealed those plans only to Che. Castro and Che did not belong to the PSP; nor did the PSP publicly support them. With the PSP inactive, the Americans concluded that they could remain on the sidelines as well.

Noncommunists, in Cuba and abroad, supported Castro's insurrection. In late March the rebels received a huge shipment of arms from a C-47 transport plane sent by President José "Pepe" Figueres of Costa Rica and piloted by Pedro Luis Díaz Lanz, a defector from the Cuban air force. Castro met the plane on a field near the Estrada Palma sugar mill, not far from the Cuban army's base of operations. One has to wonder how Batista's infantry, artillery, and air force could have allowed a transport plane to land and unload. The rebels unloaded 250 machine guns, 250 automatic rifles, 225 mortars and bazookas, and more than one million rounds of ammunition. Then they destroyed the plane. With this delivery, Castro had more weapons than he had men in the mountains, but he kept most of the weapons for his column, leaving the urban militias and even Guevara's column clamoring for a larger share of the stockpile.[54]

When M-26-7 militants seized three Havana radio stations on April 9 and announced the "final blow" against Batista, the mountains were strangely silent. Camilo Cienfuegos demonstrated some activity along the highway near Bayamo, but the guerrilla columns in the sierra generally remained inactive

---

54. Bonachea and San Martín, *Cuban Insurrection*, 205–6; Che to Camilo, April 2, 1958; Che to Camilo, April 3, 1958, in Guevara, *Obras, 1957–1967*, 2:663–64.

while the inexperienced M-26-7 militants took to the streets of Havana. Guevara's column remained in a defensive posture, trying only to hold Sánchez Mosquera at Bueycito. The normally aggressive major did not show much interest in moving anywhere. In the cities, most workers remained on the job. More than two thousand poorly armed M-26-7 activists hit the streets, thinking that the people would rise in rebellion with them. If they intended to engage in military actions, they lacked the arms, numbers, and training to confront Batista's army, police, and paramilitary units. Yet within a half hour, the strikers had engaged Batista's forces in the picturesque yet barren streets of Old Havana; within two hours, the M-26-7 leaders ordered a retreat. Strikers in other cities suffered similar fates. Casualty lists climbed into the hundreds; Batista had decimated the 26th of July Movement in the cities. Castro called the failed general strike a "moral rout."[55]

On May 3, 1958, the National Directorate of the M-26-7 met at Altos de Mompié to analyze the causes and consequences of the debacle. Che, the first participant in the meeting to later divulge anything about the heated arguments that occurred, framed the debate as the final showdown between the Sierra and the Llano, two different and antagonistic conceptions of the struggle. The leaders, Guevara charged, suffered from an "occupational deformity" that led them to the faulty conclusion that the urban struggle had greater importance than the guerrilla campaign. The urban leaders had overestimated their strength in the cities and underestimated the power of their enemy, thinking that they could topple the dictatorship simply by calling on the people to strike. The guerrillas, in contrast, had matured during their difficult and demanding campaign in the mountains, gaining an appreciation for Batista's deadly capabilities. To Che, the failure of the general strike demonstrated the fatal flaws in the strategic conception of the Llano and validated the guerrilla line of the Sierra. Che then lashed out at his enemies. He accused David Salvador, a labor organizer, of holding a subjectivist, putschist, sectarian view of the strike; he had refused to collaborate with the Communist party, a decision that weakened the M-26-7 among urban workers. Che admonished René Ramos for thinking that his untested militias could fight Batista's troops in the cities. And Faustino Pérez, though a trusted comrade of Castro, had postponed the strike, then rescheduled it at a most inoppor-

55. Guevara, *Episodes*, 310–11; Castro, "A Call to Strike," April 9, 1958, in Castro, *Revolutionary Struggle*, 378–79; Bonachea and San Martín, *Cuban Insurrection*, 210–11; "El 9 de abril de 1958," *Bohemia*, April 19, 1959; Paterson, *Contesting Castro*, 139–49; H. Thomas, *Cuban Revolution*, 206–13.

tune moment. There was only one honorable course of action: the resignation of Salvador, Ramos, and Pérez.[56]

The Llano leaders struck back hard, charging that the guerrillas had not launched the diversionary strikes they had promised, an insinuation of cowardice that no *guerrillero* could tolerate. Tempers flared in a number of heated exchanges, particularly during a violent debate about the participation of the Communist party. The Llano opposed any collaboration with the PSP in the struggle. The PSP had collaborated with Batista before, and some of the urban activists charged that the communists had even betrayed them to the police. Nevertheless, Fidel and Che insisted that the M-26-7 collaborate with the PSP.[57]

In the evening, the National Directorate relieved Pérez of his duties and replaced him with Delio Gómez Ochoa, a Sierra combatant loyal to Fidel. In addition, the directors replaced Salvador with Ñico Torres, who agreed to work with the PSP; they relieved Ramos, assigned him to the Sierra, and appointed Fidel the commander of all urban militias. Fidel emerged as the commander in chief of all the M-26-7 military forces and general secretary of the organization, which would be transferred to the Sierra. Fidel Castro and the strategy of guerrilla warfare triumphed at Altos de Mompié. Che clearly understood and took great satisfaction in the strategic implications of this decisive meeting: "The line of the Sierra would be followed, that of direct armed struggle, extending into other regions and in that way taking control of the country."[58]

The rebels wanted a bloody struggle with the army, and they were about to get it. Maneuvers around the mountains and along the coast indicated that the army intended to launch a major military offensive. In the battles to come, Fidel wanted Che by his side. Before the Altos de Mompié meeting, Fidel had relieved Che of command of Column 4 and reassigned him to the administration of a recruit training school at Minas del Frío. The reassignment was not a demotion. With Fidel now occupied with the direction of both the urban and rural wings of the M-26-7, in addition to national politics and international diplomacy, he had less time to devote to the preparation of the rebel

---

56. Guevara, *Episodes,* 316–18; Anderson, *Che Guevara,* 318–19. I interviewed two participants in the Mompié meeting, Luis Buch and Marcelo Fernández, and both men refused to discuss it, maintaining a tradition of silence.

57. Paterson, *Contesting Castro,* 144; Bonachea and San Martín, *Cuban Insurrection,* 220–21.

58. Szulc, *Fidel,* 442–44; Guevara, *Episodes,* 321 (quoted).

defenses. Fidel brought Che closer to his camp and made him his de facto military chief of staff. In addition to administering the training school, Che supervised the preparation of the rebel defenses in the sierra. Anticipating victory in the imminent offensive, Fidel then intended to dispatch Che and his trainees from Minas del Frío across the island in a final rebel offensive.[59]

59. Anderson, *Che Guevara,* 317–23.

Above: Universo Sánchez and Che Guevara, early 1957. (Photo: Cuban Collection, Manuscripts and Archives, Yale University Library)

Left: Che Guevara, early 1957. (Photo: Cuban Collection, Manuscripts and Archives, Yale University Library)

Fidel Castro recruiting peasants, early 1957. This photograph shows some of the survivors of the *Granma* landing and the rout at Alegría del Pío. *Standing, right to left, facing camera:* Ciro Redondo, Juan Almeida (hatless), Manuel Fajardo (stocky man with cap, uptilt visor), Che Guevara (with hand to face), Julito Díaz (hatless), Rafael Chao, Luis Crespo (with towel around neck), and Ciro Frias. (Photo: Cuban Collection, Manuscripts and Archives, Yale University Library)

Rebel leaders at a hut near El Hombrito. *Left to right:* A guide known as "Palmero," Marcelo Fernández (seated, wearing beret), Ciro Redondo (standing, with goatee), Fidel Castro, and Camilo Cienfuegos, 1957. (Photo: Cuban Collection, Manuscripts and Archives, Yale University Library)

A brief rest stop on a march from El Hombrito to La Plata. Che Guevara on right, then a lieutenant serving as the medical officer, smoking a cigar; Universo Sánchez (center, holding a telescopic rifle), and a young guerrilla named Peditro. (Photo: Cuban Collection, Manuscripts and Archives, Yale University Library)

Recruits on their way for combat training, fall 1958. After the rebels repelled the army's summer offensive of 1958, with government forces showing clear signs of weakness, the number of volunteers joining the rebel army rose rapidly. (Photo: Cuban Collection, Manuscripts and Archives, Yale University Library)

Rebels from Fidel Castro's Column No. 1 take Las Minas de Bueycito, early fall 1958. Although the rebels occupied the town for only twenty-four hours, it was the first real town taken by this column. (Photo: Cuban Collection, Manuscripts and Archives, Yale University Library)

Lieutenant Juan Vitalio Acuña, testing a homemade rifle-grenade launcher. Head of Che's rear guard in Cuba and promoted to Comandante in November 1958, he followed Che to Bolivia, where he was the second in command, once again heading Che's rear guard. (Photo: Cuban Collection, Manuscripts and Archives, Yale University Library)

Celia Sánchez at a safe house in Manzanillo, early 1957. Celia organized the underground network in Oriente province and provided critical assistance to the rebel forces after their disastrous encounter at Alegría del Pío. She became one of Castro's closest associates and advisers. (Photo: Cuban Collection, Manuscripts and Archives, Yale University Library)

Left: Adolfo Mena González, also known Che Guevara. This photograph appeared o the passport that Che used to enter Bolivia in November 1966. He traveled under the name of Adolfo Mena González, claiming to be a Uruguayan businessman. (Photo: Latin American Library, Tulane University)

Below: Che in camp. The woman leaning against the tree, her back to the camera and her face barely visible, is Tania, the East German/Cuban agent who collaborated with Che on the Bolivian campaign. (Photo: Latin American Library, Tulane University)

Che in camp. Che is standing, leaning against the tree. (Photo: Latin American Library, Tulane University)

La Higuera, Bolivia. The X marks the spot where Che's guerrillas battled against the Bolivian rangers. (Photo: Latin American Library, Tulane University; originally published in the Bolivian journal *La Presencia*)

Above: Che Guevara, captured, with Bolivian rangers posing next to him. The photo was taken about an hour before his execution. (Photo: Latin American Library, Tulane University; photo: Felix Rodríguez)

Opposite: Che Guevara, captured. The man with his back to the camera is Felix Rodriguez, the CIA agent who advised the Bolivian rangers and interrogated Che. (photo: Latin American Library, Tulane University; photo: Felix Rodríguez)

Che's body, with three hands grabbing locks of his hair, shortly after his execution. (Photo: Latin American Library, Tulane University; photo: Felix Rodríguez)

SIX THE CONQUEST OF SANTA CLARA

In May 1958, Castro's rebel army controlled the Sierra Maestra. Fidel had established operational headquarters at La Plata, Che had developed a school and industrial camp at La Mesa, and they had repeatedly repelled army incursions. Che had not held the army off at El Hombrito in December 1957, but that greatest rebel loss since Alegría del Pío did not result in a substantial gain for Batista. After driving Che off El Hombrito, Major Sánchez Mosquera withdrew, demonstrating that he could find the rebels but not showing that he could destroy them, a pattern followed by other officers. The army occasionally searched and never destroyed, allowing the rebels to reestablish or strengthen their defensive positions. The rebels had hit the army hard and run back to their mountain camps, daring the army to pursue them. Few army officers other than Sánchez Mosquera had taken the rebel bait, and those who did normally paid a price. Having given Castro eighteen months to establish his defensive bases while he and his men perfected the art of guerrilla war, the army high command now recognized that only a massive and coordinated incursion into the Sierra Maestra could drive the rebels off the high ground and into the plains.

Despite their relative numerical weakness, Castro and Che already contemplated a drive into the plains, knowing that final victory would only come with the capture of the Havana garrisons. Urban workers and local peasants had raised their strength to about three hundred combatants, each possessing about fifty bullets. These men had to defend only a few square miles of rebel territory, particularly Fidel's command complex at La Plata and Che's base for recruits at Minas del Frío.[1] Castro, anticipating a time when he could move from the strategic defensive to the offensive, created three new columns in the spring of 1958 and dispersed them across Oriente province. When more than one hundred recruits finished training at Minas del Frío, Che would lead them in a new column across the island, launching the third and final phase of their projected guerrilla campaign.

In the spring of 1958, Batista's generals finally realized that they had to drive Castro out of his mountain bases before his rebel army gained any more strength. Batista's forces had crushed the general strike in April, but Castro's army in the mountains still constituted a serious military threat. If the army could not defeat Castro there, then the rebel cause and the mystique surrounding the *barbudos*, as the rebels were called, would captivate more Cubans, galvanizing them to join the guerrillas in a fight against an unconstitutional government.

Batista's army began to move in early May, when it occupied two rice farms on the edge of the sierra, reinforced the coastal garrisons, and stationed navy frigates off the coast to offer artillery support in the coming offensive. On May 10, air and naval forces bombed Castro's headquarters at La Plata, where Fidel had established a field hospital, electric generators, telephones, and warehouses, making it a tempting target.[2] The bombing apparently did little damage to Castro's headquarters, but one has to wonder why, given an approximate location of the camp, the air force and navy did not bomb it every day.

With Batista's army coming after him, Fidel called on Che to meet and defeat the enemy wherever and whenever it hit the rebel lines. At no moment in his revolutionary career would Che Guevara shine as much as he did in the final phase of the Cuban insurrection. As Castro's de facto chief of staff during the army's offensive, Che directed a brilliant defensive campaign and repulsed the army's only serious effort to drive the guerrillas out of the mountains. Immediately after the army scaled back its offensive operations, Guevara launched an ambitious counteroffensive, breaking out of the sierra, march-

---

1. Anderson, *Che Guevara*, 324; Che claimed to have only two hundred "usable rifles," see Guevara, *Episodes*, 323.

2. Castro to Che, May 5, 1958; Castro to Che, May 12, 1958; Castro to Che, May 19, 1958, in Franqui, *Diary*, 316–21; Anderson, *Che Guevara*, 317–23.

ing across the island, and taking Santa Clara in a conventional campaign that brought final victory to the rebel army. The famous *guerrillero,* soon to become a modern guerrilla icon, distinguished himself in the Cuban insurrection as a defensive strategist and a rather conventional military commander.

Throughout May, Che supervised the construction of trenches, antitank ditches, antiaircraft shelters, and the placement of land mines along all the approaches to the rebel bases. He stockpiled supplies and weapons and trained new combatants at Minas del Frío. He even built a landing strip near La Plata to receive deliveries from light airplanes. Fidel retained ultimate authority over strategy and the deployment of the rebel columns, but Che held effective command of the guerrilla defenses. To meet the enemy, Che could put about three hundred men in strong defensive positions on commanding high ground, spread out among seven columns. Fidel commanded Column 1, based at La Plata. Che commanded a newly formed Column 8, composed of his recent graduates at Minas del Frío. The five-mile line between La Plata and Minas del Frío constituted the strategic heart of the rebel stronghold. Ramiro Valdés replaced Che as commander of Column 4, based at La Mesa, east of Turquino Peak. Crescencio Pérez commanded Column 7, occupying the westernmost rebel position. Three columns operated in forward positions close to the enemy bases. Camilo Cienfuegos and Column 2 operated on the northern lines near Bueycito and Juan Almeida's Column 3 held a position near El Cobre, just west of Santiago. Raúl Castro's column, based in the mountainous region east of Santiago, was too far away to provide much defensive support to Che. The seven rebel columns held a thin line from Caracas Peak in the west to the Sierra Cristal in the east, but the strategic core of the rebel defenses occupied only a few square miles on the crest of the Sierra Maestra. Less than eight miles separated Castro's La Plata headquarters from the enemy's forward position at Las Mercedes to the north. Only five miles separated La Plata from the coastal garrisons and naval artillery to the south.[3]

Meanwhile, Batista's political supporters and junior military officers lobbied for a full-scale campaign against Castro's rebels. The army had launched four previous offensives, but the only one that produced even a measure of success was the first, which resulted in the near annihilation of the original *Granma* force. The other three, embarked on in the spring and fall of 1957,

---

3. Osvaldo Herrera, "Ataque a Bayamo (el ascenso de Camilo)," in Pavón, *Días,* 47–54; communiqué of Fidel Castro, April 16, 1958, in Franqui, *Diary,* 300; Che to Camilo, April 12, 1958, in Guevara, *Obras, 1957–1967,* 2:666; Guevara, *Episodes,* 314.

produced nothing of military significance other than the removal of the attackers' ineffective field commanders. In early May, General Eulogio Cantillo presented an ambitious plan to deploy twenty-four battalions for a final assault on the Sierra Maestra. From his base at Bayamo, Cantillo intended to blockade the mountains with a military cordon stretching from Niquero in the west to Santiago de Cuba in the east. After severing the rebels' lines of communication and supply, the general intended to attack Castro from the north and northeast, hoping to force the guerrillas out of their strongholds and westward onto the plains, where troops stationed at Bayamo and Manzanillo waited to destroy them. Air and naval forces would soften up the rebels prior to the attack and pound them into dust when they left their trenches. Although Batista authorized a more limited offensive with only fourteen infantry battalions—each with a tank company assigned to it—General Cantillo still had more than twelve thousand regular troops to hunt down and destroy the rebels, whose positions were well known to the air and naval forces.[4] (See Map 7.)

General Cantillo finally brought sound strategy to the counterinsurgency campaign. The success of the summer offensive still depended on its complete execution by capable field commanders and soldiers, who had to find the enemy positions, overrun them, and keep driving toward their final objective: the rebel stronghold on the crest of the Sierra. Much depended on effective coordination and communication between the fourteen infantry battalions and the air and naval forces that supported them. Cantillo's strategy had a reasonable chance of success, assuming that Batista's officers and soldiers had the courage and motivation to execute it. They would likely suffer heavy losses in a protracted campaign effort, barring any lucky air strike directly on Fidel. The longer it lasted, the more likely that Batista would lose political and military strength. Facing dissent within the military and enjoying only qualified support from a small segment of the population, Batista lacked the political legitimacy required for a bloody and protracted counterinsurgency campaign.

He could not survive long without the support of his officer corps, and personality conflicts divided the officers and adversely affected Batista's military strategy. After Batista appointed General Cantillo chief of operations and authorized the summer offensive, he gave General Alberto del Río Chaviano command of operations in eastern Oriente province. Batista made the appointment to placate his chief of staff, General Francisco Tabernilla,

---

4. Pérez, *Army Politics,* 152–53; Bonachea and San Martín, *Cuban Insurrection,* 229–31.

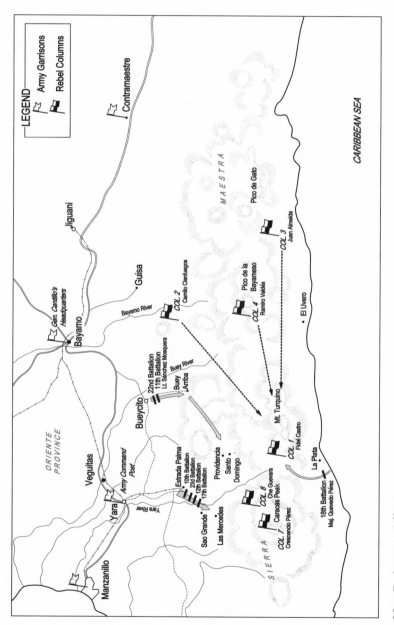

Map 7. Summer Offensive, 1958

father-in-law of the disgruntled General Chaviano. Although Cantillo retained command west of Santiago, the heart of the rebel territory, the creation of two theaters under separate commands caused more problems than it solved. Personal animosity between the two generals engendered unnecessary difficulties in command authority and diminished prospects for effective coordination between the field battalions.[5]

Still, the army troops outnumbered the rebels by a ratio of thirty or forty to one. If the battalion commanders coordinated their attacks properly, they could pound the thinly manned rebel lines with overwhelming force, trapping the rebels in their trenches or forcing them to abandon the sierra. The success of the operation hinged on the ability of Batista's armed forces to deliver continuous, concentrated, and coordinated assaults on the rebel positions, using the combined might of their air, land, and naval forces.

By mid-May, the army had established forward bases at the Estrada Palma sugar mill and Minas de Bueycito, both of which could be reinforced and supplied by rail or truck from Manzanillo or Bayamo. While the battalions gathered, B-26 and C-47 planes bombed and strafed rebel locations nearly every day, trying to soften the rebel defenses. On May 19, Colonel Raúl Corzo Izaguirre advanced from Estrada Palma toward Las Mercedes, in the first probe of the guerrillas' defensive perimeter. Crescencio Pérez and Column 7 contested Major Corzo's advance with less than a quarter mile separating the opposing forces. Fidel suddenly felt insecure about Pérez's reliability and ordered Che to take personal command of the rebel defenses at Las Mercedes.[6]

On May 24, General Cantillo launched his offensive from Las Mercedes, followed by a move from Minas de Bueycito five days later. Che arrived too late to prevent Major Corzo from taking Las Mercedes, after a thirty-hour battle. Sánchez Mosquera, now holding the rank of lieutenant colonel, advanced slowly from Bueycito, facing stiff opposition from Ramiro Valdés. What had once been a guerrilla war had now become a war of positions. The rebels had prepared their lines carefully and they moved easily between well-fortified and concealed trenches on high ground, with clear lines of fire on the advancing troops. Enemy infantry commanders had learned to fear guerrilla ambushes and land mines. With half of the battalions' strength composed of raw peasant recruits, they feared that their companies would stop or retreat

5. Bonachea and San Martín, *Cuban Insurrection*, 229–31; H. Thomas, *Cuban Revolution*, 214.

6. Quirk, *Fidel*, 184; Anderson, *Che Guevara*, 324–25.

as soon as they fell into an ambush. Che intended to punish each company that dared to advance against his lines, making the soldiers pay the highest possible price for each yard they gained. Three weeks after the offensive began with a few exploratory moves, the infantry battalions had moved only four miles south from their bases at Estrada Palma and Minas del Bueycito.[7]

Meanwhile, the air force continued to pound the rebel positions. Fidel rightly suspected that General Cantillo placed the highest priority on the destruction of his La Plata headquarters, particularly the airstrip that provisioned his army. Cantillo knew the approximate location of La Plata. The operations of the airstrip, radio transmitter, and telephone lines facilitated its detection by radar and electronic surveillance equipment. Still, the bombers did not score a direct hit on any of the major rebel installations, which were built into and between the trees to prevent easy detection from the air. The aerial assaults only affected the morale of the rebel troops. As a result of bombing and strafing runs on June 4 and 5, for example, twenty of Guevara's students at Minas del Frío left, with Guevara's permission, or deserted, broken by Batista's show of force.[8]

By June 11, Castro concluded that the enemy intended to drive directly toward La Plata. Lieutenant Colonel Sánchez Mosquera, commander of the two battalions advancing southward from Minas de Bueycito, led the maneuver by cutting diagonally across the northern slopes of the range, heading toward La Plata via Santo Domingo with Battalions 11 and 22. "A battle of enormous proportions is going to break out in the Sierra," Castro informed Camilo Cienfuegos on June 11. "They are going to concentrate the main body of their forces in order to try to deliver a decisive blow." To meet the anticipated assault, Fidel ordered Camilo to fall back and join him in Santo Domingo.[9]

General Cantillo had indeed concentrated his forces for a decisive strike on La Plata. With Lieutenant Colonel Sánchez Mosquera driving down at Castro from the northeast, General Cantillo ordered Major José Quevedo Pérez and the Eighteenth Battalion to come up from the southern coast on

---

7. Bonachea and San Martín, *Cuban Insurrection,* 230–33; Fidel Castro "Report on the Offensive: Part I (August 18, 1958)," in Castro, *Revolutionary Struggle,* 380, 402; Franqui, *Diary,* 328–43.

8. Anderson, *Che Guevara,* 326.

9. Quirk, *Fidel,* 183–86; Fidel Castro to Camilo Cienfuegos, June 12, 1958; Fidel Castro, "Report on the Offensive: Part I (August 18, 1958)," both in Castro, *Revolutionary Struggle,* 402; Fidel to Camilo, June 11, 1958, in Franqui, *Diary,* 341 (quoted).

June 16. General Cantillo's initial strategy had not called for an attack from the south, but he soon realized that a successful drive from the southern coast, easily supported by naval forces offshore, would squeeze the rebels in an iron vise. To clamp the device from the south, General Cantillo selected Major Quevedo Pérez and the inexperienced Eighteenth Battalion rather than Colonel Corzo Izaguirre and the veteran troops of the Seventeenth Battalion. Events subsequently demonstrated the folly of sending raw troops up the La Plata River toward El Jigüe, the underbelly of Castro's La Plata command center. In the northern foothills, General Cantillo had the Nineteenth Infantry Battalion at Arroyon and the Seventeenth Infantry Battalion at Las Mercedes, giving him five infantry battalions plus the air force and two naval frigates in support.[10] For some reason, Cantillo had mobilized only five of his fourteen battalions for the attack, leaving nine battalions in reserve.

Castro recalled the columns of Ramiro Valdés, Juan Almeida, and Crescencio Pérez on June 17, pulling in his defensive perimeter to engage the enemy approaching from the north and south. Castro felt the pressure most acutely on June 19, when the army battalions threatened to overrun his most forward platoons. Castro and Che moved men back and forth between their northern and southern lines, slowing the advance of the enemy until all the rebel columns had assembled west of Turquino Peak. Raúl's column remained alone in eastern Oriente province, but General Chaviano had shown little inclination to fight him there. Fidel intended to exhaust and bleed the army, giving up indefensible territory in order to defend the main rebel camps, with their armaments factories, kitchens, hospitals, warehouses, and airstrip, for as long as possible. Castro calculated that if he could resist the army incursion for three months, he could then turn the attackers away by launching a counteroffensive across the island, delivering a crippling blow to Batista. Fidel placed Che in command of the northern defenses while he kept an eye on Major Quevedo's advance from the south.[11]

The rebels faced the daunting prospect of fighting on two fronts simultaneously. With only three hundred combatants, Che could not man all the trenches and repulse advances from both directions. If, however, the infantry gave him time to move the guerillas back and forth along their interior lines,

10. "General Cantillo's Plan of Attack, June 16, 1958," in Franqui, *Diary*, 347–48; "Por qué se rindió el Comandante José Quevedo," *Bohemia*, January 18, 1959, 52.

11. Castro to Camilo Cienfuegos, June 11, 1958; Castro to Ramiro Valdés, Juan Almeida, and Guillermo García, June 17, 1958; Castro to Che, June 20, 1958, in Franqui, *Diary*, 341, 344–47, 354; Castro, "Report on the Offensive," in Castro, *Revolutionary Struggle*, 400–403.

they could move men between the fronts as needed, giving them a good chance to hold both lines. On June 23 and 24, a rebel platoon led by Captain Ramón Paz attacked elements of the Eighteenth Battalion moving up the La Plata River. The rebels sustained only three casualties, while the enemy suffered twenty-one killed or wounded as it moved upstream.[12] If Major Quevedo and the Eighteenth Battalion had continued to press northward, calling in reinforcements and air strikes as needed to break through the rebel defenses, Castro would have been forced to pull guerrillas off Guevara's northern lines to defend the southern perimeter.

As it happened, Major Quevedo advanced slowly, giving Castro time to reorganize his defenses while Che concentrated on the Twenty-second and Eleventh Battalions in the north. Lieutenant Colonel Sánchez Mosquera left Santo Domingo on June 28 and moved his two battalions to the Yara River. With nearly eight hundred men under his command, the largest force he had yet commanded, he ordered the Twenty-second Battalion to ascend the heights of the Sierra Maestra along the banks of the Yara River. Che had prepared this ground for just such a maneuver. He allowed the lead company of the Twenty-second Battalion to move four miles into his defenses before he attacked. When he unleashed the first volley from the darkness of the mountain forests, the soldiers, many of them going into battle for the first time, took cover from an enemy they could not see. The firing of .30- and .50-caliber machine guns, followed by prolonged periods of silence, kept the soldiers pinned down and terrified. When armored vehicles drove up to cover the flanks of the infantry, they ran into field mines. One sixty-pound TNT mine completely destroyed the First Company's formation. Unwilling to face the invisible guerrillas on their own, the soldiers dropped their weapons and backpacks and scattered through the forest. The second battalion never came up in support; Lieutenant Colonel Sánchez Mosquera remained at his base. Guevara had scored a decisive victory over the army in the first major engagement of the summer offensive. According to Bonachea and San Martín, "This first series of encounters with the army . . . destroyed the main thrust of the offensive, never permitting the army to penetrate more than a few miles into the Sierra Maestra."[13]

Lieutenant Colonel Sánchez Mosquera withdrew on the morning of June 30, leaving eighty soldiers on the battlefield, along with a valuable supply of war matériel that included radio equipment and the army's secret code. The

12. Fidel Castro, communiqué, June 25, 1958, in Franqui, *Diary,* 365.
13. Bonachea and San Martín, *Cuban Insurrection,* 235–36.

acquisition of this equipment and the code gave the rebel forces a decided advantage over their opponents. According to Castro, from that moment on, he and his commanders knew the objectives and tactical dispositions of the enemy battalions. The code did not change until July 25, but when it did, the rebels promptly intercepted the new code as well.[14]

Having checked the army advance from the north, Castro turned his complete attention to the south, knowing of the enemy's movements and objectives in advance. Major Quevedo, aside from leading inexperienced troops on an important and dangerous mission, had been a classmate of Fidel's at the University of Havana.[15] Castro attempted to exploit his personal relationship with Major Quevedo as soon as he learned that Quevedo commanded the Eighteenth. Castro sent a personal letter to him on June 9, writing, "What a surprise to know you are around here!" In an obvious effort to soften his adversary with expressions of friendship, Castro continued, "I write you these lines without thinking of them, without telling you or asking you anything, only to salute you and wish you, very sincerely, good luck. Your friend, Fidel Castro."[16]

Major Quevedo's troops had faced stiff resistance on the coast and throughout their march up the river, engaging rebel troops fourteen times between June 9 and July 11, when Fidel moved in for the kill with Columns 1, 3, and 4. Camilo remained at La Plata and Che on top of Minas del Frío, under strict orders to hold the northern defensive line "at all costs." With his rear secured by Camilo and Che, Castro surrounded Major Quevedo's battalion at El Jigüe on July 11. For the following seventy-two hours, neither Quevedo nor Castro moved. When Quevedo dispatched a platoon to break the encirclement and bring up supplies from the beach, Castro's squads pushed them back into the trap at El Jigüe. On July 15, Castro demanded the surrender of his former classmate, offering honorable terms that included the right of officers to keep their firearms.[17]

On July 18, Colonel Corzo Izaguirre and the Seventeenth Battalion attempted to relieve Quevedo's encircled column by driving from the Estrada

14. Ibid., 233–35; Castro, "The First Battle of Santo Domingo," in Castro, *Revolutionary Struggle*, 382–83; H. Thomas, *Cuban Revolution*, 215; Regan, "Armed Forces," 140–41; Taber, *M-26*, 264.

15. Bonachea and San Martín, *Cuban Insurrection*, 240–41.

16. Castro to Major José Quevedo, June 9, 1958, in Castro, *Revolutionary Struggle*, 381.

17. "Por qué se rindió el comandante José Quevedo," *Bohemia*, January 18, 1959; Fidel to Che, July 11, 1958; Fidel to Che, July 15, 1958, in Franqui, *Diary*, 366–67, 370; Fidel Castro to Major José Quevedo, July 15, 1958, in Castro, *Revolutionary Struggle*, 385.

Palma sugar mill to Las Vegas de Jibacoa. Che, knowing the importance of holding the line, held it fast. Castro, meanwhile, continued his efforts to bag Major Quevedo's entire battalion. One of his men, posing as an army communications officer, radioed the air force with news that the rebels had taken Quevedo's position. The air force ordered an aerial assault on the position, unaware that it had been tricked. Quevedo's besieged men, already short of supplies, suffered further demoralization. Despite orders from General Cantillo to fight his way back to the coast, Major Quevedo surrendered on July 21. After a ten-day engagement at El Jigüe, the rebels took 241 prisoners, 249 weapons (including a bazooka and a mortar), and 31,000 rounds of ammunition, at the cost of only three lives.[18]

Five army battalions still held positions on the northern front near Minas del Frío and Santo Domingo, with nine other battalions in reserve. If Cantillo could draw the rebels out of their strongholds, he still might destroy the guerrilla army. Fidel Castro's blood was up, and General Cantillo sensed it. After defeating Major Quevedo at El Jigüe, Cantillo correctly predicted that Castro would attempt to destroy the greatest army threat, the battalion commanded by Lieutenant Colonel Sánchez Mosquera, which Che had already punished when it attempted to advance from Santo Domingo. General Cantillo recognized that the remnants of Battalions 22 and 11, stationed at Providencia and Santo Domingo respectively, offered tempting bait to Castro. Despite the presence of Battalion 19 at Las Vegas de Jibacoa, 17 near Minas del Frío, and 23 at Arroyon, Castro might be lured into combat on the plains, where he could put his newly captured weapons and ammunition to use. Thus, on July 26, General Cantillo devised a new plan of operations designed to attract the rebels onto terrain that favored his army. On the plains north of the Sierra Maestra, the infantry battalions could be coordinated, supplied, reinforced, and supported more effectively. General Cantillo ordered Battalions 11 and 17 to feign a retreat northward, pulling back to Providencia and Las Mercedes, respectively, trying to bait Castro into combat on his terms with the prospect of capturing one or two more battalions.[19]

Sánchez Mosquera, now a colonel, began his withdrawal from Santo Domingo as ordered, but instead of heading directly to the Estrada Palma

18. Bonachea and San Martín, *Cuban Insurrection,* 240–43; "Por qué se rindió el comandante José Quevedo," *Bohemia,* January 18, 1959; Anderson, *Che Guevara,* 331.

19. General Eulogio A. Cantillo, "Plan de Operaciones," Puesto de Mando Zona de Operaciones, Bayamo, July 26, 1958, in Guevara, *Che,* annex 64, 254–57; Bonachea and San Martín, *Cuban Insurrection,* 251–52.

sugar mill, his men took up positions in the hills around the hamlet of Providencia, hoping to ambush pursuing rebel columns. On July 28, Castro ordered Ramón Paz to advance up a hill; as Paz marched up, Sánchez Mosquera and two hundred men swept down the hill, killing Paz and scattering the guerrillas, who panicked at the unusual sight of enemy soldiers on the attack. Major René Ramos and a squad of guerrillas drove the battalion out of Providencia in a vicious counterattack, wounding Colonel Sánchez Mosquera in the process.[20]

Emboldened even further by a costly success at Providencia, Fidel turned his sights to Las Mercedes to the west, which Colonel Corzo Izaguirre held with Battalion 17. The withdrawal of Sánchez Mosquera left Battalion 17 in a vulnerable position; Fidel called Che to an urgent meeting to discuss his plan to encircle and capture it. Fidel wanted to deploy 250 guerrillas for an attack on the plains, moving quickly from the defensive to the offensive. There is no evidence that Che opposed Fidel's offensive plans, but the strategy marked a definite departure from the defensive campaign that Che had conducted so far. In any case, Fidel ordered an all-out assault on Las Mercedes, convinced that a victory there would be "the end of Batista."[21]

The rebels attacked Battalion 17 on July 31. Che's column hit the entrenched soldiers from the southeast, swung around to the left, and destroyed one tank with a bazooka. Four other rebel units struck Las Mercedes from the north, while Camilo held a position at Cuatro Caminos, from which he could ambush any reinforcements sent from the Estrada Palma sugar mill. By the end of the day, with guerrilla units closing a noose around Las Mercedes, Fidel decided to settle in, hoping to force the surrender of yet another enemy battalion.[22]

On August 5, General Cantillo sprung the trap that he had planned for Castro. Three armored battalions, with five tanks and nearly one thousand troops, attacked the rebel trenches at Sao Grande. If the enemy broke through the lines, at least four guerrilla units—and possibly more—would be pinned down between three army battalions in Sao Grande and Battalion 17 at Las

20. Bonachea and San Martín, *Cuban Insurrection,* 251–53; Fidel to Celia Sánchez, July 28, 1958, in Franqui, *Diary,* 379–80.

21. Fidel to Che, July 29, 1958; Fidel to Lalo and Guillermo García, July 30, 1958, both in Franqui, *Diary,* 381–82.

22. Fidel to Che, July 31, 1958, in Franqui, *Diary,* 385–86; Bonachea and San Martín, *Cuban Insurrection,* 253–54; for the deployment of guerrilla forces for the July 31 attack, see Map 12 L, Batalla de Las Mercedes, July 31–August 6, 1958, in Instituto de Geografía de la Academía de Ciencias de Cuba, *Nuevo atlas nacional de Cuba.*

Mercedes. Shortly after noon, Fidel sent Che a distressing report on the engagement: "The guards got through."[23]

If General Cantillo redeployed two of his three battalions to the eastern and western flanks of the guerrillas, called in the reserves, and ordered air strikes, he would have a good chance of delivering a crushing blow to the rebels. Camilo and Che, posted to the south and east of the trap, could easily escape, but if Cantillo acted quickly, he could trap a substantial portion of Castro's rebel army. General Cantillo, however, failed to exploit the opportunity to crush Castro's rebels in the plains, a chance for which he had waited two months. Castro had to buy time, and General Cantillo inexplicably sold it to him. Castro asked Cantillo for an immediate cease-fire followed by negotiations to end further bloodshed. Cantillo, convinced that he had finally trapped the guerrillas, nevertheless agreed.[24]

Although Batista doubted that Cantillo had bagged Castro's rebel army, he authorized negotiations with Fidel. On August 6, Lieutenant Colonel Fernando Neugart arrived at Castro's headquarters for negotiations. Castro repeated his request for an immediate cease-fire and Neugart consented. Then, Castro launched into a political monologue, with Che sitting off in a corner, quietly observing the lengthy soliloquy. Neugart left that evening without getting a word in, though he agreed to return the following day. He returned as promised, only to hear a ten-hour verbal assault on the Batista regime.

On the third day, Colonel Neugart managed to pull Castro out of his monologue and proposed an immediate cease-fire, the formation of a military junta, and the prompt scheduling of general elections. The colonel left Fidel on August 8, carrying a proposal that Batista would not accept. While Castro and Neugart were negotiating, Castro pulled his units out of the trap between Sao Grande and Las Mercedes and redeployed them in more secure positions. Castro had used a clever political maneuver to correct the military error he had made by ordering an attack on the plains. If General Cantillo wanted to renew the attack, Castro and Che would be waiting for him behind fortified posts and trenches in the mountains.[25]

23. Fidel to Che, August 5, 1958, in Franqui, *Diary*, 388.

24. Bonachea and San Martín, *Cuban Insurrection*, 257; for the analysis of the battle of Las Mercedes, I am indebted to Colonel August G. Jannarone, United States Air Force, retired, a distinguished officer with twenty-seven years of service and a specialist in unconventional warfare. On May 29, 1996, in Tampa, Florida, Colonel Jannarone and I pored over a map of Oriente province and analyzed the summer offensive in general and the battle of Las Mercedes in particular.

25. Bonachea and San Martín, *Cuban Insurrection*, 258–59.

Batista's only serious counterinsurgency campaign essentially ended with these inconclusive negotiations in early August, less than three months after it began. The opposing forces had engaged in thirty skirmishes and only six major battles. The rebel army captured one entire battalion (18), and inflicted heavy casualties on three others (11, 22, and 17). The rebel army had killed 231 soldiers, taken 422 prisoners, and captured an arsenal of weapons, including two fourteen-ton tanks with thirty-seven-millimeter cannons. Castro suffered only twenty-five dead and another forty-eight wounded. On August 18, Castro claimed complete victory in a Radio Rebelde broadcast: "After seventy-six days of incessant battle," the rebel army had "repelled and virtually destroyed the cream of the tyranny's forces."[26]

Che, by contrast, did not take full credit for repelling the summer offensive, recognizing that the army lost it as much as his rebels had won it. "It was not only repelled by the men under my command, it was also humiliatingly lost by the dictatorship's army, which did not fight, retreating and leaving behind weapons and equipment."[27] Indeed, ten battalions had been held in reserve, one surrendered, and the other three usually withdrew soon after engaging the rebels. The four battalions that carried the brunt of the combat responsibilities had certainly suffered heavy casualties, but of the twelve thousand men assigned to the summer offensive, only 5 percent had been killed or wounded. General Cantillo apparently lacked confidence in his men. He estimated that 75 percent of his troops lacked adequate training for counterinsurgency operations, which demanded great physical endurance. Knowing that the guerrillas did not execute their prisoners, the inexperienced soldiers saw surrender, capture, or self-inflicted wounds as convenient means of getting out of combat. As a result, General Cantillo reported, the soldiers did not press their attacks vigorously.[28]

Still, General Cantillo and Batista shoulder the responsibility for the failure to execute a sound offensive strategy. Why, for example, did they assign only one battalion for the drive up the southern coast? General Cantillo could have designated another battalion to support Major Quevedo, or he could

26. Fidel Castro, "Report on the Offensive," in Castro, *Revolutionary Struggle*, 399–404. By one dissenting account, Castro's casualty estimates did not include the dead and wounded at Las Mercedes, where seventy rebels may have been killed. See Bonachea and San Martín, *Cuban Insurrection*, 262.

27. Che Guevara, "Interview in the Escambray Mountains," in Guevara, *Che: Selected Works*, 367.

28. General Eulogio A. Cantillo, "Plan de Operaciones," Puesto de Mando Zona de Operaciones, Bayamo, July 26, 1958, in Guevara, *Che*, annex 64, 254–55.

have deployed another battalion for a simultaneous advance up the Palma Mocha River, coordinated with Major Quevedo's advance up La Plata. Why did not Cantillo assign more battalions to the drives from Estrada Palma and Bueycito? What was the purpose of keeping nine battalions in reserve?

At least one officer on Batista's general staff recognized Cantillo's failure to deploy all the battalions under his command. On July 30, with the final battle of the summer offensive already under way, Admiral José Rodríguez Calderón submitted "Plan N," designed to encircle the rebel stronghold by placing eleven battalions in a tight military cordon around the sierra. Although the plan differed only slightly from General Cantillo's initial strategy, it showed that at least one Cuban officer recognized that a minimum of eleven battalions were required to encircle the area.[29] General Cantillo had once hoped to surround the enemy too, but he fought the summer offensive with less than half his total strength.

In addition to these strategic errors, battalion commanders did not coordinate their advances properly. When Colonel Sánchez Mosquera attacked the northern front, Colonel Corzo Izaguirre and Major Quevedo remained inactive on the southern front. When Major Quevedo walked into a trap at El Jigüe, Sánchez Mosquera remained inactive in the north. And when Castro finally walked into Cantillo's trap at the battle of Las Mercedes, Cantillo refused to bring up reserve battalions and air strikes for the kill. Cantillo's acceptance of Castro's call for negotiations, coming when the army held the upper hand for the first time in eighteen months, constituted the critical blunder of the army's summer offensive, for he halted the campaign just as it had begun to show results. General Cantillo ceded the initiative to Castro soon after he took it, and he would never get it back.

Cantillo and the forces under his command simply lacked the will to kill or die for Batista. Batista, lacking a constitutional foundation or widespread civilian or military support, needed a quick political solution to a growing military problem. His military had suffered a high number of casualties in less than two months, and as the war escalated and the casualties mounted, his civilian and military support would have dropped further. As Castro's popularity and the guerrilla mystique spread, Batista's army officers looked for ways to fight him without destroying him. Thus, the summer offensive began and ended with a whimper, as if the Cuban army never intended to destroy

29. Admiral José Rodríguez Calderón, "Plan de Operaciones 'N,'" July 30, 1958, in Guevara, *Che*, annex 66, 264–65; Bonachea and San Martín, *Cuban Insurrection*, 250–51.

the rebel army, which it seemed to have treated as a friendly foe with whom it had waged an elaborate war game. On August 12, when Fidel and Che arrived at Las Mercedes to deliver one hundred prisoners to the Red Cross, they sipped coffee with one of Batista's colonels, who admitted that the rebels would probably win. When Fidel showed interest in the colonel's helicopter, the officer invited Fidel and Che for a ride. For an astonishing fifteen minutes, one of Batista's officers flew the two highest-ranking rebel officers over the sierra.[30] It evidently did not occur to this colonel that he could have deposited the comandantes at General Cantillo's headquarters in Bayamo.

With the army's offensive operations stalled, Castro decided to launch a bold counteroffensive, a campaign that he and Guevara had been contemplating long before the army initiated its summer offensive. With ten fresh battalions still within a few miles of his northern lines, Castro decided to detach Guevara's new Column 8, formed primarily from the graduates of Minas del Frío, and march it to Las Villas province, three hundred miles away. Camilo Cienfuegos would take another column to Pinar del Río province, at the far western end of the island. The detachment of these two columns, led by two of the best rebel commanders, would weaken the rebel defenses, but it would also compel General Cantillo to send some of his battalions after them. He had enough battalions in reserve to pursue Guevara and Cienfuegos and continue the assault on Castro's depleted lines, but he had shown little interest in escalating the conflict. If Guevara and Cienfuegos succeeded in establishing new fronts in central and western Cuba, however, they would turn a regional insurrection into a national rebellion. Guevara and Cienfuegos would take the war much closer to Havana, threatening to ignite a nationwide political and military crisis as irregular warfare turned gradually into a conventional campaign, involving a fight for control of the highways, railroads, and cities leading to or guarding the approaches to Havana.

On August 21, 1958, Castro ordered Che to march his column from the Sierra Maestra to Las Villas province. Fidel warned him that a march through the barren plains of Camagüey province would expose his men to enemy planes. Guevara, confident that he had trained his men to face extreme hardships, eagerly accepted the assignment. Castro ordered Guevara to invade Las Villas province and prevent the movement of enemy troops from west to east. To carry out his mission, Guevara received absolute political and military authority over all rebel forces in the region, with the power to apply the penal

30. Szulc, *Fidel,* 448.

code and initiate an agrarian reform. Che recognized the strategic importance of his mission. He had to sever the lines of communication and supply between the army's base in Havana and the rebel fronts in Oriente province. In effect, Castro had ordered Che to cut the island in two. Che knew neither the terrain nor the people of Las Villas province and he had only 120 combatants, but Castro had put him in command of the most important offensive campaign of the entire insurrection.[31]

Castro's strategic plan corresponds with Alberto Bayo's third and final phase of an insurrection, an assault on the major cities. It also bears a superficial similarity to the strategies of the Cuban wars for independence. Che and Castro had read accounts of the wars and to them, their rebel army descended directly from the *mambises,* the peasants who waged guerrilla war against Spanish troops from 1868 to 1898. Camilo would follow in the footsteps of the legendary Antonio Maceo, who defiantly marched his cavalry from Oriente to Pinar del Río in 1896. Castro assigned Che, the only foreigner among his commanders, the role that had been occupied by Máximo Gómez, the Dominican commander of the Cuban army of liberation who fought the Spanish army in Las Villas.[32]

The first step in Che's long march to Las Villas province would have to be a break through or around the enemy's lines. Fourteen battalions still surrounded the Sierra Maestra, and their commanders knew the location of the rebel bases. On August 23, airplanes flew twelve bombing raids over the rebel camp, one of these raids coming close to the bunker in which Che had taken shelter. Che wisely chose to avoid the enemy battalions directly to the north, moving his column west, around the army's right wing.[33]

The members of Che's Column 8, veterans of the old Column 4 or graduates of his school at Minas del Frío, resembled their commander. They were highly disciplined, politically motivated, and self-sacrificing combatants who understood the importance of escaping the sierra undetected. Among them was Ramiro Valdés, his trusted deputy; Pablo Ribalta, his communist adviser; Oscar Fernández Mell, a doctor; and Harry Villegas, his bodyguard. Che

31. "En Cuba," *Bohemia,* January 11, 1959; Fidel Castro, "Che Guevara Ordered to Invade Las Villas (August 21, 1958)," in Castro, *Revolutionary Struggle,* 416; Guevara, *Episodes,* 324.

32. Judson, *Cuba and the Revolutionary Myth,* 179; Franqui, *Diary,* 440–41; Aldo Isidron del Valle and Fulvio Fuentes, "La Invasión: Column 8 'Ciro Redondo,'" *Bohemia,* October 20, 1967; Quirk, *Fidel,* 13, 85; Guevara, "Political Sovereignty and Economic Independence," in Guevara, *Che: Selected Works,* 218.

33. Iglesias Leyva, *De la Sierra Maestra,* 44–50.

also brought along his young and loyal protégés, including Joel Iglesias and Enrique Acevedo. On August 28, Che spoke to his men about the hardships that lay ahead, though he did not reveal their destination. He only told them that Castro had given them a dangerous mission, facing odds of ten or fifteen to one. "We will eat enemy soldiers for breakfast, airplanes for lunch, and tanks for dinner. Fifty percent of us will be killed," Che predicted. But even if only ten men survived, they would fight on, for honor compelled them to complete their assignment. Because of the hazardous nature of the mission, Che wanted only volunteers; he promised to transfer any man who did not want to fight in his column. One hundred and fifty men volunteered.[34]

Later in the evening on August 28, Che rode over to Cayo Espino, where the rebels had constructed a crude landing strip illuminated by means of an electrical generator. At 8:30 P.M., a bimotor Beechcraft airplane piloted by Pedro Luís Díaz Lanz sputtered to a halt in the field. Men rushed to unload boxes of arms and ammunition. An enemy plane appeared at 8:45 P.M., followed by another; within minutes, the plane and airstrip became the target of constant aerial attacks. By 6:00 A.M. on August 29, the men had unloaded most of the precious cargo, but with enemy infantry advancing on the airstrip, Che had to destroy the plane before it fell into enemy hands.[35]

In addition to the plane, Che lost a pickup truck carrying gasoline, so he had to modify his plan to transport his column in several trucks. On the morning of August 30, Che called in his squad leaders and reemphasized the need for discipline; to prevent the enemy from picking up their trail, he prohibited any eating or smoking. Then he assigned the order of march. The column moved out on August 30, hoping to sneak across the Manzanillo–Bayamo highway under cover of darkness, then jump onto three trucks and drive to Las Villas province.[36] (See Map 8.)

On September 1, a hurricane brought heavy rains to Oriente and made all roads except the Central Highway impassable. From that moment on, the soldiers proceeded on foot, while Che, Ramiro Valdés, and other members of the general staff rode on horseback. Within a week, the column had slipped several miles well south and west of the army base at Bayamo and turned west, crossing the Jobabo River into Camagüey province near the swampy

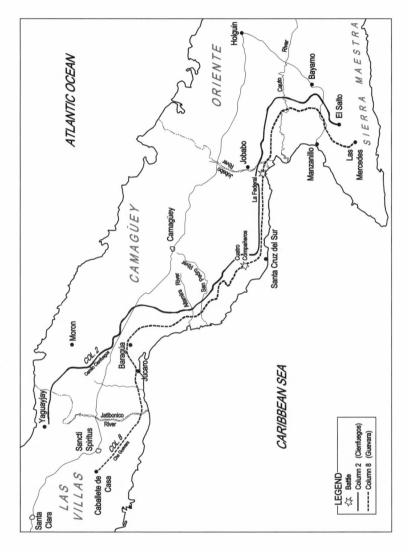

Map 8. March of Column 8 to Las Villas

coastline. Camilo followed a roughly parallel route, both commanders trying to avoid contact with the enemy.[37]

The following day, Che's column fell into an ambush at La Federal, a village several miles west of the Jobabo River. Che's well-trained combatants overran the troops, killing three and taking four prisoners. Camilo, who had learned of the ambush and diverted his line of march, rushed over to Che's headquarters. The comandantes, with more than two hundred men between them, had to decide whether to hold their ground or retreat. When Camilo, never one to shy away from battle, recommended a retreat, Che ordered his men to withdraw.[38]

The objective of Che's march, after all, was not Camagüey province; he wanted to establish a base in the Escambray Mountains of Las Villas province as soon as possible, and to that end, he had to elude the enemy wherever possible. The column hugged the Caribbean coast on its westward march, with only one army company on its trail. On September 14, Che marched into another ambush when he tried to cross a railroad line just outside Cuatro Compañeros. Che could not avoid the engagement. To get across the line, the rebels fought for nearly two and a half hours, giving the air force time to hit them with two B-26s and two C-47s. Che withdrew, leaving behind food, medical supplies, and some incriminating documents belonging to Communist party member Pablo Ribalta.[39]

Batista and his military officers tried to use the evidence to alert the Americans to the communist column marching on Havana. On September 20, chief of staff General Francisco Tabernilla announced that the army possessed evidence proving that communist agents directed Guevara's rebel column. However, only U.S. ambassador Earl Smith considered the documents credible proof of communist infiltration in Guevara's column. Smith convened a staff meeting in Havana to discuss the impact of Guevara's march through Camagüey province, but the CIA station chief could neither confirm nor deny the rumors about Guevara's communist ties. Smith, red with anger, shouted, "Well, I know that Guevara is a Communist even if you don't.

37. Iglesias Leyva, *De la Sierra Maestra,* 80–100; Che to Fidel, September 8, 1958, in Guevara, *Episodes,* 363.
38. Iglesias Leyva, *De la Sierra Maestra,* 140–41; Guevara, *Episodes,* 365–67; Rogelio Acevedo, "La Federal," in Pavón, *Días,* 307–11.
39. Guevara, *Episodes,* 368–69; Bonachea and San Martín, *Cuban Insurrection,* 270; Col. Robert Dueñas to director de Operaciones G-3, September 14, 1958; Lt. A. Suárez Suquet to Ayudante y S-1 Rgto 2 GR, September 19, 1958, in Guevara, *Che,* annexes 19 and 20, 180–81; Guevara, *Episodes,* 368–69.

And I'll tell you what I'm going to do. I'm going to burn up the wires to Washington and tell them that the Communists are marching through Cuba like Sherman's march to the sea."[40]

With the CIA and the American military observing from the sidelines, Guevara continued his march—not so much like William Tecumseh Sherman, but more like Augusto César Sandino, avoiding the enemy in pursuit. Guevara's evasive tactics angered Lieutenant Armando Suárez Suquet, his most aggressive hunter. Lieutenant Suárez Suquet reported that, like cowards, Guevara's men refused to hold their ground and fight him. He claimed that his men eagerly anticipated the day when they could destroy the communists, but he still begged for more troops to block Guevara's march to Las Villas. Having learned of Guevara's destination, Lieutenant Suárez Suquet also asked for radio minipacks to establish ground-to-air communications with the air force. Aerial assaults had been effective at Cuatro Compañeros, and the infantry desperately needed regular ground-to-air communications to search out and destroy Guevara's column.[41]

On September 29, Guevara once again found his march along the swampy coastline blocked, this time by about two hundred soldiers. Fearing another ambush, Che ordered his men to wait until nightfall, when they would try to slip through or around the enemy. The army still located Guevara's position and brought in the bombers again, forcing the column to take refuge in barren swampland while the planes bombed a heavily wooded area nearby. Finally, the young Lieutenant Rogelio Acevedo found a route around the far end of the enemy line, through a lagoon that the army officers apparently considered impassable. One hundred and forty men, a quarter of them without adequate shoes, splashed across the lagoon, just more than one hundred yards from an enemy post. Guevara's column had eluded an ambush yet again, for reasons that he attributed to the low combat morale of the dictator's soldiers.[42]

The air force continued its daily bombing raids against Guevara's suspected locations, but it failed to prevent his column from crossing the Jatibonico River into Las Villas province on October 7. Che compared his arrival in Las

40. Anderson, *Che Guevara*, 337–38; Bethell, *Losers*, 64–65 (quoted).

41. Lt. A. Suárez Suquet to Ayudante y S-1 Rgto 2 GR, September 19, 1958; Lt. A. Suárez Suquet, "Exhortación, Al Jefe de las Unidades que operan en Zona del 2do Dist. Mtar Camp. 'Agrte' y a todo el mando," September 21, 1958, in Guevara, *Che,* annexes 21 and 24, 181, 187; Guevara, *Episodes,* 327.

42. Guevara, *Episodes,* 370–71.

Villas to "the passage from darkness into light."[43] He had marched 250 miles in five weeks, surviving ambushes and bombing raids and gaining strength and popularity along the way. The rebels had demonstrated that they could win; the army had demonstrated that it could lose. The army officers had adequate intelligence about the location and direction of both rebel columns, but they could not stop their advance.

Once Che and Camilo established camps in the Escambray Mountains, the army would find it even more difficult to dislodge them. The march, however, had taken a toll on the morale of Guevara's men. After he crossed into Las Villas, Che announced that he would release any soldier who no longer wanted to fight. Several men took him up on the offer, to the delight of Che, who gladly relieved himself of the "scum" under his command.[44]

As the commander of all M-26-7 forces in Las Villas, he expected the full cooperation of all personnel. His reputation as a communist won him some support from the PSP, but it also cost him the backing of moderate M-26-7 leaders, who refused to cooperate with any communists. "If Che sends us something in writing," an M-26-7 officer allegedly told a PSP member, "we'll help him; if not, Che can go fuck himself."[45]

At this, Che restrained his anger. He had entered a new world of political combat, and without Fidel there to handle the delicate task of coordinating the activities of several rebel organizations, he risked fighting them as well as the army. There were as many as eight hundred guerrillas operating in two separate units, one under the command of Rolando Cubela of the Revolutionary Directorate (DR), the other an offshoot of this organization led by Eloy Gutiérrez Menoyo. The DR had established a guerrilla front in February 1958, but split in the summer of 1958 as a result of personal and ideological disputes between Cubela and Gutiérrez Menoyo. Che, with little experience in Cuban politics, had to proceed tactfully. To strengthen Che's position, on October 14 Fidel ordered Camilo's column to remain in Las Villas rather than march to Pinar del Río, as initially ordered. Fidel left no doubt about the command structure in Las Villas. He would only accept Che as the commander of all rebel forces.[46]

Back at La Plata, Fidel read Che's report on his march to Las Villas province. The column, he reported, had established a base in the Escambray

43. Ibid., 373.

44. Bonachea and San Martín, *Cuban Insurrection*, 275–76; Guevara, *Episodes*, 370–72.

45. Guevara, *Episodes*, 371.

46. Bonachea and San Martín, *Cuban Insurrection*, 173–87; Fidel to Camilo, October 14, 1958, in Franqui, *Diary*, 416–18.

Mountains and had already begun its difficult political tasks. Pacing back and forth in his mountain retreat, reading detailed accounts of how the column had broken through enemy encirclements at La Federal, Cuatro Compañeros, and Baragúa, Castro could hardly contain himself: "The Che is extraordinary! Really extraordinary!"[47]

Unfortunately, the other M-26-7 militants in Las Villas province did not share Fidel's high opinion of Che. Enrique Oltuski, provincial coordinator, refused to recognize Che as the supreme political and military commander in Las Villas. Oltuski got into a heated argument with Che over agrarian reform and U.S. imperialism, leading Guevara to conclude that he would have to sweep out all the "weaklings" in the organization who favored an accommodation with the United States. Marcelo Fernández Font, a national coordinator, had to mediate discussions between Che and Oltuski, who reluctantly agreed to recognize Che's authority and work with him.[48]

With the rival guerrilla organizations, however, Che had to proceed cautiously. Eloy Gutiérrez Menoyo flatly rejected Che's offer to negotiate terms of their collaboration. At one point Gutiérrez Menoyo even imprisoned an M-26-7 captain, Víctor Bordón. Fauré Chomón, the general secretary of the DR, refused to have anything to do with Gutiérrez Menoyo. Chomón and Che considered the possibility of attacking Gutiérrez Menoyo's second front before initiating offensive operations against the army, but they did not want to delay the assault on Santa Clara. Sharing Che's eagerness to conclude the war, Chomón agreed to collaborate with Che, despite the participation of PSP members in Guevara's column.[49]

Guevara's resolution of his conflicts with Chomón and Oltuski shows that he had gained some skill in and appreciation of the revolutionary political arena. In his negotiations with Oltuski and others, however, Che remained more confrontational than diplomatic. He succeeded in part because he acted with Castro's full authority, giving him a credibility he lacked on his own. Oltuski was not the first revolutionary leader to object to Guevara's rude and argumentative style, nor would he be the last.

Fortunately for the M-26-7, Che directed only military and political affairs in Las Villas province. Fidel still dictated national policy, and to the end, he

47. Quirk, *Castro,* 198.
48. Che to Oltuski, November 3, 1958, in Guevara, *Episodes,* 376; Matthews, *Cuban Story,* 246.
49. Che to Alfredo Peña, November 20, 1958; Che to Fauré Chomón, November 7, 1958, both in Guevara, *Episodes,* 378–79, 382; Bonachea and San Martín, *Cuban Insurrection,* 284; Chomón, "Cuando el Che llegó al Escambray," 354–55.

feared an American maneuver to replace Batista with a reformist politician or reputable military officer. After Guevara's march to Las Villas, however, neither the Americans nor Batista could prevent a final, decisive military battle. The ranks of the rebel army had swelled after the summer offensive, enabling Castro to deploy rebel columns in all six Cuban provinces, from Pinar del Río to Oriente. By October 1958, Fidel Castro commanded thirty-two columns, distributed in four fronts. While Fidel, Raúl Castro, and Juan Almeida commanded three fronts in Oriente—the heart of the rebellion remaining where it began—Che commanded the forces in Las Villas, the key to the entire campaign.[50]

Batista, like Ambassador Smith, clung to the slim hope of a political solution to the military crisis. He carried out presidential elections as promised on November 3. Despite alarming levels of abstention, caused largely by rebel activity, Batista still claimed a victory for his handpicked successor, Andres Rivero Agüero. Even Ambassador Smith, who had favored the candidacy of Carlos Márquez Sterling, recognized the elections as a sham, as a move that killed all chances for a peaceful solution to the crisis that raged from Havana to Santiago. The Eisenhower administration then began to search earnestly for a political resolution that would begin with Batista's departure and the installation of a government not dominated by the Fidelistas.[51]

Meanwhile, the Fidelistas moved aggressively on all military fronts. The rebels laid siege to Santiago, threatening to capture a coveted prize: the Moncada army garrison and its huge arsenal. Fidel moved out of La Plata and led the bloody battle at Guisa, on the plains north of the Sierra Maestra. The results of the battle struck fear into the Cuban army and inspired the rebels, who suffered only fifteen casualties while killing 116 soldiers and wounding another 80. As the rebels displayed increasing courage and experience in their offensive, the soldiers showed less and less willingness to fight for Batista's illegitimate regime. Batista's army had the firepower and the numbers, but it lacked the will to fight, as was concluded in a U.S. intelligence estimate in November.[52]

If the officers and soldiers in Las Villas decided to fight, they would present a formidable challenge to Che. Military needs alone mandated collabo-

---

50. For information on the formation of the columns and fronts, see the maps and charts in Guevara, *Episodes*, 462–67.

51. Paterson, *Contesting Castro*, 196; Bonachea and San Martím, *Cuban Insurrection*, 289–90.

52. Paterson, *Contesting Castro*, 199–200; CIA, Special National Intelligence Estimate no. 85-58, "The Situation in Cuba," November 24, 1958, in *Cuban Missile Crisis Collection*, document no. 00008, NSA.

ration with the DR, which had a substantial force in the field and held considerable prestige among the general public. In late November, Che and
Rolando Cubela agreed to coordinate their military forces for a final assault
on the dictatorship. In the name of Frank País and José Antonio Echeverría,
the commanders pledged "to win or die."[53]

On December 1, 1958, Che anticipated the imminent collapse of Batista's
regime. Like Fidel, he still feared that an American intervention would deny
him victory. "If foreign elements intervene," Guevara predicted, "it might
remain in power for some time. Nevertheless, the popular forces are so strong
that the collapse is inevitable."[54]

A quick and decisive military victory in Santa Clara would hasten Batista's
departure and preempt an American-backed effort to install in Havana a "third
force," a moderate civilian-military junta. The battle between Che and the
army in Santa Clara would determine Cuba's fate. Batista's regime would not
necessarily collapse if Santiago fell to the rebels. If Che conquered Santa Clara,
however, the rebels would block the shipment of army supplies and reinforcements to the battered army battalions in the eastern province. More
important, Che would have an open road to the presidential palace in Havana.

To take Santa Clara, Che applied a classical military strategy. In this final
campaign, the one that made Guevara a legend, the comandante displayed
his greatest military skills, not as a guerrilla warrior, but as a conventional
military strategist. Even if the campaign did not develop into a conventional
war of position between two well-organized forces, the strategy Che pursued
reflected the mind of a comandante who had studied classical military history and theory. Indeed, at his headquarters in the Escambray Mountains,
he read *The Decline and Fall of the Roman Empire*. He looked to the classics,
rather than Mao, for his inspiration. Guevara intended to sever Santa Clara
from the roads and railroad linking it to Havana in the west, the port of
Cienfuegos to the southwest, and Caibarién to the northeast. (See Map 9.)
The rebels would capture all the small towns surrounding Santa Clara one
by one, accumulating supplies, armaments, and volunteers as they gradually
tightened a noose around Santa Clara. The DR guerrillas would advance from
the south, while Che's forces would attack on the eastern and northern fronts,
with all forces converging on the capital for a final assault.[55]

---

53. Chomón, "Cuando el Che llegó," 355; "Pedrero Pact," December 1, 1958, in Guevara,
Episodes, 383–84; Dorschner and Fabricio, *Winds of December*, 179–80.

54. Guevara, "Interview in the Escambray Mountains," in Guevara, *Che: Selected Works*, 367.

55. "La batalla de Guisa," in Pavón, *Días de combate*, 223–48; Taber, *M-26*, 279–82;
Fernández Mell, "La batalla de Santa Clara," 362–64.

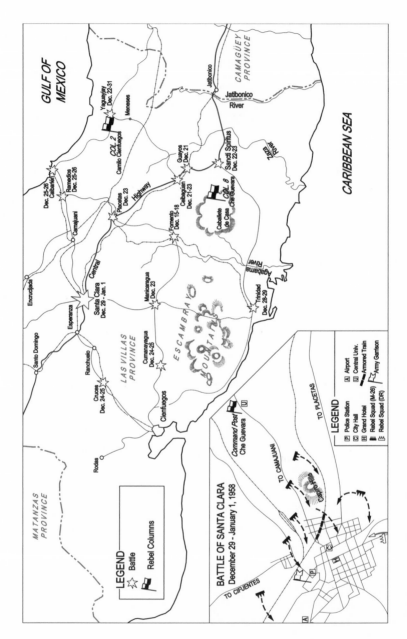

Map 9. Las Villas Campaign

Che initiated the campaign on December 14, with an attack on Fomento, a town of eight thousand southeast of Santa Clara. After his men gained control of the highway, Che telephoned the commander of the garrison and asked for his surrender. The officer refused. Che slammed the phone down and ordered his men to cut off the supply of water to the garrison. He intended to capture this garrison without a fight. On December 17, the commanding officer confessed that he would rather join the rebels than be handed over to the Red Cross. Che took Fomento in three days, thus acquiring even more weapons and recruits.[56]

Che then set out to gain control of the Central Highway. Camilo attacked Yaguayjay on the northern branch of the highway on December 19; Che attacked Guayos, on the southern branch of the highway, on December 21. It fell within two hours. Then, Che joined forces with the DR to take Caibagúan. The garrison at Caibagúan surrendered on December 23 without a fight. During the maneuvering around Caibagúan, a B-26 bomber dived low over the rebel positions, forcing Che to run for cover. Leaping over a fence to safety, he tripped and broke his arm, his third wound.[57]

With his arm in a black silk sling, Che directed Column 8 up the Central Highway to Placetas, a city of thirty thousand people less than thirty miles east of Santa Clara.[58] As the rebels advanced, the soldiers retreated to their barracks, conceding the streets to Che. The rebels fired a few demonstration shots and the army surrendered. On December 22, Che took command of Placetas, the largest city the rebel army had ever taken.[59]

Camilo remained engaged at Yaguayjay, unable to convince a stubborn officer to surrender. With or without Camilo, Che intended to press the attack until Batista capitulated; a string of rebel victories in rapid succession had given him momentum, weapons, and more volunteers. Che sent a platoon west of Santa Clara to block the arrival of reinforcements from Havana; then he advanced against Remedios on December 25 to block reinforcements from the Atlantic coast. After a few skirmishes in the streets of Remedios, the soldiers and policemen agreed to lay down their arms and return to Havana.[60]

56. Dorschner and Fabricio, *Winds of December*, 184–85, 204–5.
57. Bonachea and San Martím, *Cuban Insurrection,* 293; Dorschner and Fabricio, *Winds of December,* 258.
58. Isidron del Valle and Fuentes, "La Invasion," *Bohemia,* October 20, 1967; "Habla el Comandante Guevara," *Bohemia,* January 11, 1959.
59. Bonachea and San Martín, *Cuban Insurrection,* 293; Dorschner and Fabricio, *Winds of December,* 258.
60. Dorschner and Fabricio, *Winds of December,* 258–59, 280–81.

Batista's army was surrendering or losing on all fronts. Desertions and defections increased; defeatism spread throughout the military. In mid-December, General Francisco Tabernilla, once Batista's staunchest supporter, proposed to replace Batista with a military junta led by General Eulogio Cantillo. Ambassador Smith informed Batista on December 17 that the United States no longer supported him or any government that he put in power. The sooner he left for Spain, the better, Smith told the beleaguered Batista.[61] Political and diplomatic intrigue intensified as military affairs turned decisively in favor of the rebels. On December 24, General Cantillo offered a peace proposal to Castro in Oriente province. Castro rejected it. On December 25, Che rejected a cease-fire proposal from Colonel Florentino Rosell, the commander of reinforcements sent to Santa Clara on an armored train. This revolution would not make any last-minute compromises, Che argued.[62]

A conclusive military victory in Santa Clara would make all late political efforts irrelevant. Fidel wanted Che to attack and win, quickly. On December 26, he advised Che: "It's essential for you to realize that the political aspect of the battle at Las Villas is fundamental." By sending Che and Camilo into Las Villas, Castro put his columns in a position to march on Havana before the DR, rival political parties, or disgruntled military officers formed a provisional government. If Che and Camilo did not take Havana first, Fidel might still be writing letters by flashlight when a civilian-military junta took power in Havana. "The enemy is collapsing with a resounding crash," Castro informed his most accomplished comandante, and when the M-26-7 marches into Havana, "Camilo's column should be in the lead."[63]

Ismael Suárez, a member of the M-26-7 underground in Santa Clara, found Che at his headquarters in Remedios on the afternoon of December 27, rapidly giving orders to ten to fifteen officers. When Che stopped for a moment, Suárez asked for permission to report. Suárez was exhausted, having spent the past thirty-six hours negotiating with Colonel Florentino Rossell, who still believed that he could arrange a cease-fire with Guevara. Rossell's plans went nowhere, but the effort gave Suárez an opportunity to view the army's strength and position. Colonel Rossell had positioned an armored train near Capiro Hill, a strong defensive position guarding the northern entrance to the city. Batista had hoped to reinforce Santa Clara defenses with four

61. Paterson, *Contesting Castro,* 213–14.
62. H. Thomas, *Cuban Revolution,* 236–37; Dorschner and Fabricio, *Winds of December,* 229–31, 272.
63. Fidel to Che, December 26, 1958, in Franqui, *Diary,* 471.

hundred soldiers, machine guns, bazookas, and rifles sent out on the train. Che had to destroy or capture that train to take Santa Clara; it blocked his advance on Santa Clara and contained soldiers and supplies badly needed by the army.[64]

Several hours later, Che ordered his officers to move into Santa Clara. He ordered Lieutenant Rogelio Acevedo to occupy the university campus on the edge of the city's northern boundary, where Che intended to set up his head-quarters.[65] At dawn of December 29, Acevedo had his men in place as ordered, when Che and his general staff arrived. Che called him into his first-floor office and ordered him to push into the city. "But aren't we going to wait for nightfall?" Acevedo asked, slightly daunted by the prospect of attacking three thousand Batistiano soldiers and policemen with four hundred men. "No, no, *no*. We're going in now," Guevara insisted.[66]

Acevedo's men marched toward Santa Clara in the ditches along the road. An armored enemy column, with two tanks and infantry in support, engaged the rebels just beyond the railroad line north of town. The rebels withstood a deadly fire and drove the column back into town. Meanwhile, DR rebels attacked Barracks 31 at the southeastern edge of the city; with the arrival of other rebel platoons on the northern and western sides of Santa Clara, Che had his men in excellent position for a decisive blow.[67]

The armored train blocked the rebel advance through the north. Parked behind Capiro Hill, on which enemy trenches observed all rebel movements, it represented a formidable obstacle. Che ordered Captain Ramón Pardo Guerra to destroy the tracks behind the train, thereby preventing it from returning to the city; Captain Pardo Guerra commandeered a bulldozer and completed his mission on the morning of December 29. Later in the day, the rebels overcame resistance on Capiro Hill and attacked the train with machine guns and Molotov cocktails, converting wooden boxcars into ovens. The enemy commander ordered the train back into Santa Clara, unaware that the line had been cut. The locomotive came screeching into the break in the line, and fell over with a resounding thud. Fifteen minutes after issuing a demand

---

64. Dorschner and Fabricio, *Winds of December,* 272–74, 281–82, 291–92; Bonachea and San Martín, *Cuban Insurrection,* 297–99.

65. Dorschner and Fabricio, *Winds of December,* 292–93.

66. Ibid., 299–301; on the strength of the opposing forces, see Fernández Mell, "La batalla de Santa Clara," 365–68.

67. Acevedo, *Descamisado,* 278–80; report of Antonio Núñez Jiménez, in Franqui, *Diary,* 474–75; Bonachea and San Martín, *Cuban Insurrection,* 297; "Desde la Sierra Maestra hasta Las Villas," *Bohemia,* January 11, 1959.

for unconditional surrender, Che captured the armored train, with nearly four hundred soldiers and hundreds of wooden crates filled with arms, ammunition, and supplies. With the train went Batista's last hopes of survival.[68]

Nevertheless, a few army and police units resisted the inevitable from positions in downtown Santa Clara, in Leoncio Vidal barracks, the police station, city hall, and the Grand Hotel. The people rallied to the rebel cause, joining the rebel attack on the city center, armed with whatever weapons they could find. In vicious house-to-house fighting on December 30 and 31, the people's army tightened the circle around the last Batista strongholds, leaving comrades dead and dying in the street.[69]

Had Batista's soldiers ever fought with the conviction that untrained civilians displayed on the streets of Santa Clara, Guevara's column never would have made it out of the Sierra Maestra. When Batista treated his New Year's Eve guests to yellow rice and chicken at Camp Colombia, he knew that his army could not resist the rebel advance on Havana. Too many people had joined the rebel cause; too many generals and soldiers had deserted him. Batista resigned at midnight. He boarded a plane two hours later and fled to the Dominican Republic.[70]

By dawn, the news of Batista's resignation reached Santa Clara, where the Leoncio Vidal garrison refused to surrender. Major Candido Hernández, chief of operations at the barracks, came to Che's headquarters and asked for a truce. Che demanded his unconditional surrender. He threatened to resume the attack at 12:30 P.M. He reminded the commander that the United States might intervene militarily to prevent a Castro victory. If that occurred, Guevara suggested that the major commit suicide, since he would be guilty of "high treason against Cuba."[71] Hernández surrendered before 12:30 P.M.

Che then telephoned Fidel to get his orders. Castro wanted to capture the Havana garrisons before any reformist military officers or ambitious politicians maneuvered their way into the presidential palace. He ordered Che and Camilo to march on Havana immediately. Camilo, though he was still at Yaguayjay, sixty miles east of Santa Clara, would lead the rebel columns into Havana and take command of Camp Colombia, the strongest garrison in the

68. Ramón Pardo Guerra, "El tren blindado," in Pavón, *Días de combate*, 381–87; Guevara, *Episodes*, 336; Bonachea and San Martín, *Cuban Insurrection*, 298.

69. Fernández Mell, "La batalla de Santa Clara," 370–71; Alfredo Pino Puebla, "La batalla de Santa Clara," *Bohemia*, December 27, 1959; Anderson, *Che Guevara*, 368.

70. Dubois, *Fidel Castro*, 342–43; Quirk, *Fidel*, 207–8.

71. Fernández Mell, "La batalla de Santa Clara," 371–72 (my translation).

country. Che would march behind Camilo and take command of La Cabaña, an old colonial fortress guarding the entrance to Havana harbor.[72]

Che, second in command to Fidel Castro and the most accomplished comandante of the revolution, was denied the glory that he had won on the battlefield. Che had trained the guerrillas in the Sierra Maestra; he had launched the first independent column; he had directed the rebel defenses during the army's summer offensive; and he had marched across the island and taken Santa Clara in a brilliantly planned and executed campaign. Camilo, though wildly popular and an extraordinary fighter, had been Guevara's subordinate for more than a year and played a peripheral role in the Las Villas campaign. Yet Fidel assigned Camilo the mission of taking Cuba's most important military garrison. According to Carlos Franqui, the chief propagandist for the M-26-7, "Che was the most obvious candidate to take Colombia. What reasons did Fidel have for sending him to La Cabaña, a secondary position?"[73] The answer is stated succinctly by Jon Lee Anderson, Che's biographer. "Fidel had undoubtedly chosen the less visible position for Che because he wanted him out of the limelight. To the defeated regime, its adherents, and Washington, Che was the dreaded 'international Communist,' and it was only asking for trouble to give him a preeminent role so early on."[74]

In any case, Che gathered all available trucks and jeeps for the drive to La Cabaña with four hundred men. The column rolled out of Santa Clara on the evening of January 2, 1959, prepared for battle but finding no resistance en route to Havana. Guevara's column came to a halt outside the fortress at 4:00 A.M., January 3. Che warned his men to be cautious, given that the eleven hundred troops inside might resist. Then he noticed that the tanks at the main gate were unarmed. Comandante Che Guevara took La Cabaña without a fight.[75] The war was over.

In *Guerrilla Warfare*, Che Guevara argued that the final phase of a guerrilla campaign would assume the characteristics of a conventional war. The conquest of Santa Clara had the characteristics of a regular war, with two armies slugging it out, each one trying to annihilate the other. In taking Santa

---

72. Dubois, *Fidel Castro*, 347; Taibo, *Guevara*, 253–54.
73. Franqui, *Diary*, 502–3.
74. Anderson, *Che Guevara*, 376.
75. Dorschner and Fabricio, *Winds of December*, 440, 468; Bonachea and San Martín, *Cuban Insurrection*, 324; "Entró en la Cabaña el Com. Ernesto 'Che' Guevara," *Revolución*, January 3, 1959; Herbert L. Matthews, "Top Castro Aide Denies Red Tie," *New York Times*, January 4, 1959.

Clara and then Havana, Che had defeated elements of Batista's army, but he had not annihilated it. Che and Fidel annihilated the Batistiano army *after* they took Havana, by imprisoning, exiling, or executing the officer corps. They never had an opportunity to crush the Cuban army, because so many soldiers and officers surrendered before they even fired a shot. The Cuban army had the means to defeat the rebels; too many officers and soldiers simply lacked the will to fight them. Neither the soldiers nor the officers cared to risk their lives defending an unpopular and unconstitutional government against an increasingly popular movement that at least held out the prospect for a better political future.

In the two days before Che arrived at La Cabaña, the army disintegrated. General Cantillo and Colonel Ramón Barquín made two unsuccessful attempts to install a non-Fidelista junta after Batista's departure. With the army crumbling under them and the rebels approaching Havana, neither one could mount an effective resistance. Colonel Barquín, despite his prestigious anti-Batista record, could not rally the army. "All they left me with is shit," Barquín grumbled.[76]

In his one day in office, Barquín had appointed loyal officers to the infantry, air force, navy, national police, and La Cabaña. If he had contested the rebel advance with the battered and demoralized remnants of the army, one can only speculate about the outcome, but the casualties certainly would have been high. To avert a bloodbath he turned over command of Camp Colombia to Camilo without a fight, just as his appointee, Colonel Manuel Varela Castro, surrendered La Cabaña to Che. Thus, the insurrection did not end with a final, conventional confrontation between regular army units. Batista never rallied his men in the field, never deployed his best army units, and never concentrated his forces for a spirited offensive or defensive campaign. His army crumbled beneath him, eliminating his only base of political support and forcing him to flee in disgrace. Batista resigned a few weeks after he and his top generals realized that they could not stem the rising tide of opposition to an illegitimate, unconstitutional regime.

The military successes of the rebels in Santa Clara and Oriente, particularly the former, hastened Batista's departure and the disintegration of the army. Che's conquest of Santa Clara demonstrated that the rebels possessed the training and determination that Batista's army lacked. The rebel army, once composed of only sixteen combatants, had grown into an experienced,

---

76. Cited in Paterson, *Contesting Castro,* 230.

well-organized, dangerous military power. That Che never had the opportunity to test his seasoned veterans in combat against Batista's best does not diminish the value of his achievements. By conquering Santa Clara, Che Guevara cut down the last remaining pillar of the Batista regime, overrunning determined resistance and recording the greatest military feat of the entire insurrection.

However, many other political organizations contributed to the destruction of the Batista dictatorship. The students, middle classes, traditional politicians, and elements of the officer corps had all chipped away at the regime. The farcical presidential elections of November had damaged Batista's credibility even among his strongest supporters, including the American ambassador. The Eisenhower administration remained neutral for most of the insurrection and eventually encouraged Batista to resign. American neutrality represented the greatest of all rebel victories, for it meant that the outgunned and outnumbered rebel army never had to face American marines, military advisers, and intelligence agents. Ironically, Che Guevara subsequently advocated a strategy designed to provoke a battle with the Americans. One can measure the success of a guerrilla campaign, however, by the number of battles not fought, and Che Guevara never had to fight American troops to get into Havana. He just drove up to the gate of La Cabaña. The Americans would not let Che or any guerrilla movement he organized, sponsored, inspired, or led, drive so easily into power again.

SEVEN GUERRILLA WARFARE

Over the course of three centuries, La Cabaña had been the residence of Spanish governors, American admirals, and Cuban generals. Its thick white walls, built on a rocky point guarding the entrance to Havana harbor, now sheltered a thirty-one-year-old Argentine comandante, who seemed oddly comfortable in the colonial fortress. A tattered olive green uniform without insignia fell limply on his light frame, his oily hair dangled to his shoulders, and a revolver hung from his belt. He looked like a common soldier who had just come from the field of battle, but he sounded like a professor of revolutionary theory and practice.

"What are the lessons of the Cuban revolution?" a curious reporter asked.

"The most obvious lesson is that one can battle regular forces with troops composed of peasants, workers, and intellectuals. This is a vital experience in the fight against other dictatorships."[1]

The men and women who had served under Comandante Che Guevara during the insurrection knew that he often mixed historical or philosophical lessons into his military training. He had recorded and studied the history of the Cuban insurrection as he fought it, stuffing his knapsack with field diaries,

---

1. Herbert Matthews, "Top Castro Aide Denies Red Tie," *New York Times,* January 4, 1959.

papers, and books. No other militant in the rebel army matched Guevara's intellect, the breadth and depth of which he would now reveal in service to Cuba's revolutionary government. Some Communist party officials could match Che's intellect, but, because they had generally refused to join the fight, could not explain how the rebel army triumphed or what lessons other revolutionary movements could draw from the Cuban experience. Che's confrontation with imperialism in Guatemala, his extensive knowledge of Marxist-Leninist thought, and his combat experience in Cuba gave him the authority to speak on revolutionary theory and practice, and Cuba—soon the world— listened to him.

Over the following eight years, Che wrote and spoke prolifically on a wide range of subjects, from guerrilla warfare to the budgetary finance system. The diversity of the topics reflect the variety of positions he held in the revolutionary government, including president of the National Bank, minister of industry, comandante, instructor of the army and militia, party leader, diplomat, volunteer cane-cutter, math student, and close adviser to Fidel Castro. Somehow, in rare moments of solitude, Guevara wrote enough articles, speeches, letters, and books to fill a nine-volume compilation. This collection of Guevara's works—the most complete available—still does not include the diaries he kept from 1957 to 1966 or many of the letters and official memorandums he wrote while in government service.[2]

In this immense body of literature one will find Guevarism, the body of revolutionary strategies and tactics that begin with irregular warfare. *Guerrilla Warfare*, Guevara's first and most basic manual of guerrilla warfare, does not represent the full flowering of Guevarism. The publication of *Guerrilla Warfare* in 1960 undoubtedly established Che as Latin America's leading advocate of unconventional warfare. The popularity of the book, however, probably has more to do with the fame of the author than with the content of its pages. In this short treatise, Che presented few innovations that would distinguish him from Mao Tse-tung or Vietnamese general Vo Nguyen Giap. Che made his contributions to guerrilla strategy in briefer articles published several years after *Guerrilla Warfare*, titled "Guerrilla Warfare: A Method," and "Message to the Tricontinental." In these and other works Che articulated a revolutionary line that branded him as an international communist maverick, critical of Soviet and Chinese strategists.

Guevarism grew out of Che's combat experience and reflected his desire to liberate Latin America from American imperialism. Revolutionaries stud-

---

2. Guevara, *Ernesto Che Guevara: Escritos y discursos.*

ied his strategies and tactics carefully; his enemies did so too. Che may not have been an innovative *guerrillero,* but he was certainly influential. According to Brian Loveman and Thomas Davies, "The Cuban example, along with *Guerrilla Warfare* and his [Guevara's] later writings, fundamentally altered the course of Latin American history, of U.S. foreign policy, of international politics, and for both better and worse, the human condition in Latin America."[3]

Ironically, the man viewed by others as a great theorist thought of himself as a practical revolutionary. Guevara knew too many theorists who understood imperialist exploitation from an academic perspective and who did nothing to ameliorate this exploitation, their explanation for inaction being that the "conditions weren't right" or some other orthodox rationalization for what Che saw as cowardice. Had he followed prevailing communist theory, he would never have taken up arms against Batista. Theorists only interpret history and anticipate the future; they do not change them, according to Guevara. Theorists, like the communists whom Che often criticized, remain outside history and therefore remain slaves. The Cuban Revolution, he argued, demonstrated the importance of stepping into history precisely to transform it. The Cuban revolutionaries had taken up Marx where he had left off, picking up a rifle to fight within history. "We, *practical revolutionaries* [emphasis added] when initiating our struggle, simply fulfilled laws foreseen by Marx the scientist," Che wrote.[4]

Che Guevara combined theory and practice and this offered a living example of revolutionary praxis. He discussed philosophy with French existentialist Jean-Paul Sartre as easily as he talked to a common soldier about guerrilla tactics. He theorized reluctantly and with reservations, eager to implement the Cuban Revolution rather than discuss it as a historical abstraction. Maurice Zeitlin, a professor of sociology and anthropology at Princeton, once attempted to engage Che in a discussion of Rosa Luxembourg's critique of democratic centralism. Guevara had obviously analyzed Luxembourg's critiques of Leninist theory, but he avoided the debate, claiming that "I am not accustomed to discussing theory. I try to be pragmatic." Zeitlin persisted, questioning Che about the relevance of Lenin to the Cuban Revolution. Guevara praised the part that Lenin played in constructing the theory of imperialism, but Che seemed most interested in the practical contributions to

3. Loveman and Davies, "Guerrilla Warfare, Revolutionary Theory," 29.
4. Guevara, "Notes for the Study of the Ideology of the Cuban Revolution," in Guevara, *Che Guevara: Selected Works,* 50.

development that Lenin made in the final congress before his death, in which he discussed electrification and industrialization.[5]

Che had concluded that the Cuban Revolution contradicted the fundamental Leninist premise that there could be no revolutionary movement without a revolutionary theory. The principal leaders of the Cuban insurrection knew something about Marxist-Leninist thought, but no revolutionary theory guided them as they embarked on the *Granma*. Their unlikely victory had demonstrated that "the revolution can be made if the historical realities are interpreted correctly and if the forces involved are utilized correctly, *even if the theory is not known* [emphasis added]."[6]

In writing about guerrilla warfare, Che did not intend to revise Marx, Lenin, or Mao and construct a new revolutionary theory, model, or paradigm. He simply intended to teach revolutionaries how to make revolution. Che described *Guerrilla Warfare* as an "eminently practical" manual. He even disparaged its contributions. "It is little more than a schoolboy's attempt to arrange words one after another; it has no pretensions of explaining the great things."[7] Moreover, at the time he published the manual, the pace of revolutionary action was exceeding revolutionary thought, to the extent that he considered his manual "almost worthless here in Cuba" just months after he published it. For other countries, however, "it might be of some value, but only if it is used with intelligence, without haste or deception."[8]

To extract a theory of guerrilla warfare based solely on *Guerrilla Warfare* is to misrepresent Guevarism. It is certainly one of Che's fundamental works on the subject, but it is just a basic work, written for combatants, not intellectuals. In January 1960, Raúl Castro, minister of the Fuerzas Armadas Revolucionarias (FAR, Revolutionary Armed Forces), appointed Che the chief of the Department of Instruction. For more than a year prior to the appointment, Che had been purging the old army and organizing a new one. As comandante of the La Cabaña fortress in the spring of 1959, he prosecuted and executed hundreds of Batistianos, part of a larger campaign to eradicate counterrevolutionary elements from the military. At the same time, he initiated educational and cultural programs designed to teach and indoctrinate a new army that was loyal to the revolution. In a speech given on January 27,

5. "Interview with Maurice Zeitlin," in Guevara, *Che: Selected Works,* 394.

6. Guevara, "Notes for the Study of the Ideology of the Cuban Revolution," in Guevara, *Che: Selected Works,* 48.

7. Che Guevara to Ernesto Sábato, April 12, 1960, in Guevara, *Episodes,* 411.

8. Ibid., 413.

1959, he explained that the revolutionary army would receive training in guerrilla warfare to defend Cuba from foreign aggression. Che harbored no illusions that in the event of an American military intervention, the Cuban military could repel the first thrust onto the island. "That is why we must anticipate and prepare our vanguard with a guerrilla spirit and strategy—so that our defenses will not disintegrate with the first attack and will maintain their cohesive unity. All the Cuban people must become a guerrilla army."[9]

Che's strategy of yielding territory to a foreign invader and reorganizing Cuba's military forces for a protracted guerrilla campaign became a part of official Cuban strategy. During the missile crisis of 1962, Soviet and Cuban military strategists assumed that the Americans would overrun the coastal defenses relatively easily. After that occurred, Cuban and Soviet troops would withdraw to prearranged and stockpiled sites at three regional headquarters (Pinar del Río, Las Villas, and Oriente provinces), from which Che, Fidel, and Raúl would direct guerrilla operations against the invading forces.[10]

In addition to Che's duties with the regular army and militias, he supervised Cuba's clandestine efforts to foment revolution in the Americas. Guevara viewed the triumph of the Cuban Revolution as the first step in a war of liberation that would eventually sweep across Central and South America, and he intended to lead this continental revolution. Within a month after establishing his post at La Cabaña in January 1959, Guevara began to summon prospective Latin American revolutionaries, and aspiring guerrillas came from Nicaragua, the Dominican Republic, Haiti, and Guatemala in the spring of 1959. From a conspiracy organized spontaneously and informally by Che, the covert operations grew into a formal program administered by the Liberation Department within the Interior Ministry run by Ramiro Valdés, a Guevara loyalist and protégé who had served under Che in the Las Villas campaign. Manuel "Barba Roja" Piñeiro ran the department as a vice minister, but Che Guevara actually ran the Liberation Department. According to an anonymous source interviewed by biographer Jon Lee Anderson, "From Day One, Che was in charge of the armed liberation movement supported by Cuba."[11]

Thus, when Guevara wrote *Guerrilla Warfare,* he was organizing, training, indoctrinating, and equipping armies, militias, and guerrilla bands. To the extent that he theorized about guerrilla warfare, he did it to inspire and

9. Guevara, "Social Ideals of the Rebel Army," in Guevara, *Che: Selected Works,* 203.

10. Testimony of General Gribkov, in Blight, Allyn, and Welch, eds., *Cuba on the Brink,* 61–62.

11. Anderson, *Che Guevara,* 393–97, 759.

instruct his soldiers, which explains the practical emphasis of the manual. The origins of the manual elucidate its content, in which the focus is more on tactics than strategy, more on defensive than offensive operations. Guevara explained his strategic perspective in the first two chapters, "Essence of Guerrilla Warfare," and "Guerrilla Strategy," which constitute less than 10 percent of the book. The rest of the treatise is devoted to tactics, the methods for achieving on the battlefield the grand strategic objectives devised in the classroom. Che explained how to organize, equip, train, and discipline a rebel column. He included detailed instructions on how to build an antitank trap, what to pack in a knapsack, and how to string up a hammock.[12] Given these limitations, many of them recognized by Guevara, one should not belabor the point that *Guerrilla Warfare* contains few innovative theories about guerrilla warfare.

The basic premise of Guevarism is that the Cuban victory over Batista invalidated previous doctrines and confirmed the path of armed struggle in the Americas. Che introduces *Guerrilla Warfare* by highlighting the three fundamental contributions of the Cuban Revolution to revolutionary strategy in the Americas:

1. "Popular forces can win a war against the army."
2. "It is not necessary to wait until all conditions for making revolution exist; the insurrection can create them."
3. "In underdeveloped America the countryside is the basic area for armed fighting." (132–34)

These three proclamations represent a radical departure from the traditional policies of Latin American Communist parties. It was time to "stop crying and fight," as Che had concluded after his first meeting with Fidel in 1955. Just in case the Communists missed the meaning of his first point, Guevara made it more explicit in the second, which he directed against the "defeatist attitude of revolutionaries or pseudo-revolutionaries" who had denounced armed struggle in Cuba and elsewhere. To Che, the success of armed struggle in Cuba had demonstrated that the act of insurrection would create the conditions for revolution, an innovative political statement that contradicted the Soviet claim that the conditions for revolution did not exist

---

12. Guevara, *Guerrilla Warfare*, 132–34. Subsequent references to this work appear in the text.

in Latin America. Guevara admitted that the creation of a guerrilla front alone would not produce all the conditions necessary for revolution. "There is a necessary minimum without which the establishment and consolidation of the first center is not practicable," Che conceded. He thereby limited the applicability of guerrilla warfare in Latin America: "Where a government has come into power through some form of popular vote, fraudulent or not, and maintains at least an appearance of constitutional legality, the guerrilla out-break cannot be promoted, since the possibilities of peaceful struggle have not yet been exhausted" (51).

Latin American Communist parties, following the Soviet line, held dog-matically to the proposition that armed struggle could not succeed even when applied to brutal dictatorships. Only the organized proletariat, led by the Communist party, could possibly lead the revolutionary movement, and in Latin America, the proletariat had neither the strength nor the consciousness required to foment revolution. Given the weaknesses of the proletariat, the Communists devoted their efforts to organizing and indoctrinating, build-ing political coalitions, and participating in electoral politics, as they had done in Cuba. Castro's successful rebellion, however, had demonstrated the revo-lutionary potential of the peasants and the virtues of waging guerrilla cam-paigns from the mountains, far beyond the reach of the professional army. Guevara urged revolutionaries not to ignore the struggle of organized work-ers, but he cautioned that activists in the cities faced greater dangers than in the countryside. In strategic terms, Che recognized that the countryside offered the ideal terrain for a successful guerrilla campaign; in political terms, he saw the peasants as revolutionaries, not reactionaries.

Guevara's *Guerrilla Warfare* begins simply as a call to arms in Latin America. Wherever the necessary minimum existed, duty called on revolutionaries to establish a guerrilla front. Che did not intend to create a model of guerrilla warfare with universal applicability. He recognized that the circumstances of each country would determine the particular mode and forms of guerrilla war-fare. There were a few general principles of guerrilla war that had to be observed. "Whoever ignores them will go down to defeat," Che warned (51). Che went on to describe the general principles of guerrilla warfare, followed by some technical instructions, but he urged guerrillas to devise their own strategies and tactics carefully, based on circumstances only they could inter-pret. The guerrilla fighter had to adapt the form and timing of struggle to conditions that no general theory of guerrilla warfare could anticipate.

At the same time, Guevara noted in *Guerrilla Warfare* that guerrilla campaigns generally evolved through three distinct phases, a lesson he had learned from Alberto Bayo. In the initial phase, a small band of guerrillas initiates operations in a remote region, engaging the enemy sporadically, at times and places of the guerrillas' choosing. After registering a few victories, gaining confidence and expertise, in the second phase the guerrilla band establishes semipermanent bases, with basic industries, a communications network, supply lines, and administrative systems. In the process, the guerrilla band increases in size and expands its area of operations, gradually transforming itself into a regular army fighting a war of positions. In the third and final phase, this regular army will encircle and take the cities through conventional methods.

Che Guevara never argued that a guerrilla foco alone would lead to complete victory. The guerrilla foco was only the "embryo" of a regular army and a conventional campaign. Guerrilla warfare, Che argued, is "one of the initial phases of warfare and will develop continuously until the guerrilla army in its steady growth acquires the characteristics of a regular army. At that moment it will be ready to deal final blows to the enemy and to achieve victory. Triumph will always be the product of a regular army, even though its origins are in a guerrilla army" (54–55).

Ironically, Guevara offered few—if any—strategic or tactical lessons on how to conduct the second and third phases of the campaign. Ninety percent of *Guerrilla Warfare* deals with the conduct of the initial stage of the campaign. Guevara does not explain how to encircle and capture enemy cities, assuming that any commander would know how to execute a complicated military maneuver. Guevara described rather than prescribed the strategy of the final campaign: "It is thus that guerrillas reach the stage of attack, of the encirclement of fortified bases, of the defeat of reinforcements, of mass action, ever more ardent, in the whole national territory, arriving finally at the objective of the war: victory" (58).

The applicability of *Guerrilla Warfare* is therefore limited to the initial phase of a campaign, when the guerrillas are most vulnerable. "At the outset, the essential task of the guerrilla fighter is to keep himself from being destroyed," Guevara argued (55–56). To avoid destruction, the guerrilla band could not defend territory. The guerrillas had to be prepared to evacuate an area of operations if and when the enemy army threatened it. They had to remain in constant motion, offering the enemy no fixed target, allowing the enemy no time to monitor their movements. When moving, the guerrillas should march at night; when attacking, they must attack by surprise. The numerical inferiority of the guerrilla band made it imperative to avoid fighting at times and terrain chosen by the enemy, for the enemy's possession of superior armaments and personnel allowed it to sustain losses that the guerrillas could not afford. "No battle, combat, or skirmish is to be fought unless it will be won," Che stated emphatically (54 [quoted], 58–59).

The ultimate objective of the guerrilla band, however, remained the same as that of a conventional army. Guevara shared the strategic conception of all classical military strategists, including Clausewitz, in which the ultimate objective of war is the destruction of the enemy army. The guerrilla army, in its infancy and even in its more advanced stage, might avoid battle, but it still intended to defeat the enemy army in battle, not through a war of attrition. "The general strategy of guerrilla warfare, . . . is the same in its ultimate end as is any warfare: to win, to annihilate the enemy" (54).

No guerrilla band could survive if it did not enjoy the support of the masses, particularly the peasants living near the zone of operations. Without peasant support, the guerrillas would depend entirely on their urban ties for supplies, recruits, and intelligence, a vulnerability that an enemy could easily exploit. To attract peasants the guerrillas had to fight for the social and economic reforms they demanded, particularly land reform. Guevara emphasized that guerrilla warfare was "a war of the masses, a war of the people. The guerrilla band is an armed nucleus, the fighting vanguard of the people." Although the actual number of combatants in a guerrilla band was relatively low, it was not inferior to the professional army it fought. "Guerrilla warfare is used by the side which is supported by a majority but which possesses a much smaller number of arms for use in defense against oppression," Che contended (52).

Guevara viewed guerrilla warfare as the most effective means of fighting. Other forms of struggle, such as a general strike, could contribute to victory, but only if coordinated with the guerrilla vanguard and applied at the proper moment of the general insurrection. A general strike could paralyze entire armies and shut down the economic life of a country, after the guerrillas had already weakened the opposition, Che conceded (57).

However, Che conceived of the guerrilla band as the armed vanguard of the masses. All other revolutionary groups should recognize its leadership and provide the assistance it requires. Urban organizations should perform important auxiliary missions such as recruitment, fund-raising, supply, and communications. They should not take military action independently; they should let the guerrillas lead the armed struggle in the countryside. Guevara advocated mass mobilization and urban military actions only for the final and decisive phases of the campaign. For the earlier stages of the struggle Che limited mass organizations, including political parties, labor unions, and clandestine cells, to secondary roles. Their objective should be "to lend the army maximum help, since obviously the armed fight is the crucial factor in the triumph" (125).

Che's conception of a three-stage revolutionary campaign is similar to the Maoist perspective of a protracted war in that the campaign evolves through three distinct stages. Without using Maoist terminology, Che formulated a three-phase struggle similar to Mao's: a strategic defensive, followed by a strategic stalemate, culminating in a strategic offensive.[13] Mao's strategic defensive began, however, not as a challenge to his domestic opposition, but to expel a massive Japanese invasion. In all three Maoist phases, the Chinese revolutionaries fought a powerful and determined invader, and a strong nationalistic impulse drove all the Chinese combatants. The scale, strategy, and character of Mao's revolutionary campaigns, stretching more than two decades and involving millions of combatants in civil and international war, distinguishes it from the Cuban experience. Mao directed a brilliant and massive campaign against an immense military power. Guevara's proposition that fifty guerrillas could liberate a Latin American country from American imperialism could not have been derived from Mao.[14]

Guevara argued that this band of fifty guerrillas would increase in size and expand its operations, developing into a regular army and fighting a conventional campaign in the final offensive. Mao utilized regular army units and guerrilla bands simultaneously, in each of three phases. Mao had contributed innovative theories of guerrilla warfare, but his armies fought regular and irregular campaigns. According to one military historian, Mao was concerned with "revolutionary war, in which regular army units employ the tactics of irregulars, partisan units fight in parallel to the regular forces (with their actions sometimes considered most important), and classical full frontal assaults are launched only when the situation demands them."[15]

In a clear break with Mao, Guevara advocated a guerrilla band as the sole fighting force and guerrilla warfare as the predominant tactic. The Chinese Revolution did not begin with an armed nucleus of thirty fighters in the coun-

---

13. Mao Tse-tung, "On Protracted War," in Mallin, *Strategy for Conquest,* 71–74.
14. Guevara, *Guerrilla Warfare,* 130.
15. Chailand, *Guerrilla Strategies,* 7.

tryside. It began as a conventional war between regular armies in southern China. Mao subsequently adopted the strategy of protracted revolutionary war, in which he deployed guerrilla units to harass the Japanese invader during the first phase. Mao did not postulate, nor did the Chinese Revolution follow, a line of guerrilla struggle that Che Guevara subsequently promoted.

Che's strategic innovation consisted in his concept of the guerrilla band initiating the struggle and evolving into a regular army. Historically, military commanders have used guerrilla warfare to complement the activities of the regular army. The guerrillas in Spain (1808–12) and in the Soviet Union during World War II supported and complemented the conventional struggle, the first waged by Lord Wellington's British army on the Iberian Peninsula and the second directed by the massive Soviet Red Army. Most guerrilla campaigns, even those commanded by Colonel T. E. Lawrence, had always been coordinated with and protected by large armies, demonstrating exceptional merit fighting behind enemy lines to disrupt supplies and communications. In *Guerrilla Warfare* Che attempted to delineate a new type of guerrilla campaign, in which a guerrilla band establishes itself in a rural area as *the only* base of armed struggle. Che cannot claim originality of the concept, however, for he had learned it from Alberto Bayo, who had learned it by studying the campaigns of Augusto César Sandino.

Che argued that his strategic formulation grew out of the Cuban experience. In the history of the Cuban insurrection, Che perceived universal laws about the beginning, development, and end of a guerrilla war. Che's model begins with a small group of combatants, hiding in the most remote and inaccessible places, and striking only when they anticipated certain victory. The guerrilla band grew, established semipermanent bases, repelled the army offensive, and then launched a final assault on the cities. Because the Cuban Revolution had evolved along these lines, Che argued that other revolutionary movements could develop and triumph in a similar manner.

Che's model of guerrilla warfare and the history from which it is derived reflect the Cuban insurrection as he saw it, not as it actually occurred. For him the war began with a small group of rebels reorganizing in the mountains as a guerrilla force. For other M-26-7 activists the war began with Castro's attack on Moncada in July 1953. Che Guevara built a model of guerrilla warfare based on his personal experience as a soldier and comandante, which did not include clandestine work as a leader of an urban cell responsible for fundraising and recruitment. He subsequently inflated the importance of the Cuban Revolution, making his guerrilla strategies irresistibly seductive to Latin

American revolutionaries. "It [the Cuban Revolution] has been called by some the cardinal event in the history of America and next in importance to the trilogy composed of the Russian Revolution, the social transformations which followed the triumph over Hitler's armies, and the victory of the Chinese Revolution."[16]

The strength and validity of Guevarism rests on Che's interpretation of the Cuban insurrection. In *Episodes of the Revolutionary War*, Che wrote the history of the insurrection as he saw it or wanted it to be, a guerrilla campaign fought and led by an army of peasants in the countryside. Guevara never intended to write a comprehensive history of the Cuban insurrection. Twenty-eight of the thirty-two articles that compose *Episodes of the Revolutionary War* cover the fighting in the Sierra Maestra from December 1956 to the end of 1957. He says little about the critical summer offensive of 1958 or the decisive Santa Clara campaign that he commanded. He mentions rival revolutionary organizations only to disparage them. *Episodes of the Revolutionary War* is a partial history of the Cuban insurrection, the emphasis on the Sierra Maestra reflecting his own experience in and predilection for guerrilla warfare. From this incomplete history, Che derived fundamental principles for his treatise on guerrilla strategy and tactics.

Important events that occurred during the three-year struggle, such as the attack on the presidential palace in March 1957 and the Cienfuegos military rebellion six months later, are mentioned briefly or not at all. Since Guevara did not participate in those events, he did not feel qualified to write a history of them. At the time, however, he felt competent enough to criticize them severely in his field diaries. In his published accounts, Guevara at least praised José Antonio Echeverría, president of the Revolutionary Directorate and the intellectual author of the assault on the palace, as a "great fighter" and a "true symbol of our young people." In his diary, however, Guevara routinely referred to the Revolutionary Directorate as a "terrorist group."[17]

Guevara described the military uprising at the Cienfuegos naval base on September 5, 1957, as simply "another incident in the armed struggle." The Cienfuegos rebellion was, however, a large-scale insurrection with important political consequences. Military officers seized control of the naval base and city with the support of other opposition groups, including the M-26-7.

16. Guevara, "Cuba: Exceptional Case or Vanguard in the Struggle Against Colonialism?" in Guevara, *Che: Selected Works*, 57.

17. Guevara, *Episodes*, 265; Anderson, *Che Guevara*, 246.

Batista's army responded quickly and crushed the insurgents, who had waited in vain for other military units or insurrectionary forces to join the rebellion. According to Che, the plot failed not because other rebels did not rally to their support but because the Cienfuegos conspirators, not understanding guerrilla warfare, committed the "tragic mistake of not heading for the Escambray Mountains" and forming another "solid front in the mountains."[18]

The attack on the presidential palace and the Cienfuegos uprising, followed by waves of bloody repression, exposed the brutality of the Batista regime and reaffirmed its unconstitutional character. Batista's army and police forces hunted down, tortured, and murdered students after the attack on the palace, culminating in the gruesome execution of four DR leaders who had taken refuge in an apartment in downtown Havana. At Cienfuegos, three hundred rebels lost their lives in the bloodiest engagement yet with the Cuban military, many of them killed after surrendering. Batista exacted bloody revenge on the officers who had allegedly betrayed him. Widespread reports of grisly reprisals circulated, among them that surrendering rebels were shot on sight and wounded men buried alive. The notorious Major Jesús Sosa Blanco, naval chief of La Chorrera Fortress in Havana, presided over the torture and execution of several conspirators, including Naval Lieutenant Dionisio San Román, who was tormented for several months before being dumped at sea. The Cienfuegos uprising cannot be dismissed as simply "another incident." The number of deaths at Cienfuegos alone exceeded the total strength of Castro's rebel army in its first year.[19]

In their failure, both attacks generated opposition to an increasingly unpopular regime and contributed to a growing sense of national and international crisis. The funerals for the four murdered students became a national political protest. Batista's use of American weaponry to suppress the Cienfuegos rebellion, including tanks and B-26 aircraft, violated the terms of an agreement with the United States that specifically prohibited the use of American arms for maintaining internal security. This conspicuous violation of a treaty with the United States, combined with the barbarities associated with the repression Batista unleashed afterward, weakened his ties to the Eisenhower administration, which eventually suspended all arms shipments to him.[20] Che praised the valor of the DR rebels and the Cienfuegos officers, but he dismissed

18. Guevara, *Episodes,* 266.
19. H. Thomas, *Cuban Revolution,* 144–48; Anderson, *Che Guevara,* 280–81; Bonachea and San Martín, *Cuban Insurrection,* 127–30, 147–52.
20. Paterson, *Contesting Castro,* 97.

the political contributions that they made in their heroic failures.

Che offered many negative opinions, but he reserved his harshest criticisms for the Llano. He attributed the failure of the April 1958 general strike to "errors of judgment" committed by the urban leaders. Throughout the insurrection, the urban leaders had failed to concentrate their efforts on the organization and support of guerrilla fronts in the mountains. For Guevara, the tragic ending of the April 1958 general strike was confirmation that the urban leaders, like other opposition figures, simply did not understand guerrilla warfare. "The llano leadership had underestimated the enemy's strength and subjectively overestimated their own [in the general strike], without taking into account the methods necessary to unleash their forces," he concluded.[21]

The failure of the attack on the presidential palace, the annihilation of the Cienfuegos conspirators, and the aborted general strike all demonstrated to Che the folly of military actions in the urban centers and the great wisdom in a guerrilla campaign based in the mountains. There is little doubt that most of the casualties suffered during the three-year insurrection occurred in the cities. There are no reliable casualty figures for the Cuban insurrection; estimates range from one thousand to more than twenty thousand for the period 1953 to January 1, 1959. Whatever the total figure, historian Hugh Thomas has concluded that civilians in the cities accounted for most of the deaths.[22]

These deaths, including that of M-26-7 leader Frank País, were not in vain. Although the urban militants lost every major confrontation, they contributed to ultimate victory. Urban struggle, whether military or political, supported the guerrilla campaign directly and indirectly. Clandestine organizations based in Havana and Santiago provided valuable assistance to the guerrillas, particularly after Batista's army routed them at Alegría del Pío. Patient and dangerous covert operations in the cities, quite apart from the bloodstained dramas of the presidential palace and Cienfuegos, sustained the guerrilla struggle in the mountains during the first two stages of the campaign. While the guerrillas established their bases in the mountains, the Llano, DR commandos, naval conspirators, and others, facing agonizing death if captured, chipped away at the foundations of Batista's regime, preparing the ground for a final rebel offensive against Santiago and Santa Clara.

Yet Che believed that the rebel army deserved the exclusive credit for defeating Batista, its military victory confirming the validity of the Sierra's

---

21. Guevara, *Episodes,* 316.
22. H. Thomas, *Cuban Revolution,* 262.

strategic conception, guerrilla warfare. The victory demonstrated "the capacity of the people to free themselves by means of guerrilla warfare," Che concluded.[23] In reality, guerrilla warfare was only *one* means by which *one* faction of *one* opposition group struggled against Batista. A broadly based and loosely organized opposition emerged to contest Batista's seizure of power. Disgruntled military officers, traditional politicians, student groups, and labor unions fought Batista on all fronts, using political, diplomatic, social, and military weapons against an unconstitutional regime.

In Che's history of the insurrection, he ignores, neglects, or discredits any opposition group that did not adopt guerrilla warfare in the mountains as the primary means of struggle. In the last six months of the campaign, however, the rebel army led a nationwide assault against Batista in a battle of positions that resembled conventional warfare. By late December 1958, as many as seven thousand rebels fought in uniform, most of them under the command of the M-26-7, but they never defeated Batista's strongest military units, the garrisons in and around Havana, in a decisive, pitched battle.[24] Guevara's final assault on Santa Clara only approximates the characteristics of a battle between two military forces fighting at full strength. Batista's army disintegrated and collapsed, and its officers resigned, fled, or went to prison. Guevara could claim credit for demoralizing elements of that army and inflicting on it serious physical and psychological damage, but he and Camilo defeated only a few demoralized units of that army. If the Havana garrisons had offered resistance to Che and Camilo, those units' heavy artillery, tanks, and aircraft would have punished the outgunned rebel columns. Guevara and Cienfuegos would have found it difficult to capture the garrisons, even if they had had the entire rebel army under their command.

The regular Cuban army simply refused to fight—not for Batista, General Cantillo, or Colonel Ramón Barquín. Most of the army had not even seen combat, but its morale had been sapped by the perception that it defended an unconstitutional regime against a majority of the people. The rebel army could not take sole credit for creating this perception. Many anti-Batista groups struck hard at the illegitimate foundations of Batista's regime. Batista did not lose legitimacy or popular support solely because of the defeats his

---

23. Guevara, *Guerrilla Warfare*, 50.
24. Historian Neill Macaulay, who fought with the rebel army before launching his academic career, provided the most reliable estimate for the number of combatants. See Macaulay, "The Cuban Rebel Army"; Dickey Chapelle, "How Castro Won," in Osanka, *Modern Guerrilla Warfare*, 325–35.

army suffered at La Plata or El Uvero. He suffered other losses, including that of American military support, and the brutality of his greatest victories drained his limited reservoir of public support. The unconstitutional and brutal character of his regime legitimized armed opposition, to the extent that former president Carlos Prío Socarrás lent Castro the money he used to buy the *Granma* and induced Prío to attempt his own invasion later. The sacrifices of the DR militants in Havana garnered the sympathy of the middle and upper classes and, perhaps more important, prevented Batista from sending his best battalions to the Sierra Maestra.

Historian Che Guevara, however, claimed victory on behalf of an army of peasants who had adopted guerrilla strategy and defeated the dictatorship on the battlefield. In fact, the eighty-two men who landed with the *Granma* were not peasants. They came from the cities, and they represented all social classes. Most of the fifty-eight recruits sent to the mountains in April 1957 were not peasants either; they came from Santiago and other urban centers. Peasants began to enlist in the rebel army soon after the *Granma* landed, and Che trained many of them at Minas del Frío. Che's Column 8, coming right out of Minas del Frío into battle, contained a high percentage of peasants who were trained by and loyal to Che. Peasant participation in the M-26-7 army peaked at 50 to 75 percent in mid-1958, according to a recent estimate. However, one cannot dismiss the service of the urban middle to upper classes, particularly in the form of key leaders, most notably Che Guevara. Peasants swelled the ranks of the rebel army, but it would be inappropriate to label it an army of peasants.[25]

In developing his strategies of guerrilla warfare, Che filtered out the actions that had failed in Cuba. In *Guerrilla Warfare,* one will not find, for example, advice on how to attack a Moncada-like garrison, storm a presidential palace, or launch a general strike. All these actions had failed in Cuba. In contrast, the rebel army did not lose a single engagement after it had established a base in the Sierra Maestra and adopted a guerrilla strategy. The Cuban insurrection thereby illuminated the correct path to victory, validating one means of struggle—guerrilla warfare—and invalidating all others. Cuban revolutionaries had tried assassinations, general strikes, electoral alliances, military conspiracies, and surprise attacks on garrisons, but these had all failed. Only the guerrilla strategy succeeded, confirmation of its viability as a revolutionary strategy.

25. H. Thomas, *Cuban Revolution,* 261; Wickham-Crowley, *Guerrillas and Revolution in Latin America,* 25–26.

The applicability of Guevara's strategy to other revolutionary movements rested on the assumption that the Cuban Revolution was not a historical aberration. Soon after the publication of *Guerrilla Warfare,* critics charged that because the revolution had been shaped by exceptional circumstances, other movements that adopted the Cuban model would not succeed unless those same conditions prevailed. Each revolution, Che recognized, manifests unique characteristics, but he only conceded three exceptional features. The first and probably most important was in the person of Fidel Castro, whom Che ranked among the "greatest figures in the history of Latin America." Che also acknowledged that "North American imperialism was disoriented and unable to measure the true depth of the Cuban Revolution." The United States government, unable to interpret the ideological orientation of the Fidelista movement, pursued contradictory and ineffective policies. "When imperialism tried to react, when it realized that the group of inexperienced young men had a clear understanding of their political duty and was determined to live up to it, it was already too late," Che explained.[26]

Che also admitted that the revolutionary movement benefited from a higher degree of class consciousness among the proletariat, generated by mechanized capitalist enterprises in rural Cuba. As a result, the masses were amenable to the socialist orientation of the revolutionary movement. However, Che pointed out that the guerrillas established their first base in the Sierra Maestra, where peasants had not been transformed into a rural proletariat by capitalist enterprises. The "petty bourgeois" spirit of the Sierra Maestra peasants compelled them to join the rebel army in the hope of acquiring their own land. But Che made no other concessions to his critics: "We believe that no other factors of exceptionalism exist and we have been generous in granting this many."[27]

The objective conditions that could spawn revolution, Che argued, existed in every Latin American country. All Latin America exists in a state of "underdevelopment," the product of four centuries of colonialism and imperialism. The Latin American economies had been distorted by imperialist policies that compelled Latin Americans to produce a single product for consumption in a single industrial market. This monocultural dependence, creating a permanent state of underdevelopment, produced low salaries, unemployment, and hunger, objective conditions for developing revolutionary movements from

26. Guevara, "Cuba: Exceptional Case or Vanguard in the Struggle Against Colonialism?" in Guevara, *Che: Selected Works,* 59.
27. Ibid., 57–60.

the Rio Grande to Tierra del Fuego. The Americas lacked only the subjective conditions, primarily the "consciousness of the possibility of victory
through violent struggle against the imperialist powers and their internal
allies." In Cuba, the Fidelistas had demonstrated that the subjective conditions for a revolutionary triumph could be created by the struggle itself,
Che argued.[28]

Che cautioned other revolutionaries, however, about the character of the
upcoming struggles. Imperialism had learned from its mistakes in Cuba; it
would never again be taken by surprise in other Latin American countries.
"This means that great popular battles against powerful invading armies await."
Likewise, the Latin American bourgeoisie and the landowners would hesitate
to join a popular revolution against their imperialist allies. As a result, other
revolutionary movements would face stronger and deadlier foes.
Revolugtionaries should therefore consider the possibility of change through
the electoral process. Che would not pardon revolutionaries for failing to
explore electoral options, just as he would not excuse them for rejecting the
path of armed struggle. Che therefore urged Latin Americans to rise in rebellion everywhere, fighting on all available fronts simultaneously.[29]

Guevara's emphasis on military tactics in *Guerrilla Warfare*, however, suggested that success only required the faithful application of the proper techniques. He recognized, of course, that no revolutionary movement would
succeed where it did not enjoy mass support. But with people supporting the
armed vanguard, success would come through the application of the military
tactics that Che taught in *Guerrilla Warfare*. These tactics, however, became
outdated as soon as *Guerrilla Warfare* was published. His adversaries studied the manual and revised their strategy and tactics accordingly. The guerrillas whom Guevara inspired or put into the field had no ready guide to the
new strategic doctrines, the modified tactics, or the upgraded hardware that
their enemy would take into the battlefield. The guerrilla armies that sprang
up after the Cuban Revolution faced well-trained counterinsurgency companies equipped with sophisticated weaponry, communications equipment, and
surveillance systems.

Not coincidentally, every guerrilla band sponsored by Cuba failed until
the Sandinistas overthrew Nicaraguan dictator Anastasio Somoza in 1979.
Cuban support for the Nicaraguan revolutionaries began in the spring of 1959,

28. Ibid., 61–63.
29. Ibid., 64–70.

when Che organized a Nicaraguan column under the command of Rafael Somarriba. The group sailed from Cuba and fell into the hands of Mexican authorities on June 25, 1959, carrying documents verifying Cuban support, including one signed by Che Guevara.[30]

Under Che's leadership, Cuba organized and trained guerrilla armies throughout Latin America. His revolutionary ambitions went far beyond Cuba's shores, up to and including his native Argentina. He would not stop, and Cuba would remain isolated and endangered, until revolutionary movements rolled up a few victories on the continent. Che did not simply theorize about guerrilla warfare; he practiced it from the triumph of the Cuban Revolution on January 1, 1959, to his death in Bolivia on October 9, 1967.

Inspired and led by Che, Cuba became a "fully operational Guerrilla Central" by 1962. Through the Liberation Department, Che trained revolutionaries in guerrilla warfare and sponsored focos throughout the region. These projects, once only the product of Che's continental vision, now constituted a strategic element of Cuban foreign policy. According to Jon Lee Anderson, "The spreading guerrilla threat helped divert American pressure away from Cuba and simultaneously made Washington pay a high price for its regional containment policy."[31]

By March 1963, the CIA estimated that Cuba had provided training or political indoctrination to fifteen hundred to two thousand Latin Americans. The prospective guerrillas received training at clandestine camps and, of course, studied Che Guevara's *Guerrilla Warfare*. Representatives from every Latin American country had gone through training in Cuba. Several guerrilla groups in the field had already demonstrated particular strength, including Cuban-sponsored bands in Venezuela, Peru, and Colombia. Guerrilla groups also operated sporadically in Nicaragua and Guatemala, with a guerrilla potential emerging in Ecuador and Brazil, according to the CIA assessment.[32]

Although the guerrilla bands had only registered modest successes, Che did not lose faith in his strategy or select his targets more carefully. Instead of concentrating his revolutionary forces for an attack on the weakest regime, Che advocated warfare against all of them. In "Guerrilla Warfare: A Method,"

30. Anderson, *Che Guevara,* 393–97; C. Douglas Dillon (acting secretary of state) to American embassy, Havana, June 30, 1959, U.S. National Archives, record group 84, Diplomatic and Consular Post Records, Havana embassy, 320 Cuba-Nicaragua, box 3.
31. Anderson, *Che Guevara,* 533.
32. "Cuban Training of Latin American Subversives," March 27, 1963, memorandum, CIA, CIA Files, NSA.

published in 1963, Guevara advocated guerrilla warfare in every Latin American country, regardless of whether its government maintained any semblance of constitutionality. Armed struggle was not just *possible* in *some* Latin American countries; to Che, it was now *advisable* in *every* country. In *Guerrilla Warfare,* Che had rejected the possibility of waging guerrilla war against governments that maintained a constitutional facade. By 1963, Che had concluded that self-proclaimed democracies such as Chile simply disguised the dictatorships of the bourgeoisie. Citing Lenin again, Che urged revolutionaries not to forget the class character of allegedly democratic regimes. Those regimes, allied with imperialism, tried to maintain the dictatorship of the exploiting classes without resorting to force. "Thus," Che argued, "we must try to oblige the dictatorship to resort to violence, thereby unmasking its true nature as the dictatorship of the reactionary social classes."[33]

To those who held that there was still a peaceful road to power—among them members of some of the traditional Communist parties in Latin America—he argued that "violence is not the monopoly of the exploiters and as such the exploited can use it too." Then he invoked the revered name of José Martí to justify armed struggle in Latin America: "He who wages war in a country, when he can avoid it, is a criminal, just as he who fails to promote war which cannot be avoided is a criminal."[34]

Guevara directly attacked, just as Fidel had done in the Second Declaration of Havana, those who sat with "arms folded" while they waited for the objective conditions in Latin America to develop. When Castro initiated the armed struggle with an attack on the Moncada army barracks in Santiago, the PSP of Cuba denounced the "putschists and adventuristic activities of the bourgeois opposition."[35] Official Soviet doctrine held that the conditions for armed revolution, primarily the existence of a proletariat with a revolutionary consciousness, did not exist in Latin America. Hence, the Cuban Communists did not offer any support to Castro's rebel army until the summer of 1958, when the party dispatched Carlos Rafael Rodríguez to the Sierra Maestra as an observer and liaison, rather than combatant. Castro's military success, followed by his turn toward the Communists and the Soviet Union, so startled the Soviets that they, like their clients in the PSP, had to reevaluate their policies toward Latin America. The PSP and the Kremlin had great difficulty

33. Guevara, "Guerrilla Warfare: A Method," 189.
34. Ibid., 187.
35. *Daily Worker* (New York), August 10, 1953.

accepting the fact that Castro, not the Communist party, had led the Cuban Revolution.[36]

In *Guerrilla Warfare*, Che had not delineated the relationship between the guerrilla army and the Communist party, the latter of which, according to Moscow and its loyalists in the PSP, should lead the revolutionary struggle. In his 1963 article, Che clarified an argument that he had made by omission in his original work: the Communist party did not have an inherent right to lead the revolutionary struggle. "No one can solicit the role of vanguard of the party as if it were a diploma given by a university. To be the vanguard of the party means to be at the forefront of the working class through the struggle for achieving power."[37]

The guerrilla foco, in fact, could replace the party and fulfill the same mission. The guerrilla vanguard was the embryo of the people's army, party, and state. From the leadership of the guerrilla foco would emerge the political and military leaders who would seize power and initiate the revolutionary transition. In the course of commanding guerrilla armies, organizing mass organizations, raising funds, maintaining lines of communication and supply, spreading propaganda, and administering justice, revolutionary activists would gain valuable administrative experience that would serve them well in their capacity as the bureaucratic cadres of the revolutionary state.[38] Che obviously extracted this lesson from the Cuban experience, in which the top leadership of the guerrilla army, namely Fidel, Raúl, Che, Ramiro Valdés, and other guerrilla commanders assumed the top political positions in the revolutionary government. A government by guerrillas would follow revolutionary victory, in Che's strategic vision.

The members of the pro-Soviet Communist parties in Latin America believed that they had the right and duty to lead the revolutionary movement, but they did not advocate armed struggle, convinced that the accumulation of social and economic forces would generate a revolution at the appropriate time. The orthodox Communists had refused to promote the armed struggle on the pretext that "conditions are not yet mature."[39] Che could not tolerate such passivity, nor could he respect the Communist claim to the revolutionary vanguard. From Marx and Lenin he had learned that it

36. Szulc, *Fidel*, 453; H. Thomas, *Cuban Revolution*, 486–87; Geyer, *Guerrilla Prince*, 248–49; Quirk, *Fidel*, 396–402; Bourne, *Fidel*, 234–35.
37. Guevara, "Guerrilla Warfare: A Method," 151.
38. Ibid., 156.
39. Lowy, *Marxism of Che Guevara*, 19–20.

was not enough to interpret the world; one had to change it. Observing the development of objective conditions would not necessarily change them in favorable ways. People had to act on those conditions, following the Marxist position that "circumstances make men as much as men make circumstances." Lenin had proved that a revolutionary vanguard could act as a historical catalyst and accelerate the transition from one society to the next. In Che's worldview, individuals make their own history, not exactly as they would like, but under given conditions.[40]

One must keep in mind that Che promoted the creation of a revolutionary party in Cuba by uniting the old PSP with the M-26-7 and other organizations. He definitely saw a need for a party organization, but he opposed any orthodox party that adopted strategies imposed by the Soviet Union or that were culled from a traditional interpretation of Marx or Lenin. The Cuban revolutionaries could learn from general rules of political organization and historical experiences, but Che refused to submit to foreign mandates. He had learned Marxism-Leninism as a means of analysis rather than as a blueprint for revolution that other Communist parties had to adopt without modification. If revolutionaries looked to Marx or Lenin for eternal truths about Latin America, they would not find any, for neither man had studied the region. Marx, Che had written in 1960, had made some disparaging comments about the Mexicans, based on some unacceptable racial theories. Marxism, Guevara believed, could only work in Latin America if revolutionaries modified and applied it to the unique circumstances of time and place.[41]

Che assumed that socialism in Cuba and revolutionary movements in Latin America would develop with unique characteristics, shaped by unique historical, geographical, social, and cultural factors. Communism in Cuba and revolutionary movements in Latin America would dance to a different rhythm, the beat of the tropics. Even if Che could not dance, he would not let the Soviets' temperate orthodoxy stifle Cuba's youthful enthusiasm. The Cubans had made a revolution when the Soviet theoreticians rejected armed struggle, and they would continue to make their revolution with *pachanga,* as Che liked to say. The Cuban revolutionaries, unfettered by Communist orthodoxy, happily optimistic in "an atmosphere of a socialist carnival," would have to make their own mistakes.[42]

40. Ibid.
41. Ibid., 13; Guevara, "Notes for the Study of the Ideology of the Cuban Revolution," October 8, 1960, in Guevara, *Che: Selected Works,* 49.
42. Karol, *Guerrillas in Power,* 43; Dumont, *Cuba,* 87 (quoted).

Like Lenin, Che believed that the passage of societies through the stages of history could be accelerated. The passage from capitalism to socialism, Lenin realized, was not simply a mechanical process that would occur when the objective conditions for such a transition had been generated by the internal contradictions of capitalist society. Lenin had acted as a catalyst for revolutionary change, taking power and initiating a socialist revolution under the most unfavorable circumstances, including imperialist aggression. From Lenin's experience Che deduced that societies did not have to pass through all the historical stages identified by Marx. The vanguard could shorten or even skip some of the stages of history, as they had done in Cuba.[43]

The Cuban leaders had done this because they had developed a revolutionary consciousness before they took power. Like Lenin, Castro had acted as the catalyst for the new society, leading the people with his spirit of sacrifice and courage. If Latin American revolutionaries would simply follow the Cuban example and launch guerrilla fronts with or without the support of the Communist party, they would be revolutionized by the experience and develop a socialist consciousness during the course of a guerrilla campaign. In Che's mind, the guerrilla army and experience could fill the role previously reserved by the Communist party for its intellectual leaders. Che saw no valid reasons why the guerrilla army and its leaders could not serve simultaneously as the political and military leaders of the revolutionary struggle. As the combatants fought, they would learn more about the needs and interests of the peasants and proletariat. Che believed that a socialist consciousness would develop in the act of rebellion itself, a position that negated the raison d'être of the Communist party intellectuals.[44]

Guevara's intellectual opponents argued that consciousness emerged only when a certain stage in the mode of production had been reached. They rejected Che's idea that the Cuban Revolution could "skip some steps" in the inevitable flow of history, even though the M-26-7 had done just that by fighting Batista's army when the PSP still collaborated with the dictator.[45] Che felt that the old Communists still had not learned the obvious lessons of the revolution; some of them were still wondering how and to what extent Fidel had initiated a socialist revolution. To Che, the explanation was rather

43. Guevara, "Discurso en la Asamblea General de Trabajadores de la Textilera Ariguanabo," March 24, 1963, in Guevara, *Ernesto Che Guevara: Escritos y discursos*, 7:49.
44. Ibid., 43–44; Guevara, "The Role of a Marxist-Leninist Party," in Guevara, *Che: Selected Works*, 104–45.
45. In August 1960, Guevara had a tense argument with René Dumont, a French Marxist, about the stages of history. See Dumont, *Cuba*, 50–53.

simple: "a socialist character was acquired through a conscious act, thanks to the knowledge acquired by the leaders, the deepening of the masses' consciousness, and the correlation of forces in the world."[46]

Che Guevara, therefore, viewed the guerrilla foco as a political, military, and intellectual catalyst, a revolutionary agent that would transform the country as it transformed the combatants. He endowed the foco with powers bordering on the spiritual. It would embolden the timid, empower the powerless, and weaken the powerful. The spiritual energy generated by the foco transcended and ultimately invalidated the doctrines of the armchair revolutionaries, imprisoned by their self-imposed obsession with objectivity. If, as Fidel had proclaimed in the Second Declaration of Havana, the duty of revolutionaries was to make revolution, true revolutionaries simply had to launch a guerrilla foco and keep it alive long enough for it to generate those mystical forces that Che associated with it. The guerrillas just had to observe the three fundamental rules of "constant mobility, constant vigilance, [and] constant distrust." The fighting would gradually expand and the popular forces would gain enough strength to take the war from the countryside to the city, where they would eventually triumph over the forces of repression.[47]

Despite Che's emphasis on the guerrilla foco, he insisted that other forms of struggle could also contribute to revolutionary victories. Critics had already charged that Che dismissed the contributions that other forms of mass struggle could make to the revolution, such as organizing labor unions, political demonstrations, general strikes, or boycotts. Che insisted that guerrilla warfare and mass struggle are not mutually exclusive strategic concepts. "Guerrilla warfare is a people's war; to attempt to carry out this type of war without the population's support is the prelude to inevitable disaster." However, the guerrilla foco possessed more power and potential than any mass organization. The struggle of the masses through traditional political methods could never lead to ultimate victory. Given that (a) the objective of revolutionary warfare was the seizure of power, and (b) the enemy would fight to retain power, logic dictated that the revolutionaries must form a people's army, the only instrument with which they could take power and destroy the oppressor army.[48]

Unfortunately for aspiring revolutionary strategists, Che did not explain the appropriate strategy and tactics for the second and third stages of his rev-

46. Guevara, "On the Budgetary System," in Guevara, *Che: Selected Works,* 113.
47. Guevara, "Guerrilla Warfare: A Method," 158.
48. Ibid., 156.

olutionary campaign. "Guerrilla Warfare: A Method" reiterated the basic strategic concepts that applied primarily to the initial stages of Guevara's campaign,
emphasizing the defensive rather than offensive aspects of guerrilla warfare.
He still did not explain how the people's army would encircle and take the
cities in the final stage of the insurrection. In Che's description of the final
offensive, he only hinted that the rebel army would retain some of its guerrilla character, even when it operated as would a conventional army. "In the
final stage, the concept of maneuver is introduced. Large units attack strong
points. But this war of maneuver does not replace guerrilla fighting; rather it
is only one form of action taken by the guerrillas."[49] Unlike Mao, however,
he did not elaborate on the use of guerrilla tactics by conventional armies, one
of the Chinese leader's greatest contributions to revolutionary theory.

Because Che placed so much emphasis on the formation of guerrilla focos
with only thirty to fifty combatants, he is popularly associated with foco theory or *foquismo*. Accordingly, a well-directed guerrilla nucleus, linked to the
people, could serve as the catalyst for a mass political movement. Guevara
did not introduce foco theory. He often referred to the *foco insurreccional,*
but he never advocated a theory of anything. Che was a strategist, not a theorist. Other theorists, extrapolating from and often misrepresenting Che,
among them most notably Régis Debray, created foco theory and credited
Che with the original concept. Debray provided the most complete elabora-
tion of foquismo in *Revolution in the Revolution?* (1967) with Castro's blessing and assistance. Che, however, did not contribute to the book nor did he
ever endorse it. He actually criticized it and Debray. He read Debray's book
for the first time during his final campaign in Bolivia.[50] Che wrote extensive,
critical commentaries in the margins of the book, giving evidence that he dis-
agreed with this author who invoked his name without permission. Guevara
did not regard Debray as his equal, nor did he appreciate his skills as a combatant, though Debray served Guevara as a courier and as an advance scout.
Debray borrowed liberally from Che's writings on guerrilla warfare to establish himself as a guerrilla theorist, but he did not represent Guevara. Indeed,
he misrepresented Guevarism because he said little, if anything, about the tricontinental strategy. In doing so, he exaggerated the revolutionary potential
of the guerrilla foco to a dangerous degree. On close inspection—a view
beyond the objective of this analysis—substantial differences are revealed

49. Ibid., 160.
50. Guevara, *Bolivian Diary,* 171; Anderson, *Che Guevara,* 717.

between the foquismo propagated by Debray and Guevarism in its full and final expression.[51]

Régis Debray developed foco theory into the official strategic doctrine of the Cuban Revolution under the direct guidance of Fidel Castro in 1966. Debray obviously incorporated some of the strategic doctrines of Guevara, emphasizing the potential of the guerrilla vanguard and minimizing the role of the Communist party as the leader of the mass struggle. Although both Debray and Guevara advocated mass struggle, Debray's emphasis on the foco reduced Guevarism to its simplest terms, turning a complex strategy for international revolution into an unrealistic military strategy called "foco theory." Guevara did not introduce foco theory. Neither it nor Debray offered him much help against the Bolivian army. In any case, whatever merits or flaws Debray's *Revolution in the Revolution?* might have, it is not an accurate reflection of Che's strategic thinking.[52] Debray says nothing about the tricontinental strategy that was central to Guevara's military plans.

Che argued repeatedly that the guerrilla foco represented only the first stage of a protracted revolutionary campaign. The foco and the war would grow until the campaign acquired the characteristics of a conventional army and struggle, with final victory always coming as the product of a regular army's fighting a war of positions and destroying the enemy army. To maximize the chances of widespread success, Guevara advocated guerrilla focos in every country. One isolated guerrilla foco would face the concentrated power of the United States and a puppet army; several guerrilla focos, challenging American imperialism simultaneously, would compel the United States to divide, and consequently weaken, its forces. The continental dimensions of Guevara's guerrilla strategy gave each guerrilla foco a greater military threat than it would have if it operated in isolation. The more fronts we open, Guevara argued, the more difficult we will make it for the imperialists and the greater will be our chances of success.[53]

"The Yankees will intervene due to solidarity of interest and because the struggle in Latin America is decisive," Che claimed. Given the certainty of

51. Childs, "An Historical Critique." While I take issue with Childs's argument that there is no difference between Guevarism, *foquismo,* and Fidelismo, I have little quarrel with his theses about the evolution of foco theory.

52. Peter Worsley, "Revolutionary Theory: Guevara and Debray," in Huberman and Sweezy, eds., *Régis Debray and the Latin American Revolution,* 131.

53. Guevara, "Discurso clausura de la Semana de Solidaridad con Viet Nam del Sur," December 20, 1963, in Guevara, *Ernesto Che Guevara: Escritos y discursos,* 9:247–48.

Yankee intervention, Che saw no viable alternative to a coordinated continental campaign. No revolutionary movement could take and consolidate power if it operated in isolation. The United States supported a continental network of oppressive governments, with armies at its service. "The unity of the repressive forces must be confronted with the unity of the popular forces," Guevara asserted.[54]

Guevara's continental ambitions constituted an integral part of his revolutionary strategy. His emphasis on creating the initial guerrilla foco never implied the advocacy of a minor military front in an isolated region of one country; he advocated guerrilla fronts in every Latin American country, part of a coordinated strategy sponsored by Cuba's Liberation Department. In fact, Guevara advocated guerrilla warfare throughout the developing world—his revolutionary ambitions and strategic vision extended far beyond the hemisphere. A soldier of the Americas when he left Buenos Aires in 1952, he became a soldier of the international proletariat before he left Cuba mysteriously in 1965. Between those two dates, Che's strategic concepts evolved from the continental to the global. As he gained fame as the originator of guerrilla warfare in Latin America, revolutionaries in Africa and Asia wanted to hear what he had to say too.

54. Guevara, "Guerrilla Warfare: A Method," 157.

EIGHT THE TRICONTINENTAL STRATEGY

On the evening of August 9, 1961, 150 journalists showed up for Che Guevara's press conference, held during the Organization of American States meeting in Montevideo, Uruguay. The day before, he had delivered a scathing indictment of President John F. Kennedy's Alliance for Progress, an enticing $20-billion development package that only one of the Latin American delegates, Che Guevara, had dared to criticize. The American delegation had dismissed the content of Guevara's speech as a "pack of lies," but the rest of the world apparently enjoyed his performance. In his wrinkled fatigues and trademark beret, Che provided the press corps with the most colorful photo opportunities and story lines of the entire conference. Women longed for a glimpse of him, young men wanted to be like him, and political opponents wanted to assassinate him. The *New York Times* reported that the "eloquent and intelligent Argentine-Cuban is stealing the show."[1] Che delivered another impressive performance, answering a wide range of tough questions about Cuban politics, economic policy, and commercial relations. One of the reporters broke the trend and asked Che about his personal life: "How do you live? What do you eat? Do you drink? Do you smoke? And—if the ladies will pardon me—do you like women?"[2]

---

1. "Cuba at Punta del Este," *New York Times*, August 17, 1961.
2. Juan de Onis, "U.S. Aides at Uruguay Parley Shunning Clash with Cubans," *New*

Guevara responded: "I would stop being a man if I did not like women. Now, I would also stop being a revolutionary if I did not comply with just one of my duties as a revolutionary." He went on to explain that he worked sixteen to eighteen hours a day and slept no more than six hours a night. He never had time to go out to a nightclub or restaurant; he simply had no time for fun. Guevara suddenly turned serious and reflected on the personal sacrifices he had made for the revolution. "I am convinced that I have a mission to fulfill in this world, and on the altar of this mission I have to sacrifice my home, I have to sacrifice all the pleasures of daily life, I have to sacrifice my personal security, and I might even have to sacrifice my life."[3]

Che's few personal friends knew that he had long considered it his destiny to fight and possibly die on behalf of the people's "authentic revolution." He served the revolution diligently as president of the National Bank and as minister of industry, but in private conversations, he often talked about commanding another guerrilla campaign. He was still "howling like a man possessed," eager to fight against imperialism from any trench. His talk about guerrilla warfare did not merely reflect nostalgia for a happier time; his close comrades expected him to return to the field and they expected to go with him—anytime, anywhere. Service in the Cuban bureaucracy had not changed Che's character or his ambitions; he still thought of himself as a man of action who would fulfill his destiny fighting for the authentic revolution.[4]

Che viewed guerrilla warfare not so much as a subject for theoretical debate but as the most effective strategy to achieve his desired end: the destruction of imperialism. He intended to command one front in the anti-imperialist war, and he expected all true revolutionaries to enlist in the army, regardless of policies emanating from Moscow or Beijing. In the battle between capitalism and communism, Che allowed no compromise, retreats, or fear. Guevara's strategy placed him squarely in opposition to the Soviet policy of peaceful coexistence, but that won him few points with Moscow's ideological adversaries in Beijing. Intense international rivalry between the United States and the Soviet Union and, more important, between the Soviet Union and China, restrained Guevara's efforts to forge an alliance of African, Asian, and Latin American anti-imperialists. The success of his mission, however,

York Times, August 10, 1961; "Conferencia de prensa de Montevideo, Uruguay," August 9, 1961, in Guevara, *Ernesto Che Guevara: Escritos y discursos,* 9:118.

3. "Conferencia de prensa de Montevideo, Uruguay," August 9, 1961, in Guevara, *Ernesto Che Guevara: Escritos y discursos,* 9:118.

4. Deutschmann, *Che,* 116; Angel Gómez Trueba, interview by author, Havana, November 26, 1996; Rojo, *My Friend Che,* 152–53; Gambini, *El Che Guevara,* 299.

required military and economic support from the recalcitrant Soviets and the intractable Chinese, not to mention Fidel, Raúl, Manuel Piñeiro, and revolutionaries on three continents. Against overwhelming odds Che attempted to organize a covert network linking La Paz, Havana, Algiers, Brazzaville, Dar es Salaam, Prague, Moscow, and Beijing. Once established, this network would launch or support guerrilla bands in Africa and Latin America and increase support to the Vietnamese revolutionaries, who had illuminated the path of struggle that Che now advocated on three continents simultaneously.

This tricontinental strategy, based on the assumptions that revolutionaries on three continents would fight and the imperialists would not fight long, is the essence of Guevarism, a strategy—as opposed to a theory—designed to attack, exhaust, and ultimately overthrow imperialism. Che began to articulate this strategy in the early 1960s, long before his famous "Message to the Tricontinental" (1967) popularized the doctrine. Although that message represents the fullest explanation of his global strategy, the transcontinental parameters of his revolutionary strategies had surfaced in his earlier works. He did not *develop* into an international revolutionary; he *was already* an international revolutionary when he landed in Cuba in 1956, a soldier of the Americas. He gradually expanded his horizons until they encompassed the entire developing world. In speeches and articles throughout the 1960s, Che linked the Cuban struggle to the Asian, African, and Latin American liberation movements; he saw their participants as allies in Cuba's struggle against American imperialism. Given that imperialism operated on a global scale, revolutionaries would have to fight it in a global campaign. Hence, Guevara always advocated a fighting alliance between all those who sought to liberate their countries from American imperialism.

The anti-imperialist war consumed Che and ultimately led to his departure from Cuba. Having consolidated the Cuban Revolution and initiated the revolutionary programs, he grew frustrated. He couldn't waste any time in the Cuban bureaucracy while revolutionaries fought the war he wanted to command. Given his global ambitions, it should not be surprising that he grew impatient in his late thirties. Guevara himself had noted in *Guerrilla Warfare* that the ideal age for combatants was twenty-five to thirty-five. Although he was, by his own definition, past his prime, Castro thought that he was still in top mental and physical condition.[5] Che Guevara's return to the battlefield was only a question of when and where.

---

5. Deutschmann, *Che,* 117; Guevara, *Guerrilla Warfare,* 85.

By the spring of 1962 Che had begun to plot his return. A master chess player, he easily conceptualized long-term strategies, taking into account his moves as well as the options available to his opponents. Che exhibited his mental agility during the Congolese campaign in 1965, when he challenged one of his men to a chess match, with the caveat that he would play blind, sitting with his back to the board. Che called out his moves and Dogna, his opponent, called out his own as he shifted the pieces around the board. Che lost that match, but he got his revenge playing the same way the following day, mating Dogna in twenty-five moves.[6]

Che first plotted a return to his native Argentina in 1962, when he brought several groups of Argentine revolutionaries to Cuba for training. The recruits included Jorge Masetti, a journalist; Ciro Roberto Bustos, a painter; and his old friend Alberto Granado, who helped to recruit guerrillas in Argentina. Masetti graduated from a military school with the rank of captain and then completed several covert missions to Prague and Algeria. "Stealthily, Che was setting up the chessboard for his game of continental guerrilla war, the ultimate prize being his homeland," according to Jon Lee Anderson. "At the right time, each group would be mobilized to take its place in a united army in the Argentine campaign under Che's command."[7]

Che monitored political developments in Argentina to determine when conditions would favor the initiation of his guerrilla campaign. The military overthrew reformist president Arturo Frondizi in March 1962 and subsequently broke relations with Cuba. Che anticipated a reactionary crackdown on progressive movements, particularly on the Peronist party, a development that might favor a guerrilla campaign. An Argentine naval uprising in April 1963 revealed a serious split within the military, further evidence to Che that the objective conditions favored revolutionary action. By this time, Masetti and the Argentine guerrillas had received extensive military training in Algeria with the support of Che's personal friend Ahmed Ben Bella, who had led the campaign against French colonialism. After seven months in Algeria, Bella arranged to transport Masetti and his men to South America. Che had ordered Masetti to train at a rearguard base in Bolivia and survey the area of operations in Argentina while he waited for Che to come and take command of offensive operations.[8]

6. Testimony of Dogna, in Taibo, Escobar, and Guerra, *El año en que estuvimos en ninguna parte*, 86–88.
7. Castañeda, *Compañero*, 248–49; Anderson, *Che Guevara*, 540.
8. Anderson, *Che Guevara*, 541–43.

In June 1963, soon after Masetti established his Bolivian base, he violated Che's orders and marched into Argentine territory. The election of a civilian president, Dr. Arturo Illia, on July 7 did not deter Masetti. Operating under the nom de guerre of Major Segundo—a title and a name that implied the existence of a first major (Che)—he published a manifesto denouncing Illia for collaborating with the military. Masetti subsequently returned to Bolivia, but the move into Argentina, followed by his manifesto, had already alerted the Argentine and Bolivian security forces to the presence of his guerrilla band. In late 1963, Che ordered Masetti to do no more than explore the area of operations until Che arrived. Nevertheless, Masetti decided to initiate operations in February 1964. The Argentine secret police infiltrated the band, and the army located the guerrillas' base. By mid-April, the foco had been liquidated. Che lost one of his former bodyguards, Hermes Peña, and Masetti disappeared, presumed dead.[9]

The destruction of the Argentine foco shocked Che. He lost personal friends and comrades in arms, and even he had to question the guerrilla strategy he had advocated. Alberto Granado caught Che reflecting on the news of Masetti's disappearance. Che grumbled, "Here you see me, behind a desk, fucked, while my people die during missions I've sent them on."[10]

Che realized that he could not long delay his return to the battlefield. In his writings on guerrilla warfare, he had tried to explain how and why revolutionaries should fight imperialism. He had written the battle plan, after all, and he felt compelled by his convictions to command the armies at the front. He did not expect to destroy imperialism with one miraculous blow delivered from a remote Bolivian hamlet; he intended to shake imperialism to its foundations by launching guerrilla focos throughout Africa, Asia, and Latin America, threatening to deprive the imperialists of vital resources and markets. The imperialists would have to intervene militarily, but they could not sustain prolonged counterinsurgency campaigns on three continents. The more fronts we open, Che argued in 1963, the "greater will be our chances of success."[11]

Che Guevara devoted the last three years of his life to the formation of a tricontinental anti-imperialist front, supported by the two Communist giants, China and the Soviet Union. He envisioned much more than a political union

9. Ibid., 573–79, 587–94.
10. Ibid., 594.
11. Guevara, "Discurso clausura de la Semana de Solidaridad con Viet Nam del Sur," December 20, 1963, in Guevara, *Ernesto Che Guevara: Escritos y discursos*, 9:247–48.

of developing countries; he advocated a revolutionary alliance that transcended national boundaries, coordinating conventional and unconventional armies engaged in a global struggle against imperialism. Moreover, he expected the Soviet Union and China to put their political controversies aside and direct the revolutionary movement that they both claimed to lead. With the Communist superpowers coordinating the global campaign, each one of Guevara's little guerrilla focos would assume a strength far beyond its numbers, for the focos formed part of a tricontinental strategy backed by conventional armies and nuclear missiles.

Whatever merits Che Guevara had as a strategist, he certainly lacked the magical powers required to heal the deep rift between the Soviet Union and China. In 1964 the cold war between Moscow and Beijing turned red hot, and both the Soviets and Chinese demanded allegiance from their revolutionary comrades in Latin America. Although Cuban support for guerrilla movements in rural Latin America fell in line with Mao's conception of protracted revolutionary war, the Cubans received most of their military and economic assistance from the Soviet Union, not China, leaving them vulnerable to Soviet pressure.

Fidel Castro recognized these political realities and tried to find a comfortable middle ground with the Soviets. The first sign of a Cuban compromise came in May 1963, when Castro and Nikita Khrushchev reached an agreement on Latin American policy. Although Castro endorsed the Moscow line that the "export of revolution was contradictory to Marxism-Leninism," he also won Soviet recognition of the right of peoples to choose the path of armed struggle. Khrushchev and Castro agreed that "the practical forms and methods of the struggle for socialism in each country are to be worked out by the people of that country."[12] In exchange, the Cubans only recognized the *possibility* of a peaceful road to socialism. Che and Fidel remained convinced that the armed struggle represented the only realistic path to power, and despite Soviet opposition, they continued to promote revolution in Latin America.[13]

Latin America's Communist parties, however, opposed the armed struggle and complained repeatedly to the Soviet Union about Cuban interference in their internal affairs. The Soviets feared that Cuban subversion would

12. Crain, "The Course of the Cuban Heresy," 57.

13. Suárez, *Cuba*, 179; Jackson, *Castro, the Kremlin, and Communism*, 21–22; testimony of Castro, in Blight, Allyn, and Welch, *Cuba on the Brink*, 245; CIA, Director of Central Intelligence, "Situation and Prospects in Cuba," NIE Number 85-63, document no. 03127, Cuban Missile Crisis Collection, NSA.

drag them into an unwanted confrontation with the United States. During Castro's visit to the Soviet Union in January 1964, the Soviets apparently extracted a major concession from Fidel, who had come to them in desperate need of a commercial agreement. Castro got what he needed the most, a Soviet agreement to purchase Cuban sugar at inflated prices. In return, Castro signed a joint communiqué with Khrushchev in which he advocated relations with the United States "based on the principles of peaceful coexistence between states with different social regimes."[14]

"To Che, the term 'peaceful coexistence' was anathema," Jon Lee Anderson argues.[15] Castro's assent constituted an explicit endorsement of that Soviet policy. Fidel had apparently broken with China and his good comrade Che Guevara, the intellectual founder of Latin America's scattered guerrilla bands. Castro's pledge represented only rhetoric—not reality—for he did not agree to withdraw rebels already in the field. Still, Castro's appeasement of Moscow opened a breach between Fidel and Che and between Cuba and China. Castro, the political pragmatist, was attempting to safeguard the Cuban Revolution by sacrificing political principles that Che could never surrender. To the extent that Castro would actually practice the Soviet policy of peaceful coexistence, he would undermine Guevara's tricontinental strategy and alienate his best comandante.

By this time, many Soviet intelligence agents had already labeled Che a Maoist. To conclude that Che fit this mold, one had only to read his published works on guerrilla warfare. His advocacy of a war without quarter and his emphasis on rural guerrilla warfare linked him directly to Mao. To determine Che's political orientation, the KGB assigned an agent to spy on him; Chinese agents tagged him as well.[16] Just as he was plotting his return to the battlefield, Che found himself at the center of the Cold War and the Sino-Soviet dispute, pulled apart, suspected, and harassed by American, Soviet, and Chinese agents. He repeatedly rejected Soviet accusations that he was a Maoist, but he could not deny that his strategy followed the Chinese line. Although the Soviets respected his revolutionary commitment, he was, if not a Maoist, certainly a nuisance. "Anything to the left of the Soviet line was considered pro-Chinese and pro-Trotskyite," one Soviet analyst recalled.[17]

---

14. Halperin, *Taming of Fidel Castro*, 21.
15. Anderson, *Che Guevara*, 587.
16. Castañeda, *Compañero*, 252–53.
17. Testimony of Kiva Maidanek, cited in Anderson, *Che Guevara*, 581.

If Guevara did not embrace the Maoist line, he certainly did not endorse the policy of peaceful coexistence. In July 1964, through a *New York Times* reporter, Fidel offered to terminate Cuban support for Latin American guerrilla groups if the United States ceased its hostile actions against Cuba. He evidently hoped that Cuba could normalize relations with the United States, particularly if Lyndon Baines Johnson defeated Barry Goldwater in the upcoming presidential elections. Shortly after Fidel extended the olive branch, Guevara condemned the offer. Claiming that history had demonstrated repeatedly that nobody could "play" with imperialism, Che argued that Cuba's fundamental task was "to fight against imperialism wherever it shows its face and with all the arms we can muster. The name of the man supposedly elected by the North American people every four years does not matter."[18]

If Castro intended to drive Cuba toward the Soviet line and peaceful coexistence with the United States, Che's belligerent speech left no doubt that Fidel would not take Comandante Guevara with him. As it happened, the U.S. State Department quickly rejected Castro's overtures. Fidel, who had never really terminated Cuba's revolutionary activities anyway, then returned to Che Guevara's line of global confrontation. Over the next three years, Castro would vacillate between appeasement and confrontation, his moves reflecting the extent to which the Soviets exerted their military, diplomatic, and economic influence on Cuba. While Castro may have preferred Guevara's combative posture, Cuba's dependence on Soviet assistance prevented Fidel from pursuing Che's militant line. Castro could always use Guevara's guerrilla bands as leverage in his relations with the Soviets and Americans.

In a strange convergence of strategic interests, the Soviet Union and the United States agreed that Cuba should not promote revolution in the hemisphere. The Soviets publicly denounced Guevarism in the journal *Kommunist*, a theoretical outlet for the Soviet Communist party, in July and August 1964. The Soviets flatly rejected Guevara's theory that subjective factors could accelerate the revolutionary process and warned against premature acts that would sabotage the popular front strategies of Latin America's Communist parties. The Soviets did not even endorse the armed struggle against brutal dictatorships, maintaining that progressive forces could advance their revolutionary objectives through several other means of struggle. In Venezuela and Guatemala, where guerrilla bands had already been established, the Soviets still advocated political struggle behind a broad, anti-imperialist front, mean-

18. Guevara, "Discurso en la inauguración de la INPUD, Santa Clara, July 14, 1964," in Guevara, *Ernesto Che Guevara: Escritos y discursos,* 8:141 (my translation).

ing the formation of alliances with the bourgeoisie and even with reformist military factions.[19]

In November 1964, Guevara made his final attempt to convince the Soviets to support new guerrilla fronts in Latin America and Africa. Less than a month earlier, Leonid Brezhnev had replaced Khrushchev in a silent coup, but the same skepticism about Cuba's revolutionary strategy still prevailed in the Kremlin.[20] Latin American Communists, led by Victorio Codovilla of Argentina and Mario Monje of Bolivia, had complained to the Soviet Union about Cuban intervention in their internal affairs. The Soviets maintained that the objective conditions did not favor armed struggle, and Che wanted to convince them otherwise. Vitali Korionov, deputy chief of the Soviet Central Committee's Americas Department, listened incredulously to Guevara's revolutionary strategy. He concluded that Che and Fidel proposed nothing less than a continental insurrection, envisioning themselves as the heirs of the great South American liberator, Simón Bolívar. Korionov informed Che that because the Latin American Communists opposed the strategy, the Soviet Union could not endorse the plan either. Korionov suspected that Che would pursue the armed struggle against imperialism anyway, even without Soviet support. Che had always advocated war against imperialism, and he would not compromise or postpone his plans to launch revolutionary movements in Latin America.[21]

Thus, when Communist party leaders from Latin America convened in Havana to discuss revolutionary strategy in late November, Che did not participate. The Chinese did not attend either; they had not been invited. The pro-Soviet delegates surprisingly agreed to provide "active support" to insurgents in Venezuela, Guatemala, Honduras, Colombia, Paraguay, and Haiti. Targeting six countries for revolution represented a significant concession by the Soviets, but the "hit list" still fell far short of Guevara's expectations. In "Guerrilla Warfare: A Method," Che had advocated armed struggle against *every* Latin American government, not just the six regimes specified in the Havana resolution.[22]

19. Crain, "Course of the Cuban Heresy," 78–82.

20. *Hoy,* November 14, 1964; *Hoy,* November 19, 1964; Thompson, *Khrushchev,* 268–78.

21. Karol, *Guerrillas in Power,* 330–32; Angel Gómez Trueba, interview by author, Havana, November 26, 1996; Anderson, *Che Guevara,* 595–97, 612–15; "Entrevista desde Moscu para el Diario El Popular, de Montevideo," November 12, 1964, in Guevara, *Ernesto Che Guevara: Escritos y discursos,* 9:282.

22. Thomas L. Hughes to secretary of state, Jan. 22, 1965; George C. Denney Jr. to acting secretary of state, April 8, 1965, box 31, Cuba Country File, National Security Files,

While the Communists celebrated a bureaucratic compromise, Che delivered an inflammatory denunciation of imperialism in a November 30 speech in Santiago, far from the tepid Communists he loathed more than ever. He had come to Santiago to inaugurate a factory, a ritual he had performed countless times. After delivering the standard praise for Cuban industry, he launched into an attack on American imperialism. Six days earlier, Belgian paratroopers transported in American planes had rescued Belgian and American hostages held by Algerian-backed rebels in Stanleyville in the Belgian Congo.[23] The American intervention outraged Che, who considered the loss a setback for all revolutionaries, including those Communist ideologues in Havana who debated endlessly about armed struggle in one continent. Che identified with the fighters of the wars of national liberation in Asia and Africa. The Americans had demonstrated a bestiality that knew no frontiers, he claimed, and revolutionaries had to respond in kind. He explained that "against this class of hyenas one cannot have anything but hatred, there can be nothing other than extermination. And when patriots of the Congo or from any other country of the world take hold of the people who mercilessly assassinated thousands of unhappy women, children, and elderly men who had not participated in the battle, we must remember!"[24]

Few Cuban officials and fewer Latin American Communists shared Guevara's passion, sympathy, and outrage. Che wanted vengeance. However, he began to realize that he could not fulfill his mission as an official representative of Cuba; he would have to carry out his duties as an international renegade. He knew that Castro supported him, but Soviet opposition to his allegedly "Maoist" policies hurt Cuba's relations with the Soviet Union, threatening the survival of the revolution. Che could no longer tolerate, and Cuba could not long withstand, Soviet pressure to adopt orthodox Communist policies. Fidel could not commit himself completely to the anti-imperialist war that Che intended to wage. Fidel could offer Che covert support, including funds, recruits, supplies, training, and safe haven, but he needed to maintain a deniable distance from Che. Otherwise, Cuba would pay a heavy price

Lyndon Baines Johnson Library, Austin, Texas (hereafter NSF, LBJ); Jackson, *Castro, the Kremlin, and Communism,* 28–29; Crain, "Course of the Cuban Heresy," 62–69; Anderson, *Che Guevara,* 615; Duncan, *Soviet Union and Cuba,* 61–65; Guevara, "Guerrilla Warfare: A Method," 189.

23. Gleijeses, "'Flee! The White Giants Are Coming!'" 228.

24. Guevara, "Discurso en la conmemoración del 30 de Noviembre," November 30, 1964, in Guevara, *Ernesto Che Guevara: Escritos y discursos,* 8:233.

for Guevara's international gambits. Che and Fidel recognized this new political reality. Thus, Che offered his resignation to Fidel sometime after he returned from the Soviet Union on November 19, 1964. Fidel could not keep Che in Cuba against his wishes and had no choice but to accept the resignation. Both men agreed to keep it secret while Che embarked on an extended international mission to determine when and where he would return to the battlefront.[25]

Che Guevara did not leave Cuba because of a violent disagreement with Fidel or Raúl. The Castro brothers did not force Guevara out of Cuba because his policies had failed. When he left Cuba, first for the Congo and then for Bolivia, he did so with Fidel's blessing and support, the best and strongest indication that Cuba secretly favored Guevara's covert campaigns. The Cubans subsequently welcomed the aura of mystery that surrounded Guevara's departure, but Che always intended to return to the battlefield whenever circumstances permitted. He never intended to grow old and die in Cuba as a bureaucrat or a pathetic icon of former guerrilla glory. By the end of 1964, Che and Fidel concurred that the time had come. Fidel agreed to dispatch Che on a three-month foreign mission to New York, Africa, and China, under cover of an official Cuban mission. Secretly, Che attempted to form a tricontinental fighting front while he analyzed prospects for waging guerrilla war in central Africa.

If anybody in the American intelligence community wanted to predict Guevara's next guerrilla venture, Che's speeches offered them numerous clues. In his speech to the United Nations General Assembly on December 11, Guevara did not disguise his interest in African liberation. Wearing his traditional olive green fatigues and an unbuttoned jacket, Che proclaimed, "The hour of doom for colonialism has struck and millions of inhabitants of Africa, Asia, and Latin America are rising up to face a new life and making good their unrestricted right to self-determination and the independent development of their nations."[26]

He referred to the "tragic case of the Congo" as an example of "how the rights of peoples can be flouted with absolute impunity and the most insolent cynicism." The world had protested the German occupation of Belgium during World War II, but when the sons of those Belgian patriots murdered

---

25. Anderson, *Che Guevara*, 615–16; Castañeda, *Compañero*, 274–75.
26. Guevara, "Colonialism Is Doomed," in Guevara, *Che: Selected Works*, 334.

the Congolese, the world was silent, primarily because the Belgians had killed black people "in the name of the white race, just as they had suffered under the German heel because their blood was not sufficiently Aryan." In response to the racist attacks of imperialist "hyenas" and "jackals," Che urged "all free men . . . to avenge the Congo crime."[27]

If Che expressed the official position of the Cuban government, his belligerence hinted at international war, with Cuba allying with all nations fighting imperialism, colonialism, and neocolonialism. "The hour of doom for colonialism has struck," and Cuba's duty was to assist its Latin American neighbors in their efforts to throw off the "colonial yoke of the United States."[28] To make the dream of liberation a reality, Guevara offered to make the ultimate sacrifice: "I would be prepared to give my life for the liberation of any of the Latin American countries without asking anything of anyone, without demanding anything, without exploiting anyone."[29]

While in New York, Che met secretly with Senator Eugene McCarthy to discuss prospects for peace with the United States, a diplomatic gesture seemingly incompatible with his militant speech. Yet he had also enumerated the conditions for peace during his United Nations speech, and now he secretly awaited an American response. The Cubans had initiated the contact through Lisa Howard, a journalist who had acted as a go-between in secret negotiations between the Kennedy administration and Castro a year before. Evidently, Castro hoped to resume these talks, which had been aimed directly at the cessation of hostilities between the two countries. If Castro had authorized Guevara to offer concessions, Che quickly scuttled any chance at appeasement. He made no effort to conceal Cuba's subversive activities, McCarthy explained: "He explicitly admitted that they were training revolutionaries and would continue to do so."[30]

Guevara had descended into the bowels of the monster, to paraphrase Martí, for the second time in his life, and boasted of his covert activities. His declarations to McCarthy reflected his belligerent character, but they did not serve him well, given his intention of spawning guerrilla movements on three

27. Ibid., 339.

28. Ibid., 346.

29. Guevara, "Intervención en la Asamblea General de Las Naciones Unidas en uso del derecho de réplica," in Guevara, *Ernesto Che Guevara: Escritos y discursos*, 9:309 (my translation).

30. Memorandum of conversation, Undersecretary George Ball, [Senator Eugene McCarthy], Assistant Secretary Thomas C. Mann, December 17, 1964, container 21, Cuba Country File, NSF, LBJ; Castañeda, *Compañero*, 274.

continents. One might have expected him to deceive or confuse the Americans, hoping that he might be able to keep them off his trail for some time. Che, however, told the Americans he would fight before he went off to war. He wanted the Americans to fight back.

As he made clear in several speeches and interviews during his three-month tour, Che expected the next decisive battleground to develop in central Africa. In an interview given in Algeria on December 23, he divulged more than enough information for the CIA to track his activities over the following year. He explained, "Africa represents one of the most important fields of struggle against all forms of exploitation existing in the world—against imperialism, colonialism, and neocolonialism."[31] Guevara praised the African revolutionaries and nationalists, Cuba's potential allies in a tricontinental revolutionary alliance. With Ahmed Ben Bella in Algeria, Gamal Abdel Nasser in Egypt, and Julius Nyerere in Tanzania, Che saw a realistic chance of developing rearguard bases for revolutionary movements in the Congo, Angola, Rhodesia, and even South Africa. The Americans had a tenuous grip on Africa, leaving many of the nation-states vulnerable to a guerrilla campaign, particularly if Moscow and Beijing supported it. Hence, Guevara explained that he had come to Africa to forge a "continental front of struggle against imperialism and its internal allies." Guevara understood that this front, uniting African, Asian, and Latin American rebels, would "take some time to organize, but when it is formed it will be a very hard blow against imperialism."[32]

Guevara hoped to turn the new nonaligned movement into a holy revolutionary alliance. Under the leadership of Nasser, Tito, Jawalharlal Nehru, and Achmed Sukharno, all of whom Che had met during his first tour of Africa and Asia in 1959, representatives of nonaligned countries began to organize at conferences in Belgrade (1961) and Cairo (1964). By its very existence, the nonaligned movement presented a political challenge to imperialism, but Che longed for the day when the developing countries also developed a military potential. It was only necessary, Che argued, "for the most advanced countries to form a true front, a battle group enabling us to fight with more real means and to triumph sooner."[33]

Che certainly talked a tough line worthy of Mao, but his associates in

31. Guevara, "Interview with Josie Fanon," in Guevara, *Che: Selected Works,* 401.
32. Ibid., 404.
33. Algier's correspondent's dispatch in French to Prensa Latina, Havana, December 26, 1964; interview with Serge Michel, chief editor of daily *Alger Ce Soir,* both in Foreign Broadcast Information Service (hereafter FBIS), Cuba, December 28, 1964.

Havana had deeply offended the chairman. The Chinese Communists had been excluded from the secret Havana conference in November 1964. They interpreted the conference and its resolutions as a sign of Cuba's growing allegiance to the Soviet Union. In an effort to mollify the Chinese and convey a Latin American offer to mediate the Sino-Soviet dispute, Castro dispatched Carlos Rafael Rodríguez and a delegation of Latin American Communists to Beijing. The effort failed. On February 2, 1965, just two months after Rodríguez's failure, Che, accompanied by Emilio Aragonés and Osmany Cienfuegos, flew off to Beijing to try yet again. This time, the CIA correctly discerned the motives of Guevara's visit.[34]

The Chinese response to the Cuban mission has been described as a "snub" that might have included some "bitter verbal exchanges." Che apparently met with Premier Chou En-lai, but Mao refused to receive him. Mao probably intended to express his displeasure with Osmany Cienfuegos, who had angered some Chinese officials during previous sessions. In any case, Che got nowhere with his proposal to organize an international fighting front. Although the Chinese favored Che's militant line, they sensed that the Cuban government had drifted into the Soviet camp. The Chinese would continue to provide assistance to the revolutionary governments and movements in Africa, but they would do so independently, without any effort to coordinate revolutionary efforts with Che or Cuba.[35]

Che flew from Beijing to Dar es Salaam, Tanzania, on February 11. Under leftist president Julius Nyerere, Dar es Salaam had become a safe haven for African guerrillas; there they enjoyed the rare privilege of operating in a national capital in which there was not an American embassy. The Cubans did have an embassy, and their ambassador, Pablo Ribalta, directed a clandestine network on the eastern shores of Lake Tanganyika. During a weeklong stay in Dar es Salaam, Ribalta, who had served as Che's political commissar during the Cuban insurrection, introduced Che to Congolese rebels, including Laurent Kabila, military commander of the eastern zone.[36] To Kabila Che proposed sending thirty Cuban instructors to train Congolese

34. Castañeda, *Compañero*, 270; Peking NCNA International Service in English, 1326 GMT, February 4, 1965, FBIS, Communist China, February 5, 1965; CIA, Directorate of Intelligence, Office of Current Intelligence, "Weekly Cuban Summary," February 3, 1965, container 36, Cuba Country File, NSF, LBJ.

35. CIA, Directorate of Intelligence, Office of Current Intelligence, "Weekly Cuban Summary," March 31, 1965, container 36, Cuba Country File, NSF, LBJ; Karol, *Guerrillas in Power*, 372; Halperin, *Taming of Fidel*, 124–25.

36. Taibo, Escobar, and Guerra, *El año en que estuvimos en ninguna parte*, 18–19.

as well as Mozambican, Angolan, and other African revolutionaries, a proposal to which Kabila readily agreed, confirmation that he saw the struggle in the Congo as part of a larger continental issue. Most of the fifty African representatives from ten countries who met with Che in the Cuban embassy, however, did not embrace Che's proposals. They wanted Cuba to finance their training in Cuba, a proposal that Che dismissed as impractical and too expensive. Che offered to train all the African rebels in the Congo, where they would have an opportunity to fight imperialism. But the Africans would train only in their native country. Che argued in vain that a victory in the Congo would benefit the entire continent. The chilly response Che received did not shake his confidence. Shortly after the meeting, Che declared, "I am convinced that it is possible to create a joint fighting front against colonialism, imperialism, and neocolonialism."[37]

Che delivered his climactic critique of imperialism at the Second Seminar of Afro-Asian Solidarity on February 25. Regarded by some scholars as the speech that marked Guevara's open break with the Soviet Union and possibly with Fidel Castro, it definitely contained some harsh words for Cuba's Soviet allies. He called on his African and Asian comrades to intensify the anti-imperialist struggle across the continents: "There are no frontiers in this struggle to the death. We cannot remain indifferent in the face of what occurs in any part of the world. A victory for any country against imperialism is our victory, just as any country's defeat is a defeat for all."[38]

Che repeated his call for the formation of a "large compact bloc" that would help other countries liberate themselves from imperialism. This time, he publicly challenged the Soviet Union and China to back up their revolutionary rhetoric with arms. In the name of international proletarian duty the Soviets and the Chinese should supply arms and ammunition "without any cost whatsoever and in quantities determined by their need and availability to those people who ask for them in order to direct their fight against the common enemy." He specifically asked the Communist superpowers to send arms and ammunition to the Congo and Vietnam.[39]

The Soviets and the Chinese, accustomed to receiving something in return for their military and economic assistance, took offense at such a strident

37. Gálvez, *Che in Africa,* 36–40; "Frente común antimperialista de América Latina, Africa y Asia," *Revolución,* February 19, 1965 (quoted).

38. Guevara, "Revolution and Underdevelopment," February 25, 1965, in Guevara, *Che: Selected Works,* 351.

39. Ibid., 357.

lecture from a pretentious representative of a small island nation. The Soviets had already rejected Guevara's plans for a global campaign against imperialism. China had agreed to send a small shipment of arms to the Congolese rebels, but they did not endorse Guevara's strategy either. So in Algiers, Che let the world hear the criticisms he had probably leveled against Soviet and Chinese officials in private. Referring to economic and military assistance, he boldly charged that the Soviet Union and China had not fulfilled their international duty to underwrite the development and liberation of the Third World. In his view, the socialist superpowers behaved like capitalist powers in their commercial relations with the developing world, buying and selling goods at international market prices set by their capitalist adversaries. Like capitalists, they bought raw materials at the cheap prices set by the law of capitalist value; they sold manufactured products at the high prices set by the same capitalist marketplace. Trading in this manner, Che argued, "the socialist countries are, to a certain extent, accomplices to imperialist exploitation."[40]

Che attempted to soften the blow by praising the recent commercial agreement signed by the Soviet Union and Cuba. On the day that Che denounced Soviet commercial policies, Raúl Castro signed a new commercial agreement in Moscow whereby the Soviets agreed to purchase five million tons of Cuban sugar above market prices. While Che conceded that the agreement favored Cuba, he still expected more economic assistance from the Soviets and Chinese. Che demanded fair prices, set not by the market, but by the political and moral imperatives of advancing worldwide revolution: "Foreign trade must not determine politics, but on the contrary, it must be subordinated to a fraternal policy toward the people," Che argued.[41]

Che's admonitions about morality, commercial policy, and political philosophy alienated the benefactors he had been courting. The sermon in Algiers inflicted a mortal wound to the ambitious tricontinental strategy he had been promoting. Why, after hearing Che compare their policies to those of immoral imperialists, would the Soviets and Chinese support him? In his public speeches, interviews, and secret negotiations, Che expressed his criticisms without hesitation, bluntly condemning the countries from which he expected assistance, revealing critical shortcomings as a diplomat. To get Soviet and Chinese support for his tricontinental campaign, Che would have had to engage in patient and complicated negotiations, a task ideally suited to some-

40. Ibid., 351–52.
41. Ibid., 352.

one with Fidel Castro's political talents. As a subordinate of Fidel in the Sierra Maestra, Che did not have to handle political affairs and international diplomacy. As an independent leader, however, he would have to manage them. Honest to a fault and incessantly combative, he would anger enemies and allies excessively and needlessly.

He also displayed a stubbornness that often compelled him to reject or ignore friendly advice. Ahmed Ben Bella, perhaps his closest friend in Africa, had cautioned him about his Africa project. Che could compensate for the lack of Soviet and Chinese support through Bella in Algeria and Nasser in Egypt. They might have endorsed Che's pan-African vision, but they had serious concerns about his strategy, particularly if he decided to command a group of black Cuban troops then being trained in Cuba. Bella warned Che not to play the role of a white messiah coming to liberate the African people. "The situation in black Africa was not comparable to that prevailing in our countries; Nasser and I, we warned Che of what might happen," Bella claimed.[42]

Nasser issued similar warnings to Che in early March. Guevara clearly wanted to join the fight in the Congo, arguing that it was "the hottest spot in the world now." Che's interest in the Congo astonished Nasser. "What happened to all that you were doing in Cuba? Have you quarreled with Castro? I don't want to interfere, but if you want to become another Tarzan, a white man coming among black men, leading them and protecting them . . . it can't be done."[43]

Nasser tried to persuade Guevara that other countries would denounce the presence of Cuban or even Egyptian military advisers in the Congo as foreign interference. Nasser only wanted to provide the Congolese rebels with training and supplies. Guevara wanted to do more. He had even been thinking about joining the struggle in South Vietnam; he wanted to fight against imperialism, anywhere. At his last meeting with Nasser, he explained that he was still trying to decide "where to go, where to find a place to fight for the world revolution and to accept the challenge of death." "Why do you always talk about death?" Nasser asked. "You are a young man. If necessary we should die for the revolution, but it would be much better if we could live for the revolution."[44]

A combination of strategic, political, diplomatic, and personal factors compelled Che to leave Cuba and return to the battlefront. He had helped the

42. Anderson, *Che Guevara,* 620; Castañeda, *Compañero,* 283.
43. Heikal, *Cairo Documents,* 349.
44. Ibid., 356.

Cubans attain power, consolidate the revolution, and initiate the construction of socialism. Cuba needed his services less than did revolutionaries on other fronts. He wanted to pursue other challenges, not only because of a self-assumed revolutionary duty, but also because he intended to fulfill his personal mission. Hence, even though he failed to establish a solid international fighting front during his African travels, he could no longer remain in Cuba. When Castro greeted him at the Havana airport on March 15, 1965, Guevara's revolutionary fervor had not diminished, and he had not broken with Fidel.

Nevertheless, observers noted the cold distance that separated Che from Fidel, Raúl, Carlos Rafael Rodríguez, and President Osvaldo Dorticós Torrado at the airport. The presence of Carlos Rafael Rodríguez, Moscow's man in Havana, must have struck Che, the scourge of the Soviets, as odd. Instead of holding a press conference, the party left the airport immediately for a closed-door session that lasted forty hours. Fidel, Raúl, and Che never discussed what happened. No researcher has ever uncovered official documentation about the meeting. One popular rumor that never seems to die is that Fidel, Che, and Raúl got into a heated argument, with the latter two nearly coming to blows over Che's pro-Chinese policies. Allegedly, as a result Che decided to resign and leave Cuba.[45]

Circumstances suggest, however, that Che had decided to leave Cuba in November 1964, long before his marathon meeting with Fidel and Raúl. During Che's three-month foreign mission he had studied the political, economic, and geographic conditions for launching a revolutionary campaign in Africa. In Tanzania he had even surveyed areas in which he could establish a base for an incursion into the Congo. Meanwhile, back in Cuba, more than one hundred black Cubans were training for an international mission, a clear indication of an official Cuban interest in fomenting revolution in Africa. The Cubans already supported several Latin American guerrilla bands. Che could take command of one, start another, or launch a totally unexpected front in Africa. If there was a serious argument between Fidel and Che, it likely concerned Che's options.

The personal and ideological ties between Fidel and Che had not been severed. Fidel shared some of Guevara's criticisms of the Soviet Union, and he supported Che's revolutionary ambitions, particularly in Latin America. On March 13, 1965, just two days before Guevara returned to Havana, Fidel

45. Castañeda, *Compañero,* 296.

had endorsed Che's controversial call for the socialist countries to give the Vietnamese people all the weapons and fighters that they needed, regardless of the risks.[46] For practical reasons Fidel understood the necessity of appeasing the Soviets, but he, and the Cuban intelligence network, would continue to promote guerrilla movements in Africa and Latin America over the following three years. Cuba did not terminate its support for Che or the revolutionary movements he advocated in March 1965; Cuba's subversive efforts actually expanded and intensified in the two years after Che left the country.

Given the course of subsequent events, one cannot dismiss the possibility that the icy reception that Che received at the airport represented a deliberate Cuban effort to throw American, Soviet, and Chinese agents off Che's trail. Che and Fidel were still working in tandem, fulfilling an agreement that they had reached in late 1964.[47] Che was going deep undercover, and the stories of violent disputes within the Cuban leadership provided a perfect ruse to generate rumors that Che had been imprisoned, exiled, or even killed. Che had left no doubt in his public comments that he believed that Africa offered realistic opportunities for the development of a guerrilla foco. From any number of sources, intelligence agents could have picked up stories of Che's interest in leading a Cuban mission in central Africa. Without assistance from Cuban intelligence, Che could not have slipped out of Cuba and traveled all the way back to Africa, just after he had actually visited the base from which he would launch the Congo campaign.

The proposal for Che to take command of the Cuban contingent to Africa may have originated with Castro, as he subsequently claimed. Che undoubtedly would have preferred to go immediately to Argentina, but the guerrilla foco there had already been liquidated. Cuban agents had begun to establish a clandestine network in Bolivia, but it still lacked the strength to support a guerrilla band. Castro hoped to prevent the impulsive Guevara from walking into a death trap. Shortly after Guevara's return to Havana, the Cuban leadership agreed that Che would command the Cuban mission to the Congo, temporarily. After Manuel Piñeiro's men completed preparatory work in Latin America, the Cubans would transfer him to his native continent.[48]

Nevertheless, Che left from a base with serious cracks in its foundations and was headed toward an international front that had not even been established.

46. Anderson, *Che Guevara,* 627.
47. Ibid.
48. Deutschmann, *Che,* 118; Anderson, *Che Guevara,* 628.

Fidel had maintained a delicate balance between the Soviet line of peaceful coexistence and the militant policies favored by Che and the Chinese. Some high-level Cuban officials, including Raúl Castro and Carlos Rafael Rodríguez, may have actually opposed Guevara's tricontinental strategy.[49] The Soviet Union opposed it; China refused to embrace it; the African revolutionaries objected to it; and few Latin American revolutionaries enlisted in his campaign. Che faced overwhelming odds, but he launched his international campaign anyway, considering it a duty and a personal mission.

If Che was not a theorist, he most certainly was an idealist.[50] Shortly after he had castigated the Soviets and Chinese in Algiers, a Uruguayan journal published his most elegant expression of his utopian vision. In "Socialism and Man in Cuba," Guevara described the ideal society for which he fought. Regardless of the conditions that dimmed the prospects for revolutionary victories everywhere, Che regarded the fight as inevitable, necessary, and desirable. He expected all revolutionaries to join him on the march toward the "most important revolutionary ambition: to see man liberated from his alienation."[51]

People would not be liberated until man "produces without being compelled by the physical necessity of selling himself as a commodity." Guevara saw the construction of socialism and communism as more than a materialistic process whereby the state expropriated the means of production and distributed the products of collective labor among the masses equitably. Che's ultimate communist utopia liberated the individual from the sense of alienation experienced by workers in a capitalist setting. Each person, freed from the oppressive restraints of capitalism, would express his or her human condition through music, literature, and the arts, producing an egalitarian society in which culture and the arts flourished.[52]

In "Socialism and Man in Cuba" Che composed the romantic farewell of a man headed into battle, a soldier justifying a death that he welcomes. The nostalgic tone of the article reveals a man content with yet exhausted by what he has accomplished, happy to meet the destiny that awaits him. "It must be said with all sincerity that in a true revolution, to which one gives oneself completely, from which one expects no material compensation, the task of the vanguard revolutionary is both magnificent and anguishing."[53] Then, as

---

49. Castañeda, *Compañero,* 295–97.
50. Lowy, *Marxism of Che Guevara,* 29–34.
51. Guevara, "Socialism and Man in Cuba," in Guevara, *Che: Selected Works,* 157, 162.
52. Ibid., 162–63.
53. Ibid., 167.

if to justify the sacrifices he had made: "Let me say, with the risk of appearing ridiculous, that the true revolutionary is guided by strong feelings of love." He had done all that he had done in the name of love. Love, Che finally admitted, was the fundamental characteristic of the new man that he had always hoped to be: "it is impossible to think of an authentic revolutionary without this quality."[54]

Che had always maintained a certain detachment in all his interpersonal relationships, but he also placed his revolutionary duties above his personal interests. His fourth child, Ernesto, had been born while he toured Africa in 1965, and the pain it caused him is reflected in the bittersweet tone in which he wrote about the revolution. "The leaders of the Revolution have children who do not learn to call their father with their first faltering words; they have wives who must be part of the general sacrifice of their lives to carry the Revolution to its destiny; their friends are strictly limited to their comrades in revolution. There is no life outside it."[55]

He accepted the personal sacrifices in the name of a cause he now called "proletarian internationalism." To fulfill his self-imposed duties as a revolutionary, he had to return to the battlefront. He wrote: "If he [the revolutionary] forgets about proletarian internationalism, the revolution that he leads ceases to be a driving force and it becomes a comfortable drowsiness which is taken advantage of by our irreconcilable enemy, by imperialism, which gains ground. Proletarian internationalism is a duty, but it is also a revolutionary need."[56]

Once a soldier of the Americas, Che Guevara now fashioned himself as a commander of an international proletariat army in formation. The numerous criticisms he had received from friends and allies around the world did not deter him. On this project, so central to his character and his personal mission, Che Guevara could not delay. If Fidel had waited for the appropriate conditions to develop in Cuba, he never would have attacked the Moncada barracks. The very act of revolution, Guevara believed, could create the revolutionary consciousness that combatants required.

Fidel Castro believed in Che Guevara as well. Castro vacillated between Soviet orthodoxy and Guevarism. Having extended olive branches to the United States in accordance with Soviet policy, Fidel swung back to a more confrontational posture after Guevara's departure. He came out firing with

54. Ibid.
55. Ibid., 167–68.
56. Ibid.

an inflammatory denunciation of "peaceful coexistence" in his May Day speech of 1965. The speech marked a return to the belligerent line favored by Che. With Cuban support, revolutionaries from Africa, Asia, and Latin America pursued Che's dream of forging an international fighting front. From then until Che's death, Manuel Piñeiro's Liberation Department promoted guerrilla focos more vigorously than it had when Che supervised its operations.[57]

Moreover, Fidel pushed ahead with Che's plan to forge an international fighting front, convening the First Tricontinental Conference in January 1966. With 512 representatives from eighty-two countries and territories, the first meeting of the Organization of Solidarity of the Peoples of Africa, Asia, and Latin America (OSPAAL) was "the largest assembly of Third World militants and supporters that the world had ever known." The world's strongest liberation movements sent delegates, including from South Vietnam, Angola, Mozambique, and Palestine. In the Latin American delegations, which were selected by Cuba, pro-Cuban militants naturally dominated. Hence, Castro had little difficulty securing passage of resolutions endorsing the armed struggle in Latin America, implicitly under Cuban leadership. The Soviet representatives watched with concern, knowing, of course, that they would ultimately finance Cuba's adventures through the subsidies it provided to the island nation. Despite opposition from the Soviet and Chinese delegations, the Tricontinental Conference endorsed Guevara's cherished strategy.[58]

Behind the scenes, Cuban agents pressured the delegates to launch new guerrilla focos. Those who refused to embrace the armed struggle, the traditional communists, were passed over in favor of the more radical groups that did. Mario Monje, leader of the Bolivian Communist party, talked with Piñeiro about launching a foco in Bolivia, but he did not give the answer the Cubans wanted. With a group of Bolivians already training in Cuba, Monje still refused to break with the Soviets and endorse the armed struggle in his country. An angry Piñeiro pressed him hard, giving him two to three months to revise his views and initiate a guerrilla war.[59]

Unfortunately for Che, the first meeting of the Tricontinental would also be its last. The organization collapsed as a result of the Sino-Soviet rift as well as conflicts between the Latin American revolutionary movements, some of them generated by hostility toward Cuban leadership and policies.[60]

57. Anderson, *Che Guevara*, 677–78.
58. Halperin, *Taming of Fidel Castro*, 185–94.
59. Anderson, *Che Guevara*, 683–85.
60. Halperin, *Taming of Fidel Castro*, 185–94.

OSPAAL never developed the fighting capability that Che had envisioned for it. It only represented a temporary victory for Che's tricontinental strategy, giving him a measure of faith after his failure in the Congo and before his departure for Bolivia.

Hoping to give the movement a new impetus before it vanished, Che wrote his famous "Message to the Tricontinental," the fullest expression of his global anti-imperialist strategy. He envisioned a long and bloody war against imperialism, a struggle that demanded the highest sacrifice from all combatants. If Che had to die fighting for the liberation of another country, he would consider it an honor. He asked, "What do the dangers or the sacrifices of a man or of a nation matter, when the destiny of humanity is at stake?"[61]

In this message, Che summarized the strategy that he had been articulating in bits and pieces over the previous three years. It marked the culmination of his strategic development and established a global rationale for the war against imperialism. This rationale, and the strategic lessons he derived from it, consists of five fundamental themes:

1. Imperialism, being a world system, must be defeated in a world confrontation.
2. The foundations of imperialism are in Africa, Asia, and Latin America, from which it extracts capital, raw materials, and cheap labor, and to which it exports capital and manufactured products.
3. The people of the developing world must attack the foundations of imperialism and force the imperialists to fight outside of their natural environment. The armies of imperialism are strong and technologically advanced. Revolutionaries can defeat them only by forcing them to fight in unknown and hostile regions.
4. The United States cannot fight wars of national liberation on three continents simultaneously. With the Vietnamese war already draining the United States of men, morale, and resources, the emergence of guerrilla focos in Africa, Asia, and Latin America would drag the Americans into wars that they would lose by attrition.
5. To crush imperialism, revolutionaries must create a second or third Vietnam. (163–76)

61. Guevara, "Message to the Tricontinental," 176. Subsequent references to this work appear in the text.

Che had no illusions about the character of the war he promoted so vigorously. He warned:

> And these battles shall not be mere street fights with stones against
> tear-gas bombs, or of pacific general strikes; neither shall it be the
> battle of a furious people destroying in two or three days the repres-
> sive scaffolds of the ruling oligarchies; the struggle shall be long,
> harsh, and its front shall be in the guerrillas' refuge, in the cities, in
> the homes of the fighters—where the repressive forces shall go seek-
> ing easy victims among their families in the massacred rural popula-
> tion, in the villages or cities destroyed by the bombardments of the
> enemy. (63)

Guevarism, in its fullest and final expression in the "Message to the
Tricontinental," had evolved into a strategy of total war against imperialism,
using all available means. The tricontinental strategy did not replace the *guerra
de guerrillas* concept; it supplemented it. *Guerrilla Warfare* explained how
revolutionaries should launch a guerrilla foco and survive through the gru-
eling first phase of a longer campaign. The tricontinental strategy called for
the coordination of guerrilla campaigns across three continents. Guevara never
argued that a guerrilla foco, operating by itself in some remote corner of
Bolivia, could hope to topple imperialism. Imperialism could only be destroyed
in total, global war. Guevara's manual of guerrilla warfare was still instruc-
tive for the initial phase of the struggle, but Guevarism called for the annihilation of imperialism using every viable strategy and tactic. "We must carry
the war into every corner the enemy happens to carry it: to his home, to his
centers of entertainment; a total war," Che argued. "It is necessary to prevent him from having a moment of peace, a quiet moment outside his barracks or even inside; we must attack him wherever he may be, make him feel
like a cornered beast wherever he may move" (174).

From his Cuban experience, Guevara learned that the triumph of a revolutionary movement in one country would only weaken, not destroy, imperialism. The American imperialists, no longer disoriented, had developed more
sophisticated counterinsurgency strategies, tactics, and technology since the
Cuban Revolution. In response, revolutionaries had to change their strategies and tactics, and Che's "Message to the Tricontinental" included some
fundamental revisions in the character and scope of the war. In *Guerrilla
Warfare* he emphasized the rural guerrilla campaign over other forms of strug-

gle; in the tricontinental strategy he attached greater importance to a concept of "total war." He had never before argued for taking the war into "centers of entertainment." The earlier Guevara might have labeled such actions terrorist or even criminal. By 1967, Che had concluded that a total, global war was "almost our sole hope for victory" (175).

The success of the strategy required minimal coordination of revolutionary activity on three continents. Guerrilla bands in Latin America, already operational in Guatemala, Colombia, Venezuela, and Peru, only required more money, supplies, and recruits. In Africa, nationalistic or radical leaders in six or seven African states could promote the expansion of guerrilla activity there. The Americans had increased their military commitment in Vietnam, with the Soviets and Chinese supporting their North Vietnamese comrades. As the conflict escalated, the political, economic, and social consequences for Americans increased. Che noted how President Johnson's "Great Society" programs had "dropped into the cesspool of Vietnam." The powerful American economy already showed signs of the strain imposed by maintaining the war effort (167). With American society being ripped apart by civil rights protesters and antiwar activists, Che anticipated even graver consequences resulting from the creation of a second or third Vietnam.

Guevara's strategy, therefore, called for, welcomed, and even *required* American military intervention in Africa and Latin America. The history of the Vietnamese struggle showed how it would occur. The imperialists would attempt to crush the movement through a proxy army first, limiting American involvement to the provision of military and technical assistance. As the guerrilla war expanded, the Americans would replace the ineffective puppet army with their own regular troops, determined to prevent another Cuba. The people would resent American intervention, and nationalists would fill the ranks of the rebel army. As the war escalated, it would increase the political, economic, and social costs for the Americans at home, further weakening American war-making capability.

If the Soviet Union and China had endorsed the strategy, it could have presented a serious challenge to the United States. Che had only asked them to provide military and logistical support for the revolutionary armies. Through OSPAAL or some other organization, revolutionaries could have coordinated their efforts. They could have decided, for example, to target the most vulnerable countries in Latin America and Africa: Nicaragua, Colombia, Peru, Bolivia, Congo, and Angola. They could have increased their military commitment in Vietnam and offered more support to revolutionary bands in other Asian countries. Limiting Soviet and Chinese support to military supplies and advice, they might have been able to nibble away at imperialism without provoking a direct confrontation with the United States. If and when the wars escalated, the Americans would have to dispatch their own troops, while the Soviets and Chinese would have relied solely on the Africans, Asians, and Latin Americans to fight the wars, thereby limiting the domestic political, economic, and social consequences of their proxy wars.

To some extent, the Soviets and the Chinese were already executing this strategy. They provided military and economic assistance to Cuba, Vietnam, and several African states. They even provided military aid to the Congolese rebels, but they did all of it in a piecemeal fashion. Che advocated an organized and coordinated effort to promote their common interests by opening fronts in selected countries. All that, however, required a higher degree of solidarity than actually existed. Che knew of the divisions within the revolutionary movements, but he could not let them delay his return to the battlefield. For Che Guevara, the war against imperialism was a moral imperative.

In its final form, Guevarism implicitly endorsed forms of struggle that Guevara had earlier dismissed, including selective assassinations, bank robberies, mass strikes, and urban assaults. The guerrilla vanguard would still initiate the struggle in rural areas and lead the people's war throughout the entire struggle, but Guevara implicitly accepted all actions that contributed to the destruction of imperialism. He burned with such an intense hatred of American imperialism that he ultimately endorsed any and all attacks against the imperialists. He encouraged all revolutionaries to unleash their hatred of their enemy, for it would impel them to go "over and beyond the natural limitations that man is heir to" and transform them into an "effective, violent, selective, and cold killing machine" (174).

NINE THE HISTORY OF A FAILURE

On Saturday, September 11, 1965, Cuban, Congolese, and Rwandan combatants waited in ambush. They had been waiting eleven days under the command of Che Guevara, who insisted that they hold their positions until the enemy vehicles rolled into their sights. The Congolese rebels tried to leave several times, but the Cuban soldiers, eager for a fight, made them obey their commanding officer. The Cubans had spent most of their first five months in the eastern Congo lounging around the camps, complaining—like their prestigious commander—about the passivity of their new African allies.

Finally, at 10:45 A.M., the rebels heard an approaching car. A Rwandan soldier serving in the middle unit hit it with a bazooka, and then the rest of the soldiers opened up with everything they had. A truck filled with guards came up from one hundred yards away and engaged the rebels posted on the left flank. Many of the Congolese soldiers withdrew when the fire got hot, leaving Che with only a handful of Cubans and Rwandans to finish off the enemy. Che ordered a withdrawal after capturing six weapons, ammunition, papers, photographs, and some documents. Che berated his men for not showing the necessary discipline and courage expected of his combatants. He described the results of the engagement as "satisfactory" only because he had suffered no casualties. His men still needed much more discipline and training.[1]

1. Gálvez, *Che in Africa*, 150–52.

Although the rebel ambush did not impress Che, his adversaries certainly took note. The Congolese rebels had never fought with distinction against experienced troops, particularly the South African mercenaries hired by Premier Moise-Kapenda Tshombe. In September, American officials detected a distinct improvement, which they attributed to Cuban influence. "North of Albertville," U.S. ambassador G. McMurtrie Godley reported ten days after the ambush, "we have already seen what is most likely [the] first effect of commie mercenary presence in [the] form [of] well-laid ambushes in [the] area far from rebel concentrations." American intelligence sources estimated that there were 160 Cuban military advisers in the Congo, along with some Chinese, Russian, and Algerian "mercenaries." The Americans expected these veterans to correct the main deficiency in the Congolese rebel units, the lack of aggressive leadership. The Congolese government had relied on white mercenaries from South Africa and Rhodesia to suppress the rebellion. The arrival of Cuban veterans threatened to equalize conditions on the battlefield and escalate the conflict. "If [the] Congolese rebels can hold out, they [are] likely [to] establish something akin to [a] 'Liberated Area' so dear to [the] hearts of Chinese and Cuban Communist theoreticians," Godley predicted. The mercenaries may not be able to eliminate the reinforced rebels from the eastern Congo, the ambassador warned.[2]

Although the CIA had overestimated the Cuban presence in the eastern Congo, the agent accurately assessed the potential impact of Cuban "volunteers" on the Congolese rebellion. Che Guevara and more than one hundred Cuban combatants had arrived in the spring of 1965 to fight the Tshombe regime, backed by the United States. With Soviet and Chinese arms shipped through Algeria, Egypt, and Tanzania, and Comandante Che Guevara training and commanding troops in the field, the Congolese rebellion posed a serious military threat to the established government. A superpower conflict loomed in central Africa, just as Che had anticipated in his tricontinental strategy. The Cuban intervention threatened to transform a poorly organized rebellion into a coordinated military campaign directed by hardened combatants and officers.

The Congo had been in a state of political turmoil bordering on anarchy during its first five years of independence. Having achieved its independence from Belgium in 1960 without a bloody civil war, the Congo came under the

---

2. [G. McMurtrie] Godley (U.S. ambassador, Leopoldville) to secretary of state, September 21, 1965, container 85, Congo Country File, NSF, LBJ.

leadership of Patrice Lumumba, one of many African nationalists who had led the independence movements in the late 1950s and early 1960s. Appointed prime minister in June 1960 by President Joseph Kasavubu, Lumumba immediately confronted a national crisis when Tshombe declared the independence of Katanga province in the eastern Congo. Determined to maintain the geographic and political integrity of the newly independent state, Lumumba appealed for foreign military assistance. The Soviet Union offered aid and Lumumba accepted it, for which the United States labeled him a pro-Soviet radical, an African version of Fidel Castro. The United Nations intervened militarily and blocked Soviet aid to Lumumba, who then fell in a coup led by President Kasavubu in September 1960. Lumumba subsequently rebelled against Kasavubu and his militant premier, Colonel Joseph Désiré Mobutu, leaving the Congo government in Leopoldville (now Kinshasa) facing a rebellion in the northeast led by Lumumba, and a secessionist movement in the east, led by Tshombe. (See Map 10.) Mobutu's troops captured Lumumba in December 1960 and turned him over to Tshombe in Katanga. Two months later, the Katanga regime announced that villagers had killed Lumumba. The Congolese rebels and his foreign sympathizers, however, held Tshombe and the imperialists responsible for his assassination.[3]

With United Nations military assistance, the Kasavubu government suppressed the Katanganese secessionists in January 1963 and forced Tshombe into exile. Political stability still eluded the Congo, however, for the Lumumbists remained determined to reclaim their rightful political authority in Leopoldville. A group of reformists led by Pierre Mulele, Christophe Gbenye, and Gaston Soumaliot formed the Committee of National Liberation (CNL) to fight under the banner of the martyred Lumumba. In January 1964, with UN forces scheduled to depart that summer, the Lumumbist revolt erupted again. Mulele, who had spent several months in Beijing studying revolutionary theory and practice, commanded rebel forces in Kwilu province in the western Congo. Gbenye and Soumaliot opened another military front in the northeastern Congo. Despite political rivalries between the rebel factions, the rebellion spread rapidly throughout the Congo. To crush it, Kasavubu recalled former enemy and notorious anticommunist Moise Tshombe from Spain and appointed him prime minister in August 1964. The appointment of the hard-line Tshombe, regarded by the rebels and many African leaders as an instrument of colonialism and as the assassin of

3. Kanza, *Conflict in the Congo.*

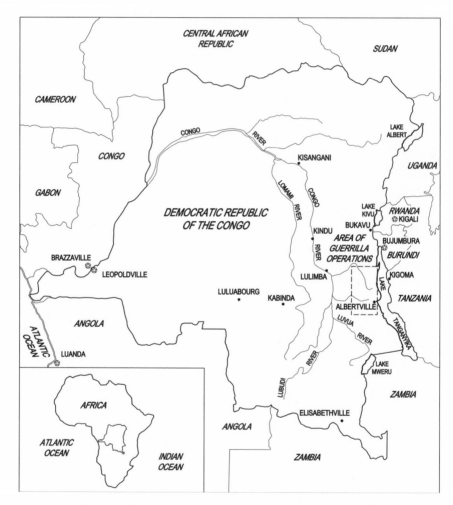

Map 10. Congo Campaign

Lumumba, escalated the conflict and threatened to rip the country and continent apart.[4]

The "radical" African states, led by Ahmed Ben Bella (Algeria), Gamal Abdel Nasser (Egypt), Julius Nyerere (Tanzania), and Kwame Nkrumah (Ghana) denounced Tshombe and mobilized their military resources in support of the Congolese rebels. Even moderate African states such as Kenya and Morocco supported the rebels against the infamous Tshombe. King Hassan II of Morocco asked, "How could anyone imagine that I, the representative of my country's national conscience, could sit at a conference table or at a banquet with the man who personifies secession?"[5] Whether moderate or radical, these African states would accept no resolution to the Congolese crisis that left Tshombe in power.

Most of the rebel arms apparently came from the Soviet Union and China via third countries. In October 1964, Algeria, Egypt, and Ghana had agreed to supply the rebels with military aid from stockpiles of Soviet and Chinese weapons, with the implicit understanding that the Soviets and Chinese would replenish the military warehouses later. Bella opened an arms pipeline to the rebels. The Algerians loaded the weapons onto Soviet aircraft in Algeria; Soviet crews flew them to Juba in southern Sudan, from where truck crews transported the weapons to rebels at the Congo border. By the end of the year, the rebels had received about three hundred tons of military equipment.[6]

With only minimal amounts of military aid from the Soviet Union and China, the Congolese rebels mounted a serious military threat to Tshombe. The United States, alarmed at the imminent collapse of an anticommunist ally in central Africa, decided to commit its resources, but not its troops, to the defense of Tshombe's government. After Belgium and other European countries rejected an American request to send troops to Tshombe, the Johnson administration decided to help him recruit mercenaries for his army. At a National Security Council meeting on August 11, 1964, President Johnson agreed to arm and transport mercenaries recruited by Tshombe. Belgium and the United States would pay them. Tshombe, who had employed mercenaries while leading the Katangan war of secession, turned to Colonel Mike Hoare, who recruited vigorously in South Africa. The United States' reliance on mercenaries did not reflect a lack of determination to eradicate the alleged

4. Kelly, *America's Tyrant*, 93–95; Gleijeses, 'Flee!' 211–12.
5. Cited in Gleijeses, 'Flee!' 212.
6. Ibid.; Greig, *Communist Challenge to Africa*, 180.

"communist" threat to the Congo. The Johnson administration hoped to crush the rebellion by any means short of a full and direct American military intervention. CIA agents and American military advisers would provide intelligence and military assistance to the mercenaries. If they got the job done, American troops would not be needed. The Congo was the Cold War battleground that Che had anticipated, but the Johnson administration was not going to let it turn into the second Vietnam that Che advocated.[7]

Johnson's measured response produced the desired results. By November, Tshombe's army included four hundred mercenaries and a small air force piloted by anticommunist Cuban exiles. To drive the rebels from their base in Stanleyville (now Kisangani), the Americans unleashed Operation Dragon Rouge. American planes dropped Belgian paratroopers in and around Stanleyville, while the mercenaries drove against the city from land bases. The coordinated campaign cleared the rebels out of the city, but not before they had looted a Belgian mining company and made off with a huge reserve of gold. Although the rebels lost Stanleyville, they survived the counteroffensive. On December 31, 1964, the CIA offered a bleak assessment of the counterinsurgency campaign: "Despite the loss of Stanleyville and little sense of cohesion among the rebels, much of the countryside remains under the sway of their adherents."[8]

Biographer Jorge Castañeda argues that Operation Dragon Rouge had crushed the Congolese rebellion by the time Che arrived in April 1965.[9] Although the mercenaries had routed the rebels from their bases in Stanleyville and the northeastern Congo in early 1965, the Congolese rebellion flared up again in the eastern Congo, partly the result of Che Guevara's intervention with Cuban troops. After the rebels withdrew from the northeastern region, they reestablished a new front in the eastern Congo, from bases located west of Lake Tanganyika. There, drawing Chinese and Soviet supplies from a line going across the lake and down to Dar es Salaam, the rebels continued the struggle against Tshombe and his Belgian and American sponsors.

The Soviet Union and China pursued their own strategic interests in central Africa, regardless of Che Guevara's tricontinental strategy. The Soviets, brushed aside by the United Nations in their previous campaign to support Lumumba, saw an opportunity to destabilize a pro-Western regime in the

---

7. Greig, *Communist Challenge to Africa*, 215–17.

8. CIA, Directorate of Intelligence, "The Congo: Assessment and Prospects," December 31, 1964, container 87, Congo Country File, NSF, LBJ.

9. Castañeda, *Compañero*, 276.

heart of Africa, and they took advantage of it. Seeing little risk in supporting a war through third-party proxies (Algeria and Egypt), the Soviets may have encouraged the radical African states to support the rebellion, though they had little intention of getting directly involved. As long as they kept a low profile, they had little to lose and everything to gain, despite their dissatisfaction with the rebel leadership. Reports received by the CIA indicated that "the Soviets regard the Congolese rebels as a venal and undisciplined rabble, but they evidently believe they can be used to serve Moscow's interests in the Congo[,] which at present are to diminish Western influence and presence, and to foment trouble for the Leopoldville government."[10]

The Chinese displayed a similar reluctance and for similar reasons. They had been aggressively courting the radical African states for several years, in a campaign highlighted by the visit of Premier Chou En-lai to Africa in 1964. The Chinese provided military and economic aid to Algeria, Egypt, Tanzania, Ghana, and Congo (Brazzaville), and supported liberation movements in other countries with arms and training. Their aggressive actions, in fact, may have compelled the Soviets to match Chinese efforts on the continent, simply for fear of losing influence. The Chinese nevertheless opened a small-arms pipeline to the rebels through Tanzania. Like the Soviets, they harbored serious doubts about the rebel leaders. The Chinese wanted the rebels to demonstrate enough military power to hold a province before they dispatched substantial quantities of arms and ammunition.[11]

American intelligence agents unknowingly concurred with the Chinese and Soviet assessments of the Congolese rebel leaders. The CIA dismissed the rebel leaders as a "motley collection of left-wing politicians." Gbenye, nominal head of the CNL, lacked prestige and faced numerous internal challenges to his authority. The only rebel leader who exercised any authority over the rebel fighters, according to the CIA, was the "poorly educated and ruthless" General Nicolas Olenga, commander of the rebel forces in and around Stanleyville.[12]

The rebel forces, however, lacked competent military leadership, and it did not matter how many Chinese or Soviet-made weapons they received,

10. CIA, Directorate of Intelligence, "The Congo: Assessment and Prospects," December 31, 1964, container 87, Congo Country File, NSF, LBJ.

11. Larkin, *China and Africa*, 73–74; CIA, Directorate of Intelligence, "The Congo: Assessment and Prospects," December 31, 1964, container 87, Congo Country File, NSF, LBJ.

12. CIA, Directorate of Intelligence, "The Congo: Assessment and Prospects," December 31, 1964, container 87, Congo Country File, NSF, LBJ.

they did not know how to use them. The Congolese rebels desperately needed training and experienced leadership. With foreign military assistance, the rebels could turn the tide of war against Tshombe, whose army relied on foreign mercenaries and advisers. "The appearance in the Congo of combat 'volunteers' from the radical African states would create a new, more ugly and dangerous situation there," the CIA warned in December 1964.[13]

Che Guevara and a Cuban military contingent could provide the military catalyst that the American observers feared. Cuban support for African liberation movements dated back to 1963, when Castro dispatched a military mission to Algeria at the request of President Ahmed Ben Bella, then embroiled in a border dispute with Morocco. Castro, eager to assist a comrade-in-arms, in October 1963 sent an expeditionary force that included 686 men, 22 tanks, and an artillery group. Under the command of Cuban veteran Efigenio Ameijeras, former commander of Column 6 on Raúl Castro's second eastern front, the Cubans came prepared to fight and equipped to make an impact. Recognizing the strength of the Cuban contingent, the Algerians positioned the Cubans at the spearhead of an attack across the Moroccan border scheduled for October 29, 1963. At the last moment, Bella resolved the dispute with the Moroccans and called off the attack, leaving Ameijeras furious. He had come to fight, not to tour North Africa.[14] A similar fate awaited Che and his expeditionary force.

Che went to Africa with the understanding that the Congolese rebels intended to continue their struggle and that a group of African states wanted to help them. Che could have supported another African revolutionary movement, but he and Fidel thought that the veteran Cuban soldiers could play a decisive role at a critical moment in the insurrection. Based on his personal inspection of the area and discussions with the Congolese rebels and their foreign allies, he concluded that one hundred Cuban combat "volunteers" could tilt the balance against Tshombe. Training alone could correct some of the rebel deficiencies. With inspired and experienced leadership the rebels might actually defeat Tshombe. Che was certainly a match for Colonel Mike Hoare, the South African mercenary, and the rebels already had an established supply line linking them to Soviet and Chinese stockpiles in Tanzania, Egypt, and Algeria. If he and the Cuban volunteers intervened with newly trained Congolese units before the enemy detected it, the rebels could roll

13. Ibid.
14. Gleijeses, "Cuba's First Venture in Africa," 159–96.

up a few victories before Tshombe's American and Belgian supporters responded.

The success of the mission depended in the first place on getting Comandante Che Guevara out of Cuba and into the heart of Africa. To complete this important mission, Cuban intelligence cooperated with Soviet, eastern European, Egyptian, and Tanzanian intelligence and military officers. The mysterious disappearance of Che Guevara in Havana, followed by rumors of serious disputes at the highest levels of the Cuban government, provided a perfect cover for Guevara's departure. He was last seen in public at a funeral on March 30, 1965. After leaving the cemetery, Che went incognito. He shaved his entire head and beard, put on a pair of black-framed eyeglasses, and inserted a prosthesis in his mouth. To test his new disguise, Che made his first appearance at the secret training camp in Pinar del Río province, accompanied by Osmany Cienfuegos. Víctor Dreke, the commander of the camp, who had fought with Che in the Escambray, could not identify the man introduced to him as "Ramón." Che Guevara had disappeared.[15]

Ramón Benitez, aka Ernesto Guevara, entered Dar es Salaam, Tanzania, on April 19, 1965. On May 6, a CIA informant passed on several rumors about Che Guevara's location. He was either under house arrest in Havana, imprisoned at La Cabaña, seeking asylum in the Mexican embassy, or a Soviet prisoner in Algiers. Two weeks later the CIA received another report that Che had gone to Moscow to receive treatment for throat cancer. In late May, one rumor had Che returning to the front lines, not in Africa, but in the Dominican Republic, where he had secretly attempted to lead the rebellion that the American marines crushed in April 1965. Rumors of Che's imprisonment in Cuba continued to intrigue the CIA throughout the summer and fall of 1965, with the agency also considering reports of Che's appearance in Colombia, the Dominican Republic, Guatemala, and Peru. In December 1965, after Che had withdrawn the Cuban contingent from the Congo, a CIA informant reported with certainty that Che was in Guatemala.[16]

Che Guevara got into and out of the Congo without being detected by the CIA. Lawrence Devlin, the CIA station chief in the Congo, claims that he reported Guevara's presence in the country in October 1965, but his superi-

---

15. Testimony of Víctor Dreke, in Taibo, Escobar, and Guerra, *El año en que estuvimos en ninguna parte*, 26–29; Carrasco, "Tatu: Un guerrillero africano," 257–58.

16. For these and other CIA rumors about Che, see Ratner and Smith, *Che Guevara and the FBI*, 139–81.

ors never believed him.[17] In fact, the CIA lost the trail of Che Guevara for two years. The agency did not locate him until the summer of 1967, months after the Bolivian army first engaged Che's guerrilla band in southeastern Bolivia.

Cuban intelligence undoubtedly planted rumors to throw the CIA off Guevara's track. With American agents sniffing around Havana for evidence of Che's imprisonment or execution, Che left Havana at dawn on April 1, 1965. According to the few details released in the official Cuban history, Che and two comrades boarded a Cubana flight at José Martí International Airport, the last passengers to board the plane. They sat in one row, Víctor Dreke in the window seat, Che in the middle, and José María Martínez Tamayo guarding the aisle. Che wore a hat and glasses, a winter overcoat draped over his arm. His disguise worked so well that Luis Gómez Wagemert, a journalist who had interviewed Che several times and now sat in the aisle across from him, did not even recognize him.[18]

The journey from Cuba to Dar es Salaam took Che, on many stopovers, through Newfoundland, Prague, Milan, Cairo, and Nairobi. Cuban agents met them at every stop and facilitated their passage through customs and immigration, though they did not even know the identity of the travelers. The fact that the group landed in Prague and stayed two days in a house outside the city suggests that the Cubans received help from eastern European and possibly Soviet officials. The Soviets, in fact, never objected to Che's mission to the Congo. Shortly after Che left Cuba, Fidel informed Soviet ambassador Alexandr Alexiev that Che had departed Cuba to lead a revolutionary movement in Africa. Alexiev discreetly relayed this information to Soviet premier Leonid Brezhnev, who showed little interest in Che's mission to Africa.[19] All evidence, especially the deliveries of Soviet arms to the rebels via third countries, indicates that the Soviet Union, despite its public opposition to Cuba's "adventures" in the Third World, provided some support to Che's Congolese campaign.

Che kept a low profile throughout the long journey, spending most of his time reading and writing while on the plane and in his various rooms. The Cuban intelligence officer who picked Che up at Cairo thought that he was a "weird" agricultural technician. In Dar es Salaam, Ambassador Pablo Ribalta greeted Che and his escorts at the airport on April 19 and took them directly

---

17. Castañeda, *Compañero*, 313.

18. Testimony of Víctor Dreke, in Taibo, Escobar, and Guerra, *El año en que estuvimos en ninguna parte*, 28–29, 34–35; Carrasco, "Tatu: Un guerrillero africano," 258.

19. Anderson, *Che Guevara*, 639.

to a hotel. Even he did not recognize Che, his former commander. Che Guevara's disguise and the covert journey from Cuba to Africa had worked perfectly.[20]

Cuban intelligence also worked considerable magic in getting a full company of black Cuban soldiers, armaments, and supplies to Africa. In the wake of Che, though following other routes, came an additional 8 officers, 19 sergeants, 11 corporals, and 72 privates. Che would eventually command a Cuban column of 112 men divided into three infantry platoons and one artillery unit. They arrived in small groups over the following two months, some of them going through Moscow, Algeria, and Egypt, on their way to Dar es Salaam.[21]

The terms governing the command and deployment of these Cuban troops, however, remained ambiguous. Although Presidents Nyerere of Tanzania and Nasser of Egypt had accepted Cuba's proposal to provide military aid to the Congolese rebels, neither they nor the rebels had agreed to accept a Cuban combat force commanded by Che Guevara. They had only agreed to accept Cuban military instructors. When Che arrived, however, he intended to lead a combat unit into battle. He did not solicit the approval of Laurent Kabila, Nyerere, or Bella for this substantial change in the Cuban military mission. Che went to the Congo as an uninvited guest and unauthorized to command troops in battle, but expecting the African rebels to follow him into battle. As Che explained it, "I . . . figured that it would be difficult for them to refuse [his presence]. I was blackmailing them with my presence."[22]

The Congolese rebels never approved the presence of Che, and they never approved any Cuban combat mission. The Congolese asked for and approved thirty Cuban military instructors. There is no evidence that the rebel command authorized these instructors to engage in combat. In his meetings with Kabila, military commander of the region, and with Gaston Soumaliot, minister of defense of the rebel government, Che had only proposed to train Congolese and African rebels in the eastern Congo—and some of the Africans expressed opposition to that idea. He did not propose that a Cuban column would join the fight against the Tshombe government.[23]

20. Testimony of Dreke and Rivalta, in Taibo, Escobar, and Guerra, *El año en que estuvimos en ninguna parte,* 34–37.
21. Testimony of Nane, Dreke, Rivalta, and Kumi in Taibo, Escobar, and Guerra, *El año en que estuvimos en ninguna parte,* 34–37.
22. Gálvez, *Che in Africa,* 55.
23. Ibid., 37–38.

Che did not see any difference between training and fighting, convinced that soldiers learned how to fight by fighting. The Congolese may have understood training to be much like what they had experienced in China and the Soviet Union, where they studied and practiced in noncombat situations. But when Che offered instructors, he expected them to fight on the front lines. Revolutionary soldiers "can't be created in a military academy," Che argued. "Someone can get a degree from a military academy, but their real graduation, like that of any other professional, comes in the exercise of their profession, through their reaction to enemy fire, suffering, defeat, continuous attacks and adverse situations."[24]

The lack of agreement on two fundamental issues—Che's command authority and the combat duties of the Cuban column—limited the impact that Guevara's column would have on the Congolese rebellion. He did not even have the authority to order his own troops into battle, let alone the disparate Congolese rebel factions. He had arrived on his own initiative. Without a clearly defined mission and authority, Che would languish in the mountains for the following nine months, frustrated by Congolese leaders who refused to submit to his blackmail. The Congolese did not have to accept him, and they certainly did not have to submit to his command.

The only troops Che commanded in the Congo were Cubans. If he ordered them into battle without Congolese approval, he would convert a civil war into a war between Cuba and the Congo. At any rate, Castro had not authorized Che to do that, either, though his men would clearly fight if ordered. Che informed his men that they had come to liberate the Congo from imperialism, in a struggle that could last as long as five years. So before he sent his men into the country, he presumptuously assigned his men war names corresponding to numbers in Swahili. Dreke became Moja (one), Martínez Tamayo became Mbili (two), and Che became Tatu (three).[25]

After a few days in Dar es Salaam gathering supplies, Che and thirteen Cuban volunteers left for the Congo in a Land Rover, three Mercedes Benzes, and two jeeps. The backpacks and arms went in the truck; the men strapped a small launch to a trailer and covered it with a tarp. Everybody, including Che, took turns driving over one thousand miles of dirt roads through towns and hamlets from Dar es Salaam to Kigoma, a city of about seventy thousand

---

24. Ibid., 40.

25. Testimonies of Nane and Kumi, in Taibo, Escobar, and Guerra, *El año en que estuvimos en ninguna parte*, 37–40. To simplify the narrative, only the real names of the combatants in the Congo and Bolivia will be used.

people on the eastern shore of Lake Tanganyika. The Cuban team arrived in Kigoma on the evening of April 22, 1965.[26]

Kigoma, the staging area for shipments of Soviet and Chinese arms, lacked the port facilities required to receive and store military supplies safely. Che noted boxes of Soviet and Chinese equipment strewn about the waterfront, exposed to the elements. The poorly organized port facilities matched the undisciplined character of the Congolese troops. Che noted with disgust how many rebel officers and soldiers frequented Kigoma's brothels and bars. Che never would have granted his soldiers weekend passes to a den of such iniquity, as did the Congolese leaders. "The revolutionary leadership [of the Congo] never sufficiently assessed the nefarious influence of Kigoma—with its brothels; its liquor; and, above all, the certain refuge it offered," Che concluded later.[27]

Unlike the rebel combatants in Kigoma, Che wanted to get across the lake and to the front as soon as possible. The journey across the lake would expose the rebels to enemy fire. To intercept arms shipments across the lake, the Tshombe government had acquired two 180-ton, armor-plated landing crafts, equipped with machine guns and small cannons. The ships were slow but more than a match for the fishing boats that smuggled supplies and combatants across the lake. Just before midnight on April 23, the fourteen Cubans boarded two launches with outboard motors. They were dressed in combat uniforms with olive green berets and carried FAL automatic rifles, prepared to engage the enemy if necessary. During the six-hour journey, they spotted the lights of what could have been enemy vessels, but they arrived undetected at Kibamba on April 24. Che Guevara had arrived in Congolese rebel territory.[28]

The following day the Congolese rebel leader, Antoine Godefri Tchamlesso, introduced Moja, Mbili, and Tatu to several military leaders of the eastern front. Tchamlesso, not knowing the true identity of the Cubans, introduced Che as a doctor and a French translator. He then asked the Congolese leaders to include Moja, the alleged leader of the Cuban contingent, in all future general staff meetings. Che noted that this proposal did not please the Congolese officers.[29]

26. Testimonies of Che, Rivalta, Dreke, and Kumi, in Taibo, Escobar, and Guerra, *El año en que estuvimos en ninguna parte,* 42–43.

27. Gálvez, *Che in Africa,* 61.

28. Testimony of Dreke, Ilanga, Che, and Kumi, in Taibo, Escobar, and Guerra, *El año en que estuvimos en ninguna parte,* 47–49.

29. Gálvez, *Che in Africa,* 65–66.

After the meeting, Che pulled Tchamlesso aside and revealed his true identity. He could not remain in disguise any longer if he expected to exert influence over military affairs. Tchamlesso was floored, according to Che. Convinced that Che's presence in the Congo would cause an international scandal, he urged Che to conceal his identity. Che told him to go back to Dar es Salaam and tell Kabila that he was in the Congo. Tchamlesso left that night.[30]

While he waited for Kabila's response, Che made a formal military proposal to the general staff of the northern front, based at a camp overlooking Kibamba and the lake. He proposed to initiate a five-week training program for companies of one hundred men, divided into groups of twenty. The Cubans would teach them the rudiments of infantry fighting, armaments, field engineering, communications, and reconnaissance. Upon completion of their training, Martínez Tamayo would lead a company into combat. While that company served at the front, another one would continue training. When the first company returned, the second one would depart for the front. In this way, Che hoped to train and fight simultaneously, weeding out the worst soldiers and identifying officers at the same time. The Congolese staff asked Tatu, whom they knew only as a doctor, to put the proposal in writing, which Che promptly did.[31]

Che waited for a response from Kabila for the following six weeks. While many of the Congolese leaders debased themselves with alcohol and prostitutes in Kigoma, idleness consumed Che. One day he would climb up to a rebel mountain base at Luluabourg, and the following day he would climb back down for a visit to Kigoma. He went up and down the hills so often that one of his Congolese comrades asked himself, "What's up with this shit-eating white man, are there no hills in his country?"[32]

The news that Che Guevara and 120 Cubans had arrived in the eastern Congo frightened Laurent Kabila. He had been expecting thirty Cuban instructors; a group of 120 Cuban veterans represented a combat force powerful enough to overrun Tshombe's mercenaries. Kabila, however, refused to exploit his unexpected military advantage. Instead of going immediately to the front to unleash an offensive with his augmented force, he remained in Dar es Salaam and sent Leonard Mitudidi to serve as his military liaison with Che. According to Tchamlesso, Kabila lacked the training and temperament

30. Ibid., 67.
31. Ibid., 69.
32. Testimony of Ilanga, in Taibo, Escobar, and Guerra, *El año en que estuvimos en ninguna parte*, 62.

required of a guerrilla commander.[33] He would send word that he would arrive at the front shortly, and then he would not show up. This went on, day after day, for weeks. With such leaders as Kabila, Che was not surprised to find that his soldiers lacked discipline, training, and the fighting spirit required of a guerrilla. They had plenty of Soviet and Chinese arms and ammunition; they just did not know how to use them or have the expertise of their Cuban allies.

Mitudidi arrived at the front with a group of eighteen Cuban combatants on May 8, 1965. He authorized Che's request to establish a separate base camp near Luluabourg area, nearly five thousand feet above sea level and two miles from Kibamba. About two weeks later, Mitudidi issued his first formal military order to Che. He commanded him and the Cubans to attack Albertville, held by a large, well-supplied contingent of regular Congo army soldiers and foreign mercenaries. Che denounced the order as "absurd." The rebels had not made any of the necessary preparations; they did not know the terrain, strength, or location of the enemy forces; and Che had only thirty combat veterans to throw into the battle (and ten of them were sick). He met Mitudidi on May 23 and talked him out of what could have been a suicidal assault. Instead, he sent out scouting parties to determine the strength and location of all forces in the area—including his allies.[34]

Che spent most of his first two months in the Congo reading, learning Swahili, teaching, playing chess, and fighting boredom. The Congolese rebels, well supplied and situated in fortified positions on high ground, did not seem too interested in fighting. The rebels had simply set up a camp and relaxed, evidently trusting that the enemy would not attack them if they did not attack first. Che described them as a parasitic army, living off the supplies provided by local peasants, while making no preparations to engage the enemy.[35]

Che had come to the Congo to fight imperialism, but only two months into the campaign he concluded that the Congolese would not fight. Barring significant changes in leadership, strategy, and tactics, Che predicted, the insurrection was "irreversibly condemned to failure." Prospects for the movement diminished considerably in Che's eyes on June 7, when the one leader he trusted, Mitudidi, drowned while crossing Lake Tanganyika. In this "stupid accident," Che lost a thirty-year-old man who had just begun

33. Testimony of Tchamlesso, in Gálvez, *Che in Africa*, 69–70.
34. Gálvez, *Che in Africa*, 77–80.
35. Testimony of Taibo, Escobar, and Guerra, in Taibo, Escobar, and Guerra, *El año en que estuvimos en ninguna parte*, 66–76.

to impose order out of the "terrible chaos" that had prevailed at the Kabimba rebel base.[36]

On June 17 Kabila finally ordered Che to attack the enemy. He commanded Che to attack Front de Force (or Fort Bendera), the strongest garrison in the southeastern region, defended as it was by three hundred Congolese soldiers and one hundred mercenaries. Che strongly objected to the order, considering it as absurd as Mitudidi's plan to attack Albertville. He detailed his concerns and issued strategic recommendations in an extensive report to Kabila. Che believed that the rebels, driven out of their bases in the northeastern region, needed to reorganize and prepare to meet a concentrated effort by the American imperialists to crush them during this period of relative weakness. He expected the imperialists to hit them hard, first by neutralizing the lake and cutting off their supply lines. They had to organize quickly and select their targets carefully, Che explained to Kabila: "The time factor is of key importance for consolidating and developing the revolution, which cannot be done except by hitting the enemy hard. Passivity is the beginning of defeat" (92).

Instead of attacking Front de Force, Che urged Kabila to concentrate on training and organizing the rebel army into a force capable of striking the enemy hard. They had no experience in conducting large-scale operations that required the coordination and mobilization of units at the battalion level. There was no central military command "with real power over all the fronts, to bring what in military terms is called the unity of doctrine." In the absence of unified military command, local chiefs exercised excessive tactical and strategic independence, making it impossible for the commanders to coordinate large troop movements. The rebels had plenty of combatants and armaments, but they lacked discipline and training. "All this results in an inability to carry out major tactical actions and, therefore, strategic paralysis" (92).

Che then proposed measures to correct the weaknesses of the rebel forces. He recommended that the rebels fight in mixed units commanded at first by Cubans. In a series of well-defined, selected tactical actions, the Cubans would train the Congolese soldiers and gradually extend their radius of action. At the same time, the Cubans would establish a central training base, organize and train a true general staff, and complete other complementary work such as establishing a health care system. If Kabila accepted this proposal, he would effectively cede strategy and command to Che, agreeing to replace his tradi-

---

36. Gálvez, *Che in Africa,* 91. Subsequent references to this work appear in the text.

tional military strategy with guerrilla warfare under Che's command. Che asked for Cuban command of the rebel units "because we would guarantee direction of the fighting in line with our concept of guerrilla warfare" (92–93).

The Congolese leaders held tightly to a concept of conventional warfare. They could not see beyond Albertville, the base of enemy operations, and hence, their primary target. They wanted to attack Albertville as soon as possible with all their forces. Che shared the objective of taking Albertville, but he argued that it had to be done through a "slow and tenacious" process. He advocated attacking its lines of communications and supply through ambushes and sabotage. The rebels would demoralize the enemy systematically, attacking only when conditions favored them, selecting poorly defended enemy outposts first and rolling up a series of small victories. By gradually tightening a noose around Albertville, the rebels would force the enemy to abandon the town rather than drive them out of it in a costly and bloody siege (94).

To Che's great dismay, Kabila insisted on the attack at Front de Force and ordered Cuban troops into battle under the command of a rebel known as Mudandi, a Rwandan Tutsi who had been trained in China. Che opposed the attack, but he yielded to Kabila. At least 450 men, possibly as many as 700, defended Front de Force, which was built around a hydroelectric power plant on the Kimbi River. Che did not know the exact strength of the garrison. When he saw it a month later, he described it as a "veritable bastion" (132). At the time, the rebels had not even reconnoitered the area, which alone demonstrated Kabila's inexperience. Yet Che submitted to Kabila's orders because his men wanted action. Che longed for battle too, but Kabila refused to let him risk his life at the front. Thus, when forty-four Cuban troops first marched off into battle on June 20, accompanied by 160 Congolese and Rwandan Tutsis, Che was not with them.[37]

At 5:00 A.M. on June 29, 1965, the rebels attacked in four groups, opening up with cannons, mortars, machine guns, and antiaircraft weapons. The enemy responded in kind, and the two sides exchanged heavy-weapons fire for the following two hours. In most of the units, the African soldiers fled when the firing became heated, leaving weapons and wounded and dead comrades behind them. The Cubans held their ground and performed honorably, making the best out of a bad situation before they called off the ill-advised

37. Testimony of Dreke and Che, in Taibo, Escobar, and Guerra, *El año en que estuvimos en ninguna parte*, 95–100.

attack. The results were nevertheless disastrous, much as Che had anticipated. Four Cubans and fourteen Rwandans lay dead on the field.[38]

In the knapsack of one of the fallen Cubans, the South African mercenaries found a diary and a Cuban passport, which detailed the itinerary from Havana to Africa. Colonel Mike Hoare had suspected that the unusually audacious attack had to reflect the presence of foreign military personnel. The discovery of the diary and passport erased all doubts. The South African passed on this valuable information to his American advisers. On July 6, the U.S. embassy in Leopoldville first disclosed the presence of Cuban troops to Washington. Soon, newspapers in Dar es Salaam published reports of the Cuban presence. The attack on Front de Force had been doubly disastrous; it produced no positive results, and it blew the cover off the Cuban mission.[39]

The debacle at Front de Force further demoralized the Cubans under Che's command. "Each of our combatants," Che wrote in his diary, "had the sad experience of seeing how the troops that went to the attack dissolved in the moment of fight. . . . They had also observed the lack of comradeship among them, leaving the wounded to their fate."[40] Many of the Cubans, seeing no reason to fight a war that the Congolese themselves refused to wage, discussed returning home. If the Cubans remained, they would have to intensify their training efforts. The Congolese attributed their defeat, not to their inexperience, but to the mysterious *dawa* that was not with them on that day. The Congolese believed that dawa, which means "medicine" in Swahili, protected them against the bullets of their enemies. The Cubans tried to convince them that no magical spirit could possibly protect them from enemy fire, but the Congolese believed that the Cubans had a very powerful dawa that they had brought with them from Cuba. The fact that four Cubans had died in combat did not persuade them that dawa did not exist; it only suggested that the dawa did not protect them on that day.[41]

A week after ordering his men into a battle they should not have fought, Kabila made his long-expected and oft-announced trip to the front on July

38. Testimony of Dreke, Nane, and Che, in Taibo, Escobar, and Guerra, *El año en que estuvimos en ninguna parte,* 109–19; Carrasco, "Tatu: Un guerrillero africano," 265; Anderson, *Che Guevara,* 650; Gálvez, *Che in Africa,* 101–6.

39. Gleijeses, "'Flee!'" 220–21; CIA, "Cuban Negroes Trained for Guerrilla Activities in the Congo," January 19, 1966, report no. 00-K-323/00185-66, CIA Files, NSA; Testimony of Dreke, in Taibo, Escobar, and Guerra, *El año en que estuvimos en ninguna parte,* 116–17; Castañeda, *Compañero,* 309, 313.

40. Gálvez, *Che in Africa,* 107.

41. Testimony of Che, Dreke, and Ilanga, in Taibo, Escobar, and Guerra, *El año en que estuvimos en ninguna parte,* 119–20, 130–32.

7. Che now had an opportunity to press for the necessary changes in leadership, strategy, and tactics, all of which hinged on his principal request: to take personal command of training and fighting at the front. Kabila responded cordially that a world-renowned revolutionary such as Che could not risk his life on the front line. Che insisted that he knew how to take care of himself and that he did not seek glory on the battlefield. Perhaps Kabila recognized behind Che's request a bid to take command, not of the combatants, but of the rebel strategy. If he authorized Che to take command of units at the front, he would give Che the opportunity to select the targets and the tactics, responsibilities that Kabila then held in his hands. Naturally, Kabila refused to do so.[42]

Che had better luck with Ildefonse Masengo, who had replaced Mitudidi as head of the eastern front. Masengo accepted Che's proposals and allowed him to form mixed teams of Congolese, Cuban, and Rwandan combatants to set small-scale ambushes. Che ordered Martínez Tomayo to set an ambush on July 17, in territory that Cuban scouts had inspected carefully. A team of fifty men attacked one truck containing five soldiers, only one of them armed. The rebels killed the five enemy soldiers and captured their vehicle. The behavior of the rebels during and after the skirmish, however, diminished the value of this first victory. Many of the Rwandan soldiers had fled when the shooting began, only to return to take possession of several cases of beer and whiskey in the truck. Then, on the way back to camp, one of the Rwandans killed an innocent peasant. With such victories, Che predicted, it would take at least five years for the revolutionary movement to triumph, "unless something changed in how the war was directed—an ever more distant possibility."[43]

One can presume that Che privately wished for a change in leadership and military strategy. The leaders of these rebel forces, namely Soumaliot and Kabila, had little or no military training. They ordered undisciplined troops to attack well-defended positions, violating the principal tenet of guerrilla warfare that no battle or skirmish is to be fought unless it can be won. But they were neither guerrillas nor revolutionaries. They emphasized the political struggle over the military campaign, which explains why they spent most of their time at conferences in Cairo or diplomatic sessions in Dar es Salaam. They seemed, in fact, to spend more of their time fighting each other than battling the enemy, Che admitted in an open letter to his men. Despite the many Congolese shortcomings, Che pleaded with his men to honor their

42. Gálvez, *Che in Africa,* 113–14.
43. Ibid., 123.

revolutionary commitments. They would have to lead by example.[44]

The most effective boost to Cuban morale, and a possible turning point in the rebellion came in mid-August, when Che decided to take command in the field without Kabila's consent. He could no longer subordinate himself, his troops, or his mission to Kabila. He never confronted or challenged Kabila directly, but he told Pablo Ribalta that he did not have "any confidence in Kabila." Che had also concluded that unfortunately, "all the others who were there [the political leaders in Dar] were worse, not even being intelligent." Following the old military maxim that a general cannot lead from the rear, Che arrived at Front de Force on August 18, determined to inspect the troops and terrain; take stock of the rebel army's arms, supplies, and morale; and initiate military action.[45] He did not want his Cuban soldiers to fight as an independent unit but the idleness of the Congolese had forced his hand. The appearance of Che, who was wearing his customary olive green uniform and black beret and carrying his Soviet pistol and M-1, produced a visible surge of confidence in the Cuban troops. "I couldn't get Kabila to come," Che told his men. "If he wants me to return to the base, he will have to come here."[46]

Che was now the de facto commander of an independent mixed column of about forty Congolese, ten Rwandans, and thirty Cubans, and it was the most effective combat unit in the entire rebel army. On the eastern front, which encompassed the towns of Uvira, Fizi, Baraka, Lulimba-Kabambare, and Kasongo, the rebels had more than two thousand rifles and several cannons, plus mortars, bazookas, and antiaircraft guns.[47] Kabila certainly did not know how to deploy these weapons in a coordinated campaign, so Che decided to do it. In early September, he carefully prepared an ambush. He divided his column into three groups and placed one of them at the center and the others at the left and right flanks of the road. The rebels planted a mine in the road and assigned a small unit to destroy a plank bridge after the enemy crossed it, cutting off the retreat and preventing reinforcements from coming up. It was a simple tactic, used often in the Sierra Maestra, but more organized and "professional" than the rebels' previous tactics. When the enemy convoy fell into the ambush on September 11, it essentially represented an act of war perpetrated by the government of Cuba against the Congo,

44. Ibid., 127–29.
45. Ibid., 130–31, 135.
46. Testimony of Dreke, in Taibo, Escobar, and Guerra, *El año en que estuvimos en ninguna parte*, 150–51.
47. Gálvez, *Che in Africa*, 131.

since Che, not Kabila, had ordered it. As noted earlier, the execution of the ambush disappointed Che, but he had finally fired his first shot of the Congolese revolution. When Dreke, the bodyguard assigned by Fidel to protect Che, attempted to remove Che from the front, Che responded brusquely, "I am the chief."[48]

Some of Che's African comrades, however, had serious reservations about accepting the command of a foreign white man. They wondered why a white man would come from so far away to help African rebels. The leaders, for reasons of pride or racism, also had trouble accepting Che's military advice. In the days since he had decided to fight, with or without approval, he had devised a strategic plan to concentrate the rebel forces for an elastic encirclement of Lulimba-Kabambare. With fifty-three men defending it, he expected support from other units, but no other rebel leader would join him in the attack. Frustrated by the passivity of the Congolese rebels, Che effectively abandoned his alliance with Kabila and the local rebel leaders by the end of September. From that time on, Che concentrated his efforts on the "creation of a perfectly armed, well-equipped, independent column that can be both a shock force and a model. If this is achieved," Che predicted, "it will have changed the panorama considerably. Until this is done, it will be impossible to organize a revolutionary army; for the low quality of the chiefs prevents it."[49]

He might have selected the right country to launch his tricontinental campaign, but he had allied with the wrong leaders. Laurent Kabila, an avowed Marxist with ties to the Soviet Union and China, never demonstrated the fortitude or aggressiveness that Che expected of a military leader. Soumaliot, the nominal president of the CNL, was no better, yet Fidel Castro feted him in Havana in early September without Che's knowledge. Che only learned of the trip after Soumaliot returned to Africa. He had warned Pablo Ribalta not to give any money to Soumaliot without his approval, but that warning reached Havana too late. Soumaliot somehow convinced Fidel that his rebel armies had already made significant progress. On a series of trips to other African countries, he had asked for more military support for launching a new offensive in the eastern Congo, with more heavy weapons and torpedo boats for a naval campaign on the lake. From Fidel he asked for only fifty doctors, to which Fidel acceded.[50]

---

48. Ibid., 140–41; Testimony of Dreke, in Taibo, Escobar, and Guerra, *El año en que estuvimos en ninguna parte*, 159.
49. Gálvez, *Che in Africa*, 172.
50. Ibid., 139; Anderson, *Che Guevara*, 659.

To correct the distortions presented by Soumaliot, Che drafted a long, characteristically blunt report to Fidel on October 5, 1965. "Soumaliot and his comrades have sold you a huge streetcar. It would be tiresome to list the large number of lies they have told," he began. The reality is, Che explained, that there were only two zones where there was actually an organized revolutionary movement: his own and near the Kasai River in the western Congo, where Pierre Mulele—the "great unknown"—directed an independent rebellion. Other bands survived in the forest, lacking leadership and fighting spirit. As an example of the miserable state of affairs, Che mentioned the recent loss of Baraka, an important lakefront town defended by one thousand rebels. Facing the opening move in Colonel Hoare's offensive, the rebels surrendered this strategic town without firing a shot. Che had two hundred reliable combatants, but he warned Fidel that they alone could not "liberate a country that doesn't want to fight." Sending any more men to the Congo would be harmful "unless we decide, once and for all, to fight on our own. In that case, I will need a division, and we will have to see how many the enemy will throw against us."[51]

Che's enemy, now alerted to and concerned about the presence of the Cuban contingent, had initiated an offensive campaign designed to eliminate the rebels from the "Fizi pocket." Colonel Hoare had wanted to launch an offensive the previous May, but Tshombe's financial problems left his mercenaries unpaid and unhappy. Colonel Hoare knew the exact location of all the rebel camps—their coordinates were given in a telegram from Ambassador Godley—but he lacked the men and matériel to launch offensive operations. After the discovery of communist volunteers, however, Tshombe's American and Belgian supporters initiated military and diplomatic actions to crush the rebellion. Military advisers arrived in Albertville to inspect the area and develop a strategic plan. By taking Baraka and launching a fleet of jerry-rigged gunboats on Lake Tanganyika, Che's enemy obviously intended to sever his lines of communication and supply to Dar es Salaam. To complete this task, Ambassador Godley urged the State Department to apply diplomatic pressure on President Nyerere of Tanzania. Godley believed that Nyerere would terminate aid to the rebels if the Americans, the British, and other African leaders demanded it.[52]

51. Che to Fidel, October 5, 1965, cited in Gálvez, *Che in Africa*, 183.
52. CIA, Directorate of Intelligence, "The Situation in the Congo," August 26, 1965; Godley to State, September 21, 1965, container 85, Congo Country File, NSF, LBJ.

The enemy's military and diplomatic offensive produced quick results. In early October, Hoare's motorized division, supported by Cuban American pilots flying T-28s and B-26s provided by the United States, attacked the rebel base at Fizi. Hoare received transportation, communications, and field maintenance support from U.S. Army units stationed just outside the combat zone. While Colonel Hoare subsequently reported that his column met surprisingly stiff resistance from the Cuban veterans defending Fizi, Che's diary indicates that Fizi fell without much of a fight. The rebel commander of Fizi blamed everybody but himself for not resisting the attackers. Thus, Oscar Fernández Mell reported on October 10 that "the soldiers are advancing on Fizi, and there's nothing to stop or even delay them."[53]

Che could not mount a viable defense. With Fizi and Baraka in enemy hands, he recognized that the mercenaries controlled the western shore of Lake Tanganyika, making it nearly impossible for him to receive supplies or reinforcements. Even a retreat across the lake began to look more precarious. The Congolese soldiers began to talk of retreating before it was too late. Che's bodyguard began to fear for the life of his commander, but Che was determined to fight on, despite the risks.[54]

On October 13, President Kasavubu dismissed controversial prime minister Tshombe, offering the opening gambit in a bid to end hostilities. The dismissal, coming after months of political struggle between the two men, opened the door for a political settlement. Tshombe's appointment had compelled many African leaders to support the rebellion, for they held him responsible for the assassination of the venerated Lumumba. With Tshombe out, African support for the rebel movement quickly softened. When Kasavubu arrived in Ghana for the meeting of the Organization of African Unity (OAU) on October 19, he received a warm welcome. More important, he promised to send all foreign mercenaries home and to establish friendly relations with the governments of other African countries, including the leftist regime of Congo-Brazzaville. Kasavubu's proposal formed the foundation for a political settlement. The OAU passed a resolution calling for the withdrawal of all foreign forces from the Congo, including Hoare's mercenaries and the Cuban volunteers, leaving the Congolese to negotiate a settlement without any foreign involvement.[55]

53. Kelly, *America's Tyrant,* 159–66; Gálvez, *Che in Africa,* 193–94.
54. Taibo, Escobar, and Guerra, *El año en que estuvimos en ninguna parte,* 191–95.
55. Kelly, *America's Tyrant,* 166.

With this rapid turn of events, Congolese volunteers began to desert, and as they left, Cuban morale dissipated. Che convened a meeting of all Communist party members to decide on a course of action. The Cuban volunteers expressed serious doubts about the prospects for victory under the current leadership. Che asked how many people still believed that the revolutionary movement had a chance to succeed. Only six people raised their hands. They had not voted to leave the Congo, but their will to fight had suffered an irreversible decline. Some of Che's loyal men would follow him to the bitter end if necessary, but he refused to sacrifice them for a losing cause.[56] He could only hope for a withdrawal with Cuban honor intact.

On October 24, the sound of artillery and gunfire signaled the advance of enemy soldiers on the Cuban camp. Che intended to hold his ground. His Congolese volunteers fled as the enemy approached. Just as he was about to organize his defenses, he learned that a large number of enemy soldiers were about to surround them. If he ordered his men to dig in and fight, he might lose his entire column; if they retreated, he would probably lose a large part of his supplies and equipment. Che wanted to put up a stiff resistance until nightfall and then retreat under cover of darkness with as much matériel as his men could carry. When he learned that the enemy had overrun his outer line of defense, he had no choice but to retreat. The enemy had penetrated so far that Dreke, Che's bodyguard, felt certain that Che would have been killed or captured if Che had waited any longer to retreat.[57]

With Colonel Hoare hot on Che's heels and the Congolese rebels running away, the other African states withdrew their support for the insurrection. Ahmed Ben Bella, overthrown in June 1965, could no longer muster African support for Che and the rebellion. At the end of October, President Nyerere asked Ambassador Ribalta, in accordance with the OAU resolution, to withdraw the Cuban forces from the Congo. This was the "coup de grace for a dying revolution," Che wrote.[58]

Only Che wanted to continue the fight. Even Fidel wanted to pull Che out of the Congo before he lost him. On November 4, Che received a letter from Fidel, urging him to withdraw. If he decided to stay, disregarding the OAU resolution, Castro promised to send all the men and material resources Che required. Fidel nevertheless asked him to "do everything except the

---

56. Taibo, Escobar, and Guerra, *El año en que estuvimos en ninguna parte*, 195.
57. Testimony of Che, Dreke, Mena, and Genge, in Taibo, Escobar, and Guerra, *El año en que estuvimos en ninguna parte*, 196–97.
58. Gálvez, *Che in Africa*, 238.

absurd." If Che decided to leave, Castro promised him that he could return to Cuba and resume his duties in the party and the government. He would support whatever decision Che made.[59]

As Che responded to Fidel on November 4, Colonel Hoare pressed his troops closer to Che's camp. The Cubans had reestablished a solid line of defense, and Che, convinced that his men could resist the advancing troops, preferred to fight and die where he stood rather than allow his forces to flee in disgrace. He refused to withdraw unless and until the Congolese explicitly asked him to do so.[60]

Now General Joseph Désiré Mobutu, recognizing an opportunity to crush the Cuban volunteers before the OAU resolution took effect, gave Colonel Hoare time to complete his offensive operations. As a result, Che's life and the survival of the Cuban column remained in danger. If Che did not act quickly, Hoare's forces would block his exit and strike directly against his camp. Many of the Cubans, recognizing the imminent danger, talked openly about retreating, and Che was inclined to let them go. He considered the possibility of selecting a group of highly motivated combatants to maintain a nucleus of guerrilla resistance indefinitely. On the evening of November 17, however, the Cubans suffered another military setback when enemy forces overran their outer line of defense. The following day, Che learned that the Congolese leaders had approved an immediate cease-fire. Che asked for confirmation in writing, but with the enemy pressing his lines, he could no longer delay the inevitable. He ordered a withdrawal. His men no longer wanted to fight for a country that did not want to be liberated.[61]

The evacuation began at dawn on November 19 with the burning of the house that had served as Guevara's residence for seven months. He did not want any documents to fall into enemy hands. Even after that, he still thought about reorganizing a guerrilla band with his best combatants. He thought that at least twenty men would have followed him, enough to constitute a foco. As about two hundred men prepared to load up in several launches for the dangerous lake crossing on the night of November 20, Che was still thinking about staying behind. It would not have been a difficult sacrifice for him to make, but he could not bring himself to ask others to do the same.[62]

59. Fidel to Che (received November 4, 1965), in Gálvez, *Che in Africa*, 239.
60. Gálvez, *Che in Africa*, 241–42.
61. Ibid., 264–72.
62. Ibid., 271–73, 291–92.

Around two o'clock on the morning of November 21, three launches evac-
uated the Cubans from the Congo. As the boats moved quietly across the
lake, Che contemplated an uncertain future. He did not know where to go.
In his farewell letter to Fidel, he had resigned all his positions and renounced
his Cuban citizenship.[63] Despite Fidel's invitation to return to Cuba, Che
still felt compelled to fight on the front lines. Che saw nothing attractive in
returning to the Cuban bureaucracy. He wanted to fight. Once again, the
only question was where.

As the boats approached the Tanzanian shore, Che bid farewell. The decision of the Congolese to suspend the struggle has obliged us to withdraw, he
explained. He asked them to honor the memory of their fallen comrades. If
Fidel asked any of them to go on an international mission again, he hoped
that they would accept their duty without hesitation, despite their experience
in the Congo. However, the time had come for them to separate: "I won't
land with you, for we must avoid any kind of provocation," Che told his men.[64]

Che made it back safely to Dar es Salaam, took up residence on the top
floor of the Cuban embassy, and began to write his account of the Congo
campaign. He began: "This is a history of a failure." As usual, he severely
criticized his own performance. He had been too complacent with the
Congolese leaders and too hard on his own men. He thought that as a result
of his farewell letter to Fidel, some of his men viewed him as a foreigner, just
as they viewed the Congolese. "My function was to be their real leader, leading them to the victory that would promote the development of an authentic people's army," Che wrote. Seen as a foreigner, he never assumed the
authority that the revolutionary movement so desperately needed. "If I had
been a better soldier, I would have been able to have a greater influence," he
concluded.[65]

Despite the disastrous experience in the Congo, Che remained faithful to
his strategy of guerrilla warfare. The failure of the Congolese rebellion reflected
no faults in his strategic conceptions, because the rebels had never applied
his strategy. In the few skirmishes in which Che's men applied guerrilla tactics, the men performed well enough to impress their adversaries. Had the
Congolese leaders given Che the opportunity to train a guerrilla force and
direct its operations, the outcome in the Congo could have been different.

63. Che to Fidel, March 31, 1965, in Guevara, *Che: Selected Works*, 422–23.
64. Gálvez, *Che in Africa*, 275.
65. Ibid., 292–93.

But the Congolese rebels and their African supporters, unwilling to give Che combat command, gave up before he had an opportunity to launch a true guerrilla campaign. The one great military disaster of the short-lived campaign occurred at Front de Force, where Kabila ordered an ill-advised conventional assault on a well-fortified position. The negative results of that action, combined with the incompetent leadership of Kabila and Soumaliot, confirmed Che's faith in guerrilla warfare and his ability to command it. If he failed in the Congo, he failed because he refused to take a command that the Congolese never offered to him. "I have left with more faith than ever in guerrilla struggle, but we have failed. I bear a great responsibility; I won't forget the defeat or its most valuable teachings."[66]

Yet the experience that weighed most heavily on Che was his decision not to fight to the death. "I didn't demand the maximum sacrifice at the decisive moment. I was held back by something in my psyche." Perhaps it was neither the time nor the place to make the sacrifice, but he could have done it easily. "I think I should have overcome that self-critical analysis and told a given number of combatants that we should make the final gesture and should have remained."[67] Nearly two years later, when faced with a choice between leaving and dying, Che chose the latter.

66. Ibid., 293.
67. Ibid., 291–92.

TEN HERE I AM ADVISER TO NO ONE

Mario Monje arrived in Havana in December 1966, determined to persuade Fidel Castro not to launch a guerrilla campaign in Bolivia. He had learned that a group of Cuban combatants had already set up camp in southeastern Bolivia, although he—the leader of the Partido Comunista de Bolivia (PCB, Bolivian Communist Party)—had not requested or approved Cuban military assistance. In a private meeting with Fidel, Monje insisted that only Bolivians could lead the armed struggle in Bolivia, and that only the PCB had the authority to initiate and direct a guerrilla campaign. Castro concurred, then asked Monje to meet Che Guevara at an unspecified location along the Bolivian border for further discussions. Monje accepted the invitation enthusiastically, understanding that Che would arrive from a country near Bolivia. Monje returned to La Paz on December 24, received secret instructions, and left for Camiri on December 29.

Two days later, Monje arrived at Ñancahuazú, a camp located on the river of the same name in southeastern Bolivia. Che pulled Monje aside and walked with him to a secluded location. He apologized immediately, confessing that he had deliberately deceived him, but he could not change his plan to fight in Bolivia, now that he had arrived.

"I am here, this is my liberated region, and I shall not leave it even if I am left with only those who came with me," Che declared.[1]

1. Mario Monje, "Castro Reneged on Promise of Nonintervention," *Presencia* (La Paz),

Monje suddenly realized that the Cuban revolutionaries had decided to initiate guerrilla operations in his country, with or without PCB approval. "As long as the guerrilla struggle takes place in Bolivia, I insist on having absolute leadership," Monje responded.

"That is a narrow and absurd view of proletarian internationalism," Che asserted firmly. "The type of struggle we are calling for goes beyond the national framework."

Che explained that Bolivia offered the best opportunities for a guerrilla campaign in South America. He intended to establish a new front with hardcore combatants from Cuba and elsewhere, hoping to spark a confrontation with the United States by developing a guerrilla front in the heart of South America. American intervention in Bolivia, Che asserted, would generate opposition from progressive and nationalistic forces, leading to the development of other guerrilla bands across the continent. The fight against imperialism in South America might last ten or fifteen years, but his sense of fate and duty compelled him to fight Yankee imperialism anywhere, to the death, if necessary. Although Che invited Monje to join the struggle as its titular head, he insisted on retaining overall command because Monje had no military experience. Monje, however, would not yield to anybody on Bolivian territory, even if Lenin came from the grave to command the guerrillas.

"I am here now, and the only way I will leave is dead. This is our territory," Che insisted.

Monje was equally adamant. "Leadership has to be real, and from the beginning it must be in my hands. Owing to my lack of experience I will ask your advice and your suggestions until I have acquired the leadership capacity and can take charge of the guerrilla struggle. You can be my most important adviser."

"Here I am adviser to no one," Che stated calmly.[2]

Che's determination to maintain absolute political and military authority over the guerrilla band grew out of his negative experiences in the Congo. There, he had deferred to the Congolese leaders, with disastrous consequences. He came to Bolivia determined to control strategy and tactics and was unwilling to risk his revolutionary project to Monje or any other inexperienced leader. After Monje gained experience, Che might cede leadership to him and

---

July 25, 1968; "Communist Party Leader Discusses Che Guevara," *Expreso* (Lima), July 20 and 22, 1968, both in FBIS.

2. Peredo, "My Campaign with Che," 339–41. In all accounts of the argument, there is accord that the fundamental disagreement between the two men was over the leadership of the movement.

move on to another front, but he intended to direct operations in the critical start-up phase of a guerrilla campaign.

Che Guevara controlled all aspects of the Bolivian campaign, from start to finish. He conceived of the tricontinental strategy, chose southeastern Bolivia as the place to initiate it, selected his combatants, trained them, and led them into battle. If the revolutionary strategy contained fatal flaws, Che drafted it. If the combatants lacked training, Che trained them. If the urban support network failed him, Che organized it. Che, who insisted on wielding supreme command of the Bolivian foco, bore the ultimate responsibility for the mission.

After leaving the Congo, Che wanted to go directly to Argentina to revive the guerrilla movement in his native country. Fidel and other officials argued against the proposal, asserting that conditions in Argentina did not favor the establishment of a guerrilla band. Jorge Masetti's guerrilla foco had been crushed; a civilian government possessed constitutional legitimacy; and the Argentine Communist party, led by Victorio Codovilla, opposed Che's militant line. Fidel asked Che to return to Cuba and wait for covert operatives to establish clandestine urban networks, develop lines of communication and supply, build support among the labor unions and peasant organizations, scout the terrain, and recruit volunteers. Che, reluctant to return to Cuba after Fidel had already announced his resignation, preferred to wait in Tanzania. Eventually, through Aleida, Che's wife; Ramiro Valdés; and others, Fidel persuaded Che to fly to Prague and wait there. He left for Czechoslovakia sometime in February or March 1966.[3]

During the spring and summer of 1966, with Che in Prague, Cuban officials carefully surveyed the revolutionary situation throughout Latin America. In the wake of the First Tricontinental Conference, held in Havana in January 1966, the Cuban government aggressively promoted guerrilla movements. The Cubans had been training Latin American guerrillas since 1959, but they could not claim victory in any country. To score a victory over American imperialism, the Cubans offered arms, training, and men, including Comandante Che Guevara, their best commander. Castro, eager to protect Guevara and Cuba's prestige, did not want to waste lives and efforts in a losing cause, so he ordered Piñeiro to select the most appropriate place from which his anxious comandante could launch the continental revolution.[4]

3. Anderson, *Che Guevara,* 581, 596, 613, 675–80; Castañeda, *Compañero,* 326–31.
4. Anderson, *Che Guevara,* 698.

Most Latin American governments in 1966 ruled within a constitutional framework. Even Nicaragua—which had the closest thing to the Caribbean-style dictatorship that the Cubans had overthrown in 1959 and where the reform-minded Luis Somoza Debayle and his reactionary brother Anastasio ruled through the civilian administration of René Schick Gutiérrez—maintained at least a fiction of representative democracy. The Guatemalan military also played the game of constitutional democracy, yielding power to the elected government of Julio César Méndez Montenegro in 1966. In Colombia, the Liberal and Conservative parties maintained power through the National Front agreement, alternating the presidency every four years. Raúl Leoni, democratically elected president of Venezuela, took a softer line on a growing crisis by offering amnesty and a negotiated peace to the guerrilla bands supported by Cuba. In Peru, President Fernando Belaúnde Terry also came to power through an election, in 1963, replacing a military junta. The Brazilian military regime and the Paraguayan dictatorship of General Alfredo Stroessner did not hide behind democratic masks either, but no guerrilla bands operated in either country.[5]

Bolivia, however, had entered a political crisis in November 1964, when General René Barrientos Ortuño came to power by a military coup, effectively ending twelve years of revolutionary changes under the Movimiento Nacional Revolucionario (MNR, National Revolutionary Movement). Although Barrientos initially promised to continue the revolution, in May 1965 he launched an assault on the militant miners' unions, the heart and soul of the Bolivian revolution since 1952. The army invaded the mining camps and overran the militias, then Barrientos exiled or jailed the union leaders, liquidated the unions, and forced the rank-and-file members underground. He retained high levels of support among the peasantry, however, and he reclaimed some constitutional legitimacy through an election in July 1966.[6]

Without a Batista-style dictatorship anywhere, the Cubans had no easy target. In any country, they would test Guevara's proposition that guerrilla warfare would "unmask" the reactionary nature of nominally democratic regimes. The guerrilla movements in Colombia and Venezuela had failed to do so in their first few years, but they had gained considerable strength by 1966. According to one U.S. estimate, eight hundred guerrillas operated in Colombia and another four hundred in Venezuela. Guatemala, with only three hundred

5. For a brief survey of revolutionary movements in Guatemala, Nicaragua, Colombia, Venezuela, Peru, Bolivia, and El Salvador, see the case studies in Guevara, *Guerrilla Warfare*.
6. Dunkerley, *Rebellion in the Veins*, 120–28; Prado Salmón, *Defeat of Che Guevara*, 45.

estimated combatants, occupied third place in the list of active guerrilla movements.[7] The Peruvian guerrilla foco suffered a devastating setback in early 1966, when its leader, Luis de la Puente, fell in combat. Moreover, the Peruvian Communist party opposed this and other Cuban-sponsored focos.[8]

Through a process of elimination, four countries appeared on Che's list of targets: Guatemala, Venezuela, Colombia, and Bolivia. The movements in the first three countries, though strong in combatants, suffered from internal and international political disputes. Some objected to Cuban interference in their affairs, holding that only they could determine when and how to promote the armed struggle in their country. With each movement divided into quarreling factions, whether Soviet, Trotskyite, Fidelista, or Maoist, none of the guerrilla movements possessed the organizational strength and direction that would have made it an obvious choice to receive the command of Che Guevara. There is no evidence that the Guatemalan or Colombian guerrillas would have submitted to Guevara's command, even though they had lost important leaders during counterinsurgency campaigns in February and March 1966. In Venezuela, the Communist party had already opted for the "legal struggle," which they did partly in response to the government's offer of amnesty and a negotiated political solution.[9]

Bolivia, a landlocked country in the heart of the continent, offered the brightest prospects for launching Che's revolutionary campaign. The Cubans had been training Bolivian cadres on the island for several years. By the time Mario Monje attended the Tricontinental Conference in Havana in 1966, the Cubans had already decided to activate the Bolivian guerrillas. During the conference, Castro and Piñeiro exerted intense pressure on Monje to begin a guerrilla campaign with the combatants they had trained. Monje reluctantly agreed to enroll himself in a guerrilla-training program, but he vigorously contested Fidel's and Piñeiro's suggestion that conditions favored the armed struggle. The Bolivian Communists, in fact, had divided into pro-Soviet and pro-Chinese factions. Oscar Zamora, leader of the Maoist wing, had met with Che in April 1965 and attended the Tricontinental Conference as the head of a delegation contesting Monje's authority and policy. The Cubans treated Monje as the official representative of Bolivia, but they had indicated in no

7. Walt Rostow (national security adviser) to president, June 24, 1967, "Guerrilla Problem in Latin America," container 2, Intelligence File, NSF, LBJ.

8. Castañeda, *Compañero*, 331–32.

9. Anderson, *Che Guevara*, 678.

uncertain terms that they would endorse another man if Monje did not fall in line with their revolutionary strategy.[10]

Che sent José María Martínez Tamayo from Prague to Bolivia in March 1966 to survey conditions in Bolivia. Cuba's Liberation Department, under Che's direction, had been laying the groundwork for a Bolivian campaign for several years. Che had also discussed the possibility of a guerrilla movement with Roberto and Guido Peredo, two Bolivian Communists who had visited Cuba in 1962 and again in 1965.[11]

In March 1964, Che had sent Tamara Bunke under deep cover to La Paz, with instructions to establish ties to the army and government, survey the political conditions in the countryside, and make contacts with miners, peasants, and workers. Born in Argentina and raised in East Germany, Tamara, also known as Tania, met Che during his first visit to Berlin in December 1960. At the time (and even thereafter) she may have worked for East German security. She arrived in Havana in May 1961, took a job as a translator, joined the revolutionary militia, and studied journalism at the University of Havana. Rumors about an intimate relationship between Che and Tania spread as they socialized frequently. In March 1963, Cuban intelligence cleared Tania for clandestine work. From March 1964 until Che's arrival in late 1966, Tania worked under cover as Laura Gutiérrez Bauer, an Argentine ethnologist. She worked in the Ministry of Education, married a Bolivian, and established political contacts, including with Gonzalo López Muñoz, press secretary to President Barrientos.[12]

In early 1966, Tania received top-secret instructions from Piñeiro to leave Bolivia for a meeting with a Cuban agent. Che might have recalled Tania to Prague for a debriefing and possibly to consummate their love affair.[13] Martínez Tamayo's visit to Bolivia and Tania's presence in La Paz formed part of a long-term, clandestine Cuban operation to determine the feasibility of launching a guerrilla foco in Bolivia, involving Fidel, Che, and Piñeiro. After Martínez Tamayo submitted a positive report on Bolivia, Che selected that country for the site of his South American guerrilla foco. In the summer of 1966, Che sent Harry Villegas and Carlos Coello to La Paz to organize

10. Ibid., 682.
11. Villegas, *Pombo*, 67; Gott, *Guerrilla Movements*, 301–4.
12. Rojas and Rodríguez Calderon, *Tania*, 100–103; Anderson, *Che Guevara*, 549–51, 688. Anderson's impressive research in East German, Soviet, and Cuban intelligence sources did not turn up any evidence that Tania was a double agent.
13. Castañeda, *Compañero*, 330–31.

and prepare the foco. Che returned secretly to Cuba in July 1966 and took up residence in a safe house in eastern Havana.[14]

The benefits of hindsight allow observers to second-guess Guevara's choice of Bolivia. At the time, few people could have convinced Che that any other country offered better prospects for establishing one of his tricontinental fronts than did Bolivia. The Bolivian army, with approximately seven thousand men under arms, exercised poor control of its borders on five countries. Army officers had some training in counterinsurgency warfare, but the peasants drafted into the rank and file did not.[15] In the event of a serious military threat, Bolivia would require immediate American military training and assistance. However, the Americans might not provide aid in a timely manner, given that they had fewer economic or strategic interests in Bolivia than in Central America, Venezuela, or Colombia. The distance between the United States and Bolivia, combined with the relative absence of vital interests there, might give Guevara sufficient time to establish his base and prepare for the American intervention he anticipated.

Geography favored Bolivia for other reasons. Che conceived of the Bolivian campaign as the initial phase in a protracted continental struggle, aimed not solely at the Barrientos dictatorship but at all the pro-American regimes in South America. Che intended to liberate the entire continent, not just Bolivia. According to Manuel Piñeiro, Che designed the Bolivian foco as a "mother column," with combatants from several Latin American countries. "'From his viewpoint, this guerrilla struggle [Bolivia] should be a training school for Latin American cadre, above all those from the Southern Cone—among them, Argentines—which would help to extend the armed struggle to bordering countries,' Piñeiro explains."[16] As the Bolivian foco gained strength and expanded, Che would create new guerrilla fronts in neighboring countries, with Bolivia continuing to serve as a safe haven, rear guard, and training ground for Latin American guerrillas. The continental crisis would escalate with each new band, gradually drawing the Americans into war on terrain and terms that did not favor them.[17]

---

14. Anderson, *Che Guevara*, 675–82; Gott, *Guerrilla Movements*, 305–7; Villegas, *Pombo*, 67; testimony of Pombo, in Guevara, *Bolivian Diary*, 421–23.

15. Prado, *Defeat of Che Guevara*, 44–45.

16. Suárez Salazar, *Che Guevara*, 19.

17. Peredo, "My Campaign with Che," 326–27; Gott, *Guerrilla Movements*, 307–8; Harris, *Death of a Revolutionary*, 60–67, 89–93; Prado, *Defeat of Che Guevara*, 43–44.

Che outlined his strategic vision in his "Message to the Tricontinental." Written prior to his departure from Cuba, the message explained how the proliferation of guerrilla bands in South America would gradually escalate into a war with the United States, following the example of Vietnam. Che clearly intended to fight the American military:

> Little by little, the obsolete weapons, which are sufficient for the repression of small armed bands, will be exchanged for modern armaments, and the U.S. military aides will be substituted by actual fighters until, at a given moment, they are forced to send increasingly greater numbers of regular troops to ensure the relative stability of a government whose national puppet army is disintegrating before the impetuous attacks of the guerrillas. It is the road of Vietnam; it is the road that should be followed by the people.[18]

All this was as likely to occur in Bolivia as in any other Latin American country. Given the strategic objective of fomenting a continental revolution, Bolivia offered the best opportunity to get the war started. According to Fidel, Piñeiro, and Harry Villegas, three Cuban officials closely associated with the Bolivian campaign from its inception, Che selected Bolivia on his own.[19] The Cubans clearly chose Bolivia after informed deliberations and analysis involving the highest officers in the Cuban revolutionary network, most important among them Fidel, Che, and Piñeiro. These and other high-ranking officials surveyed conditions in Latin America and decided to deploy a veteran contingent of guerrillas in Bolivia. Che did not select Bolivia on his own. The Bolivian project represented a high foreign policy objective of the Cuban government, to which Fidel dedicated valuable resources and combatants.

The decision to plant the guerrilla foco in southeastern Bolivia, however, remains questionable. In September 1966, Guevara ordered Villegas and Coello to select a site in the Alto Beni, a tropical region northeast of La Paz. By that time, his advance scouts had already surveyed three zones for possible guerrilla operations, including an area around Las Yungas River in the Alto Beni. They had also surveyed a zone around Chapare, northeast of Cochabamba, and the area around Camiri, in the department of Santa Cruz, southeast of Sucre. Castro commissioned his own geopolitical survey of Bolivia from Régis Debray, who had just caused an international sensation with the publication

18. Guevara, "Message to the Tricontinental," 172.
19. Anderson, *Che Guevara*, 680–82; Suárez Salazar, *Che Guevara*, 20.

of *Revolution in the Revolution?* Although Debray subsequently claimed that he traveled to Bolivia as a journalist, he was, in fact, performing a clandestine mission for Cuba. Debray's survey of Bolivia also confirmed the Alto Beni as the most appropriate place in which to launch Che's foco. He delivered an extensive report to Piñeiro, arguing that the climate, geography, political history, and economic conditions of the Alto Beni made it an ideal place for the conduct of a guerrilla campaign.[20]

However, Villegas and Coello, assisted by the PCB, had already purchased a farm near Camiri, in the department of Santa Cruz. At the time, the Bolivian Communists had no idea that Che intended to command a foco on their territory. Thinking that the Cubans simply wanted a secure base near the Argentine border for a secret meeting with Che, Monje helped the Cubans purchase a farm on the Ñancahuazú River. Not wanting to offend their Bolivian hosts, Villegas and Coello urged Che to establish his first base at the farm, arguing that the tropical terrain, on the eastern slopes of the Andes, offered good cover for guerrilla operations. Moreover, the government's agricultural colonization project had resettled a large number of peasants in the area, giving the Cubans a base from which to draw recruits. They also attached undue economic importance to the area, asserting that the region's oil industry linked it directly to the United States via a pipeline to Chile. The site in the Alto Beni, close to La Paz and the mining camps, also offered several advantages, but it would also expose the band to the risk of early detection. Southeastern Bolivia, relatively isolated and underpopulated, gave the guerrillas a good opportunity to establish a base before the Bolivians discovered it.[21] Che reluctantly agreed to accept the Ñancahuazú as the initial base, but he insisted that it would serve only as a temporary headquarters.

According to Villegas, Che never intended to launch the actual guerrilla campaign from southeastern Bolivia. Che's strategic plan envisioned a war of liberation waged from the more densely populated Alto Beni. As Villegas explains: "The zone in which we later conducted operations was not the one we had originally foreseen. Che's aim was to conduct operations a little farther north, and the base at the Ñancahuazú had been chosen as an extreme rear, to be used for organizing the guerrilla unit. Later on, avoiding any confrontation with the army, we were to advance toward the north, on our way to a more centrally located region."[22]

20. Villegas, *Pombo,* 100–102; Castañeda, *Compañero,* 345.
21. Villegas, *Pombo,* 101–2; Anderson, *Che Guevara,* 693–95.
22. Testimony of Pombo, in Guevara, *Bolivian Diary,* 422.

As a rear guard base or training camp, the Ñancahuazú offered certain advantages for the development of a guerrilla foco. The Bolivian army, with relatively few people or resources to defend, maintained a light presence in southeastern Bolivia. The Fourth Division of the Bolivian army, based in Camiri, possessed a total strength of 1,103 men, the majority of them draftees who spent most of their nine-month tours serving as farm laborers and construction workers.[23] If the guerrillas kept a low profile, they could establish a base at and supply lines to the Ñancahuazú farm without being detected by the army. If the army did discover the guerrillas and challenge them, the Bolivian conscripts should not present a serious challenge to Che's battle-tested combatants.

Of the sixteen Cubans selected for this special mission, three men served on the Central Committee of the Cuban Communist party: Juan Vitalio Acuña, Antonio Sánchez, and Eliseo Reyes. All of them had served in the M-26-7 rebel army; ten had served under Che's command. Three men held the rank of comandante, the highest rank in the Cuban army; five men were lieutenants, and six were captains. All these men had occupied important government positions, including vice minister of industry, vice minister of sugar, and head of the G-2 intelligence service. They had distinguished themselves in combat, government service, and clandestine operations.[24] Che obviously selected from an experienced and talented pool of internationalist volunteers. Any one of them could take command of an independent guerrilla column, if and when Che decided to branch out from the mother foco, as they had done in Cuba.

Despite their background and experience, Che still put them through extensive training in Cuba and again in Bolivia. A few of them might have gained a few pounds since their days in the Sierra Maestra, but they knew how to wage guerrilla war. Fourteen men had already commanded troops in battle. Che, however, disciplined and trained them for several months in Pinar del Río province under the command of Antonio Sánchez, the highest-ranking officer in the group. Che insisted that his men learn guerrilla warfare anew, putting ranks aside and becoming common soldiers again, performing everyday tasks such as sentry duty, cooking, and cleaning.[25]

Castro apparently attached a high priority to the Bolivian expedition. Not only did he allow several high-ranking officials to leave their posts; he also

23. Prado, *Defeat of Che Guevara*, 72–73.
24. For biographical profiles of all the volunteers, see Guevara, *Bolivian Diary*, 435–54.
25. Testimony of Benigno, in Guevara, *Bolivian Diary*, 428–30.

committed Cuba's intelligence services to the project. Manuel Piñeiro's Liberation Department prepared disguises and fake passports and transported Che and others through circuitous routes designed to throw foreign intelligence agencies off his trail. The Bolivian mission became a foreign policy priority for Fidel Castro, as he indicated in his several visits to the Pinar del Río training camp. He attempted to keep Che in Cuba until Piñeiro's agents completed the guerrilla infrastructure, but Che insisted on commanding the guerrillas during the first critical stages of the campaign. He had already delayed his departure for ten months; by late October 1966, he was ready to leave. When Fidel saw him for the last time, Che was Adolfo Mena González, an Uruguayan businessman wearing a single-breasted business suit with high, thin lapels; horn-rimmed glasses; and, on his bald head, a fedora hat. Fidel, sporting the full beard and fatigues that he had never worn with the panache of Che, still looked like the commander of the M-26-7 movement. Having achieved complete anonymity, Che said good-bye to Fidel with a rather awkward, unaffectionate hug.[26]

Che assumed that Cuban intelligence agents, particularly the advance team he had sent to Bolivia, would build an underground network in Bolivia before he arrived in La Paz. He relied heavily on Martínez Tamayo, Villegas, and Coello to select the base of operations and establish an urban organization. For both tasks, particularly the latter, the Cubans required the assistance of Mario Monje and the PCB. However, during ten months of preparatory work, the Cubans never told Monje that Che Guevara intended to command a guerrilla band in his native country. Neither Monje nor the PCB ever formally agreed to collaborate with the Cuban campaign to launch a continental revolution from southeastern Bolivia. At most, Monje assented in May 1966 to Castro's personal request to provide an escort for an "international comrade" who would soon pass through Bolivia en route to a third country. Monje knew that in this request Castro was referring to Che, but he did not know that Che intended to establish a base in Bolivia. Monje claims, in fact, that Fidel always promised him that Cuba would not interfere in Bolivia's internal affairs, agreeing that the Bolivians should lead their own revolutionary movement.[27]

Monje and the PCB, however, vacillated on the issue that divided the Latin American Left, the feasibility of armed struggle. At a regional conference of

26. Deutschmann, *Che*, 132. See also the last photograph of Che and Fidel following p. 122.

27. Monje, "Castro Reneged on Promise of Nonintervention," *Presencia* (La Paz), July 25, 1968, FBIS; Anderson, *Che Guevara*, 686–87.

the PCB in May 1966, the Bolivian Communists had formally approved a resolution that confirmed the armed struggle as the only possible means of liberating the country. In the national elections held two months later, however, the PCB attained the highest vote totals in its history, nudging the vacillating Monje toward electoral struggle and away from the path of armed struggle that his party had recently endorsed. A group of Cuban-trained guerrillas within the party, including the Peredo brothers, encouraged Monje to begin a guerrilla campaign. In the summer of 1966, the PCB began to select and train personnel for a guerrilla foco under Bolivian command. At a secret meeting in La Paz with Villegas and Martínez Tamayo on July 25, however, Monje opposed the initiation of a guerrilla campaign. On July 28, Villegas and Martínez Tamayo pressed the indecisive Monje again, asking his support for a general uprising coordinated with a guerrilla offensive. Although Monje did not endorse the plan, he promised to provide the Cubans with twenty Bolivian cadres. But on August 8, when Martínez Tamayo asked him for the twenty men, Monje asked, "What twenty?"[28]

Monje had been duplicitous with the Cubans since the First Tricontinental Conference in January. He alternately endorsed and opposed the armed struggle, always balking at the alleged Cuban interference in Bolivia's internal affairs, never showing too much enthusiasm for Che's militant line. The Cubans claim that he had promised to support Che's campaign; Monje denies that he ever formally endorsed the project. The available evidence cannot resolve the critical issue—whether Monje betrayed Che. Monje certainly discussed revolutionary options with Martínez Tamayo and Villegas in Bolivia prior to Guevara's arrival. He knew or suspected that the Cubans were developing a military apparatus parallel to but independent of that of the PCB. At no point prior to Che's arrival in Bolivia did Mario Monje or the PCB or any other Bolivian political institution formally agree to support Guevara's guerrilla foco. Monje had not promised to provide Guevara with any combatants, supplies, funds, or even sympathetic propaganda. The Cubans never even asked for Monje's endorsement, concealing their true objectives from a person and party they fully expected would serve them as allies. Che apparently intended to present the Bolivians with a fait accompli, just as he had done with the Congolese. If they did not rally behind his command, they would become pariahs in Latin America's revolutionary movements, disgraced by cowardice and dishonor.

28. Anderson, *Che Guevara,* 694; Villegas, *Pombo,* 90 (quoted).

Cuban agents proceeded with plans to start a guerrilla campaign, with or without Monje and the PCB. By mid-September, relations with the PCB had deteriorated to such an extent that Che ordered a temporary cessation of contacts with the party. Villegas thought that only direct discussions between Che and Monje would resolve their problems. In the meantime, Che ordered his men to work with Moisés Guevara, leader of a dissident Communist faction, whose collaboration with the Cubans could only aggravate relations between Monje and Che.[29]

When Che left Cuba on October 23, 1966, the guerrilla infrastructure had not been constructed. The PCB did not expect him and nothing indicated that the party would rally to his cause. Cuban agents had been operating in the country for several years, but they had not built the revolutionary infrastructure. If and when Che arrived, he would not have an urban network prepared to send him recruits, money, arms, and supplies. The three Cuban agents he had in La Paz, Martínez Tamayo, Villegas, and Coello, and three of the four Bolivians who worked with them, would go with Che to the Ñancahuazú farm, leaving only Tania and Rodolfo Saldaña in La Paz. Given that Che had designated Tania as a liaison with other Latin American Communist parties, she could not organize an urban network. Saldaña could do little without the support of the PCB, and in October 1966, the Bolivian Communists decided not to support Che's guerrilla foco.[30] The withdrawal of the PCB left Che without an urban support system.

Villegas and the other agents had attempted to organize a supply and information network in Santa Cruz, with the support of the PCB. With the party's assistance, they had purchased the farm on the Ñancahuazú, and they acquired a house in Santa Cruz where they stockpiled weapons and supplies.[31] The withdrawal of the PCB in October, however, negated all these efforts. In a fatal deviation from the Cuban revolutionary model, Che took the field before an urban network had been consolidated. When the *Granma* landed in December 1956, an institutional revolutionary network already existed, with dedicated leaders such as Celia Sánchez and Frank País prepared to keep the rural guerrillas alive through their urban networks. Before Che arrived in La Paz on November 3, the urban network had already begun to collapse. No Bolivian had invited him, no Bolivian political institution had endorsed his

29. Villegas, *Pombo*, 97–99.
30. Saldaña, *Fertile Ground*, 55.
31. Villegas, *Pombo*, 102.

revolutionary project, and only the slimmest foundation for urban organization had been established.

Unless and until Che established an urban network, through an alliance with the PCB or some other institution, his survival depended exclusively on the combatants and supplies he had brought with him. This dependency had significant military repercussions later in the campaign, for if and when the Bolivian army threatened to destroy or capture the supplies he had stored in and around his base camp, which included his asthma medicine, he would have to defend them.

The establishment of a support network would have required political skills and a temperament that Che Guevara lacked. As a military commander under Fidel, he rarely had to engage in purely political affairs, because Fidel and others handled those matters. Che simply demanded obedience from true revolutionaries. The implementation of his tricontinental strategy, however, required careful coordination between revolutionary movements and their backers in Moscow and Beijing. All evidence indicates that Che had not properly coordinated his Bolivian mission with Bolivian or other Latin American revolutionaries or with their Soviet or Chinese counterparts. The deterioration of relations between the Cubans and the Bolivian Communists in the fall of 1966 should have given Che enough cause to delay his departure, for his guerrilla foco needed some kind of institutional support. If Monje or his Soviet backers actively opposed the Cuban project, they could create serious problems for Che.

The Soviets appeared indifferent or unconcerned about Cuban subversion in Bolivia. They may have even provided some support for Che, given that his travel to Bolivia took him through Moscow and Prague. His safe arrival in La Paz on November 3, 1966, represented another triumph for Cuban intelligence and yet another Cuban initiative not endorsed by Cuba's presumed allies. The following day, Tania gave Che his credentials, a document signed by Gonzalo López, director of information in the presidential palace, that certified Adolfo Mena as a special envoy of the Organization of American States.[32]

At 6:30 P.M. on November 5, Che left La Paz with Alberto Fernández, Villegas, Coello, and Jorge Vásquez Viaña, a member of the Bolivian Communist party. Traveling in two jeeps for two days, they reached the Ñancahuazú farm on the evening of November 7. En route, Che revealed his

---

32. Cupull and González, *Un hombre bravo*, 311–12; Harris, *Death of a Revolutionary*, 97–98.

identity and plans to Vásquez, his driver. He explained that he had come to Bolivia to establish a base for a guerrilla campaign that would gradually engulf the continent. Che believed so firmly in his revolutionary strategy that he told Vásquez that he would only leave Bolivia in a coffin or shooting his way across the border. After learning that he had joined a continental revolution commanded by Che Guevara, a stunned Vásquez drove the jeep into a ditch, forcing him and his new commander to walk the last ten miles to the camp.[33]

Late in the evening of November 7, in a tin-roofed ranch house buried in southeastern Bolivia, Che wrote his first Bolivian diary entry. It began: "Today a new stage begins."[34]

Che spent his first two weeks at the tin house fighting off gnats, mosquitoes, and ticks. The four-man column dug tunnels and scouted the area while waiting for the arrival of their Cuban comrades. Antonio Sánchez arrived with Eliseo Reyes on November 20. A week later six more Cubans joined them; among the new arrivals was Juan Vitalio Acuña, commander of Che's rear guard during the Las Villas campaign. The first two Bolivians who arrived at the camp, Freddy Maymura and Guido Peredo, were the only men without previous combat experience.[35]

By the end of November, there were twelve men in Che's guerrilla foco, ten Cubans and two Bolivians. The men had arrived safely but slightly behind schedule. "The general picture appears good in this remote region; everything indicates we shall be able to stay here practically as long as we wish," Che noted in his diary.[36]

The activities of the Cubans over the following few weeks suggested that they intended to make a permanent home there. In addition to the so-called zinc house on the Ñancahuazú farm, Che built a main camp and two subsidiary camps (Bear Camp and Monkey Camp), along with a network of caves, tunnels, and paths stretching nearly ten miles north of the zinc house. (See Map 11.) The men built a mud oven, a meat-drying hut, log tables and benches, latrines, and a medical dispensary. In the caves the Cubans installed two enormous World War II–era radio transmitters, which required their own electrical generator.[37]

33. Cupull and González, *Un hombre bravo*, 312; Villegas, *Pombo*, 125–26; Guevara, *Bolivian Diary*, 77–78.
34. Guevara, *Bolivian Diary*, 77.
35. Ibid., 77–85, 108.
36. Ibid., 87.
37. Ibid., 122; Anderson, *Che Guevara*, 702; Castañeda, *Compañero*, 365.

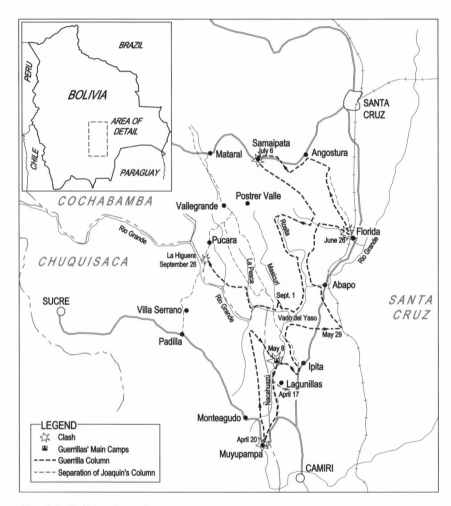

Map 11. Bolivian Campaign

In the first stages of the Cuban insurrection the rebels had been constantly on the run. In Bolivia, however, Che began by digging in, constructing a network of camps, caves, storage facilities, ammunition dumps, and field kitchens that invited detection by the Bolivian authorities. From the outset of the Bolivian campaign, Che tied his foco to the terrain, a reflection of his total dependency on the supplies he brought with him. While his men built the camps, three Bolivian recruits brought more arms, ammunition, and supplies from La Paz to Ñancahuazú. This supply line, however, would not last long. After setting up the camps, three of the Bolivians, Roberto Peredo, Jorge Vásquez, and Julio Luís Méndez, joined the guerrillas for good, weakening the tenuous link between the camps and the city. If Che could not sustain his men with the supplies he brought or produced, the foco would not survive.

Che had absolutely no experience in or understanding of clandestine urban operations. He had experienced urban operatives on his team, including Gustavo Machín, Orlando Pantoja, Martínez Tamayo, and Alberto Fernández, but he did not assign them to urban work. Only a dozen agents, including Tania, supposedly supported the guerrilla operations from La Paz and other cities, but judging by their subsequent inactivity, they produced little of any value to the guerrillas.[38]

Che's immediate fixation with digging caves and cutting trails through the forests reflects his excessive faith in the ability of a guerrilla foco to generate the objective and subjective conditions for guerrilla warfare, including an institutional network. By creating a disciplined and self-sacrificing team of combatants, Che evidently expected to inspire other people and institutions to volunteer for service under his command, as guerrillas, couriers, fund-raisers, and recruiters. Hence, instead of focusing on the development of an urban infrastructure, Che established a rural base and organized his guerrilla command, assuming that others would complete the urban network for him. With only twelve men in his band, Che hardly had enough men to operate a single column, but he nevertheless appointed Juan Vitalio Acuña as his second in command. Che had evidently lost confidence in Antonio Sánchez, who had been in command of the Cuban volunteers in Pinar del Río. The highest-ranking Bolivian was Guido Peredo, who assumed responsibility for maintaining the morale of the men as the political commissar. Che made it clear that he held absolute political and military authority.[39]

38. In the list of guerrilla combatants and sympathizers provided with the *Bolivian Diary*, only a dozen urban agents are identified. See Guevara, *Bolivian Diary*, 435–54.

39. Ibid., 93; Villegas, *Pombo*, 81–84.

Che seemed determined to establish and defend a fixed base in a desolate region. His men spent most of their time digging caves and tunnels, cutting trails, and setting up a radio station at a new camp several miles from the tin house. The men relocated there permanently on December 16. "The fundamental characteristic of a guerrilla band is mobility," Che had written in *Guerrilla Warfare*. With no shortage of arms, ammunition, supplies, or money in rural Bolivia, however, Che spent his first six weeks as if he were preparing to defend a fixed position with only twenty combatants.[40]

He knew that he needed more fighters, especially Bolivian recruits, and when Mario Monje arrived at his camp on December 31, 1966, Che still believed that he could convince him to join the insurrection. Che would not yield command to anybody, least of all the inexperienced and ambivalent Monje. He invited Monje and the Bolivian Communists to join the guerrilla campaign, but he demanded that they submit to his military authority, arrogantly assuming that no Latin American revolutionary would even dare to think that anyone could command a guerrilla band with the legendary Che Guevara in it. Che offered to recognize Monje as the political leader of the Bolivian revolution, but he refused to relinquish military command. Monje could take Che's offer or leave it. Before Monje left it, he asked to speak to the Bolivian volunteers. He explained that as secretary general of the PCB, he must have total political and military command, a demand that Che had rejected. He urged the Bolivians to leave with him, warning them that the guerrilla campaign would fail. "When the people learn that this guerrilla movement is led by a foreigner," Monje predicted, "they will turn their backs and refuse to support it. I am sure it will fail because it is led by a foreigner, not a Bolivian. You will die very heroically, but you have no prospects of victory."[41]

Monje departed the following day, alone. "He left looking like a man being led to the gallows," Che thought. The failure to win official PCB support for the campaign would make things more difficult, Che announced to the men on January 1, but he still hoped to win the support of Moisés Guevara and other dissident Communists.[42]

Che intended to begin his continental revolution from a remote base in southeastern Bolivia, a strategic ambition that the nationalistic Monje did not support. Che could not allow Monje to impose national boundaries on a con-

40. Guevara, *Bolivian Diary*, 94–96; Guevara, *Guerrilla Warfare*, 58 (quoted).
41. Peredo, "My Campaign with Che," 335–36.
42. Guevara, *Bolivian Diary*, 102–5.

tinental campaign. Because he conceived the campaign in continental terms, the Bolivian foco being the source from which other guerrilla bands would spring, any citizen of the Americas could fight in it. Thus, in early January, Che sent Tania to Argentina to recruit Ciro Roberto Bustos and Eduardo Jozami, two survivors of Masetti's Argentine campaign. Che also recruited actively from the remnants of Peru's guerrilla movement, enlisting Juan Pablo Chang (Chino), a Peruvian revolutionary of Chinese ancestry. Chino had discussed strategy with Che in early December and promised to return with more Peruvian volunteers after his trip to Cuba.[43]

While he waited for international volunteers to join him, Che concentrated on building a "steeled nucleus" of combatants. Having constructed a network of camps and storage facilities, he decided to defend them, despite his well-known prohibition against defending fixed positions in the early stages of guerrilla warfare. He designed defensive fortifications, including trenches, and a plan to defend an area adjacent to the Ñancahuazú River. If the Bolivian army attacked his territory, Che would defend it.[44]

Moisés Guevara arrived at the camp on January 26, 1967. Che did not intend to treat him any differently from how he had treated Monje, although Guevara had combatants whom Che needed. Che explained that Moisés would have to disband his group prior to his enlistment. Che would not offer Moisés or any of his men any rank, nor would he tolerate any discussion of the Sino-Soviet dispute or allow polemics on any other divisive international issue.

"I have not come here to impose conditions; I come only to request enlistment as just another soldier," Moisés explained. "For me it is an honor to fight alongside Che, the revolutionary I most admire."[45] Unlike Monje, Moisés Guevara accepted the conditions and promised to return with a group of Bolivian volunteers.

Loyola Guzmán, a young militant of the PCB who had accompanied Moisés to the camp, impressed Che even more. She supported the guerrillas by organizing an underground network in the cities, earning demerits with the PCB leadership in the process. Che reimbursed her seventy thousand pesos for the expenses she had already incurred, indicating that she had engaged in substantial fund-raising and other supportive activities, but he encouraged her to do even more. He gave her lengthy and detailed instructions

43. Ibid., 89–90, 105–6.
44. Diary of Rolando, in Guevara, *Bolivian Diary*, 416, also 108–16.
45. Guevara, *Bolivian Diary*, 118–19; Peredo, "My Campaign with Che," 343 (quoted).

for organizing urban cells. One leader, taking orders directly from Che, would manage the urban network, with six subordinates in charge of supplies, transport, information, finances, urban actions, and contacts with sympathizers. The central command of the network would reside in La Paz, with satellite organizations in Cochabamba, Santa Cruz, Sucre, and Camiri, forming a rectangle around the area of operations. Che directed the urban cadres in these centers to organize grocery stores, trucking firms, shoemaking shops, machine shops, and farms.[46]

At the time, the urban network to which Che gave these ambitious instructions probably consisted of only six persons, including Tania. The idea that these six individuals could have carried out all these tasks reflects a total ignorance of urban operations. Che simply gave orders and expected them to be carried out, without lifting a finger to turn his organizational chart into a functioning system.

At least Loyola left the guerrilla camp promising to make an effort. In contrast, Monje began to undermine the guerrilla movement. "The [Communist] party has now taken up arms against us," Che noted in his summary for January 1967. The desertion of the PCB, according to Guido Peredo, then a leader of the PCB, left the guerrillas with "virtually no [urban] organization." Peredo recognized the precarious state of the combatants that resulted from the "shameless desertion of the Communist Party." "We were on the eve of a war, and for this it was necessary to put together a clandestine network that would function in La Paz, branching out to other cities and towns all the way to the center of our military operations. These were the tasks assigned to the Communist Party of Bolivia."[47] The Cubans may have assigned the PCB these tasks, but no document has ever been produced to confirm that the Bolivian Communists ever formally accepted the assignment.

To make it worse for Che, the CIA had penetrated his weak urban network. According to Gustavo Villoldo, a Cuban-born CIA agent who arrived in Bolivia in February 1967, the Americans had three "assets" in the urban network, two Bolivians and one Peruvian. These agents, still living under CIA protection thirty-five years later, gave the American agents the information they needed to neutralize the urban activists. "That entire mechanism, that logistical support," Villoldo explained, "left the guerrillas completely isolated.

---

46. Guevara, "Instructions for Cadres Assigned to Urban Areas," January 22, 1967, in Guevara, *Bolivian Diary,* 299–304.

47. Guevara, *Bolivian Diary,* 120–21, 299–304; Peredo, "My Campaign with Che," 344.

We completely penetrated the urban network." From these agents, the CIA station chief in Bolivia learned of Guevara's presence before the Bolivians first detected him in late March 1967.[48]

Even without a strong urban network, Che believed, his fifteen Cuban veterans and a dozen Bolivians could spark a revolution. Having established his base of operations, he decided to train the men and explore the surrounding region. On February 1, twenty-seven guerrillas set out on a training and exploratory march designed to last twenty-five days. Sánchez commanded the vanguard, Acuña the rear, and Che the center.[49] One has to wonder why the Cubans, all of them with command or combat experience, plus another training session in Cuba, needed additional instruction. Some of the Bolivians obviously required training, but even among those, some had already undergone training in Cuba. A lengthy march risked an engagement with the Bolivian army, and Che did not intend to fight yet. He could have trained his men by other means, and if he needed to survey the region, he could have sent smaller reconnaissance teams or recruited a local guide. But Che, a bit anxious and bored, ordered his men on a lengthy march, not knowing, of course, that it would end in disaster.

The men battled with fatigue and illness as they marched northward along a path parallel to the Ñancahuazú, the veterans quickly recognizing their poor physical condition. Che lost fifteen pounds and marched with an "unbearable" pain in his shoulders. Seeing their beloved comandante ill, some of the men tried to help him out, but their kindness only angered him. He would suffer through the pain, just like his men.[50]

On February 10, the guerrillas contacted their first peasant, Honorato Rojas. Guido Peredo introduced himself as a hunter, and Che, posing as his assistant, asked Rojas about buying food and supplies in the area. Although Rojas promised to help the men, Che noted that he was "potentially dangerous."[51]

The guerrillas made slow progress over the following week, fighting heat, heavy rains, exhaustion, and hunger as they continued northward toward the village of Masicuri. Che described an uneventful February 19 as a "wasted day." His men made "slow and uneven progress" the following day. The

48. Cited in Castañeda, *Compañero,* 367.

49. Villegas, *Pombo,* 92; Peredo, "My Campaign with Che," 350–51; Gott, *Guerrilla Movements,* 327.

50. Guevara, *Bolivian Diary,* 122–25; Peredo, "My Campaign with Che," 354.

51. Guevara, *Bolivian Diary,* 127.

Cubans, veterans of more dangerous campaigns in Cuba and the Congo, became frustrated and irritable, sensing a lack of purpose and direction. Che remained determined to march on, testing the Cubans and training the Bolivians. When he reached the top of a high hill on February 23, under a sun hot enough to "split open rocks," he began to feel faint. From that moment on, he "walked under the power of sheer determination."[52]

Benjamín Coronado, a twenty-six-year-old teacher from La Paz, lagged behind the men as they marched along the rocky banks of the Rio Grande on February 26. Che sent Leonardo Tamayo back to help him. Benjamín stepped out on a ledge, lost his footing, and splashed into the river. Unable to swim, he could not fight the swift current. His comrades were rushing down to save him when he disappeared. Eliseo Reyes dove in after him, but he gave up after five minutes. The men had witnessed an absurd "baptism of death," Che noted.[53]

Their sagging spirits received another staggering blow on February 28, when a raft carrying Antonio Sánchez and the forward detachment across the Rio Grande drifted away from the main body. With provisions running as low as the morale of his men, Che decided to return to his base camp, his men increasingly discouraged and tired. On March 9, Che learned that Sánchez had passed through the village of Tatarenda, carelessly parading his weapons before the curious villagers.[54]

Even worse, the guerrillas asked some workers of the state oil company for information and supplies. On March 9, these workers informed Captain Augusto Silva Bogado of the Bolivian Fourth Division that they had seen some "big bearded men carrying backpacks and arms with foreign accents and with plenty of money." The workers told Captain Silva that the men had 40 or 50 million pesos. Captain Silva relayed this information to his division commander, Colonel Humberto Rocha Urquieta, who immediately ordered aerial reconnaissance. On March 11, the reconnaissance team spotted four men on a Rio Grande beach. The following day, Captain Silva left with a six-man patrol to hunt down the questionable individuals. The Bolivian army had now detected a suspicious presence, and it would not let the unidentified foreigners rest until it had captured, killed, arrested, or dispersed all of them.[55]

---

52. Villegas, *Pombo*, 141–49; Guevara, *Bolivian Diary*, 133.
53. Guevara, *Bolivian Diary*, 134–35.
54. Ibid., 139–44.
55. Prado, *Defeat of Che Guevara*, 56–59.

Guevara's weary marchers ate the last of their provisions on March 14, making a return to the base camp imperative. When they arrived at the Ñancahuazú River at a site less than thirty miles from the camp, Che felt "as if a boulder had fallen on top" of him. He nourished his frail body with horse-meat and pushed on. His battered unit suffered another tragedy on March 16, when the rear guard lost another man, six rifles, ammunition, and several knapsacks, all of them swallowed by the swift, swollen Ñancahuazú River.[56]

Two days earlier, police in Lagunillas had apprehended two men suspected of selling weapons. The prisoners subsequently informed their interrogators that a group of men commanded by Che Guevara had started a guerrilla campaign against the Bolivian government. They also identified the location of the camp at the Ñancahuazú. On the basis of this information, the Bolivian Fourth Division sent another patrol to the Ñancahuazú camp. At 3 P.M. on March 17, the patrol entered the encampment and advanced toward the zinc house, unaware that Captain Silva was approaching the camp from another direction. Captain Silva reached the camp first, surprising Antonio Sánchez and the vanguard at 4:00 P.M. The guerrillas, who had arrived at the base camp in violation of Che's direct orders, ran off as the army approached, firing a few shots before they fled. Jorge Vásquez, the Bolivian Communist and a recruit, fired the first shots of the campaign, wounding one soldier. Salustio Choque, another Bolivian, was captured without a struggle.[57]

Che did not learn of these events until March 19, when Chino arrived from the base camp. By this time, Che already knew that the area had come under continuous aerial surveillance, a development not as alarming to him as the information that Sánchez had not held the main camp. The only good news was that Moisés Guevara and eleven of his men had arrived, along with Tania; Régis Debray; and Ciro Roberto Bustos, the Argentine.[58]

The following day, Che arrived at the Bear Camp, a few miles north of the main camp. "A mood of defeat was in the air." There had already been one confrontation at the zinc house, and with sixty soldiers patrolling the area, another engagement was likely. Nobody knew what to do; there was a sense of "total chaos." Che, however, knew what to do. Infuriated by Sánchez's decision to abandon the camp, he ordered him back with the admonition that "wars are won with bullets."[59]

56. Guevara, *Bolivian Diary*, 144–47.
57. Prado, *Defeat of Che Guevara*, 67–70.
58. Guevara, *Bolivian Diary*, 147–48.
59. Ibid., 149; Testimony of Régis Debray, in Gott, *Guerrilla Movements*, 329–31.

Antonio Sánchez, former commander of Camilo Cienfuegos's rear guard and holding the rank of comandante, had to wonder why Che criticized him for abandoning the camp. He had not learned guerrilla warfare as a war of positions; guerrillas did not defend territory unless and until they had gained the size and strength to engage the enemy in regular war, and that only occurred in the final phases of a campaign. Given that Che intended to transfer his base of operations to the Alto Beni, using the Ñancahuazú bases as a temporary site to assemble and train his combatants, it did not make any sense for him to attack the Silva patrol when it surprised him on March 17. Sánchez had every reason to expect Che to order a redeployment of the guerrilla forces, now numbering about forty-seven men and women. However, with no support structure in the cities, Che needed the supplies stored in the camps and caves around the zinc house. If the army captured those supplies, the guerrillas would have to acquire their supplies elsewhere. To Che, Sánchez's withdrawal represented such an egregious error that he relieved him of command of the vanguard and assigned him to the rear guard as an ordinary combatant. He replaced him with Miguel Hernández, who had commanded one of Che's units in the Las Villas campaign.[60]

Che recognized only one viable option: fighting. He had forty-seven combatants and enough weapons to arm more. Redeploying them to the Alto Beni, several hundred miles away, would take time and considerable effort, and the move would not necessarily raise morale. The war had come to Che, and he had to fight back, ready or not. His mobility limited by the supplies on hand, Che did not have enough guerrillas and firepower to defend positions. His guerrillas would have to be on the move, but they could not move very far. It would be like fighting a guerrilla campaign with his feet tied together.

In contrast, the Bolivian army responded to the challenge with General Operations Order 1/67 on March 21, this order designed to locate and destroy guerrilla groups around the Ñancahuazú River. The army sent Major Hernán Plata and a company of sixty-six men to search the river from the zinc house to its source. Another sixty-six-man unit would establish a blocking force along the Ñancahuazú River. Although many of these soldiers had no combat experience and little training, the quick, aggressive response of the Bolivian Fourth Division spelled trouble for Guevara's guerrillas.[61]

60. Prado, *Defeat of Che Guevara*, 71; Peredo, "My Campaign with Che," 360–61; Diary of Rolando, in Guevara, *Bolivian Diary*, 417–19; Rodríguez and Weisman, *Shadow Warrior*, 152.

61. Prado, *Defeat of Che Guevara*, 72–73.

The presence of three noncombatants—Debray, Bustos, and Tania—in Che's column, only weakened the guerrillas. Che valued all of them, but they could serve him better elsewhere; in his camp, they represented a burden, three more mouths to feed. Frustrated by the unfortunate turn of events, Che ordered a five-man ambush set along the river on March 22. If the army patrol approached again, his men would drive them back.[62]

At dawn on March 23, Major Plata marched off in search of the guerrillas. He divided his unit into a vanguard, center, and rear guard, matching the guerrillas' organizational structure and their mobility. Just seven hundred meters into the search, as it attempted to cross the river, Captain Silva's vanguard fell into the guerrilla ambush. The guerrillas, having selected their positions carefully, inflicted immediate and heavy losses on the soldiers, pinning them down along the banks of the river. The soldiers returned the fire, but they could not fight their way out. Major Plata, Captain Silva, and twelve soldiers surrendered, leaving six soldiers dead. The guerrillas had won their first engagement with the Bolivian army, capturing three mortars, sixteen Mauzers, three Uzis, and a .30-caliber machine gun.[63]

In winning this first battle, the guerrillas lost the war. Che had ordered his men into battle before he had consolidated the foco with a strong urban support system. In this and many subsequent battles, because of their experience and training, the Cuban combatants prevailed over the Bolivians, but they would not be able to sustain offensive operations for long. Their supplies of food, ammunition, recruits, and cash were finite; in contrast, the Bolivian army had virtually unlimited supplies and soldiers to throw into the field against them. Although the first Bolivian army patrol surrendered too easily, the other army units showed more determination and resolve. Moreover, President Barrientos responded immediately. Unlike Batista, who never stepped in the battle zone of eastern Cuba, Barrientos visited Fourth Division headquarters at Camiri on March 26, just three days after the battle. Once he had personally inspected the zinc house and the guerrilla camp, he ordered the "drastic and immediate eradication of this insurgent foco characterized as a Castro-communist guerrilla war."[64]

This was not Cuba. The Fourth Division held its position at the zinc house and attacked the presumed locations of the guerrillas with planes and mortars in the days after the first engagement. An aggressive commander such as

62. Guevara, *Bolivian Diary*, 150–61.
63. Ibid.; Prado, *Defeat of Che Guevara*, 73–74.
64. Prado, *Defeat of Che Guevara*, 75.

Che Guevara would not even consider a retreat or redeployment now. Thus, Che drafted the first communiqué of the Ejército de Liberación Nacional (ELN, National Liberation Army of Bolivia). Beginning with a condemnation of the "military thugs who have usurped power," the communiqué detailed the "true" results of the March 23 ambush. The "hour of truth" was approaching, the unidentified commander of the ELN announced. "We call upon all who believe that the time has now come to respond to violence with violence, to rescue a country being sold piece by piece to the U.S. monopolies, and to raise the standard of living of our people, who with each passing day suffer more and more the scourge of hunger."[65]

Che's call to arms, published in a Cochabamba newspaper on May 1, fell on deaf ears. Without massive popular support, Che's forty-seven combatants would face more than one thousand Bolivian soldiers and their American military advisers alone, and in inhospitable terrain. Guevara assumed that his Bolivian adversary would show the same degree of military incompetence that the Cuban army had displayed. The Bolivian army and its American advisers, however, brought into the field technology, strategies, and tactics that Che had never faced. Much had changed since the Cuban Revolution. To prevent another Cuba, the United States had developed the equipment, strategies, and tactics required for counterinsurgency campaigns and provided military assistance to all Latin American countries, including Bolivia. Che held fast to a model of guerrilla warfare that had grown out of the exceptional experience of Cuba, where the Cuban revolutionaries never fought against an army assisted by American intelligence agents. Che and Fidel had committed tactical errors in Cuba, but the Cuban army rarely exploited those mistakes. The Bolivian army, and the American agents who advised it, knew how to make Che pay for his mistakes.

Che Guevara had gained a reputation as a master in guerrilla warfare before he defeated any troops with advanced training in counterinsurgency strategy and tactics. Batista's army lacked the organization, training, morale, and equipment required for irregular warfare. Only the summer offensive of 1958 reflected the strategic sophistication and coordination required for a successful counterinsurgency operation and, even then, poorly trained troops and inexperienced commanders failed to execute the strategic plan. In the Congo, Che engaged Colonel Hoare and the South African mercenaries in the final two months of the campaign, but Che's troops were already on the run,

---

65. Ibid.; Gott, *Guerrilla Movements*, 331–32.

knowing that the Congolese campaign was coming to an inglorious end. Until Che engaged the Bolivian Second Rangers in September 1967, he had never had his strategic conceptions and command tested by troops trained to fight a counterinsurgency campaign.

The Bolivian campaign, Che Guevara's first independent mission, got off to an inauspicious start. The Cuban insurrection had begun with the disastrous engagement at Alegría del Pío, but a national network organized before the *Granma* "invasion" replaced the rebel losses with men and matériel. No such organization existed in Bolivia, yet Che initiated the campaign anyway, his naturally aggressive instincts compelling him to fight. Logic might have dictated a withdrawal, but Che sent his men into battle, adviser to no one— and advised by no one.

ELEVEN NOT ANOTHER VIETNAM

"We must not underrate our adversary," Che warned in the "Message to the Tricontinental." "The U.S. soldier has technical capacity and is backed by weapons and resources of such magnitude that render him frightful."[1] Ironically, Che wanted to fight that which he feared most, the American soldier. He expected the Americans to intervene militarily as soon as they confirmed his presence at the head of a guerrilla band in southeastern Bolivia. The Americans obliged him in ways he did not anticipate, with results he never expected.

President Barrientos appealed personally to Douglas Henderson, American ambassador to Bolivia, on March 15, 1967, the day after the Bolivians apprehended two guerrillas at Lagunillas. The information obtained from the captives, corroborated by intercepted radio transmissions in the guerrilla zone, convinced Barrientos that he faced a serious guerrilla movement, though he did not believe that Che Guevara directed it. Ambassador Henderson did not believe it either, but he promised to look for radio-locator equipment that Barrientos requested. Hoping to stall Bolivian requests for extraordinary amounts of hardware, he asked Barrientos to submit a detailed list of the assistance his army required to support counterinsurgency operations. The

1. Guevara, "Message to the Tricontinental," 173.

Bolivians submitted their detailed requests the following evening. To crush the sixteen guerrillas, Barrientos asked for enough arms, clothing, and ammunition to outfit fifteen hundred additional reservists.[2]

After the guerrillas ambushed the Bolivian patrol on March 23, Ambassador Henderson reluctantly agreed to send two members of the U.S. Special Forces, the group known as the Green Berets, to Camiri to inspect the rebel camp. He wanted firsthand information to evaluate the Bolivians' increasingly exorbitant demands for American military assistance. When the State Department learned that American officers had visited a combat zone, Secretary of State Dean Rusk immediately ordered Henderson to keep all American personnel, including Peace Corps volunteers, out of any combat areas. According to Henderson, the State Department "did not want another Vietnam-type operation."[3]

As the Americans contemplated their military options, the Bolivian army used the resources already at hand to search out and destroy the guerrilla foco. Che maintained a defensive posture, prepared to repel advancing patrols. From the air, Che faced AT-6 aircraft supplied by the United States. In late March and early April, the planes pounded the guerrilla camps with such accuracy that Che concluded that the army had fixed his position with "absolute precision." Radio reports indicated that the Bolivian army had launched counteroffensive operations designed to crush the guerrilla foco before it took root. Che correctly deduced that the army intended to surround him. General Alfredo Ovando Candia, commander in chief of the Bolivian armed forces, deployed three companies totaling 245 men, each company ordered to perform reconnaissance in a different direction, under orders to search out and destroy the guerrillas. Even Che recognized his vulnerability at the time. Some of the recruits brought in by Moisés Guevara had failed their combat training. With the enemy mobilizing, the situation was "not good," Che reported in his diary. He had to discard the foreign visitors and rejects, gather his supplies, and move out.[4]

The Bolivian army held the initiative, however, and Che never regained it. As ineffective as the army patrols had been in combat, they put Che in a defensive posture. He had set ambushes along the routes leading to his camp and held them in place since the engagement on March 23. If the Bolivian

2. Ryan, *Fall of Che Guevara*, 44–48.
3. Ibid., 51.
4. Prado, *Defeat of Che Guevara*, 77–78; Guevara, *Bolivian Diary*, 160; Peredo, "My Campaign with Che," 363.

soldiers advanced again, they would pay. The soldiers fell into his trap at the Iripiti River on April 10. Guevara's veterans carried the day again, killing ten soldiers and losing only one man. Jesús Suárez Guayol, a veteran of Che's Santa Clara campaign, took a bullet in the head and died in camp.[5]

After this second straight rebel victory, General Ovando realized that his men faced an organized and experienced enemy. In two clashes, the army had lost eighteen dead and eighteen wounded. It had killed one guerrilla at Iripiti, but Ovando could not produce one foreign body to prove the existence of a Cuban-sponsored foco. He would suffer higher casualties if he attempted to drive Che out of his position. The army patrols could reach the camp only by marching along the banks of the Ñancahuazú River or its tributaries, all of which, hemmed in by rocks and lush vegetation, provided perfect settings for ambushes. Although the bombing raids had impressed Che with their precision, the terrain made it difficult for the pilots to spot guerrilla troops and separate them from advancing army patrols. Thus, General Ovando called a halt to the search-and-destroy missions and assigned defensive missions to the four companies operating in the Fourth Division. According to General Operations Order 4/67, "They [the four companies] should be organized defensively, undertaking patrols with a short radius of action in their respective areas, under conditions that will prevent guerrilla groups from obtaining vital supplies. They should isolate the probable area occupied by the guerrillas."[6]

Given that Che's foco lacked a vital lifeline to any city, the army's plan to confine the guerrillas to its current area of operations represented a viable strategy to weaken the guerrillas through attrition. When the army gained strength and experience, it could move in for the kill. The Bolivian army did not show any reluctance to fight, but in its first two engagements the army had suffered heavy casualties, revealing a lack of experience in counterinsurgency warfare. Bolivian and American observers concluded that the Bolivians needed training, advice, and equipment.

The Bolivians had already agreed to receive a Green Beret Mobile Training Team (MTT) to instruct a Bolivian ranger battalion in counterinsurgency warfare. The detection of the Cuban-sponsored guerrilla band convinced the Americans and Bolivians to dispatch the Green Berets a year earlier than scheduled. The U.S. Southern Command, based in Panama and commanded by

5. Guevara, *Bolivian Diary,* 168–71.
6. Prado, *Defeat of Che Guevara,* 81.

General Robert Porter, took an immediate interest in Bolivia as soon as reports filtered in about guerrilla activities. General Porter proposed to send a team of sixteen officers to analyze the military situation, but because of Ambassador Henderson's concerns about keeping the American profile low, agreed to send only air force brigadier general William Tope and one aide. In the meantime, Southern Command accelerated plans to dispatch the Green Berets to commence training of the Bolivian rangers.[7]

Major Ralph (Pappy) Shelton, leader of the MTT, was in Panama when he heard news of the Bolivian guerrillas. A decorated Korean War veteran, he joined the Special Forces, or Green Berets, in 1961. Under the Kennedy administration, the focus of American military policy in the Americas had changed dramatically, moving from hemispheric defense against external aggression to internal security and counterinsurgency. The United States, and the Latin American armies it trained, had not had much experience in counterinsurgency warfare prior to the Cuban Revolution. After the Bay of Pigs debacle, President Kennedy developed what one journalist described as an obsession with guerrilla warfare and counterinsurgency techniques. He read Mao Tse-tung's and Guevara's theories of guerrilla warfare, and he encouraged others to do the same. Thousands of State Department and Pentagon officers studied Mao and Che in special courses on counterinsurgency that Kennedy established at U.S. embassies in the developing world. He created a high-level "Special Group for Counterinsurgency" to coordinate all military and economic programs. He brought in Colonel Edward Lansdale to develop new counterinsurgency strategies and tactics based on the U.S. experience in South Vietnam. And, in his most famous response to the Latin American guerrilla challenge, Kennedy ordered a dramatic increase in Special Forces strength and stipulated that the elite troops wear the green beret, the symbol of his counterinsurgency program. The navy and air force followed this example by creating their own elite counterguerrilla units and training their best troops for unconventional warfare. In the six years prior to the arrival of the Green Beret team in Bolivia, the United States had developed strategies, tactics, and technology that would be used in a global campaign against wars of national liberation and guerrilla warfare.[8]

Major Shelton, after a stint training special forces in Laos, requested Spanish-language training and an assignment to Panama. In 1965 he took

---

7. Ryan, *Fall of Che Guevara*, 82–83.

8. Klare, *War Without End*, 38–41; Loveman and Davies, "Guerrilla Warfare, Revolutionary Theory," 21.

MTT to the Dominican Republic and served eight months. Ironically, Che Guevara had unwittingly given him and the Green Berets a decided advantage in the guerrilla wars that he led or inspired. Shelton could study Guevara's manual and devise the appropriate counterinsurgency strategy and tactics. With combat experience, ranger and airborne training, and Spanish-language skills, Major Shelton arrived in Bolivia in early April with all the skills and experience to train the Bolivian ranger battalion.[9]

In the twenty-five months of the Cuban insurrection (December 1956 to January 1959), no unit of the Cuban army ever received any counterinsurgency training by any American special forces. American counterinsurgency specialists certainly existed, but the Eisenhower administration, determined to remain neutral in the conflict, refused to provide military assistance. Intelligence agents collaborated with Batista's secret police, but in the first year of the conflict, when the guerrilla foco in the Sierra Maestra was the most vulnerable, the Americans sat on the sidelines, observing and criticizing the Cuban army. Although American assistance might not have changed the outcome of the Cuban insurrection, a limited amount of American aid turned the Bolivian army into a more formidable opponent than Che or Fidel had ever faced in Cuba. Yet when the Bolivian government announced the arrival of five American counterinsurgency experts on April 13, Guevara welcomed the news, confident that events were developing as he had predicted. "We are perhaps witnessing the first episode of a new Vietnam," he noted after he learned of the arrival of U.S. military advisers.[10]

Che recognized, however, that his foco could not remain long in the Ñancahuazú camps. Army patrols and airplanes still threatened the guerrillas. Che contemplated an early move "toward the north," possibly the Alto Beni, where he had intended to establish his base of operations. Before he moved out of the area, he wanted to relieve the foco of two of the noncombatants, Debray and Bustos. He would have preferred to get Tania out of his camp too, but she had been uncovered and could not return to La Paz. Debray, for one, wanted to get out of camp as soon as possible. He had once asked to join the guerrillas, but now, with the enemy threatening to encircle the guerrilla camps, Debray explained—with "excessive vehemence," according to Che—"how useful he would be abroad."[11]

9. Ryan, *Fall of Che Guevara,* 89–91.
10. Guevara, *Bolivian Diary,* 172.
11. Ibid., 158.

Che decided to march the main body south to Muyupumpa, from which the two foreigners would have to find their own way out. To protect his rear, Che left Acuña and the rear guard behind, with instructions to obstruct any enemy troop movement and to wait three days for his return. Surprisingly, Che did not set a rallying point at which the main body could reunite with the rear guard, in the event that the two groups lost contact. Aside from this fundamental error, one must also question why Che risked another engagement with the enemy and worse, separation from his rear guard, for the safety of two unwelcome guests. Che recognized the risks of the strategy. "In returning along the same road we risk clashing with army units alerted in Lagunillas or with a column coming from Ticucha. However, it is necessary to run this risk to avoid becoming separated from the rear guard."[12]

Che assumed that he could complete the mission without being detected, another sign that he underestimated his opponents. Che's forward and center units marched out of camp on the evening of April 17, hoping to reunite with the rear guard three days later. On the afternoon of April 19, two children from Lagunillas followed the guerrillas' tracks to their camp, bringing Andrew Roth, an English journalist, with them. From the two boys Che learned that the news of his march toward Muyupumpa had been relayed to the army in Lagunillas. On the night of April 19, the vanguard clashed with an army patrol. The guerrillas prevailed yet again, but the army presence made it too dangerous to proceed as planned. Che then "washed his hands" of Debray and Bustos. He would let them decide what to do, but he could no longer risk the security of his entire force for them. He turned away from Muyupumpa before dawn on April 20, leaving Debray and Bustos to walk into the village on their own.

At 1:00 P.M. on April 20, a three-man delegation from the village arrived at Che's camp to ask the guerrillas to lay down their arms and leave the area, because they did not want any trouble. Guido Peredo, representing the guerrillas, not only rejected the request; he demanded that the townspeople provide the guerrillas with food and medicines. He gave them until 6:00 P.M. to return with the supplies. The delegates warned that the army would not allow them to return. They also informed Peredo that the army had already captured Debray and Bustos. The situation looked bleak for the guerrillas, but Che stayed in position, waiting for the food and medicines. His wait ended at 5:30 P.M., when three AT-6 aircraft bombed the camp, forcing Che to with-

12. Ibid., 173–75.

draw. He diverted the column westward toward Ticucha, still hoping that he could circle around and reunite with his rear guard.[13]

This latest bombing, like all previous attacks, inflicted only minor damage on the guerrillas, but it put them on the run, and worse, put distance between Che and the rear guard. The Bolivian army kept the pressure on, clashing with the guerrillas at Taperillas on April 22 and again at El Mesón on April 25. The engagements delayed the guerrillas and prevented them from reuniting with the rear guard. Moreover, Che lost Eliseo Reyes at El Mesón. Reyes, former head of the G-2, the undercover division of Cuba's police, was "the best man in the guerrilla unit, one of its pillars," Che wrote.[14]

Although the Bolivian army had killed only two guerrillas in a month of sporadic skirmishes, it had Che Guevara on the run and, by a stroke of good fortune, divided the small guerrilla band. The performance of the army patrols in combat had been discouraging, but none of the units then engaged had had any counterinsurgency training. In response to the threat, the army had transferred about one hundred soldiers with some antiguerrilla training to Camiri. But President Barrientos still wanted and needed more training, equipment, and advice from the Americans.

On April 18, Brigadier General Tope arrived in Bolivia from the Southern Command to analyze the situation and evaluate the Bolivians' needs. The general's twelve-day visit, the first of six by an American general or admiral, indicated that the United States attached the highest priority to the eradication of the guerrilla band. President Barrientos shared that objective, but he wanted automatic weapons, communications equipment, and aircraft to complete the task. The Bolivian army still used Mausers dating to the Chaco War, against Paraguay (1932–35). Barrientos asked General Tope to replace them with automatic weapons that could "fill the air with lead." In a meeting with Barrientos on April 22, General Tope argued that an "untrained conscript will drop a modern weapon just as quickly as he will a Mauser."[15]

The Bolivians routinely requested high-tech military hardware; the Americans regularly stressed the need to train the army in counterinsurgency warfare. General Tope, in three meetings with the president, tried to impress on Barrientos the need for training, communications, and maintenance. The failure to provide any one of these three elements, he argued, would bring

13. Ibid., 177–79; Prado, *Defeat of Che Guevara*, 88–90.
14. Guevara, *Bolivian Diary*, 182–83.
15. Douglas Henderson (U.S. ambassador to Bolivia) to State, April 22, 1967, container 8, Bolivia Country File, NSF, LBJ.

failure to the entire campaign. Although Barrientos and his advisers nodded in agreement, their subsequent comments indicated that they did not understand the principle or simply did not want to apply it. General Tope warned his superiors that the Americans might have to intervene more directly, because the Bolivian army lacked everything required for success, adequate field intelligence, communications equipment, training, leadership, and weaponry. General Tope even anticipated the need to place American military advisers in the field to compensate for the incompetence of the Bolivian officer corps.[16]

Despite General Tope's recommendation, the Johnson administration remained determined to keep American advisers and soldiers out of the conflict. A "no-go" area had been established in April, as a result of which two American military advisers at Camiri had to be withdrawn. On April 28, 1967, Colonel Kenneth T. Macek, chief of the United States Military Group in Bolivia, and General Ovando signed an agreement for the activation, organization, and training of the Second Ranger Battalion, conceived as a battalion-size rapid reaction force, trained specifically for counterinsurgency operations in the jungle. The memorandum specifically prohibited all American advisers from "participating in actual combat operations either as observers or advisors with members of the Bolivian Armed Forces." Further, "U.S. military personnel must be careful to avoid the assumption, either directly or indirectly, of functions that should be performed by Bolivian military personnel during the conduct of counterinsurgency combat operations and related support activities."[17]

Hence, Major Pappy Shelton, ordered to stay out of the combat zone, set up his training camp at La Esperanza, a hamlet located forty-five miles north of Santa Cruz. Shelton's Green Berets never got within one hundred miles of Che's guerrilla band. From May 8, the day he began training the Second Rangers, until September 26, Major Shelton focused on teaching the Bolivians how to fight the guerrillas. Throughout the four-month training program, Shelton reported directly to General Porter in Panama. Porter, determined to prevail in a war by proxy against a Cuban-sponsored guerrilla foco, provided Shelton with all the money, men, and supplies he required.[18] He even

16. Ibid.; General Tope to Southern Command, "Meeting with President René Barrientos Ortuño, etc.," May 3, 1967, cited in Ryan, *Fall of Che Guevara*, 84.

17. U.S. Army, memorandum of understanding concerning the activation, organization, and training of the Second Battalion, Bolivian Army, April 28, 1967, Electronic Briefing Book no. 5, National Security Archive, available: <www.gwu.edu/~nsarchiv/NSAEBB /NSAEBB5/che14_1.htm>; Ryan, *Fall of Che Guevara*, 53.

18. Ryan, *Fall of Che Guevara*, 91–93.

visited La Esperanza once, another sign of the American resolve to defeat Che Guevara.

The CIA shared the Pentagon's determination to get Che Guevara. The agency had lost track of Che since he had left the Congo. The station chief in Bolivia picked up his trail in Bolivia in February or March 1967, but his superiors at headquarters in Langley, Virginia, would not confirm his presence in Bolivia until later that summer. Nevertheless, the CIA responded quickly and effectively, setting up a communications center in Santa Cruz and utilizing its agents in the urban underground. The agency assigned several Cuban exiles and an American case officer to Bolivia to collect and analyze intelligence; one agent served in the Ministry of Government in La Paz. More important, at least two Cuban-born agents accompanied Bolivian units in the field. The no-go zone established by the Americans did not apply to Felix Rodríguez and Gustavo Villoldo, both recruited by the CIA in the early 1960s. Rodríguez and Villoldo ran an intelligence network that linked the *campesinos* of southeastern Bolivia to Santa Cruz, La Paz, and beyond. In the final months of the campaign, Guevara's guerrillas could not buy supplies in any hamlet without their movements being detected and reported to the Bolivian army.[19]

Che Guevara faced an enemy with higher morale and better training than Batista's army, which never fought with the tenacity displayed by the Bolivians in 1967. Rodríguez and Villoldo, in hot pursuit of the number-two man on their hit list, would not let him rest. They had lost family and property in Cuba. In February 1959, Villoldo's father had committed suicide after Che confiscated his automobile dealership. The young Villoldo left Cuba a month later and joined the anticommunist exiles organizing in Miami. He served as the chief of intelligence and security for the Brigade 2506 air force and flew two B-26 missions over the Bay of Pigs. When Villoldo joined the CIA in 1964, he wanted revenge.[20]

Che Guevara, facing forces he did not anticipate or respect, expected to have to consolidate his guerrilla band before he engaged American forces. But the Bolivian army, despite its repeated complaints that it lacked the hardware that it needed, had him on the run *before* the Green Berets and the CIA exerted much influence over the counterinsurgency campaign. By the end of April 1967, Che's band was divided into two units and totally cut off from the outside. The guerrillas had had no luck in recruiting local peasants into

19. Ibid., 96.
20. Juan O. Tamayo, "Yo enterré al Che," *El Nuevo Herald* (Miami), September 21, 1967.

their army, and the performance of the Bolivian army was improving. Even Che noted that the army patrols had improved their techniques.[21] Che's only hope was to reunite with the rear guard, leave his Ñancahuazú bases, and relocate his foco in the Alto Beni.

Che marched his two units back to the Bear Camp, still hoping to reunite with Acuña and the rear guard there. The army's air and land pursuit of the guerrillas, however, had forced him to veer northwest, away from Acuña. When the main body returned to the Bear Camp on May 7, the rear guard was not there. Che clashed with an army patrol near the main camp the following day.[22]

By this time, American and Bolivian intelligence had received more compelling evidence that Che Guevara commanded the guerrilla foco. After several days of rough treatment at the hands of the Bolivian army, Debray and Bustos were transferred to the Green Beret training base at La Esperanza. Although Captain Gary Prado Salmón, commander of a Bolivian Ranger company, denies that any American intelligence agents participated in the interrogations, Felix Rodríguez claims that a Cuban-born CIA agent known as Gabriel García, operating under cover in the Bolivian ministry of the interior, interrogated Debray. Che had asked Debray and Bustos not to divulge his presence or objectives, but both men broke under pressure. Debray confessed that he had been in contact with Castro and that Che commanded the guerrilla band. Even worse, he identified the location of the camps and other sites where the guerrillas had stored arms, ammunition, and supplies. Debray also described Che's strategic plan to spawn guerrilla movements throughout the continent and thereby provoke American military intervention. Bustos added another gem: sketches of all the guerrilla combatants, including Guevara, and maps of the camps and caves. According to Gustavo Villoldo, the information provided by Debray and Bustos was not entirely new. He had already learned of Guevara's presence, thanks to his informants in the urban underground. Debray's testimony, however, might have convinced the Americans to pull out all the stops in their efforts to capture Che Guevara. According to Felix Rodríguez, Debray's testimony "helped convince the Agency to lay on a concentrated effort to capture the elusive revolutionary."[23]

21. Guevara, *Bolivian Diary*, 186–87; Rostow to president, May 11, 1967, container 8, Bolivia Country File, NSF, LBJ.

22. Guevara, *Bolivian Diary*, 192–93.

23. Prado, *Defeat of Che Guevara*, 95–96; Castañeda, *Compañero*, 368; Thomas L. Hughes to secretary of state, October 12, 1967, "Guevara's Death—The Meaning for Latin America";

Meanwhile, the Bolivian army closed a circle around the combat zone, determined to prevent the guerrillas from receiving outside assistance or moving out of the region. Che suspected that the army, knowing the location of his camps, would advance toward them soon. He had no choice but to move out of the area. Thus, in late May, Che led his band of twenty-five men eastward, across the Pirienda Mountains. Arriving at the town of Caraguatarenda on May 28, the guerrillas took several prisoners, two jeeps, two trucks, and some supplies. Che now had the means to move his men rapidly east and northward, farther from the army patrols.[24]

However, the arrival of the guerrillas frightened the residents, who relayed the news of these strangers to the authorities. The army sent two motorized companies under the command of Lieutenant Colonel Augusto Calderón after the rebels, who reached the Santa Cruz–Yacuba railroad on May 30. Local residents spotted their movement, however, forcing Che to post an ambush for the army patrol that he expected to follow. Army patrols fell into ambushes on May 30 and May 31. Although the guerrillas repelled each advance, the vigorous pursuit by the army prevented Che from crossing the railroad and moving into the mountains to establish another base of operations.[25]

Blocked to the east, Guevara turned the column to the north, heading toward El Limón and Puerto Camacho. His main objective was to lose the army units on his tail and reunite with the rear guard. He had to rely completely on his own resources because he could not expect any more help from Havana or La Paz. The radio transmitter had broken down; he could receive but not send messages. The foco was coming apart, and Che, like his guerrillas, had been weakened by several straight weeks of forced marches and illness, and his morale had begun to suffer. When an army truck fell into his ambush on June 3, Che spotted two young Bolivian soldiers lying down in the back, wrapped in blankets. He "did not have the heart to shoot them." He later told his men that "it would have been a crime to shoot those little soldiers."[26]

Che began to doubt that he was still a "cold killing machine." His troops exchanged fire with an army patrol as they tried to cross the Rio Grande on

---

CIA, Directorate of Intelligence, "The Bolivian Guerrilla Movement: An Interim Assessment," August 8, 1967, both container 8, Bolivia Country File, NSF, LBJ; Rodríguez and Weisman, *Shadow Warrior,* 135–36.

24. Guevara, *Bolivian Diary,* 201–3.

25. Ibid., 203–4; Prado, *Defeat of Che Guevara,* 114–15.

26. Guevara, *Bolivian Diary,* 208 (quoted); Peredo, "My Campaign with Che," 375.

June 10, but knowing the weakness of his position, he withdrew and turned westward. He was tired and on the run on June 14, his thirty-ninth birthday. He felt that he had reached an age at which he had to consider his future as a guerrilla.[27]

Ironically, American intelligence analysts shared Che's pessimism. One report, dated June 14, 1967, berated the government's "total inability to cope with the guerrillas." The officers and soldiers had little or no training in guerrilla tactics and had no knowledge of the terrain, according to the analyst. Communications between the field commanders and headquarters in La Paz was "extremely unreliable," meaning that "no one in the Army command has an accurate understanding of events in the guerrilla area."[28]

Although the Bolivian army had not prevailed in any engagement with the guerrillas, it held the upper hand. By mid-June, the Fourth Division had divided Guevara's column, severed its ties to the outside, and sent Guevara running. Che certainly knew that circumstances favored his enemy, which possessed unusually accurate information about the size, location, and movement of his band. A government communiqué of June 12 had announced that there were seventeen Cubans and three Peruvians in a band of thirty-eight guerrillas. The number of Cubans and Peruvians was accurate. Che wondered how the army had obtained such precise information.[29]

Che suspected that the deserters—Debray or Bustos—had given up too much information, and they had. Knowing that Guevara commanded an elite guerrilla column designed to serve as an international base from which to launch a continental revolution, the Johnson administration decided to crush him. In a memorandum to President Johnson, National Security Adviser Walt Rostow explained that "we have put Bolivia on top of the list." There were several hundred more insurgents fighting in Colombia, Venezuela, and Guatemala, but Che, commanding fewer than fifty combatants arrayed against an army that the Americans considered weak and ineffective, became the primary target.[30]

Rostow informed Johnson that intelligence agents were monitoring radio communications between Havana and Guevara. "We also know that they [the

27. Guevara, *Bolivian Diary*, 210–12.

28. "Cuban Inspired Guerrilla Activity in Bolivia," June 14, 1967, container 2, "Guerrilla Problem in Latin America," Intelligence File, NSF, LBJ.

29. Guevara, *Bolivian Diary*, 212.

30. Rostow to president, June 24, 1967, container 2, "Guerrilla Problem in Latin America," Intelligence File, NSF, LBJ.

guerrillas] have radio contact with Cuba using the same procedures taught by the Soviets," Rostow reported. In the field, the guerrillas communicated through walkie-talkies or field radios, and the Americans also detected those transmissions. American intelligence monitored radio traffic through ground stations, airborne systems, and satellites. The first RC-135, an airborne platform designed specifically to collect signals intelligence, came into service in December 1965. In addition, the United States operated ground stations throughout the world to monitor communications emanating from or within the Soviet Union, China, Vietnam, the Middle East, and Latin America. If American intelligence did not utilize satellite or airborne collection systems in Bolivia, the agents could have established covert listening posts in Santa Cruz or La Paz. In the late 1960s, a covert listening post set up in the American embassy in Moscow intercepted radio-telephone communications of Soviet Politburo members, including calls placed by Leonid Brezhnev as he drove around the city in his limousine.[31]

Unfortunately, we have little evidence from radio communications and surveillance during the Bolivian campaign. The Cubans apparently used some kind of field radios or walkie-talkies. We know from Villegas's diary, for example, that Guido Peredo carried a radio in his backpack.[32] Although the Cubans' radio transmitter broke down by June, the receiver worked until the end. The Americans apparently monitored all this radio traffic. They also could have pinpointed the location of the guerrilla band by triangulating on the position of the transmission. According to Richard Clement, an American intelligence agent contracted by the Bolivian government in 1967, he was assigned the job of tracking the radio signals of the guerrilla forces to pinpoint their location. He presumes that a general in Washington had overall command of the operation. Clement improvised a method of collecting electronic intelligence from a piper plane flying over the area of operations. His job was to pick up transmissions between the guerrilla units and relay the information to the ground forces. In the final phase of the Bolivian campaign, Clement played a decisive role in the capture of Che Guevara.[33]

Even without sophisticated communications surveillance, the Bolivian army received enough information from local residents to track Guevara's column. Army patrols had no trouble following Guevara; they just could not defeat

---

31. Richelson, *U.S. Intelligence Community*, 167–97.
32. Villegas, *Pombo*, 213.
33. Richard Clement, interview by author, Tampa, Florida, June 18, 1999; George Coryell, "Shadow Man," *Tampa Tribune*, June 16, 1999.

the guerrillas in battle. In June, Guevara's column continued marching north, with the army in pursuit, engaging again at Florida on June 26. In the battle, Carlos Coello, Che's bodyguard and friend, suffered a fatal wound to his abdomen. The loss of this comrade inflicted another serious blow to Che's morale: "With his death I have lost an inseparable comrade and companion over all the recent years. His loyalty was unwavering, and I feel his absence almost as if he were my own son."[34]

The situation of Guevara's column was grim and growing worse. Che marched northward to the Cochabamba–Santa Cruz road then turned west, the army still in pursuit. A detachment of guerrillas arrived in Samaipata on July 6 to pick up badly needed supplies of food and medicine. The guerrillas briefly occupied the town, killing one soldier and taking nine prisoners. In full view of the town's seventeen hundred residents, the guerrillas confiscated some supplies, but they could not find any asthma medicine for Che. Knowing that the army would soon learn of their appearance, Guevara turned the column south, heading toward his original base of operations. He had to risk a return to the Ñancahuazú area because he needed more supplies, particularly asthma medication. Che's asthma was running "full throttle" and weakened him so much that it was affecting the movement of the column.[35]

Unknown to Che, he was marching right into a trap set by the Bolivian army. Che's movement north had brought him into the Eighth Division's area of operations. Units of the Eighth Division, in fact, had blocked his attempt to cross the Cochabama–Santa Cruz road and then pursued him south. Meanwhile, the Fourth Division, based in Camiri, continued its pursuit from the south, with the result that two army divisions came at Che, one from the north and the other from the south. After blocking the exit routes east and west, the two divisions would then concentrate on a reduced area of operations north of the Rio Grande. This new strategy became official in Operations Directive 13/67, issued on July 28. The Fourth Division would occupy and close off escape routes east and west of the Ñancahuzaú River, then comb the area from south to north, particularly the Bear Camp, advancing to the Rio Grande. Meanwhile, units of the Eighth Division would comb north to south. After the units reduced the area of operations, the army would bring in the Second Ranger Battalion, then being trained at La Esperanza, for the kill.[36] (See Map 12.)

34. Guevara, *Bolivian Diary,* 219.
35. Ibid., 229–45.
36. Prado, *Defeat of Che Guevara,* 138–39.

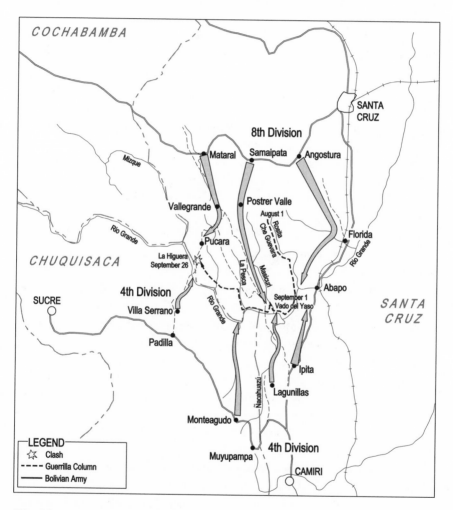

Map 12. Counterinsurgency Strategy

The new strategy, requiring coordination of at least six different units simultaneously, produced the first successes for the Bolivian army. One unit of the Eighth Division attacked the guerrillas with mortar fire on July 27. In a predawn raid on July 30, an army patrol hit the guerrilla camp by surprise, killing José María Martínez Tamayo and a Bolivian. Che escaped the army's attempt to encircle him, but he paid a high price for it. Martínez Tamayo, described by Che as an "extraordinary fighter," had been with Che since the inception of the Bolivian campaign. He also lost fifteen knapsacks containing valuable medicines, a radio, and a tape recorder. According to Captain Prado, the battle "affected Che and his men deeply because for the first time they had been surprised, followed, and hunted down vigorously by army troops."[37] Even Che noted that "the army still cannot do anything right, but several units appear to be more combative."[38]

As the military situation deteriorated for the guerrillas, Che saw a slight glimmer of hope in the political crisis that engulfed Barrientos in June. He had always hoped to attract the militant miners to his cause, and after the Bolivian military fired on workers at the Siglo XX mines that month, he expected the unions to rally to the armed struggle. A leftist challenge to Barrientos, coming from students, miners, and the remnants of the MNR, could destabilize the regime and open opportunities for the guerrilla movement. However, American intelligence detected no interest among the miners in joining the guerrillas, and the army had Che confined to an area far from the mining centers. After two parties withdrew from the governing coalition in mid-July, Che hoped for the disintegration of the government, but Barrientos remained strong.[39]

The Bolivian army certainly showed no signs of dissatisfaction with their president. In early August, Lieutenant Colonel Augusto Calderón of the First Infantry Battalion of the Fourth Division deployed four companies in four directions, all destined to converge on the Bear Camp and the storage caves around it. A map of the camps and caves drawn by Bustos guided the companies toward these critical storage facilities. Between August 6 and 9, the companies confiscated virtually everything left behind by the guerrillas— machine guns, rifles, mortars, grenade launchers, medicines, a radio, clothing, and even an electrical generator.[40] Without these supplies or the ability

37. Ibid., 139–42.
38. Guevara, *Bolivian Diary*, 244–45.
39. Ibid., 217–18, 233; George C. Denney Jr. to acting secretary of state, "Crisis Management in Bolivia," June 23, 1967, container 2, Intelligence File, NSF, LBJ.
40. Prado, *Defeat of Che Guevara*, 143–47.

to replace them from other sources, Che would have to rely solely on the supplies his men carried on their backs.

The army announced the confiscation of these guerrilla supplies on August 8, compelling Che to discuss this terrible loss with his men. Weakened considerably by constant asthma attacks, Che used his last anti-asthma injection on August 2, leaving him with a ten-day supply of tablets. The men, demoralized by the illness of their commander and the recent reverses, were growing irritable. Some talked about abandoning the struggle, an increasingly viable option. Che presented his men with a critical choice. "We have reached a moment when great decisions are called for. This type of struggle provides us the opportunity to become revolutionaries, the highest level of the human species. At the same time, it enables us to emerge fully as men." He admitted that he was a "real mess" and that he had occasionally "lost control," but he was determined to fight to the end. He let each man decide whether to leave or fight. They all decided to stay.[41]

Che could not go on, however, if he did not find some anti-asthma medication. There was still a slight chance that the army had not discovered the cave with his medicines in it, so he ordered three men to proceed with great caution to that cave. The more prudent move would have been away from his former base of operations, but Che's deteriorating health forced him to move toward the army's greatest strength, violating a cardinal rule of guerrilla warfare. On August 14, with the group en route to the cave, the radio carried the news that the army had confiscated the cave with Che's medication in it. Che now felt "condemned to suffer from asthma indefinitely. . . . This is the hardest blow they have yet dealt us," Che noted on August 14. "Someone talked. The question is who." Che had no idea that Bustos had drawn maps of his caves and camps.[42]

Things could get worse, and they did. On the afternoon of August 31, Acuña and the rear guard cautiously approached the Rio Grande, hoping to reunite with the main body, then just a day's march away. Honorato Rojas, who had first met the guerrillas in February, had led them to believe that they could cross safely near Vado del Yeso, at the confluence of the Masicuri and Rio Grande. In reality, Rojas had been convinced by Captain Mario Vargas Salinas to betray the guerrillas. Captain Vargas had deployed his forty-one men in ambush positions that morning. Eleven hours later, ten guerrillas waded single file into breast-deep water, completely unaware of the trap into

41. Guevara, *Bolivian Diary,* 250 (quoted); Villegas, *Pombo,* 174–76.
42. Guevara, *Bolivian Diary,* 251–53.

which they had marched. The army opened fire without warning, killing nine guerrillas within twenty minutes. The only survivor was José Castillo, one of the Bolivian "rejects" who had been trying to leave the guerrillas since March.[43]

In addition to destroying the rear guard, the Bolivian army captured valuable intelligence, including photographs, documents, and diaries, and one terrified Bolivian prisoner. The Bolivians asked the CIA for assistance in analyzing the astonishing stash of intelligence, which included some communications intelligence that the United States kept classified (as it is to this day). In the meantime, CIA agent Felix Rodríguez flew from Santa Cruz to Vallegrande to interrogate Castillo. Rodríguez, recognizing the potential value of the captive, convinced the Bolivian officers not to execute Castillo. Rodríguez tended to Castillo's wounds, treated him fairly, and gained the prisoner's confidence. Over the following two weeks, Felix obtained valuable intelligence from Castillo, including the fact that Manuel Hernández commanded Che's vanguard. Felix knew that if and when the army contacted Hernández, Che would be following about one thousand meters behind him with the main body, moving slowly and cautiously up steep ravines or through thick jungle undergrowth.[44]

The information acquired by the army in its raids on the camps, followed by the destruction of the rear guard, helped the Bolivian government to identify the small network of urban activists and sympathizers, including Loyola Guzmán. The CIA had already penetrated the group, and now, with the guerrillas on the run, the Bolivian authorities shut it down completely. The police arrested Guzmán and eleven others, destroying the remnants of Guevara's ineffective urban network.[45] If by some miracle Che's combatants broke out of the army's encirclement, they would find no safe haven in any Bolivian city.

It was now only a matter of time before the army clamped the vise around Che's fragile unit and hammered it. Che moved cautiously west and north,

43. CIA, "The Elimination of the Rear Guard of the Bolivian Guerrillas," September 5, 1967, container 8, Bolivia Country File, NSF, LBJ; Gott, *Guerrilla Movements,* 348–49; González and Sánchez Salazar, *Great Rebel,* 168–73; Harris, *Death of a Revolutionary,* 147–49; Prado, *Defeat of Che Guevara,* 150–53.

44. CIA, memorandum for deputy inspector general, June 3, 1975, debriefing of Felix Rodríguez, Electronic Briefing Book no. 5, National Security Archive, available: <www.gwu.edu/~nsarchiv/NSAEBB/NSAEBB5/che15>; Covey T. Oliver to Mr. Kohler, September 2, 1967, container 2, Intelligence File, NSF, LBJ; Rodríguez and Weisman, *Shadow Warrior,* 144–56.

45. Ryan, *Fall of Che Guevara,* 116; Prado, *Defeat of Che Guevara,* 165.

constantly looking for signs of an enemy ambush. The guerrillas clashed with the army on September 3 and again on September 6. On September 8, Che posted two ambushes while he sent out scouts to look for an escape route. On September 10, he lost his shoes while swimming across a river; instead of taking shoes away from one of his subordinates, he wrapped his feet with swaths of leather.[46] Ravaged by asthma, hunger, and thirst, and with planes and helicopters flying over the area, Che had to take increasingly desperate risks. The guerrillas entered the village of Alto Seco at dawn on September 22 and held it for the following twenty-four hours. To defend themselves, the guerrillas dug trenches at the entrance to the town. Che convened a meeting of all adult males that evening. Guido Peredo spoke to the men about the objectives of the guerrilla band. Then Che spoke directly to the Bolivian people for the first time in the entire campaign. He spoke anonymously and, apparently, unimpressively. He invited his audience to join the revolution, but nobody accepted the invitation.[47]

News of the guerrillas' occupation of Alto Seco reached the army command in Vallegrande on the afternoon of September 22, while the guerrillas still held the town. The army's network of informants provided them with critical intelligence, while the guerrillas received neither supplies nor recruits from the local population. At 10:00 A.M. on September 26, the guerrillas occupied the hamlet of La Higuera and cut the telephone lines, hoping that they could delay reports of their movements. However, they were already under the observation of Second Lieutenant Eduardo Galindo, commanding a company of the Fourth Division, then camped on some heights less than two miles away. At 1:00 P.M. the vanguard left La Higuera in broad daylight, observed by dozens of suspicious peasants. "This movement by the guerrillas in plain daylight through an open area with no vegetation and with considerable population cannot be explained," Captain Prado concluded.[48]

Under normal circumstances, Che would not have moved during the day. However, the army had him on the run, forcing him to take unusual risks. As the vanguard advanced along the rocky heights north of La Higuera, Second Lieutenant Galindo observed them and quickly organized an ambush. Within thirty minutes, the guerrillas marched straight into Galindo's trap.

46. Guevara, *Bolivian Diary,* 265–74.
47. Ibid., 282; Peredo, "My Campaign with Che," 389; González and Sánchez, *Great Rebel,* 178–79; Prado, *Defeat of Che Guevara,* 168–69.
48. Guevara, *Bolivian Diary,* 284–85; González and Sánchez, *Great Rebel,* 178–81; Prado, *Defeat of Che Guevara,* 171.

Hernández, the commander of the vanguard, fell, as did Roberto Peredo and another Bolivian. Two other Bolivian volunteers defected after this engagement. Che knew that he had to move out of La Higuera in a hurry. He set the mules loose and proceeded down into a nearby ravine, where he found a safe place to spend the night and contemplate the disastrous defeat.[49]

Felix Rodríguez rushed over to Pucara to identify the three guerrillas killed in the ambush at La Higuera. From his interrogation of José Castillo, Felix had learned that Hernández commanded Che's vanguard. Deducing that Second Lieutenant Galindo had just destroyed Che's vanguard, Rodríguez advised Colonel Joaquín Zenteno of the Eighth Division to send a detachment from the recently trained Second Ranger Battalion after Che. The Second Rangers had completed their special forces training and moved to Vallegrande on September 26. With Che on the ropes, 650 Bolivian rangers moved in for the kill, the first American-trained troops to go into battle.[50]

The sixteen guerrillas who were left with Che tried in vain to climb out of the canyon the following day. Captain Prado and a Ranger company with 145 men, along with another squadron of 37 men, kept the guerrillas pinned down for three consecutive days. The guerrillas, seeing soldiers on the hills above them, managed to move out of one ravine only to find themselves pinned down in another one, the Yuro. Meanwhile, radio reports indicated that as many as two thousand soldiers were tightening a circle around them."[51]

The guerrillas kept looking for a way out of the Yuro ravine, marching at night on October 4 and 5, but they passed a well-populated area in broad daylight on October 6. A farmer spotted seventeen heavily armed men passing by his field near La Higuera and reported the news to the Bolivian army. At 5:30 A.M. on October 8, the men arrived at the confluence of two ravines, the Yuro and San Antonio. Che sent out three teams to explore escape routes along the left flank (the Jaguey ravine), the center (up the Yuro canyon), and the right (La Tusca). They found that army squads blocked their exit in any direction.[52] (See Map 13.)

The guerrillas were trapped at the bottom of the Yuro ravine, confined to a stretch of about two hundred yards bordered by steep slopes that rose to

49. Guevara, *Bolivian Diary*, 284–85; Prado, *Defeat of Che Guevara*, 170–72.

50. Rodríguez and Weisman, *Shadow Warrior*, 155; Prado, *Defeat of Che Guevara*, 170–72.

51. Prado, *Defeat of Che Guevara*, 173; Guevara, *Bolivian Diary*, 293; Villegas, *Pombo*, 206–11.

52. Guevara, *Bolivian Diary*, 293–97; Peredo, "My Campaign with Che," 395; Villegas, *Pombo*, 211–12; Prado, *Defeat of Che Guevara*, 174–75.

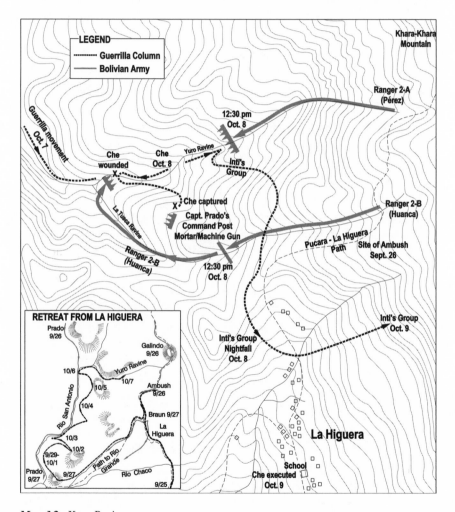

Map 13. Yuro Ravine

open fields above. They might remain undetected beneath the vegetation, but they could not advance up the canyon, retreat back toward the San Antonio River, or move through their flanks. There was no alternative; they would have to fight their way out. At 8:30 A.M., Che divided his force into three units and placed them in defensive positions. He assessed his chances in the following way. If the army attacked between 10:00 A.M. and 1:00 P.M., the guerrillas would have a minimal chance of surviving the rest of the day; if the attack came between 1:00 and 3:00 P.M., they had a good chance to neutralize the enemy; if the army offensive began after 3:00 P.M., Che thought that his men would have the advantage.[53]

The battle began around 10:30 A.M., when the seven-man vanguard, led by Villegas and Guido Peredo, exchanged fire in the upper Yuro canyon, determined to hold their position at all costs to cover the retreat of Che and the other nine men. Around one o'clock in the afternoon, Che tried to slip out of the valley, and the army pushed him back with heavy-mortar and machine-gun fire. A bullet pierced Che's black beret; another hit his M-1 carbine and rendered it inoperable; another bullet struck his right calf.[54]

Enemy squads moved in for the kill. One squad moved down La Tusca ravine to get in Che's rear and advance up the Yuro ravine to close the trap on Che and the wounded guerrillas. Che could not rally his dispersed men. They were under assault from all sides. Che, trapped at the bottom of the ravine with Simón Cuba, a Bolivian volunteer, tried to escape by the only path left open to him. He struggled up the side of the canyon, hiding behind the few bushes that offered any cover. If attacked, Cuba had a submachine gun; Che had only a nine-millimeter pistol with one clip. Around four o'clock in the afternoon, they walked into the barrel of two rifles pointed directly at their chests.

"HALT! SURRENDER!" Bolivian soldiers demanded.

Che raised his hands. "Don't shoot! I am Che Guevara, and I'm worth more to you alive than dead." Cuba dropped his submachine gun.[55]

The Bolivians took the two prisoners to their captain, Gary Prado. Che, a prisoner for the first time, looked like a man who had been chased through woods and ravines for seven months. Wild, unwashed hair fell below his shoul-

---

53. Prado, *Defeat of Che Guevara*, 176; Peredo, "My Campaign with Che," 396.

54. Prado, *Defeat of Che Guevara*, 176–77; Gott, *Guerrilla Movements*, 351; Peredo, "My Campaign with Che," 395–96.

55. Prado, *Defeat of Che Guevara*, 177; Harris, *Death of a Revolutionary*, 157–58; González and Sánchez, *Great Rebel*, 189.

ders, and his torn and ragged fatigues barely concealed his emaciated body. Leather straps covered his tired feet; his lower leg was red from his bleeding calf wound. Che asked Prado for medical attention and the Bolivian had the calf bandaged, but with a battle still raging in the ravine, he could not give more attention to the comandante. He had the hands and feet of the prisoners tied and ordered the guards to shoot them if they attempted to escape.

"Don't worry, Captain, it's all over . . . ," Che assured him.[56]

By dusk, the firing in the canyon had stopped. Captain Prado pulled his men back to positions blocking the exit routes, determined to finish off the remaining guerrillas the following day. For the moment, he knew only that his men had killed two guerrillas and taken two prisoners, one of them Che Guevara. He sent a coded message to his superiors at Vallegrande with the news that he had captured Che. He was told to keep him alive.[57]

When Captain Prado arrived in La Higuera with his famous prisoner, all three hundred residents came out of their humble homes to observe the most exciting event in the history of their uneventful town. Prado imprisoned Che in a mud-brick schoolhouse in the center of town. Over the following day he, Felix Rodríguez, and others attempted to interrogate Che, while their Bolivian and American superiors debated the fate of the fallen comandante.[58]

At 10:00 A.M. on October 9, General Ovando ordered Colonel Zenteno, commander of the Bolivian Eighth Division, to execute Che. Rodríguez had been instructed by his CIA handlers to keep Che alive so that he could be taken to Panama for interrogation. Colonel Zenteno told Rodríguez that he could not disobey a direct order. Rodríguez could only convince Zenteno to give him three hours to interrogate Che.[59] In a semiofficial Cuban version of Che's execution, the CIA allegedly issued the order to execute Che. However, evidence suggests that the Americans wanted to keep Guevara alive. On October 11, Walt Rostow informed President Johnson that General Ovando had ordered the execution. "I regard this as stupid," Rostow wrote.[60]

Che Guevara would not have submitted to interrogation—in Bolivia, Panama, or anywhere else. When Rodríguez attempted to question Guevara,

56. Prado, *Defeat of Che Guevara*, 177–78; González and Sánchez, *Great Rebel*, 189–90 (quoted).

57. Prado, *Defeat of Che Guevara*, 177–78.

58. Ibid., 250–51; Rodríguez and Weisman, *Shadow Warrior*, 160–62.

59. Rodríguez and Weisman, *Shadow Warrior*, 160–62.

60. Cupull and González, *La CIA contra el Che*, 94–95; Walt Rostow (national security adviser) to president, October 11, 1967, container 8, Bolivia Country File, NSF, LBJ.

he got an unambiguous response: "Nobody interrogates me!"[61] Che talked with Rodríguez and Captain Prado about the origins and objectives of his Bolivian campaign, but he divulged nothing that was not already public knowledge.

Bolivian air force general Jaime Niño de Guzmán, who claims that he was the last person to talk with Che, claims that Che said, "Fidel betrayed me," several times before his execution.[62] The allegation, if true, would cast new light on the reason for Guevara's failure in Bolivia. The rumors of Fidel Castro's betrayal gained new life in Jorge Castañeda's biography, *Compañero*. Castañeda considers the possibility that Castro, under Soviet pressure, cut off Guevara in the summer of 1967. Accordingly, the Cubans had organized a group of volunteers to rescue or reinforce Guevara if the situation deteriorated any further. The Soviets, however, opposed Guevara's Bolivian mission, concerned about American retaliation elsewhere. To dissuade the Cubans from supporting Guevara, Brezhnev dispatched Aleksey Kosygin to Havana in late June. During a series of meetings with Castro, Kosygin criticized Cuba's support for Latin American guerrillas. After the Kosygin visit, "an operation to boost the Bolivian foco became unthinkable," Castañeda maintains. Fidel, recognizing his total economic dependency on the Soviets, allegedly buckled, convinced that Guevara would serve the Cuban Revolution better as a martyr than as a guerrilla leader. He therefore disbanded the commando unit and let Che attempt to fight his own way out.[63]

However, in the same evidence cited by Castañeda, there is no indication that the Soviets actually demanded a Cuban withdrawal from Bolivia. From unidentified sources, American intelligence learned that Kosygin and Castro had indeed argued over the armed struggle, but they had agreed to disagree. Despite their opposition to Cuban adventurism, "the Soviets indicated [to Castro] that they were willing to continue to supply Cuba with considerable amounts of economic aid and that military aid programs, especially those concerned with the modernization of the Cuban armed forces, would be continued."[64]

In any case, would it have been possible for Fidel to rescue or reinforce Che? There were certainly Cuban soldiers prepared for another Bolivian mis-

61. Rodríguez and Weisman, *Shadow Warrior*, 166.

62. "Guevara Felt Betrayed by Castro," *USA Today*, May 1, 1998.

63. Castañeda, *Compañero*, 380–86.

64. CIA, Intelligence Information cable, "Background of Soviet Premier Alexsey Kosygin's Visit to Havana," October 17, 1967, Electronic Briefing Book no. 5, National Security Archive, available: <www.gwu.edu/~nsarchiv/NSAEBB/NSAEBB5/che3_1.htm>.

sion, but how could they have carried out their mission? Five guerrillas broke out of the Yuro ravine and returned to Cuba, demonstrating that the guerrillas could have escaped the Bolivian trap. Castañeda also points out that the Cubans had extracted a band of guerrillas in Venezuela in 1968, showing, at least to his satisfaction, that Cuba had the capacity to execute a relief mission.[65]

However, the situation in Bolivia in 1967 is no comparison to that of Venezuela a year later. According to Manuel Piñeiro, there was no organizational structure in Bolivia that could have been used to facilitate extraction or deploy reinforcements.[66] Moreover, the United States knew that Che Guevara, the number-two man in the Cuban Revolution, was within the grasp of the Bolivian Rangers. The American military and intelligence community was in active pursuit of Che, and its allies in Argentina, Brazil, Chile, and Peru had also been alerted to Cuban activity in southeastern Bolivia, presenting even graver logistical problems for the Cubans. If the Cuban commandos miraculously slipped into Bolivia, it is quite likely that the Americans would have responded with a direct strike against Cuba, with the concurrence of most Latin American nations. Neither Che nor his Cuban comrades had a viable military option.

Che's defeat in Bolivia cannot be blamed on Fidel Castro. Che committed a series of costly strategic and tactical errors that cost him his life and doomed the campaign. He initiated hostilities before he had established an effective urban network. He separated the rear guard from the main body without establishing a rallying point. He failed to move out of the area after the army took his camps and confiscated his supplies. He actually returned to his base after he knew that the Bolivian army had established a presence there. He marched his men in broad daylight through a succession of towns, giving away his strength, location, and direction to his adversary. During the start-up phase of his foco, when he should have been patient and cautious, Che made bold and aggressive moves. "During this [start-up] phase," according to Piñeiro, "the guerrillas must depend on their own strength, plus the backing they can get from the urban networks—which at that time had been beaten. So the idea that we could have just sent in military reinforcements is absurd; it was logistically impossible—that's pure fantasy."[67]

65. Ibid.
66. Suárez Salazar, *Che Guevara*, 22.
67. Ibid.

Che Guevara fell in battle trying to open another front in a global struggle against imperialism. He essentially challenged the American military to fight him in guerrilla warfare, on terrain he selected. That challenge represents a fundamental deviation from the Cuban model of insurrection. The Americans did not train Cuban army units in counterinsurgency warfare, as they did in Bolivia. They did not send intelligence officers into the field to collect and analyze data on the strength and movements of the guerrilla forces, as they did in Bolivia. Fidel Castro had effectively neutralized the United States and kept American military forces out of the conflict. Had American forces intervened militarily in the early stages of the conflict, they could have contained or crushed the rebellion in eastern Cuba. Yet in Bolivia, Che actually wanted the Americans to intervene. The Americans denied Che the direct military confrontation that he sought, but they provided critical and timely military assistance.

In the final stages of the conflict, Richard Clement's radio signal intelligence operations played a decisive role. After discovering that Che was transmitting radio messages in code and bursts, he returned to Washington to devise a way to track and pinpoint those radio signals. Returning to Bolivia, Clement and the Bolivians strung copper wires over the jungle to help them track the radio signals. Using Honeywell equipment rigged in his piper plane, Clement flew over the area of operations trying to intercept the signals, then triangulate on the position of the transmission. Corroborating evidence for this operation comes from the diary of Alberto Fernández, who fell in the Yuro ravine on October 8. In his diary entry of October 1, Fernández refers to a plane flying overhead at 9:00 A.M., "apparently looking for information by radio."[68]

On October 8, Clement picked up a coded signal, triangulated the position, and relayed the information to the Bolivian Rangers. The Rangers advanced on that position and captured Che within sixty minutes. The guerrillas disabled the piper plane with ground fire, forcing Clement to bail out. A guerrilla hit him with a .30-caliber Garand as he was hanging in a parachute, but he survived the fall, having pinpointed Che's position.[69]

Nevertheless, one should not conclude that this or other sophisticated surveillance techniques resulted in the capture of Che Guevara. Others have alleged that the CIA pinpointed Che's location by using infrared sensors to

68. Cited in Prado, *Defeat of Che Guevara*, 173.
69. Richard Clement, interview by author, June 18, 1999, Tampa, Florida.

pinpoint rebel campfires.[70] Such technology and more, including seismic detection devices, was certainly available, but there is no evidence that American agents used them or that they provided the Bolivian Rangers with information that they did not already have. By the time the Rangers went into action, Che Guevara was already pinned down in a ravine. With the Rangers blocking all exits, they could have waited for Che to reveal himself. He would have had to make an effort to break out of the trap.

The Bolivian army had already defeated Che by the time the Rangers and their American advisers went into action. Regular army units of the Bolivian Fourth Division had pursued Che for seven months, confiscating his supplies, inflicting casualties, and isolating him from potential bases of support in the cities. American training and intelligence played a decisive role only at the end of a counterinsurgency campaign conducted by the Bolivians. The Bolivians pursued Che's band relentlessly, making mistakes as they advanced, but showing the determination that Batista's army had lacked in Cuba. Che underestimated the strength of the Bolivian army and made the critical mistakes that led him into the Yuro ravine. In the end, Captain Gary Prado's Rangers got the credit for capturing Che, but Che had been defeated long before that.

The Bolivian army, not the CIA, defeated Che Guevara. It accepted Che's challenge and treated it seriously, and Generals Barrientos and Ovando decided to crush the foco before it took root. Although they initially lacked the special training and equipment that the Americans later provided, they designed and executed a viable counterinsurgency strategy. They knew that Che was most vulnerable during the start-up phase, so they reacted quickly to the first reports of a Cuban presence in southeastern Bolivia. Then, they mobilized the companies of the Fourth Division to seek out and destroy the guerrilla foco. These companies often performed badly in combat, falling into guerrilla ambushes again and again, but they persisted. In contrast to what occurred in Cuba, they fought primarily in small, mobile companies, matching the strength and mobility of the guerrillas.

In Cuba, the army usually fought in battalion-level strength, accompanied by tanks and heavy artillery, hoping to engage the guerrillas in conventional battle. The Bolivian army fought in company-level strength, which was one hundred soldiers or less, armed with machine guns, bazookas, and radio

70. Prado, *Defeat of Che Guevara,* 211–12; Andrew St. George, "How the U.S. Got Che," *True,* April 1969.

equipment. These units operated independently, and regional commanders coordinated their movements through the effective use of intelligence and communication. And, unlike the Cuban army, the Bolivian army did not retreat after a skirmish with the guerrillas. They took their losses and pushed on, determined to use their advantage in men and matériel to overwhelm the guerrillas. The Bolivian army put up a tougher fight than either Che or the Americans had anticipated.

Che's failure in Bolivia, however, does not necessarily lead to the conclusion that his tricontinental strategy was a failure. He committed so many tactical errors in the field that it is difficult to evaluate his strategy, which never got off the ground. The Bolivian army hunted Guevara for seven months, trapped him in a canyon, then captured and executed him. By making him a martyr, the Bolivian army did not disprove or diminish the significance of Guevara's strategy of revolutionary warfare. In war, particularly the kind of war Che practiced, one tactical mistake can result in complete destruction. Che's legend lives on many years after his death, and for good reasons. Che made many mistakes and fell in Bolivia, but neither his reputation nor his legacy should be determined solely by his last, disastrous campaign.

Instead of saying that Che lost in Bolivia, we might state the case positively: the Bolivian army defeated Guevara. That possibility has not been explored in the new biographies about Che, perhaps because so few people care to give any credit to the Bolivian military. Yet the evidence suggests that the Bolivians, with limited but critical American advice, applied and executed a well-coordinated and well-conceived strategy. More important, the Bolivians responded quickly, decisively, and effectively. In Cuba, Batista had claimed victory before he actually defeated Castro, and the Americans never even dispatched military advisers to provide much-needed advice on how to conduct an antiguerrilla war. The Americans might not have been able to alter the course of events in the Cuban insurrection, but they undoubtedly strengthened Che's foe in Bolivia.

If Che had faced the same enemy he had encountered in eastern Cuba, his guerrilla foco might have survived. Che faced a different adversary in Bolivia, with more sophisticated counterinsurgency tools and methods. The Bolivian army's quick response to the guerrilla foco kept the initiative away from Guevara, who dodged army patrols and air attacks for the last seven months of his legendary life. When Che committed many mistakes, the Bolivian army exploited them, pressured by their superiors in La Paz and Washington to crush Che Guevara's band. In 1967, the Bolivians and the Americans made the eradication of Che their highest priority, targeting him as they never did Castro ten years earlier.

But the Americans maintained a low profile, determined to deny Che the next Vietnam he craved. Americans decided that the primary responsibility for the campaign rested with the Bolivian army. The United States provided the Bolivians with arms, ammunition, and advice, but they refused to commit American combat troops. They had read Che's articles and speeches too, so they knew that Che intended to drag the United States into a Vietnam-like quagmire. As a result, the Americans applied a limited yet effective counterinsurgency strategy in Bolivia, providing just enough support to allow the Bolivians to defeat Che Guevara.

CONCLUSION

From the fact that Che Guevara and hundreds of his followers failed in their guerrilla campaigns in Africa and Latin America, a number of observers have concluded that he promoted a fatally flawed theory of guerrilla warfare. One military expert on guerrilla warfare notes, "The theory of the foco . . . has led most Latin American movements straight into the grave."[1] Biographer Jorge Castañeda indicted Che for raising false hopes among a generation of idealistic young Latin Americans: "Che endowed two generations of young people with the tools of that faith [in guerrilla warfare], and the fervor of that conviction. But he must also be held responsible for the wasted blood and lives that decimated those generations."[2]

Nevertheless, thousands, if not millions, of people still defend Che and his contributions to revolutionary theory and practice in Latin America. Thirty years ago a scholar of guerrilla warfare argued that Mao Tse-tung, Vo Nguyen Giap, and Guevara "provided the basic thoughts and practical tactics that have played fundamental roles in the guerrilla campaigns of the past twenty-five years."[3] The biographies published on the thirtieth anniversary of Guevara's death did not destroy or dent his reputation as Latin America's

1. Chailand, *Guerrilla Strategies,* 26.
2. Castañeda, *Compañero,* 193–94.
3. Mallin, *Strategy for Conquest,* 27.

leading guerrilla soldier and strategist. Guevara remains firmly entrenched in the pantheon of revolutionary leaders. His bust occupies a prominent place in the hall of twentieth-century guerrilla warriors, alongside those of Mao, Giap, and others. Although his strategic and tactical contributions to guerrilla warfare may have gone little beyond Mao or Giap, Brian Loveman and Thomas Davies argue that "his influence on the course of Latin American history in the last half of the twentieth century was monumental."[4]

Che Guevara's record as a guerrilla soldier, strategist, and comandante sustains all these interpretations. The guerrilla movements Che organized or inspired generally failed. He inspired young men and women to take up arms for a holy cause and many of them went to early graves. At the same time, he taught guerrilla warfare to a generation of Latin Americans and launched guerrilla movements in almost every Latin American country. He undoubtedly influenced the history of Latin America and the United States. Whether a brilliant strategist or a misguided revolutionary, Che Guevara inspired people, and his legacy lives on, in Web sites, popular musical groups, and T-shirts and other paraphernalia.

Guevara's actual record as a soldier, strategist, and commander is more complicated and controversial than the mythology that surrounds him. Separating myth from reality is difficult, particularly in the case of this legendary icon. There are no easy answers, no catchy phrases that succinctly summarize Guevara's contributions. Given the shortage of studied, deliberate appraisals of Che Guevara's military life and contributions, this analysis can only conclude with a modest attempt to evaluate Guevara's contributions to guerrilla warfare and his place in revolutionary history.

One cannot judge the skills and contributions of a military figure such as Che solely by battles won or lost. General Robert E. Lee made monumental mistakes at Gettysburg and his army suffered a crushing defeat as a result, but those mistakes do not erase the brilliance of the military campaign he had directed just two months earlier at Chancellorsville. General Ulysses S. Grant ultimately triumphed over Lee after a long and brutal campaign in Virginia, but his victory did not make him a better general than Lee. No military commander, neither Napoléon nor Guevara, has an unblemished record. Unlike observers in the ivory tower, they often pay for grave mistakes with their lives.

However, Guevara's military record does not place him in the same category of military leaders as that of Lee, Grant, or Napoléon. Mao and Giap

---

4. Brian Loveman and Thomas M. Davies Jr., introduction to Guevara, *Guerrilla Warfare*, 33.

commanded hundreds of thousands of soldiers in conventional and unconventional battles against superior Japanese, French, and American forces. George Washington, Simón Bolívar, and Pancho Villa led larger armies and won greater battles than did Che. If the size of the armies a commander puts into the field and the power of the enemy in his front measures military greatness, Che Guevara was a second- or third-rate comandante.

Che never commanded more than a regimental-size unit, and that was during the final phase of the Cuban insurrection, when volunteers swelled the ranks of his column to take Santa Clara. He did not move army corps across hundreds of miles; devise new military tactics; or coordinate complicated air, naval, and ground campaigns. There is not a Chancellorsville, Vicksburg, Austerlitz, Long March, Tet Offensive, Yorktown, or Ayacucho associated with his name; nor does his name conjure up even an ignoble association such as that of Columbus, New Mexico, with Pancho Villa's. The conquest of Santa Clara, the highlight of Che's career and the triumphal campaign of the Cuban insurrection, is not studied in military academies around the world.

However, it would be wholly unfair to denigrate Che's military career just because he did not command large forces or score impressive military victories. He never sought command of a large conventional force. During the Cuban missile crisis, he commanded Cuban forces on the western part of the island, but did not lead these conventionally organized units into battle. The basis of his entire military strategy was that a small, mobile force of combatants could win a prolonged war of attrition against an enemy with superior firepower and resources. He never advocated mass movements of troops for a decisive blow against the enemy, except for the final stages of an insurrection. Che was not like General Robert E. Lee or even the Confederate master of irregular warfare, General Nathan Bedford Forrest. Ironically, judging by his performance in the battle of Santa Clara, he probably would have made a great conventional general. However, Che was a soldier of the Americas, not West Point. The countries for which he fought did not have the resources to challenge their enemies on conventional terms. Che represented and advocated irregular warfare in developing countries, part of a global strategy to destroy imperialism by chipping away at its foundations.

The size of the armies he commanded, and the scale of the battles he fought, pale in comparison to those of many other military leaders, but few military leaders have contributed so much with so little. Che was a bright, innovative commander who accomplished feats that affected the world as much as did the actions of many officers who held a higher rank or commanded larger armies. Like the island country for which he fought, Che

Guevara exerted a magnified influence on Latin America, the United States, and the world; his went far beyond the size of the battles he won and lost.

Che Guevara was the principal military architect of the Cuban Revolution. Before Che became Castro's top military adviser, Fidel lacked a viable military strategy, as was evident in the disastrous attacks on Moncada and the *Granma* expedition of December 1956. As a common soldier under the command of Fidel Castro, Guevara—like the other soldiers—was lucky to survive Castro's mistakes. Che took his first bullet before he fired a shot in battle, yet he recovered quickly from the battle of Alegría del Pío, showing a physical tenacity and endurance uncommon for a man suffering from severe asthma. His aggressiveness in battle, in fact, may have reflected a determination to overcome his personal weaknesses. In the first rebel victory at La Plata, Che voluntarily ran across a clearing to set fire to the enemy's quarters. At the battle of El Uvero, Che led an attack on the enemy's right flank under heavy machine-gun fire, again demonstrating a willingness to expose himself to deadly risks. His courage in battle, as soldier and commander, is beyond dispute. He never shied away from a fight.

He was, in fact, too aggressive in battle. In combat, Che was "impulsive, very courageous, very daring, at times, even reckless," according to Castro. "He volunteered for the most difficult actions and suggested them in the midst of combat." Che wanted to fight; perhaps he even wanted to die. Several times Fidel had to order Che to stay out of combat to save the life of his trusted military adviser. "If we hadn't followed this policy, Che—because of those character traits of his—would not have come out of the war alive," Castro claims. Without the restraining hand of Fidel, Che often attacked when he should have retreated, as he did when he ambushed a Bolivian army patrol in March 1967. Che's aggressive character contradicted his own military dictates about being cautious during the initial phases of a guerrilla campaign. The Bolivian army revealed the fatal consequences of his offensive character.

Che's courage and audacity, however, earned him the first promotion to comandante in Castro's rebel army. Castro recognized the power of Che's calculating intellect when they first met. Fidel saw him develop into the best combatant of all his volunteers. When Che stepped on Cuban soil for the first time in 1956, he was already a trusted adviser to Castro and an instructor to his troops. Fidel consulted with Che on military strategy during the first six months of the Cuban insurrection, learning from Che the lessons he should have learned directly from Alberto Bayo in Mexico. Partly as a result of Che's influence, Castro's military strategy improved dramatically. Having suffered two military defeats, first at Moncada in 1953 and again at Alegría del Pío, Castro had to discard his conventional preferences and adopt the less conventional techniques that Che favored. Castro retained ultimate authority over rebel strategy, but he relied on Che for military guidance, particularly after he promoted him to comandante of the first independent rebel column. While there is insufficient evidence to determine the precise extent to which Che influenced Castro's strategy during the insurrection, it can hardly be coincidental that Che rose to the rank of comandante at the same time that Fidel shifted to an unconventional military strategy.

Fidel Castro only embraced guerrilla warfare after he met defeat. Che Guevara embraced guerrilla warfare before he tasted victory. Fidel favored bold but conventional military strategy, as was evident not only in his first two assaults, but also in the first great victory over Batista's army, the battle of El Uvero (May 1957). Che opposed Castro's plan to launch a frontal attack on that well-fortified position. Yet Fidel recognized the political aspects of a military campaign, more so than Che. He attacked El Uvero to send a message to Batista and the general public. It turned out to be a costly victory for the rebels, but he scored an invaluable political and psychological victory as a result. With Fidel in command of the general insurrection, leaving Che to concentrate solely on military affairs, Che accomplished the greatest feats of his military career and the Cuban insurrection.

As comandante of Column 4, in 1957 he punished several army columns in a series of ambushes at El Hombrito (August), Pino del Agua (September), and Altos de Conrado (December). He excelled at organizing and executing ambushes, though his men occasionally disappointed him by failing to kill or capture the soldiers who fell into his trap. He learned the tactic from Alberto Bayo and perfected it in the Sierra Maestra. Even soldiers trained in counterinsurgency warfare had difficulty avoiding or fighting their way out of Che's ambushes. In the Congo, Colonel Mike Hoare's mercenaries certainly took note of an impressive ambush set by Che in September 1965. In a losing effort in Bolivia, Che repeatedly ambushed the army patrols sent after him.

Che's ambushes, in fact, virtually saved Castro's rebel army from destruction during the summer offensive of 1958. Major Sánchez Mosquera led off the military offensive with a thrust at Santo Domingo (June), where Che met his eight-hundred-man battalion with mines, machine guns, and mortars. Che drove the battalion back, confiscated valuable weapons, killed eighty troops, and sent a message to the advancing troops about the dangers of advancing into rebel territory. When Che directed defensive operations, placing ambushes and waiting for the enemy to come at him, he performed brilliantly. When Fidel got his blood up and ordered an attack on Las Mercedes, the rebel army met with disaster. Thanks to Che, the rebels held their defensive lines and repelled almost every army incursion into their territory, even though they were outnumbered and outgunned in every battle. Che's defensive campaign in the summer of 1958 was second only to his Santa Clara campaign in terms of contributions to rebel victory.

Che's march across Cuba at the command of Column 8, followed by the capture of Santa Clara, won the war for Castro, and Che deserves full credit for it. He marched 120 men across terrain he did not know, established a base in the Escambray Mountains, and proceeded to divide the island in two. Pursued by the army and air force, marching into and out of ambushes all along the way, he demoralized the enemy and excited the general population by accomplishing a nearly impossible task. He encircled the city first by taking the towns and garrisons on the roads leading to it. As he cut off the lines of communication and supplies, he gradually tightened a noose around the city before sending in about one thousand men in a conventional assault on the town center. Ironically, the master of guerrilla warfare gained his reputation and his greatest victory by applying a classical military strategy. When Santa Clara fell, all of Cuba fell into Castro's hands. It was Che, not Fidel, Camilo, or Raúl, who scored the most important victory of the entire Cuban insurrection.

Fidel's skillful direction of the political insurrection contributed to and complemented Guevara's military campaign. Castro gradually established himself as the premier leader of an increasingly militant and broadly based anti-Batista coalition. Batista lacked constitutional legitimacy and popular support, making it difficult for him to rally the armed forces to his defense. As the rebels rolled up victories on the battlefield, they sapped the soldiers and officers of their morale. In the final month of the campaign, many garrisons surrendered to Che without a fight. The insurrection, beginning as a guerrilla war and culminating in a nationwide campaign with the characteristics of a conventional civil war, gradually eroded Batista's slim base of support. A sense of national political crisis engulfed the island, and with it, Batista. His army refused to fight for him, sensing that the prevailing political currents favored the rebels. The army surrendered to Che before they fought him, saving Che's column from several bloody confrontations, including a siege of La Cabaña, Havana's colonial fortress. The soldiers surrendered, not because they lacked the means to contest Guevara, but because Castro had already won the political insurrection, forcing Batista to resign without fighting for Havana.

Fidel and Che made a powerful revolutionary team. Fidel managed the politics and diplomacy; Che managed the war. Fidel orchestrated the political offensive that rallied popular opinion against an unconstitutional regime. Che directed the military offensive that shattered the military foundations of the dictatorship. Fidel waged a propaganda war from the Sierra Maestra, bringing international reporters to the sierra, where they saw heroic rebels fighting for a just cause. Che took the war from the sierra to central Cuba, showing the Cuban people that Castro's rebel army posed a real military threat to Havana. The Santa Clara campaign required careful coordination of troop movements, communications, and supplies in hostile territory. Che moved cautiously and deliberately. He avoided unnecessary engagements and attacked only when there was a certainty of victory. He took Santa Clara, cut the island in two, and forced Batista to resign. Che did all this without losing a single engagement. Given Castro's military record, one wonders whether he could have achieved what Che did in Las Villas province. Given Che's weak political skills, one wonders if he could have done what he did without Fidel.

During the Cuban insurrection, Che benefited from political developments to which he contributed only indirectly. Che lacked the political sophistication and charms that Fidel used effectively in discussions with allies and rivals, his prestige augmented by his willingness to fight and, as the war progressed, his ability to win. Che won many of those battles for Fidel, gaining a measure of political power in the process, as military commanders often do. However, a nationwide political crisis generated by years of struggle by a number of organizations, most notably the M-26-7, facilitated Che's conquest of Santa Clara. As the people rallied to the rebel cause, the Cuban army began to defect or lay down their arms. Che fought an enemy that did not want to fight, not because the rebels outgunned or outnumbered them, but because they did not want to defend an illegitimate, brutal, and unpopular president.

Che argued in *Guerrilla Warfare* that final victory would come when the guerrilla band was transformed into a regular army, attacked the enemy in its fortifications, and annihilated it. This did not happen in Cuba. Che and Camilo took the major fortresses in and around Havana because Batista's demoralized army did not want to fight back. Recognizing the inevitability of their defeat because their adversary possesses superior weaponry, numbers, or other advantages, military commanders often surrender their army before the enemy destroys it. Batista held a decisive advantage in weapons and numbers, but he never concentrated his forces against the rebels. A pitched battle between Batista's best and the rebel veterans never occurred. Che never "annihilated" the enemy on the battlefield; Batista's army disintegrated before Che arrived. Some of the officers and soldiers undoubtedly surrendered because they feared Che, but political factors, such as Batista's waning popular support, contributed equally to the demoralization of the Cuban army. Che cannot take credit for the sharp shift in political affairs in the final two months of the insurrection. He only contributed to that political reversal by marching to Las Villas and conquering Santa Clara, the decisive military campaign of the insurrection.

When Che assumed complete command of political and military affairs, as he did in Bolivia (and to a lesser extent in the Congo), his performance suffered because he lacked Fidel's political skills. As the political and military chief of guerrilla focos in the Congo and then in Bolivia, Che consistently mismanaged politics and diplomacy. He never forged effective political alliances, and he alienated potential allies. He failed in his diplomatic approaches to the Soviet Union and China, with the result that the international fighting front he envisioned for his tricontinental strategy never materialized. The result of these political failures in the Congo and Bolivia was a weak military campaign. A guerrilla foco, being the vanguard of a mass struggle, requires popular support. The two people who could have organized the foundations of a mass struggle in the Congo and Bolivia, Laurent Kabila and Mario Monje, did not support Che's military operations. Che went into battle without their support and failed.

Che was an excellent field commander, but he was not a great commander in chief. Given his unpolished political skills, he needed a reputable Bolivian politician to lead the struggle, filling the role played by Fidel Castro in Cuba. But Guevara once argued that Castro was one of three exceptional features of the Cuban insurrection, a proposition substantiated by his absence in Bolivia. Mario Monje was not an exceptional political leader. Che refused to cede leadership of the revolutionary movement to him, instead demanding the subservience of Monje and the Communist party. Consequently, Che lost the institutional network that he needed so badly to keep his combatants in the field. His guerrillas ambushed Bolivian army patrols time and time again on their way to defeat. Without a political network to support the guerrillas, he could not replace the men or supplies he lost along the way.

By the time Che arrived in Bolivia, even he was captivated by his own mystique. Che expected others to rally to his cause, believing that his appearance on the front lines would inspire confidence and courage among all revolutionaries. His faith in himself reached such unrealistic levels that he initiated the military campaign before an institutional network had been created, convinced that others would create it for him. When he arrived in Cuba, Frank País was running a network of underground cells from Santiago to Havana. Che had no idea how País organized and administered that network. Hundreds of activists worked in the face of grave danger in the cities, and many of them died to keep the guerrillas in the mountains. Che expected the same to be done for him in Bolivia, but as the supreme commander of the rebel movement, he had the responsibility to organize that urban network. The greatest flaw in Che's career as a comandante was his total ignorance of what was required to establish and run an urban underground. He paid for that ignorance with his life.

He excelled in Cuba because the revolutionary movement had been so effectively organized and compartmentalized before the guerrillas established a base in the Sierra Maestra. He did not have to concern himself with the organization of an urban network, because it had already been done for him. He did not have to recruit the first volunteers after Alegría del Pío; Frank País sent them to him. Che only had to train those troops, and there is little doubt that he was an excellent instructor. The troops he took with him to Las Villas were those that he had trained, either in the original Column 4 or at his school at Minas del Frío. They were disciplined, highly motivated, and loyal troops, both loving and fearing their commanding officer.

In his entire military career, Che rarely commanded more than one hundred troops in battle. For that reason alone, it is difficult to compare Che Guevara to Mao Tse-tung and General Vo Nguyen Giap, both of whom commanded millions of troops in conventional and unconventional warfare. The size of the armies commanded by each of these revolutionary leaders is not, however, the measure of the man or his contribution to victory. In relative terms, the Cuban insurrection was not a major war. Compared to the military activity in China and Vietnam, the war in Cuba looked like a series of skirmishes, with a handful of battles and a relatively low number of casualties. Yet the triumph of the Cuban Revolution had a substantial impact on Latin America, the United States, the Soviet Union, and China. Cuba became a major player in the Cold War, bringing the superpowers to the brink of nuclear disaster and also widening the breach between the Soviet Union and China. Che Guevara, second in command to Fidel Castro, was the principal military architect of the Cuban insurrection, and by training the Cuban army and militia, he helped to defend it against American intervention. In that sense, Che was as important to his adopted country as Mao and Giap were to their own nations.

In terms of his contributions to revolutionary theory, Guevara deserves recognition alongside Mao and Giap. He certainly wrote more on the subject than either man did, and if he did not make significant tactical innovations in guerrilla warfare, he added a few controversial strategic wrinkles. Che Guevara advocated guerrilla warfare as the primary means of attacking the enemy. Mao, Giap, and Colonel T. E. Lawrence conceived of irregular warfare as a vital part of a larger military strategy. They commanded large bodies of organized, disciplined soldiers, approximating the structure of a conventional army if not always using it in the conventional way. Che Guevara saw a guerrilla band as the primary weapon to use against the enemy. It would eventually grow in size and strength, adopting more conventional methods as it did, but the revolutionary movement would begin with an armed nucleus of fighting men and women. The notion that a vanguard group of twenty to forty combatants could spark a general insurrection by initiating a guerrilla campaign in a remote, inaccessible region is one of Guevara's contributions to revolutionary strategy.

Viewed in isolation, the concept is ludicrous. Nobody could reasonably expect a team of forty combatants to defeat an army of forty thousand. Guevara, however, aimed to do much more than that. He advocated the destruction of imperialism, and to that end, he recommended a global military campaign against the United States, waged on three different continents simultaneously. This tricontinental strategy is Guevara's second contribution to revolutionary strategy, and it is inextricably linked to his concept of the guerrilla foco. He never argued that forty guerrillas could topple a Latin American dictatorship, let alone imperialism. He believed, however, that guerrilla bands, fighting simultaneously on several African, Asian, and Latin American fronts, could gain such strength as to force American military intervention. Forced to fight on several widely separated fronts, the United States would find its resources and resolve stretched too thin to sustain combat. Becoming bogged down in a second or third Vietnam would drain the American economy, provoke political conflicts in the United States, and sap the American people of their will to fight. Che envisioned the destruction of imperialism through a protracted, global conflict with economic, political, and military weapons used against the imperialists.

Mao and Giap certainly spoke of destroying imperialism, and they even contributed military aid to other liberation movements. They did not, however, conceive of a strategy whereby a network of coordinated guerrilla focos, supported militarily and economically by the socialist superpowers, would drag the United States down. They thought of engaging the United States in grand battles, involving nuclear weapons, large conventional armies, and guerrilla warfare. Moreover, their fields of battle were relatively restricted compared to those contemplated by Che, who recognized no national or international boundaries. His military record, Che serving as he had in three rebel armies away from his native Argentina, reflects a true proletarian internationalism that is not found in other revolutionary leaders.

Guevara's manual, *Guerrilla Warfare*, as well as his revisions to that manual, published as "Guerrilla Warfare: A Method," should be read in conjunction with the analyses of imperialism that he developed from 1960 to 1966, particularly in his "Message to the Tricontinental." In this message Guevara fully expressed his strategy for a coordinated tricontinental guerrilla campaign, financed and supported by the Soviet Union and China. This strategy, while embraced by unorthodox revolutionaries in Africa, Asia, and Latin America, depended upon support from the Soviet Union and China, the only countries with the means to equip guerrilla armies on three continents. If the Communists had accepted Che's proposal, the guerrilla movements in Africa and Latin America would have acquired the strength needed to present a formidable and alarming challenge to the United States government.

In the Congo, the Soviets and Chinese provided some of the assistance that Che expected of them. At the First Tricontinental Conference in Havana (1966), the strategy became the official doctrine of Cuba and the revolutionaries it sponsored, but the campaign never got far off the ground. This failure reflects the irreconcilable ideological differences that tore the socialist world apart in the mid-1960s. One can only wonder what would have happened if the Chinese and Soviets had put real firepower and resources behind Che's tricontinental strategy. To formalize his international fighting front, Che would have had to heal the rift between the Soviets and the Chinese, and that was far beyond his meager political talents.

Che's blessing and misfortune was an iron will. He launched his tricontinental campaign before he organized the alliance designed to support it. He believed that the act of insurrection could create the conditions necessary for success, including the urban support network and the international coalitions designed to sustain guerrillas on three continents. If he had waited for these conditions to develop, he may have died an old bureaucrat in Havana, a fate worse than death for the combative comandante.

His appearance on a Bolivian battlefield so alarmed the United States that it mobilized its Special Forces to hunt him down and kill him. That counterrevolutionary movement indicates the extent to which Guevara influenced the course of American and Latin American history. No Latin American military leader made a greater impact than did Che Guevara. Thousands of Latin Americans, inspired by him and guided by his doctrines, established guerrilla bands in virtually every Latin American country. In response, the United States increased military aid throughout the region; organized covert operations; developed counterinsurgency strategies, tactics, and equipment; and dispatched military advisers wherever a Cuban-sponsored guerrilla movement emerged. The United States spent millions of dollars combating the guerrilla threat that Che organized, commanded, and personified. Hundreds and perhaps thousands of people lost their lives fighting a war that is typically recorded in the military history books as a collection of small, insignificant skirmishes. Yet when the United States discovered that Che Guevara had taken personal command of a guerrilla foco with only forty combatants, President Lyndon B. Johnson; National Security Adviser Walt Rostow; and General Robert Porter, head of the U.S. Southern Command in Panama, immediately placed Bolivia at the top of their security concerns in Latin America. The United States, through its Bolivian allies, went to war against a *man*, not a country, because the master of guerrilla warfare in Latin America represented a grave threat to American hegemony.

Ironically, Che Guevara did not consider himself a theorist, and certainly not a master of guerrilla warfare. He considered himself a man of action or, better yet, praxis. He acted upon the principles that he propagated, and he died for his anti-imperialist cause. In the end, the inspiration and assistance he provided to revolutionaries around the world might be Guevara's greatest contribution. His tricontinental guerrilla strategy may have been too ambitious. His writings on guerrilla tactics may have been derivative of Mao or even Sandino, but unlike so many other Latin American revolutionaries of his day, he fought. "Pseudorevolutionaries" angered Che as much as did the imperialists. If one believed in social justice for the proletariat and peasants, then there was no alternative but war. Che acted on that belief and died for it, and that is the message that still resonates with millions of followers today. He also killed for his principles, and that is the message that his enemies have not forgotten.

BIBLIOGRAPHY

PRIMARY SOURCES

Works by Ernesto Che Guevara

Gálvez, William, ed. and comp. *Che in Africa: Che Guevara's Congo Diary.* New York: Ocean Press, 1999.

Guevara, Ernesto Che. *The Bolivian Diary of Ernesto Che Guevara.* Edited by Mary-Alice Waters. New York: Pathfinder Press, 1994.

———. *Che.* Havana: Instituto del Libro, 1969.

———. *Che: Selected Works of Ernesto Guevara.* Edited by Rolando E. Bonachea and Nelson P. Valdés. Cambridge: MIT Press, 1969.

———. "Development of a Marxist Revolution." In Ernesto Che Guevara, *Che: Selected Works of Ernesto Guevara.* Edited by Rolando E. Bonachea and Nelson P. Valdés. Cambridge: MIT Press, 1969.

———. *Episodes of the Cuban Revolutionary War, 1956–1958.* Edited by Mary-Alice Waters. New York: Pathfinder Press, 1996.

———. *Ernesto Che Guevara: Escritos y discursos.* 9 vols. Havana: Editorial de Ciencias Sociales, 1985.

———. *Guerrilla Warfare.* 3d ed., rev. Edited by Brian Loveman and Thomas M. Davies Jr. Wilmington, Del.: Scholarly Resources, 1997.

———. "Guerrilla Warfare: A Method." In *Guerrilla Warfare.* 3d ed., rev. Edited by Brian Loveman and Thomas M. Davies Jr. Wilmington, Del.: Scholarly Resources, 1997.

———. "Message to the Tricontinental." In *Guerrilla Warfare.* 3d ed., rev. Edited by Brian Loveman and Thomas M. Davies Jr. Wilmington, Del.: Scholarly Resources, 1997.

———. *Motorcyle Diaries: A Journey Around South America.* Translated by Ann Wright. London: Verso, 1995.

———. *Obras, 1957–1967.* 2 vols. Havana: Casa de las Américas, 1970.

———. *Reminiscences of the Cuban Revolutionary War.* Translated by Victoria Ortiz. New York: Grove Press, 1968.

Guevara, Ernesto, and Raúl Castro. *La conquista de la esperanza: Diarios inéditos de la guerrilla cubana, diciembre de 1956–febrero de 1957.* Edited by Heinz Dieterich and Paco Ignacio Taibo II. Havana: Casa Editora Abril, 1996.

Taibo, Paco Ignacio, II, Froilán Escobar, and Félix Guerra, eds. and comps. *El año en que estuvimos en ninguna parte (la guerrilla africana de Ernesto Che Guevara).* Buenos Aires: Ediciones del Pensamiento Nacional, 1994.

Interviews

Buch, Luis. Interview by author. Havana, Cuba, November 27, 1996.
Clement, Richard. Interview by author. Tampa, Florida, June 18, 1999.
Fernández Font, Marcelo. Interview by author. Havana, Cuba, November 27, 1996.
Gómez Trueba, Angel. Interview by author. Havana, Cuba, November 26, 1996.
Vilaseca, Salvador. Interview by author. Havana, Cuba, November 25, 1996.

Memoirs, Documents, Speeches, and Correspondence

Acevedo, Enrique. *Descamisado*. Havana: Editorial Cultura Popular, 1993.
Almeida, Juan. "El ataque a Uvero." In *Días de combate*, edited by Luís Pavón. Havana: Instituto del Libro, 1970.
Almeida Bosque, Juan. *La Sierra Maestra y más allá*. Havana: Editora Política, 1995.
Alvarez Tabio, Pedro. *Diario de la guerra: Diciembre de 1956–febrero de 1957*. Havana: Oficina de Publicaciones del Consejo de Estado, 1986.
Ameijeras Delgado, Efigenio. *Más allá de nosotros: Columna 6 "Juan Manuel Ameijeras," II Frente Oriental "Frank País."* Santiago: Editorial Oriente, 1984.
Bayo, Alberto. *Mi aporte a la revolución cubana*. Havana: Imprenta del Ejército Rebelde, 1960.
———. "One Hundred Fifty Questions to a Guerilla." In *Strategy for Conquest: Communist Documents on Guerrilla Warfare*, edited by Jay Mallin. Coral Gables: University of Miami Press, 1970.
———. *Tempestad en el Caribe*. Mexico, n.p., 1950.
Bornot Pubillones, Thelma, Verónica Álvarez Mola, Magaly Chacón Romero, and Oscar de los Reyes Ramos, Sección de Historia de la Dirección Política Central de las Fuerzas Armadas Revolucionarias. *De Tuxpan a La Plata*. Havana: Editorial Orbe, 1979.
Cabrera Alvarez, Guillero, ed. *Memories of Che*. Translated by Jonathan Fried. Secaucus, N.J.: Lyle Stuart, 1987.
Carrasco, Juana. "Tatu: Un guerrillero africano." In *Testimonios sobre el Che*, edited by Marta Rojas. Havana: Editorial Pablo de la Torriente, 1990.
Castro, Fidel. *Revolutionary Struggle, 1947–1958*. Vol. 1 of *The Selected Works of Fidel Castro*. Edited by Rolando E. Bonachea and Nelson Valdés. Cambridge: MIT Press, 1972.
Casuso, Teresa. *Cuba and Castro*. New York: Random House, 1961.
Chomón, Faure. "Cuando el Che llegó al Escambray." In *Días de combate*, edited by Luís Pavón. Havana: Instituto del Libro, 1970.
Cienfuegos, Camilo. *Diario de campaña*. Havana: Municipio de la Habana, 1961.
Crespo, Luis. "La batalla del Uvero: 'Aquella fué nuestra primera gran victoria frente a la tiranía.'" *Bohemia* 55 (May 24, 1963): 4–6.
Cubillas, Vicente. "El combate de El Uvero: La primera gran victoria del Ejército Rebelde." *Revolución*, May 28, 1958, 8.
Deutschmann, David, ed. *Che: A Memoir by Fidel Castro*. Melbourne: Ocean Press, 1995.
Fernández Mell, Oscar. "La batalla de Santa Clara." In *Días de combate*, edited by Luís Pavón. Havana: Instituto del Libro, 1970.

Franqui, Carlos, ed. and comp. *Diary of the Cuban Revolution*. New York: Viking Press, 1980.

———. *Family Portrait with Fidel: A Memoir*. New York: Vintage Books, 1984.

———. *The Twelve*. New York: L. Stuart, 1968.

Gadea, Hilda. *Ernesto: A Memoir of Che Guevara*. Translated by Carmen Molina and Walter I. Bradbury Garden City, N.Y.: Doubleday, 1972.

Granado, Alberto. *Con el Ché por Sudamérica*. Havana: Editorial Letras Cubanas, 1986.

Guevara Lynch, Ernesto. *Aquí va un soldado de América*. Buenos Aires: Sudamericana/Planeta, 1987.

———. *Mi hijo el Che*. Havana: Editorial Arte y Literatura, 1988.

Iglesias Leyva, Joel. *De la Sierra Maestra al Escambray*. Havana: Editorial Letras Cubanas, 1979.

López-Fresquet, Rufo. *My Fourteen Months with Castro*. New York: World, 1966.

Llerena, Mario. *The Unsuspected Revolution: The Birth and Rise of Castroism*. Ithaca: Cornell University Press, 1978.

Macaulay, Neill. *A Rebel in Cuba: An American's Memoir*. Chicago: Quadrangle, 1970.

Masetti, Jorge Ricardo. *Los que luchan y los que lloran: El Fidel Castro que yo ví*. Buenos Aires: Editorial Freeland, 1958.

Núñez Jiménez, Antonio. *En marcha con Fidel*. Havana: Editorial Letras Cubanas, 1980.

Pardo Llada, José. *Fidel y el Che*. Barcelona: Plaza & James Editores, 1989.

Pavón, Luís, ed. *Días de combate*. Havana: Instituto del Libro, 1970.

Peredo, Inti. "My Campaign with Che." In *The Bolivian Diary of Ernesto Che Guevara*. Edited by Mary-Alice Waters. New York: Pathfinder Press, 1994.

Prado Salmón, Gary. *The Defeat of Che Guevara: Military Response to Guerrilla Challenge*. New York: Praeger, 1990.

Rodríguez, Felix, and John Weisman. *Shadow Warrior: The CIA Hero of a Hundred Unknown Battles*. New York: Simon & Schuster, 1989.

Rojas, Marta, ed. *Testimonios sobre el Che*. Havana: Editorial Pablo de la Torriente, 1990.

Rojo, Ricardo. *My Friend Che*. Translated by Julian Casart. New York: Dial Press, 1968.

Saldaña, Rodolfo. *Fertile Ground: Che Guevara and Bolivia, a Firsthand Account by Rodolfo Saldaña*. Edited by Mary-Alice Waters. New York: Pathfinder Press, 1997.

Smith, Earl T. *The Fourth Floor: An Account of the Castro Communist Revolution*. New York: Random House, 1962.

Smith, Wayne S. *The Closest of Enemies: A Personal and Diplomatic History of the Castro Years*. New York: W. W. Norton, 1987.

Suárez Salazar, Luis, ed. and comp. *Che Guevara and the Latin American Revolutionary Movements: Manuel Piñeiro ("Red Beard")*. Translated by Mary Todd. Melbourne: Ocean Press, 2001.

Villegas, Harry. *Pombo: A Man of Che's Guerrilla: With Che Guevara in Bolivia, 1966–68*. New York: Pathfinder Press, 1997.

Urrutia Lleó, Manuel. *Fidel Castro and Company, Inc.* New York: Praeger, 1964.

Papers and Records at U.S. Archives and Presidential Libraries

Lyndon B. Johnson Presidential Library, Austin, Tex.
 National Security Files.
 Bolivia Country File.
 Congo Country File.
 Cuba Country File.
 Intelligence File.
National Security Archive, Washington, D.C.
 Che Guevara Files.
 Central Intelligence Agency Files.
 Cuban Missile Crisis Collection.
Electronic Briefing Book no. 5. Available: <www.gwu.edu/~nsarchiv/NSAEBB/
 NSAEBB5/che14>.
U.S. National Archives, Washington, D.C., and Bethesda, Md.
Record group 59. Department of State Records.
Record group 84. Diplomatic and Consular Post Records.

SECONDARY SOURCES

Books

Alexander, Robert J. *Communism in Latin America*. New Brunswick: Rutgers
 University Press, 1957.
Ameringer, Charles D. *The Caribbean Legion: Patriots, Politicians, Soldiers of Fortune,
 1946–1950*. University Park: Pennsylvania State University Press, 1995.
———. *The Democratic Left in Exile*. Coral Gables: University of Miami Press, 1974.
Anderson, Jon Lee. *Che Guevara: A Revolutionary Life*. New York: Grove Press,
 1997.
Angelucci, Enzo, and Paolo Matricardi. *World War II Airplanes*. Vol. 2. Chicago:
 Rand McNally, 1977.
Asprey, Robert B. *War in the Shadows: The Guerrilla in History*. Rev. ed. New York:
 William Morrow, 1994.
Benjamin, Jules R. *The United States and the Origins of the Cuban Revolution: An
 Empire for Liberty in an Age of National Liberation*. Princeton: Princeton
 University Press, 1990.
Bethell, Paul. *The Losers*. New Rochelle, N.Y.: Arlington House, 1969.
Blight, James G., Bruce J. Allyn, and David A. Welch, eds. *Back to the Brink:
 Proceedings of the Moscow Conference on the Cuban Missile Crisis, January
 27–28, 1989*. Cambridge, Mass.: Center for Science and International Affairs,
 Harvard University; Lanham, Md.: University Press of America, 1992.
———. *Cuba on the Brink: Castro, the Missile Crisis, and the Soviet Collapse*. New
 York: Pantheon Books, 1993.
Bonachea, Ramón L., and Marta San Martín. *The Cuban Insurrection, 1952–1959*.
 New Brunswick, N.J.: Transaction Books, 1974.

Bonachea, Rolando E., and Nelson P. Valdés, eds. *Revolutionary Struggle, 1947–1959.* 2 vols. Cambridge: MIT Press, 1969.

Bonsal, Philip W. *Cuba, Castro, and the United States.* Pittsburgh: University of Pittsburgh Press, 1971.

Bourne, Peter G. *Fidel: A Biography of Fidel Castro.* New York: Dodd, Mead, 1986.

Brugioni, Dino A. *Eyeball to Eyeball: The Inside Story of the Cuban Missile Crisis.* New York: Random House, 1990.

Castañeda, Jorge. *Compañero: The Life and Death of Che Guevara.* Translated by Marina Castañeda. New York: Knopf, 1997.

Chailand, Gérard, ed. *Guerrilla Strategies: A Historical Anthology from the Long March to Afghanistan.* Berkeley and Los Angeles: University of California Press, 1982.

Chomsky, Aviva. *West Indian Workers and the United Fruit Company in Costa Rica, 1870–1940.* Baton Rouge: Louisiana State University Press, 1995.

Cupull, Adys, and Froilán González. *La CIA contra el Che.* Havana: Editora Política, 1993.

———. *Entre nosotros.* Havana: Ediciones Abril, 1992.

———. *Ernestito vivo y presente: Iconografía testimoniada de la infancia y la juventud de Ernesto Che Guevara, 1928–1953.* Havana: Editora Política, 1989.

———. *Un hombre bravo.* Havana: Editorial Capitán San Luis, 1994.

Debray, Régis. *Revolution in the Revolution? Armed Struggle and Political Struggle in Latin America.* Translated by Bobbye Ortiz. New York: Monthly Review Press, 1967.

Dorschner, John, and Roberto Fabricio. *The Winds of December: The Cuban Revolution, 1958.* New York: Coward, McCann & Geoghegan, 1980.

Dosal, Paul J. *Doing Business with the Dictators: A Political History of United Fruit in Guatemala, 1899–1944.* Wilmington, Del.: Scholarly Resources, 1993.

Dubois, Jules. *Fidel Castro: Rebel, Liberator, or Dictator?* Indianapolis: Bobbs-Merrill, 1962.

Dumont, René. *Cuba: Socialism and Development.* New York: Grove Press, 1970.

Duncan, W. Raymond. *The Soviet Union and Cuba: Interests and Influence.* New York: Praeger, 1985.

Dunkerley, James. *Rebellion in the Veins.* London: Verso, 1984.

Espinosa Goitizolo, Reinaldo, ed. *Atlas histórico, biográfico y militar Ernesto Guevara.* Havana: Editorial Pueblo y Educación, 1990.

Farber, Samuel. *Revolution and Reaction in Cuba, 1933–1960: A Political Sociology from Machado to Castro.* Middletown, Conn.: Wesleyan University Press, 1976.

Fermoselle, Rafael. *The Evolution of the Cuban Military, 1492–1986.* Miami: Ediciones Universal, 1987.

Foner, Philip S. *Antonio Maceo: The "Bronze Titan" of Cuba's Struggle for Independence.* New York: Monthly Review Press, 1977.

———. *The Spanish-Cuban-American War and the Birth of American Imperialism.* 2 vols. New York: Monthly Review Press, 1972.

Gambini, Hugo. *El Che Guevara.* Buenos Aires: Paidos, 1968.

Geyer, Georgie Ann. *Guerrilla Prince: The Untold Story of Fidel Castro.* Boston: Little, Brown, 1991.

Gleijeses, Piero. *Shattered Hope: The Guatemalan Revolution and the United States, 1944–1954.* Princeton: Princeton University Press, 1991.

González, Luis J., and Gustavo A. Sánchez Salazar. *The Great Rebel: Che Guevara in Bolivia*. New York: Grove Press, 1969.

Gott, Richard. *Guerrilla Movements in Latin America*. Garden City, N.Y.: Doubleday, 1971.

Greig, Ian. *The Communist Challenge to Africa: An Analysis of Contemporary Soviet, Chinese, and Cuban Policies*. Sandton, South Africa: Southern African Freedom Foundation, 1977.

Gribkov, Anatoli I., and William Y. Smith. *Operation Anadyr: U.S. and Soviet Generals Recount the Cuban Missile Crisis*. Chicago: Edition Q, 1994.

Gunston, Bill, ed. *The Encyclopedia of World Air Power*. New York: Crescent Books, 1980.

Halperin, Maurice. *The Taming of Fidel Castro*. Berkeley and Los Angeles: University of California Press, 1981.

Handy, Jim. *Revolution in the Countryside: Rural Conflict and Agrarian Reform in Guatemala, 1944–1954*. Chapel Hill: University of North Carolina Press, 1994.

Harris, Richard. *Death of a Revolutionary: Che Guevara's Last Mission*. Rev. ed. New York: W. W. Norton, 2000.

Heikal, Mohammed Hassanein. *The Cairo Documents: The Inside Story of Nasser and His Relationship with World Leaders, Rebels, and Statesmen*. New York: Doubleday, 1973.

Henry, Robert Selph. *Nathan Bedford Forrest: First with the Most*. New York: Konecky & Konecky, 1992.

Hernández, José M. *Cuba and the United States: Intervention and Militarism, 1868–1933*. Austin: University of Texas Press, 1993.

Hinckle, Warren, and William W. Turner. *The Fish Is Red: The Story of the Secret War Against Castro*. New York: Harper and Row, 1981.

Hodges, Donald. *The Intellectual Foundations of the Nicaraguan Revolution*. Austin: University of Texas Press, 1986.

Huberman, Leo, and Paul M. Sweezy, eds. *Régis Debray and the Latin American Revolution*. New York: Monthly Review Press, 1968.

Instituto de Geografía de la Academía de Ciencias de Cuba. *Nuevo atlas nacional de Cuba*. Havana: Academía de Ciencias de Cuba, 1989.

Jackson, D. Bruce. *Castro, the Kremlin, and Communism in Latin America*. Baltimore: Johns Hopkins Press, 1969.

James, Daniel. *Che Guevara: A Biography*. New York: Stein and Day, 1969.

Judson, C. Fred. *Cuba and the Revolutionary Myth: The Political Education of the Cuban Rebel Army, 1953–1963*. Boulder: Westview Press, 1984.

Kanza, Thomas R. *Conflict in the Congo: The Rise and Fall of Lumumba*. Harmondsworth: Penguin, 1972.

Karol, K. S. *Guerrillas in Power: The Course of the Cuban Revolution*. Translated by Arnold Pomerans. New York: Hill and Wang, 1970.

Kelly, Sean. *America's Tyrant: The CIA and Mobutu of Zaire*. Washington, D.C.: American University Press, 1993.

Klare, Michael T. *War Without End: American Planning for the Next Vietnams*. New York: Alfred A. Knopf, 1972.

Larkin, Bruce. *China and Africa, 1949–1970: The Foreign Policy of the People's Republic of China*. Berkeley and Los Angeles: University of California Press, 1971.

Levesque, Jacques. *The USSR and the Cuban Revolution: Soviet Ideological and Strategical Perspectives, 1959–77*. New York: Praeger, 1978.

Liss, Sheldon. *Marxist Thought in Latin America*. Berkeley and Los Angeles: University of California Press, 1984.

Loveman, Brian, and Thomas M. Davies Jr. "Guerrilla Warfare, Revolutionary Theory, and Revolutionary Movements in Latin America." In Ernesto Che Guevara, *Guerrilla Warfare*. 3d ed., rev. Edited by Brian Loveman and Thomas M. Davies Jr. Wilmington, Del.: Scholarly Resources, 1997.

Lowy, Michael. *The Marxism of Che Guevara: Philosophy, Economics, and Revolutionary Warfare*. New York: Monthly Review Press, 1973.

Macaulay, Neill. *The Sandino Affair*. Durham: Duke University Press, 1985.

Mallin, Jay, ed. *Strategy for Conquest: Communist Documents on Guerrilla Warfare*. Coral Gables: University of Miami Press, 1970.

Matthews, Herbert. *The Cuban Story*. New York: Braziller, 1961.

———. *Revolution in Cuba: An Essay in Understanding*. New York: Charles Scribner's Sons, 1975.

Musicant, Ivan. *Empire by Default: The Spanish-American War and the Dawn of the American Century*. New York: Henry Holt, 1998.

Osanka, Franklin Mark, ed. *Modern Guerrilla Warfare: Fighting Communist Guerrilla Movements, 1941–1961*. New York: Macmillan, 1962.

Page, Joseph A. *Perón: A Biography*. New York: Random House, 1983.

Paterson, Thomas G. *Contesting Castro: The United States and the Triumph of the Cuban Revolution*. New York: Oxford University Press, 1994.

Pavlov, Yuri I. *Soviet-Cuban Alliance, 1959–1991*. Coral Gables: University of Miami North-South Center, 1994.

Pérez, Louis A. Jr. *Army Politics in Cuba, 1898–1958*. Pittsburgh: University of Pittsburgh Press, 1976.

Perez-Stable, Marifeli. *The Cuban Revolution: Origins, Course, and Legacy*. New York: Oxford University Press, 1993.

Philips, R. Hart. *Cuba: Island of Paradox*. New York: McDowell, Obolensky, 1959.

Poppino, Rollie E. *International Communism in Latin America: A History of the Movement, 1917–1963*. London: Free Press of Glencoe, 1964.

Pustay, Major John S. *Counterinsurgency Warfare*. New York: Free Press, 1965.

Quirk, Robert. *Fidel Castro*. New York: W. W. Norton, 1993.

Ratliff, William E. *Castroism and Communism in Latin America, 1959–1976: The Varieties of Marxist-Leninist Experience*. Washington: American Enterprise Institute and the Hoover Institution on War, Revolution, and Peace, 1976.

Ratner, Michael, and Michael Steven Smith, eds. and comps. *Che Guevara and the FBI: The U.S. Political Police Dossier on the Latin American Revolutionary*. Melbourne: Ocean Press, 1997.

Richelson, Jeffrey T. *The U.S. Intelligence Community*. New York: Ballinger, 1989.

Rock, David. *Argentina, 1516–1987: From Spanish Colonization to Alfonsín*. Berkeley and Los Angeles: University of California Press, 1987.

Rojas, Marta, and Mirta Rodríguez Calderón. *Tania: The Unforgettable Guerrilla*. New York: Random House, 1971.

Ryan, Henry Butterfield. *The Fall of Che Guevara: A Story of Soldiers, Spies, and Diplomats*. New York: Oxford University Press, 1998.

Sauvage, Leo. *Che Guevara: The Failure of a Revolutionary*. Englewood Cliffs, N.J.: Prentice Hall, 1973.

Schneider, Ronald. *Communism in Guatemala, 1944–1954*. New York: Praeger, 1958.

Suárez, Andrés. *Cuba: Castroism and Communism, 1959–1966*. Cambridge: MIT Press, 1967.

Suchlicki, Jaime. *University Students and Revolution in Cuba, 1920–1968*. Coral Gables: University of Miami Press, 1969.

Szulc, Tad. *Fidel: A Critical Portrait*. New York: William Morrow, 1986.

Taber, Robert. *M-26: Biography of a Revolution*. New York: Lyle Stuart, 1961.

Taibo, Paco Ignacio, II. *Guevara: Also Known as Che*. Translated by Martin Michael Roberts. New York: St. Martin's Press, 1997.

Taylor, Maxwell D., et al. Introduction by Luis Aguilar. *Operation Zapata: The Ultrasensitive Report and Testimony of the Board of Inquiry on the Bay of Pigs*. Frederick, Md.: University Publications of America, 1981.

Thomas, Emory. *Robert E. Lee: A Biography*. New York: W. W. Norton, 1995.

Thomas, Hugh. *The Cuban Revolution*. New York: Harper and Row, 1977.

Thompson, William J. *Khrushchev: A Political Life*. New York: St. Martin's Press, 1995.

Welch, Richard E., Jr. *Response to Revolution: The United States and the Cuban Revolution, 1959–1961*. Chapel Hill: University of North Carolina Press, 1985.

Wickham-Crowley, Timothy P. *Guerrillas and Revolution in Latin America: A Comparative Study of Insurgents and Regimes Since 1956*. Princeton: Princeton University Press, 1992.

Wilkins, Frederick. "Guerrilla Warfare." In *Modern Guerrilla Warfare: Fighting Communist Guerrilla Movements, 1941–1961*, edited by Franklin Mark Osanka. New York: Macmillan, 1962.

Wyden, Peter. *Bay of Pigs: The Untold Story*. New York: Simon & Schuster, 1979.

Articles

Aaron, Harold R. "Guerrilla War in Cuba." *Military Review* 45 (May 1965): 40–46.

———. "Why Batista Lost." *Army* 15 (September 1965): 64–71.

Ameringer, Charles D. "The Auténtico Party and the Political Opposition in Cuba, 1952–1957." *Hispanic American Historical Review* 65 (May 1985): 327–52.

Childs, Matt. "An Historical Critique of the Emergence and Evolution of Ernesto Che Guevara's Foco Theory." *Journal of Latin American Studies* 27, no. 3 (1995): 593–624.

Farber, Samuel. "The Cuban Communists in the Early Stages of the Cuban Revolution: Revolutionaries or Reformists?" *Latin American Research Review* 18, no. 1 (1983): 59–84.

Gleijeses, Piero. "Cuba's First Venture in Africa, 1961–1965." *Journal of Latin American Studies* 28, no. 1 (February 1996): 159–96.

———. "'Flee! The White Giants Are Coming!' The United States, the Mercenaries, and the Congo, 1964–65." *Diplomatic History* 18, no. 2 (1994): 207–37.

Handy, Jim. "The Most Precious Fruit of the Revolution: The Guatemalan Agrarian Reform, 1952–4." *Hispanic American Historical Review* 68, no. 4 (1988): 675–705.

Kling, Merle. "Cuba: A Case Study of Unconventional Warfare." *Military Review* 42, no. 12 (1962): 11–12.

Luxenberg, Alan H. "Did Eisenhower Push Castro into the Arms of the Soviets?" *Journal of Interamerican Studies and World Affairs* 30 (spring 1988): 37–71.

Macaulay, Neill. "The Cuban Rebel Army: A Numerical Survey." *Hispanic American Historical Review* 43 (May 1978): 284–95.

————. "I Fought for Fidel." *American Heritage* 42 (November 1991): 78–92.

Mallin, Jay. "Castro's Guerrilla Campaign." *Marine Corps Gazette,* January 1967, 30–34.

Martin, Dolores Moyano. "The Making of a Revolutionary: A Memoir of the Young Guevara." *New York Times Magazine,* August 18, 1968, 48.

Suárez, Andrés. "The Cuban Revolution: The Road to Power." *Latin American Research Review* 7 (Fall 1972): 5–29.

Thomas, Hugh. "Cuba: The United States and Batista, 1952–58." *World Affairs* 149 (spring 1987): 169–77.

Newspapers

Bohemia, 1957–72
Granma, 1973–74
Hoy, 1959–65
New York Times, 1959–67
Revolución, 1959–65
Verde Olivo, 1961–64

Dissertations and Theses

Crain, David Allan. "The Course of the Cuban Heresy: The Rise and Decline of Castroism's Challenge to the Soviet Line in the Latin American Marxist Revolutionary Movement, 1963–1970." Ph.D. diss., Indiana University, 1972.

Regan, Carl John. "The Armed Forces of Cuba: 1933–1959." Master's thesis, University of Florida, 1970.

Videorecordings

Ernesto Che Guevara: The Bolivian Diary. Directed by Richard Dindo. Produced by Ciné-Manufacture, Les Films D'Ici. Fox Lorber Home Video, 1997.

Mi hijo el Che. Produced by Fernando Birri. Video documentary. 60 minutes. Distributed by PICS/The University of Iowa, 1984.

INDEX

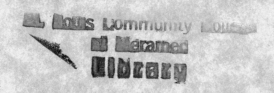